LANDSCAPE AND EMPIRE, 1770–2000

Landscape and Empire, 1770–2000

Edited by
GLENN HOOPER
Mary Immaculate College,
Limerick, Ireland

ASHGATE

Published by
Ashgate Publishing Limited
Gower House
Croft Road
Aldershot
Hants GU11 3HR
England

Ashgate Publishing Company
Suite 420
101 Cherry Street
Burlington
Vermont, 05401–4405
USA

Ashgate website: http://www.ashgate.com

British Library Cataloguing in Publication Data
Landscape and Empire, 1770–2000
    1. English literature – 20th century – History and criticism. 2. English literature – 19th century – History and criticism. 3. Colonies in literature. 4. Landscape in literature.
    I. Hooper, Glenn, 1959– .
    820.9'358

US Library of Congress Cataloging in Publication Data
Landscape and Empire, 1770–2000 / edited by Glenn Hooper.
    p.   cm.
    Includes bibliographical references and index.
    1. English literature – History and criticism. 2. Imperialism in literature. 3. English-speaking countries – Intellectual life. 4. Literature and society – English-speaking countries.
    5. Commonwealth literature (English) – History and criticism. 6. Landscape in literature.
    I. Hooper, Glenn, 1959– .
    PR408.I53L36 2004
    820.9'358–dc22

2004011460

ISBN 0 7546 0687 2

This book is printed on acid free paper.

Typeset by DC Graphic Design Ltd, Swanley, Kent.

Printed and bound in Great Britain by MPG Books Ltd, Bodmin, Cornwall.

Contents

List of Illustrations   vii

Notes on Contributors   ix

Introduction
Glenn Hooper   1

1 Planning Control: Cartouches, Maps and the Irish Landscape, 1770–1840
Glenn Hooper   17

2 African Land for the American Empire: The Proto-imperialism of Benjamin Stout
David Johnson   45

3 Landscape, Empire and the Creation of Modern New Zealand
Cheleen Ann-Catherine Mahar   65

4 Ireland in Ruins: The Figure of Ruin in Early Nineteenth-Century Irish Poetry
Sean Ryder   79

5 'A hot place, belonging to Us': The West Indies in Nineteenth-Century Travel Writing by Women
Evelyn O'Callaghan   93

6 Undeveloped Estates: Dominica and the Landscape of the New Imperialism
Peter Hulme   111

7 Reading Romance, Reading Landscape: Empires of Fiction
Mary Condé   127

8 Landscape and the Foreigner Within: Katherine Mansfield and Emily Carr
Angela Smith   141

9 Streets, Rooms and Residents: The Urban Uncanny and the Poetics of Space in Harold Pinter, Sam Selvon, Colin MacInnes and George Lamming
Gail Low   159

Contents

10 The Landscape of Insurgency: Mau Mau, Ngugi wa Thiong'o
    and Gender   177
    Brendon Nicholls

11 The Garden and Resistance in Diasporic Literature: An
    Ecocritical Approach   195
    Cynthia Davis

12 Geographies of Liberalism: The Politics of Space in Colm
    Toibin's *Bad Blood: A Walk along the Irish Border* and *The
    Heather Blazing*
    Conor McCarthy   207

    Select Bibliography   225

    Index   239

Illustrations

Colour Illustrations

3.1 Arthur Sharpe, A View of Wenderholme, Auckland, 1880. Watercolour on paper, 635 × 946 mm. Fletcher Holdings collection, Auckland (reproduced by kind permission of Collins Publishers, Auckland).

3.2 William Hodges, Waterfall in Dusky Bay, New Zealand, 1775. Oil on canvas, 1524 × 2108 mm. Admiralty House, Whitehall, London (reproduced by kind permission of Collins Publishers, Auckland).

Black and White Illustrations

1.1 John Rocque, cartouche, 'A Plan of the City and Suburbs of Dublin' map (1773). Courtesy of the Royal Irish Academy. 23

1.2 Alexander Taylor, cartouche, 'A New Map of Ireland' (1783). Courtesy of the Royal Irish Academy. 27

1.3 Alexander Taylor, cartouche, 'A New Map of Ireland' (1783). Courtesy of the Royal Irish Academy. 28

1.4 Daniel Augustus Beaufort, cartouche, 'A New Map of Ireland' (1797). Courtesy of the Royal Irish Academy. 30

1.5 James Williamson, cartouche, 'A Map of the County of Down' (1810). Courtesy of the Royal Irish Academy. 33

1.6 James Williamson, cartouche, 'A Map of the County of Down' (1810). Courtesy of the Royal Irish Academy. 35

1.7 Alexander Bath, cartouche, 'Map of Cork' (1811). Courtesy of the Royal Irish Academy. 37

1.8 Alexander Bath, cartouche, 'Map of Cork' (1811). Courtesy of the Royal Irish Academy. 39

1.9 Samuel Lewis, title page, *Atlas of Ireland* (1837). Courtesy of the Royal Irish Academy.   41

2.1 Shipwreck. Engraving in G. W. Barrington, *Remarkable Voyages and Shipwrecks. Being a popular collection of extraordinary and authentic sea narratives relating to all parts of the Globe* (London: Simpkin, Marshall, Hamilton, Kent and Co., n.d. – c.1880), facing p. 123.   49

5.1 Bog Road. Postcard, from the collection of Dr Karl Watson, University of the West Indies, Cave Hill, Barbados. Reproduced by kind permission.   101

5.2 Home Sweet Home. Jamaica. Postcard, from the collection of Dr Karl Watson, University of the West Indies, Cave Hill, Barbados. Reproduced by kind permission.   109

6.1 A Dominican Valley. Engraved from a sketch by Froude. In James A. Froude, *The English in the West Indies: or The Bow of Ulysses* [1887] (London: Longmans, 1909), facing p. 136.   113

6.2 Dominica. Showing route taken by survey for proposed interior main road. In Henry Hesketh Bell, 'Imperial Grant to Dominica: Scheme for Expenditure', C.O. 152/249 (Letter to the Governor of the Leeward Islands, 26.x.1899).   117

8.1 Emily Carr, Tanoo, 1912. Watercolour, pencil on paper, 76.4 × 55.5 cm. Vancouver Art Gallery, Emily Carr Trust, VAG 42.3.94 (Photo: Trevor Mills).   144

8.2 Emily Carr, Big Raven, 1931. Oil on canvas, 87.3 × 114.4 cm. Vancouver Art Gallery, Emily Carr Trust, VAG 42.3.11 (Photo: Trevor Mills).   150

8.3 Emily Carr, Zunoqua of the Cat Village, 1931. Oil on canvas, 112.5 × 70.5 cm. Vancouver Art Gallery, Emily Carr Trust, VAG 42.3.21 (Photo: Trevor Mills).   151

Contributors

Mary Condé is a Lecturer in the Department of English, Queen Mary, University of London. She is the author of numerous essays on Caribbean and Indian fiction, is co-editor (with Thorunn Lonsdale) of *Caribbean Women Writers: Fiction in English* (Macmillan, 1999) and has been a frequent contributor to *The Journal of the Short Story in English*.

Cynthia Davis grew up in Addis Ababa, Ethiopia, and she now teaches Caribbean and African-American literature at Barry University in Miami. Her research interests include ecoliterature, and the intersections of gardening, agriculture and the writing of the African diaspora. She has published in *The Langston Hughes Review* and the *Journal of Industrial Teacher Education*, and her book *Where the Wild Grape Grows*, co-authored with Verner Mitchell, is forthcoming from the University of Massachusetts Press.

Glenn Hooper is a Lecturer in the Department of English, Mary Immaculate College, University of Limerick. He is co-editor of *Ireland in the Nineteenth Century: Regional Identity* (Four Courts, 2000), editor of *Harriet Martineau's Letters from Ireland* (Irish Academic Press, 2001) and *The Tourist's Gaze: Travellers to Ireland, 1800–2000* (Cork University Press, 2001), and co-editor of *Irish and Postcolonial Writing: History, Theory, Practice* (Palgrave, 2002) and *Perspectives on Travel Writing* (Ashgate, 2004).

Peter Hulme is Professor in Literature at the University of Essex. He is the author of *Colonial Encounters: Europe and the Native Caribbean, 1492–1797* (Methuen, 1986) and *Remnants of Conquest: The Island Caribs and Their Visitors, 1877–1998* (Oxford, 2000), and joint editor of *Wild Majesty: Encounters with Caribs from Columbus to the Present Day* (Clarendon, 1992), *Colonial Discourse/Postcolonial Theory* (Manchester University Press, 1994), *Cannibalism and the Colonial World* (Cambridge University Press, 1998), *'The Tempest' and Its Travels* (Reaktion, 2000) and *The Cambridge Companion to Travel Writing* (Cambridge University Press, 2002).

David Johnson is a Senior Lecturer in the Department of Literature at the Open University. He has published on many aspects of South African writing, law and postcolonial theory, and is the author of *Shakespeare and South Africa* (Clarendon, 1996) and co-author of *Jurisprudence: A South African Perspective* (Butterworths, 2001). His *A Historical Companion to Postcolonial Literatures*, co-edited with Prem Poddar, is forthcoming from Edinburgh University Press.

Gail Low is a Lecturer in the Department of English, University of Dundee. She has written extensively on postcolonial and commonwealth literature, has published in *Research into African Literatures*, *Women*, *Kunapipi* and *New Formations*, and has been a contributor to *Contemporary Writing and National Identity* (ed. Tracy Hill and William Hughes; Sulis, 1995) and *Literature at the Intersection of Race and Gender* (ed. Deborah Masden; Pluto, 1999). She is the author of *White Skins/Black Masks: Representation and Colonialism* (Routledge, 1996).

Cheleen Ann-Catherine Mahar is Professor of Anthropology and Chair of International Studies at Pacific University in Oregon. She is co-editor of *An Introduction to the Work of Pierre Bourdieu* (Macmillan, 1990) and publishes in the fields of migration and social theory. Her book, *The Strategy of Urban Life: Reinventing Practice in the Disenchanted World*, is forthcoming from the University of Texas Press.

Conor McCarthy has taught at the University of Liverpool, St. Patrick's College, Maynooth, and NUI Galway, and is currently a Lecturer in the Department of English at the Mater Dei Institute, Dublin. His research interests include contemporary Irish theory and culture, drama and cinema. He has published in *Textual Practice*, *Current Writing* and the *Irish University Review*, and is the author of *Modernisation, Crisis and Culture in Ireland, 1969–1992* (Four Courts, 2000).

Brendon Nicholls is a Lecturer in English at the University of Leeds. His research focuses primarily on gender, race, psyche and culture in African and American literatures, and he has published in the *Australian Humanities Review* and has been a contributor to *Emerging Perspectives on Tsitsi Dangarembga* (ed. Jeanette Treiber and Anne Elizabeth Willey; Africa World Press, 2002). At present he is working on a book on Ngugi wa Thiong'o and has articles forthcoming in *Modern Fiction Studies* and *Kunapipi*.

Evelyn O'Callaghan is Associate Professor in the Department of English, University of the West Indies, Barbados, and has published extensively on West Indian literature, including *The Earliest Patriots* (Karla Press, 1986), *Barbados and Abroad* (Karla Press, 1986) and *Woman Version: Theoretical Approaches to West Indian Fiction by Women* (Macmillan, 1993). She reviews regularly for *Ariel*, *Caribbean Quarterly* and *The Journal of West Indian Literature*, and has an analysis of early narratives of the West Indies in press.

Sean Ryder is a Lecturer in the Department of English at the National University of Ireland, Galway. He has published widely on various aspects of nineteenth-century Irish nationalism and culture, and on Irish cinema, and is currently engaged on a project on nineteenth-century Irish popular culture for the Centre for the Study of Human Settlement and Historical Change, at NUI Galway. He is editor of the *Selected Writings of James Clarence Mangan* (UCD Press, 2004), joint editor of

Gender and Colonialism (Galway University Press, 1995) and co-editor of *Ideology and Ireland in the Nineteenth Century* (Four Courts, 1998).

Angela Smith is Professor of English Studies and Director of the Centre of Commonwealth Studies at the University of Stirling in Scotland and has taught widely at universities in England and Wales, the USA and Malawi. Her books include *East African Writing in English* (Macmillan, 1989), *Katherine Mansfield and Virginia Woolf: A Public of Two* (Clarendon, 1999) and *Katherine Mansfield: A Literary Life* (Palgrave, 2000). She has also edited *Jean Rhys, Wide Sargasso Sea* (Penguin, 1997) and *Katherine Mansfield: Selected Stories* (Oxford World's Classics, 2002).

Introduction

Glenn Hooper

Arrival

From the long list of almost endless variables that constituted imperial experience there was always one, fairly constant, element for colonists to consider: how to physically combat and control the environment. Landing at one new territory after another the first impulse of the Spanish conquistadors was to read aloud the *requerimiento*, a spectacularly bold announcement of arrival and ownership. But after this the most immediate task facing these new arrivals was how best to deal with native and environmental issues, and with the sense of intractability they individually, and jointly, presented. Natives who were amenable to the newly arrived presence were used to further the colonial project, such as La Malinche, a pragmatic individual who worked as a translator at a time when Spanish military penetration was still precarious.[1] For many others, however, the choice was stark: either conform, which in Spanish eyes meant convert to Christianity, or perish.

Nevertheless, the pressures on these early adventurers, despite their technical advantages, were manifold, and the environmental challenges facing not only the Spanish, but also the British, Dutch and Portuguese throughout the New World, as well as in Africa, Asia and the South Pacific, were many. The land was often inhospitable and dangerous. Moreover, although it frequently contained ecological, not to mention zoological challenges of a high order, it never ceased to fascinate its newest inhabitants. Threatening one moment, filled with unsurpassed potential the next, the physical space encountered was a constant source of surprise and challenge. Not for nothing, then, were the energies of many taken in different directions. For some it was a matter of priority that the settlement be protected against possible invasion from within, and they strove to maintain their hold on the country by building forts and keeps, and, above all, ensuring safe passage between one settlement and another. Sir Thomas Smith, for example, as he planned and publicized his colonization of the

---

[1] For a discussion of the at times controversial figure of La Malinche, see Tzvetan Todorov, *The Conquest of America: The Question of the Other* (New York: Harper & Row, 1984), pp. 100–23; see also Mary Louise Pratt, 'Yo soy la Malinche': Chicana Writers and the Poetics of Ethnonationalism', in P. Verdonk, ed., *Twentieth-Century Poetry: From Text to Context* (London: Routledge, 1993).

1

Ards peninsula in the north-east of Ireland in 1572, advised his colonists to proceed 'slowely, inhabite, builde, and fortifie … Then after the store house and key of his countrey [is] built, and left sufficiently garded … remove v. or vj. more or lesse miles, as the countrey shall serue, and there erecte uppon the liste an other fortresse.'[2] For Smith the Irish landscape was something both alien and unknown, to be scheduled through the cumulative effect of steadily advancing military fortifications.

Although the primary responses to land throughout the early modern colonial period were very practical ones, with the security and preservation of the colony paramount, one wonders whether later colonists, from say the eighteenth and early nineteenth century, fared any better, or had different concerns, or transformed the land and landscape in other ways. As this collection will demonstrate, although distinctions between rival empires and across historical periods are noticeable, a surprisingly similar set of attitudes towards the colonial landscape nevertheless emerges. It is true that with industrial changes such as the advent of the railway, or the fact that better maps facilitated a greater understanding of the extent of land under one's control, or the way in which census and other classification systems generally brought more colonial territory within the ken of metropolitan comprehension, that changes to the landscape continued in dramatically different ways at a variety of locales. Nevertheless, many of the same attitudes – of desire, incomprehension, ardent attachment and fear – persist. Indeed, it is almost as though, against all rational thought and despite years of possession and experience, colonists must make, and remake, what they have physically taken possession of. Sometimes arrogantly, at other times nervously, the landscape is remodelled by colonists, not just because it needs to be contained, yield a profit or support the community who live there, but because it is also regarded as a very visible marker of ownership and authority.

The story of landscape, however, is an ever-enlarging and complex one. In Richard Muir's opinion the 'spectrum of approaches to the study of landscape is remarkably broad. Some approaches, like geomorphology and the aesthetic approaches to landscape, differ from each other greatly.'[3] In an essay on the ideology of landscape representation, Susanne Seymour suggests that the 'concept of "landscape" has in recent years constituted a highly contested terrain of study and interpretation both within geography and beyond', though she herself goes on to present a rich account of the way landscape has been used to maintain colonial power.[4] Meanwhile, Denis

---

[2]   Sir Thomas Smith, 'Tract on the Colonisation of Ards in County of Down', in G. Hill, ed., *An Historical Account of the Macdonnells of Antrim* (Ballycastle: Amergin, 1978), p. 413. See also David Beers Quinn, 'Sir Thomas Smith (1513–1577) and the beginnings of English colonial theory', *Proceedings of the American Philosophical Society*, 89:4 (December 1945) and Nicholas Canny, 'Introduction', in Nicholas Canny, ed., *The Origins of Empire*, Vol. I (Oxford: Oxford University Press, 1998), especially pp. 7–8.

[3]   Richard Muir, *Approaches to Landscape* (Basingstoke: Macmillan, 1999), p. 1.

[4]   Susanne Seymour, 'Historical Geographies of Landscape', in Brian Graham and Catherine Nash, eds, *Modern Historical Geographies* (Harlow: Pearson, 2000), p. 193.

Cosgrove suggests that many 'studies exist of the changing European use of the earth, the moulding of land by human labour into visibly distinct regions we call landscapes', while others 'have examined how Europeans have represented their world as a source of aesthetic enjoyment – as landscape'.[5] However, these mutually exclusive perspectives, he notes, miss out on one very important distinction.

> The argument here is that the landscape ... is a way of seeing that has its own history, but a history that can be understood only as part of a wider history of economy and society ... historically and theoretically it is unsatisfactory to treat the landscape way of seeing in a vacuum, outside the context of a real historical world of productive human relations, and those between people and the world they inhabit.[6]

It is all very well to follow the aesthetic line and to make connections to painting and the sublime, landscape gardening, architecture and taste, or alternatively to take the path of traditional historical geography, for whom 'field systems, settlement patterns or population distributions' are of singular interest.[7] Which is not to suggest that Cosgrove fails to appreciate the attractions of both, because he in fact maintains a link to traditional historical geography, as well as to aesthetics and art, in the course of his own study, producing a highly integrated, overlapping narrative pattern. Alert to the dangers of de- and ahistoricizing perspectives, Cosgrove simply avoids the pitfalls of those historical geographers who have mired landscape appreciation in positivistic analysis, while at the same time side-stepping the seemingly anecdotal, apolitical interpretations offered by at least some art historians.

Although this collection contains essays that discuss gardens and planting, architecture, ruins and the sublime force of nature, contributors are also keenly aware of the historical context of landscape and make efforts to integrate their arguments along the lines plotted by Cosgrove. With Cosgrove they largely agree that 'in landscape we are dealing with an ideologically-charged and very complex cultural product' and, moreover, that it is 'in the origins of landscape as a way of seeing the world that we discover its links to broader historical structures and processes and are able to locate landscape study within a progressive debate about society and culture'.[8] Which is another way of suggesting that despite the variety of approaches and individual studies here undertaken, the specificities of empire necessarily ground these essays in ways that preclude, indeed practically prohibit, ahistorical analysis.

But history isn't the only influence upon these essays. Geography, too, helps to shape them in quite distinct ways, for these are landscapes that are different from Britain, and in many instances far removed from Europe. From the mid to

---

[5] Denis E. Cosgrove, *Social Formation and the Symbolic Landscape* (London: Croom Helm, 1984), p. 1.

[6] Cosgrove, *Social Formation*, pp. 1–2.

[7] Cosgrove, *Social Formation*, p. 4.

[8] Cosgrove, *Social Formation*, pp. 11, 15.

late eighteenth century – coincident with the first of these essays – landscape was a determining feature within European cultural discourse. In Britain the landscape was frequently associated with the English country house, itself seen as articulating something solid and coherent about national values and the British way of life. Writers such as William Gilpin traversed some of the most scenic parts of Britain in a search for the most picturesque or sublime landscapes, which he would describe – and sometimes sketch – in painstaking detail. And these scenes or monuments, situated in the Wye Valley, North Wales and the remoter parts of Scotland, became the focus for the touristic and leisured interests of others, all of whom were drawn to the beauty of the scene and the landscape.[9] A thing to admire and exalt, despite the fact that for many it also represented the physical consolidation of elite interests in the form of estate houses, parkland, formal and garden space, the landscape embodied taste, refinement and aesthetic pleasure.[10]

Whatever the various developments taking place within eighteenth- and early nineteenth-century British landscape discourse – how Brown's flowing lines, which largely replaced the more geometric and rectilinear fashions of the earlier eighteenth century, were themselves soon ridiculed as too pretty or manufactured by Uvedale Price and Richard Payne Knight – these are debates that impinge sometimes only tangentially upon the landscapes of Africa, India and the Caribbean.[11] The colonial landscape, at once strange and domestic, a place belonging to Britain yet abroad, created an altogether different set of problems. It could be beautiful, lavish and lush, but so too could it confront the viewer with epistemological difficulties that destabilized meaning and certainty. And when that viewer stepped up to the landscape

---

[9] A useful discussion of the Home Tour may be found in Barbara Korte's *English Travel Writing: From Pilgrimages to Postcolonial Explorations* (London: Macmillan, 2000), pp. 66–81.

[10] An impressive and considerable literature exists on the intersections of English landscaping, aesthetics and politics. See, for example, Christopher Hussey, *The Picturesque: Studies in a Point of View* (Hamden: Archon, [1927] 1967); H. F. Clark, *The English Landscape Garden* (Gloucester: Sutton, 1980); S. R. J. Woodell, *The English Landscape: Past, Present, and Future* (Oxford: Oxford University Press, 1985); John Dixon Hunt, *Gardens and the Picturesque: Studies in the History of Landscape Architecture* (Cambridge, Mass.: MIT Press, 1992); Tom Williamson, *Polite Landscapes: Gardens and Society in Eighteenth-century England* (Baltimore: Johns Hopkins University Press, 1995); Andrew Ballantyne, *Architecture, Landscape and Liberty: Richard Payne Knight and the Picturesque* (Cambridge: Cambridge University Press, 1997).

[11] 'Brown's influence on the face of the English countryside is unquestionable. His work inside parks consisted in treating them as *formally* as their natural materials allowed, which in its turn alerted his clients and their friends to the natural capabilities of the countryside … But there were many contemporaries who found Brown's designs dull … Richard Payne Knight and Uvedale Price, who prescribed fidelity to the vision of Salvator Rosa, were at one in their dismay at Brown's work.' John Dixon Hunt and Peter Willis, eds, *The Genius of the Place: The English Landscape Garden, 1620–1820* (London: Elek, 1975), p. 31.

as a colonist, imbued with authority, expected to impose his or her will upon a foreign land as a matter of routine, or because change was deemed imperative, then questions not unnaturally arose. These essays, which discuss the landscape in relation to how colonists saw it, discovered it and as often as not looked to reconfigure it to suit their own tastes, engage with several of these issues. As will become apparent, these were not landscapes necessarily available to eighteenth-century polite discourse; they were territories seen through the optic of colonial endeavour, a perspective that saw land to be cultivated, improved, planted and, above all, secured.

The interpretation of landscape here offered, then, is sensitive to local and regional particularities, but contextualized with reference to a range of aesthetic classifications and developments. Indeed, Cosgrove's interpretation of landscape as a 'cultural concept' and his warning that it is 'historically and theoretically ... unsatisfactory to treat the landscape way of seeing in a vacuum, outside the context of a real historical world of productive human relations' are principles to which all of the contributors in this volume would subscribe.[12] Whether they consider the male, romantic attachment to the Indian landscape, the history of botanical gardening, the Irish ruin or road-building in Dominica, these essays profitably situate landscape in relation to the wider contexts of their time. Their aim is to broadly consider how forms of knowledge were applied to the lands and landscapes under imperial (in some instances, post-imperial) control. They begin in the middle of the eighteenth century, when even in Britain landscape was coming to dominate many aspects of cultural life, and the authors draw upon theoretical approaches from within, among others, historical geography, art history and migration.

Malcolm Andrews has successfully demonstrated how even those picturesque enthusiasts of the late eighteenth and early nineteenth centuries, despite the effete intentions of many to see in landscape nothing other than pleasurable instruction, were involved in specific renderings of landscape that showed less than the full picture: loosening a sometimes varied topographical vista from its agricultural surroundings, framing or cropping a scene so that it conformed to a particular aesthetic category,[13] depopulating the landscape and/or importing certain motifs – the ivy-clad ruin, the meandering stream, the oak tree – in order to harmonize the more unruly aspects of nature.[14] While contributors to this volume are alert to the rationale historically presented in such cases and are keenly aware of the aesthetic arguments made in its defence, their interest lies principally in examining landscape as part of the development, as well as the legacy, of empire.

---

[12] Cosgrove, *Social Formation*, pp. 1–2.

[13] 'The landscape painter in the eighteenth century was torn between topography and fantasy, between his instinct for recording actual views and visions of idealized scenery.' John Dixon Hunt, *The Figure in the Landscape: Poetry, Painting, and Gardening during the Eighteenth Century* (Baltimore: Johns Hopkins University Press, 1976), p. 200.

[14] See Malcolm Andrews, *The Search for the Picturesque: Landscape Aesthetics and Tourism in Britain, 1760–1800* (Aldershot: Scolar, 1989), especially pp. 24–67.

Writing

Although one of the more intellectually provocative developments within the history of cartography in recent years has been the degree of attention paid to map symbolism, such innovation may be traced largely to one figure: the historical geographer J. B. Harley. By suggesting that maps functioned on a series of levels, were cultural as well as scientific artefacts, but more importantly by assigning peripheral details such as lettering, cartouche and other decorative detail a more central role, Harley focused attention on the totality of the map. Taking the work of Harley and others as a guide, Glenn Hooper's essay argues for a similar re-appreciation of late eighteenth- and early nineteenth-century Ireland, suggesting that the cartouche imagery of several maps allows for almost identical interpretations of the Irish land and landscape. Hooper suggests that several maps of Ireland adopted an equivalent attitude towards the land as those published of parts of North America, namely Carolina and Virginia: identifying it as *terra incognita* one moment and as a place of potential and abundance the next; a territory in need of protection, but a site also of concord, physical malleability, even welcome. Unlike early modern representations of the Irish landscape, which many British commentators associated with a very immediate sense of intractability – the term used for the native Irish, 'woodkerne', linked environmental and ethnic difficulties tellingly together – this later period in Irish history favoured a broader range of interpretations, but a range that nevertheless reconstituted many anxieties about how best to control the landscape, and by extension the populace who resided there. Not unlike paintings or sketches from the same period, these cartouches, Hooper argues, may be read as part of a visual repertoire that required the Irish landscape to appear contained and controlled, even though several also reveal a sense of disquiet about a place that, despite residing on the very margins, was frequently uppermost in eighteenth- and nineteenth-century British political discourse.

In a recent essay collection focusing on the intersections between romanticism, space and travel, Amanda Gilroy accurately identifies travel writing as one of the most crucial genres in the development of 'Britain's colonial project', a form that emerged 'as perhaps the most capacious cultural holdall, a hybrid discourse that traversed the disciplinary boundaries of politics, letter-writing, education, medicine, aesthetics, and economics'.[15] In David Johnson's essay we discover a narrative formed out of a similar culture, but one that crossed possibly even wider terrain than that described by Gilroy. Benjamin Stout's *Narrative of the loss of the ship, 'Hercules'* (1798) manages to entertain with its heroics of self-discovery and adventure along the coast of the eastern Cape, but also positions itself as a piece of promotional writing that argues for the imperial domination of Southern Africa. Partaking of a range of discourses – travel narrative, masculinist high seas adventure, shipwreck fable,

---

[15] Amanda Gilroy, 'Introduction', in A. Gilroy, ed., *Romantic Geographies: Discourses of Travel, 1775–1844* (Manchester: Manchester University Press, 2000), p. 1.

proto-imperial and promotional treatise – Stout reinforced the urgency developing in many minds about the consequences of allowing too free a hand to the Dutch in their development of the Cape. Indeed, Stout's invitation to American president John Adams to colonize the western Cape, despite the Gilpenesque cleansing periodically attempted, is one built on presenting the land as significantly empty and uncontested, a combination judged to have just the sort of appeal for an American appetite.

Although the lack of human agency, the use of elevated and promontory views, and the argument that ceaseless opportunity awaited America if it should only capitalize on such attractions was relentlessly stressed by Stout, such an emphasis was not specific to the Cape. Indeed, something of the desire to transform what was perceived as an empty, if fertile, wilderness by Stout also animated much emigrant discourse pertaining to New Zealand throughout the nineteenth, and well into the twentieth century. In Cheleen Ann-Catherine Mahar's essay she argues that a constant among the emigrant narratives and paintings to emerge from this period was the transformation of a land judged ready for speculators in search of a 'New Britain'. Ironically, although the New Zealand landscape was seen as a true Arcadia, a place aestheticized in the work of artists such as Alfred Sharpe and William Hodges, this was a land especially equipped for conversion. Using examples of topographical landscape painting to illustrate the appeal of selling New Zealand to intending migrants, Mahar demonstrates the way in which artists successfully maintained interest in some of Britain's furthest colonies. These painters, she argues, 'discovered' the New Zealand countryside, and presented it as a place of pastoral plenty, even though the colonial authorities vested time, effort and money stressing that whatever else it might signify, the landscape was an economic venture above all. Despite the difference in emphasis, the disregard shown to both the Maoris and their culture, and the unappealing male culture that grew up around many frontier settlements, the images of arcadian pleasure produced by the likes of Sharpe and Hodges were sharply undercut. Landscape might yet hold out the allure of empty, fertile lands, but the environmental ravages, especially the road-building schemes that desensitized the landscape, and the culture of aggressive settlerdom that endured for long after ensured a more varied appreciation of the New Zealand landscape than many could have predicted.

Painting the landscape, prevailing aesthetic and ideological determinants notwithstanding, involved a process of selection, as well as the consideration of certain formal and compositional criteria. And in Elizabeth Bohls's largely eighteenth-century account of aesthetics and the role of the female travel writer, she writes of how after the 1757 publication of Edmund Burke's *The Sublime and the Beautiful*, the ruin featured as a dominant motif within sublime discourse and, moreover, how ruin imagery was valued for its ability to impart a sense of tasteful irregularity, the way in which it 'perfectly answered the criteria of picturesque composition'.[16] The ivy-clad ruin, set tastefully into a particular scene by any

---

[16] Elizabeth Bohls, *Women Travel Writers and the Language of Aesthetics, 1716–1818* (Cambridge: Cambridge University Press, 1995), p. 99.

number of visual artists, imparted antiquarian richness and history, while at the same time giving a sense of how the ideal landscape should appear. Although the vogue for the ruin was foremost among British painters and writers – with Gilpin's scenic tourism especially prevalent and influential throughout the 1770s and 1780s – it was also promoted in places other than Britain. In Sean Ryder's essay, for example, the ruin is noted as having become central to much Irish aesthetic discourse, but with one notable difference: the Irish ruin was associated with trauma and cultural concussion to a degree that British ruins were not. If the ruin in the British landscape was an aesthetic trope used to evoke certain feelings and sensitivities, then in Ireland, in the writing of Thomas Moore, for instance, it reminded readers of Ireland's difficult history, the ruinous state emblematic of a now defunct Gaelic order. The same image, differently constructed and perceived, was significantly altered amidst an Irish landscape, revealing a rupture not always easy to control. At times representative of Irishness itself, the Irish ruin was at once an expression of loss and vanquished hopes, and a gloomy reminder of what might have been.

Although the Irish landscape is read by Ryder as an, at times, more difficult terrain than routinely thought, a similarly troubled attitude towards parts of the Caribbean is evoked in Evelyn O'Callaghan's essay, which focuses on British 'lady travellers' to the West Indies. As O'Callaghan demonstrates, the British attitude towards parts of the Caribbean was even more conflicted than in places such as Ireland, for many saw the landscape itself, rather than native attitudes, as bewildering, exotic and potentially threatening. See-sawing between different modes of address – the West Indies is 'ours', but also alien – several late nineteenth- and early twentieth-century British travel narratives reveal a commitment to a particular place, but one routinely compromised by the narrative restraints imposed on women travellers. Unable to discourse as confidently about imperial authority as men, women travellers to the West Indies, argues O'Callaghan, worked at the intersection of colonial and feminine discourses, and not surprisingly with some difficulty. However, there was one area with which female-authored writing could imaginatively engage: the landscape, especially if reflected in terms of already established aesthetic criteria, and if couched in the language of historical adventure, romance or even sublime discourse. The landscape aesthetics developed in Britain in response to Burke, as well as the arguably more refined picturesque and romantic discourse of the late eighteenth and early nineteenth century, were profitably employed by female travel writers to the West Indies at a later date, but used as much for the purpose of furthering their participation in what was frequently regarded as a predominantly male genre, as for making less 'strange' the sub-tropical vegetation and climate of their surroundings.

Although a number of essays in this collection deal with representations of landscape, or write of the different phases of landscape appreciation, or even the ways in which various locales require regionally-specific analysis and consideration, several studies deal with how landscape was promoted and reinvented in very physical terms. Harbours, coastal defences, 'new' towns and walls are all part of the physical apparatus of empire: what ensures its safety, protects it from attack, gives it character and presence and immediacy. At least so the theory goes. In J. M. Coetzee's *Waiting for the Barbarians* (1980) we see how the colony turns in on itself, becomes dependent on recreational violence, destruction and torture, and all because of a belief that a much greater fear resides elsewhere. Stockaded behind high walls, detached from the surrounding countryside, the Magistrate and his fellow inhabitants become the true barbarians, feeding on one another's paranoia, waiting for the attack that never materializes. Or think of Joyce Cary's *Mister Johnson* (1939), the prompt for Chinua Achebe's *Things Fall Apart* (1958), and of how Cary revealed the fundamental instability behind the narrative that was colonial 'authority'. In Cary's depiction, the British compound that is Fada Station is shown to be an altogether less robust presence than might have been imagined. Grimy and worn, physically permeable and under constant threat from the elements, the compound elicits nothing less than impermanence, uncertainty and doubt. Meanwhile, Major Rudbeck's road-building schemes, done for his own blurred vision of heroic self-will, are seen as pointless incursions on the landscape. What purpose the road might serve, what it will ultimately lead towards, whether the human and economic cost involved in its construction will prove worthwhile when local traders have enjoyed reasonable success thus far without it are shown by Cary to be questions worth raising, but questions rarely voiced.

At the tail end of the nineteenth century, Peter Hulme informs us, there were plans for a new road to be constructed across one of the less accessible parts of Dominica. At around the same time that the travelogues discussed by O'Callaghan were being published, testifying to the exotic beauty of several of the Caribbean islands, British officials were constructing a report for the reinvention of Dominica. Often thought to be potentially one of the richest of the West Indian islands, but neglected by successive Colonial Secretaries, Dominica was to be regarded as a test-case for the 'New Imperialists' of the late 1890s. Focusing on the relatively underdeveloped interior, they argued that here lay the perfect opportunity for some rigorous reclamation. And the way to its heart, they suggested, lay in the construction of a road that would access it from the coast, encourage settlers to build new estates, but also ensure an influx of white migrants to restock a diminishing community. Perhaps unsurprisingly, there were numerous dangers and difficulties associated with such a scheme, and despite the ambitions of Joseph Chamberlain and Hesketh Bell, Colonial Secretary and Administrator of Dominica respectively, the proposal ultimately failed. Nevertheless, this scheme for developing the interior of the island forcefully reminds us of how crucial the control of the landscape had become, how it was linked to greater economic authority, but also to the health and, ultimately, expansion of the settler community.

Although these plans for Dominica must be seen as part of a failed policy to encourage resettlement of several parts of the island, Hulme sees in Jean Rhys's short story 'Pioneers, Oh Pioneers' not only a foreshadowing of the life of the inexperienced settler, but a critique of precisely the sorts of imperial road-building ambitions that were promoted by politicians and administrators such as Chamberlain and Hesketh Bell. For Rhys, the demystification of empire, with an especial focus on the shattered world of a not-so-centred, central character, says much about the belief, or fantasy, of the 'easy' life on the colonial plantations. Associated with instability and, later, madness (although the real problem concerns his inability or unwillingness to conform), the character Rhys constructs, contrary to Chamberlain and Hesketh Bell, implicitly insists upon the complexities of landscape.

At around the time Jean Rhys was working as a chorus girl in England, her peripatetic existence forming the basis of experiences that would appear in several early works, Britain was still in thrall to the romance of empire.[17] True, the sceptical gaze turned towards it by the likes of Somerset Maugham, with his critique of planter society and its stifling codes, was not that far away.[18] But as Martin Green has ably demonstrated, the 'light reading' of a generation of Britons was nevertheless being still formed from often heroically and lavishly narrated tales of empire.[19] And just as Rhys would travel backwards and forwards, at times uncomfortably, between Paris and London – displaying, surely, as much postcolonial as modernist anxiety in early novels such as *After Leaving Mr McKenzie* (1930) – so too were others travelling. They travelled throughout the Empire in search of self-discovery, money and greater knowledge, or because they had little choice, or because the opportunity simply presented itself. Sometimes they travelled for adventure and excitement.

In Mary Condé's essay we find the emphasis, or imperial drive, to be less on the metaphysical problems of the protagonist – the sort of preoccupation routinely examined in Rhys's fiction – than on the daily struggle with the physical difficulties of settlement and landscape. Moreover, in Condé's view many romance narratives associated the rugged challenges of the colonial landscape with specifically male adventures. Above all else, it seems, strong heroes were required for the difficulties of the Orient and the hardships of sub-Saharan Africa. They saw the land as something to be tamed, and themselves as conquering heroes, travellers to distant territories who could be relied upon to put things to right, whatever the circumstances. However, although the male, land-controlling prerogative in such fiction frequently dominates, suggests Condé, the heroines in such novels were just as keen to assert their respect and understanding of the landscape as their male counterparts. Indeed, much like the differences across the landscape itself, these female novelists produced heroines who responded to their environment in all its complex and varied forms: at times puzzled

---

[17] Jean Rhys arrived in Britain from Dominica in 1907, aged 17, and after some time training as an actress joined a chorus in 1909, 'the heyday of the English stage'. Carole Angier, *Jean Rhys: Life and Work* (London: Andre Deutsch, 1990), p. 53.

[18] Maugham made five journeys to Indo-China, the Federated Malay States and China with Gerald Haxton, his lover, between 1916 and 1926, although some of his most memorable stories, largely drawn from the Malayan trilogy – 'Red', 'The Pool', 'The Outstation' – date from the 1920s and early 1930s. See Anthony Curtis, *The Pattern of Maugham* (London: Hamish Hamilton, 1974) and Frederic Raphael, *Somerset Maugham and his World* (London: Thames and Hudson, 1976).

[19] Martin Green, *Dreams of Adventure, Deeds of Empire* (London: Routledge, 1980), p. 3.

by its overwhelmingly 'exotic' nature and its unrecognizable shrub and plant-life, they were also exhilarated by veldt and bush. The almost irrational male attachment to land and landscape so decisively ridiculed in later writings – in Doris Lessing's *The Grass is Singing* (1950), for example – does not preside here. In Condé's opinion, the early twentieth-century female writer of romance fiction saw in the landscape, and its *derivatives*, an opportunity to situate both male and female characters within a conveniently lush environment that had instant appeal and, moreover, one that could be converted into a relatively easy romantic shorthand: the veldt was arid, but physically available; the heat unbearable, yet sensuously languorous; the smells pungent and overwhelming, but also intoxicating. No longer to be associated with physical incomprehension and difficulty only, the totality of the environment was presented by such writers as an immediately accessible signification system that helped to sell empire, and sometimes sex, to its readers.

Recent critical efforts to situate modernism in relation to empire have produced some provocative readings, especially of figures and texts frequently regarded as contextually unavailable. James Joyce, for example, after a period in which his work appeared all but lost to post-structuralist excess, has been rehabilitated as a figure conditioned by empire, in all its guises. Indeed, the stylistic playfulness of his work is now routinely read as a postcolonial tactic or strategy, a form perfectly adapted, and modulated, to accommodate the richness of a life conditioned as much by the British as the Roman Empire.[20] In an essay that engages with the work of two women modernist writers – Emily Carr and Katherine Mansfield – Angela Smith reinforces this view that modernist writers and painters (and Carr and Mansfield worked in both forms) were keenly attuned to the political realities of their era and not simply caught up within escapist formalism. Indeed, Smith argues that both writers not only indicate in their work a deep awareness of the plight of the colonized Other, but situate such an understanding of the Other firmly, and emphatically, within the Self. And since non-European landscapes were the common experience of both – Canada and New Zealand – Smith finds that it is this aspect of their lives, how they choose to represent these different territories and in what form, that provides them with an altogether greater clarity about their own values and beliefs. As Smith sees it, when Carr militates against the idea of the 'English' garden, with its emphasis on tidiness, symmetry and co-ordination, and looks to American landscapes that suggest entanglement and wilderness, she foregrounds spaces that lead to a self-empowering release from European structures and knowledge. While the experience of giving oneself over to the allure of the 'foreign' also occurs within Mansfield's writing, a feeling that can evoke an uneasy sense of self-recognition, Smith argues that the internalization of the Other landscape ultimately liberates these artists towards other forms, and forms of knowledge.

---

[20] As an exemplary instance of such a position, see Declan Kiberd's edited and annotated James Joyce, *Ulysses* (London: Penguin, 1992). See also Emer Nolan, *James Joyce and Nationalism* (London: Routledge, 1995).

Not for nothing, then, did both Carr and Mansfield – hybrid figures acutely aware of the duality of their lives – find experimental art something of an answer to the complexity of their lives. Yet modernism was marked by more than just an emphasis on the self, or on the forms subsequently developed and adopted. Indeed, one 'of the more striking features of Modernism', suggests Malcolm Bradbury, is its 'wide geographical spread, its multiple nationality'.[21] The shock of the new, the various feelings of wariness, hostility and euphoria that characterized modernist art in all its guises, argues Bradbury, was something shared by many cultures and nations. In Berlin, Prague, New York and London there was a need for constant interaction between artists, across disciplines and throughout cultures. But in addition to the sense that for many the formally new, or radical, was rather better served within cities was the fact that many of its practitioners actually travelled from place to place in the service of modernism. Paul Fussell, working with a somewhat more enlarged chronology, though reduced set of geographical referents than Bradbury, writes of the 'great flight of writers from England in the 20s and 30s which deposited Gerald Brenan in Spain and Robert Graves in Majorca … Lawrence Durrell in Corfu; Aldous Huxley in California … Somerset Maugham and Katherine Mansfield on the Riviera'.[22] Fussell's book, which takes the reader up to the outbreak of the Second World War, gives an account of the degree to which many writers of this generation regarded travel, and travel writing, as an instinctive, indeed for some intrinsic, part of their work.

Around the time Fussell writes of remembering the transatlantic liners that used to nuzzle the island of Manhattan – 'their classy, frivolous red and black and white and green uttering their critique of the utility beige-grey of the buildings', most of them visiting North America from Europe – an altogether different cargo of travellers was setting sail in the opposite direction.[23] In Gail Low's essay we are reminded of that momentous event in Black British history: the arrival of *Empire Windrush* into Tilbury docks in 1948 and the true beginnings of Caribbean post-war migration to Britain. Invited to Britain by an economy rapidly accelerating towards full employment, however, such migrants became within only a decade a source of concern for many white Britons. Indeed, by the mid-1960s a number of sociological studies of their relationship within, and towards, the host community had been published, studies that specifically detailed the impact Caribbean communities were having on British city life, especially in terms of employment opportunities and housing.[24] And not surprisingly several writers of the day, British and Caribbean both, began to examine such interaction by focusing on space, especially the spaces of home and street. It was

---

[21] Malcolm Bradbury, 'The Cities of Modernism', in Malcolm Bradbury and James McFarlane, eds, *Modernism: A Guide to European Literature, 1890-1930* (London: Penguin, 1991), p. 95.

[22] Paul Fussell, *Abroad: British Literary Traveling between the Wars* (Oxford: Oxford University Press, 1980), p. 11.

[23] Fussell, *Abroad*, p. 37.

[24] The apparent lack of containment and regulation appears to have been especially noted: 'The West Indian passengers came ashore last … They went quickly through passport control

in those places that immigrants achieved greatest visibility and where disagreements about territoriality and ownership were likeliest to erupt. It is the contribution and change brought *to* the landscape of London, then, that came to preoccupy many writers and is the subject of Low's essay. Her study shows how new cultures and landscapes – prosthetic to begin with, genuinely hybrid after a period – were necessarily formed out of old. That said, the transition to full, even partial, acceptance was far from easy throughout these early years, and although these Caribbean communities brought vitality and energy to largely dull and dreary post-war cityscapes, they were increasingly perceived as interlopers rather than guests. In an examination of several of the works of Pinter and MacInnes, Selvon and Lamming, Low shows how within the boarding-house culture of the time, on the very edge of 1950s and 1960s British sub-culture, such communities had to simply learn to survive.

If for some alarming changes were taking place within Britain throughout the 1950s and 1960s, for many more the concern lay not at home but overseas, where the fabric of empire was unravelling messily. Of course Britain was not the only European power with problems on its hands: France, too, was reaping the harvest of allowing too many injustices to be perpetuated in the name of the *mission civilisatrice*. Frantz Fanon's *Black Skin, White Masks* was first published in French in 1952, while the stirrings of anti-colonial resistance began to take shape in Algeria in 1954, a resistance that would lead to an especially brutal campaign waged until 1962. But for Britain the rapidly changing events took many by surprise. For some, Indian independence in 1947 seemed an almost unbelievable development, certainly not the precedent and example it was to become. But precedent it was, and in 1948 Burma and Ceylon became independent, with Libya, Sudan and the Gold Coast achieving self-government in 1951, 1956 and 1957 respectively. Indeed, so portentous was the topic, both abroad and at home, that in 1960 Harold Macmillan famously described the empire as becoming subject to a 'wind of change'. Domino theorists, it seemed, were on to something after all, for this was not so much the landscape changed as simply repossessed, and Cyprus, British Somaliland and Nigeria all gained independence that very year.[25]

Of the various anti-colonial groups the British campaigned against throughout these years, however, it was their engagement with the Kenyan Mau Mau resistance

---

... Two coaches on the boat-train had been reserved for the West Indian party so that the two officials could go around and ask everyone whether they had a place to go ... at Victoria station the platform was crowded. There was a mass of dark people; about a hundred friends and relatives were waiting to greet the newcomers. Soon they were all dispersed. No official body has a record of where they have gone to; and no official body knows for certain where they are now.' Ruth Glass, *London's Newcomers: The West Indian Migrants* (Cambridge, Mass.: Harvard University Press, 1961). See also R. B. Davison's *Black British: Immigrants to England* (London: Oxford University Press, 1965).

[25] For an accessible and compact introduction, see W. David McIntyre, *British Decolonization, 1946–1997: When, Why and How did the British Empire Fall?* (Basingstoke: Macmillan, 1998).

fighters that was marked by especial brutality. Active from 1952, Mau Mau confronted British authority – and there are parallels, here, of prestige and incredulity with French-occupied Algeria – on one of its most hallowed sites. Moreover, since many of those who made up the officer class in the country were, as Edgerton suggests, part of a 'still more highly conservative body of officers and their families who left India in 1947', the stage was set for a bloody conflict.[26] Those upper levels of British society who had links to Kenya, in other words, were in no mood to see one of its most prized, and lucrative, possessions abandoned to African nationalism[27] and were encouraged by the arrival of these hardened, Indian veterans. It is of this rather fraught and highly charged arena – of recently shipped troops, embattled settlers and the developing nature of physical force nationalism – that Brendon Nicholls writes. His reading of the increasing emphasis placed by the British military on the control of the Kenyan landscape as a way of combating Mau Mau insurgency complements other essays in this volume at a number of levels.

For example, if Mau Mau took to operating a guerrilla style operation and spatially contested British authority in direct ways, then the military would strike back by ordering internment camps, where many thousands were incarcerated, to be constructed. If Mau Mau could, with only limited success, be harassed by hot-pursuit British forces across the Aberdare mountains, then the British airforce would simply strafe the place as an effective counter-measure. Literally inscribed with violence, then, the period of the Mau Mau Emergency saw the Kenyan landscape disfigured with the mechanics of warfare, an experience which, despite the passage of time, continues to preoccupy one of the country's greatest novelists and critics, Ngugi wa Thiong'o. Although from the 1960s onwards, suggests Nicholls, Ngugi has engaged in a number of critical and political debates, he has frequently concentrated on representations of landscape, which he has consistently, almost intimately, linked to ideology. It is true that various phases of his writing have evoked occasionally gendered responses to landscape, but he has also connected landscape to land ownership and productivity, and read it in conventionally political terms throughout any number of critical and imaginative works. Of course, Ngugi is also concerned with African historiography and offers a combative challenge to those who have taken possession of the 'past' and made redundant or ineffectual the story of Mau Mau insurgency. But the desecration of the landscape enacted by the British, and now by their successors, nevertheless colours much of his writing.

In Cynthia Davis's essay the emphasis is less on the destruction or temporary mutilation of an indigenous habitat than on growing and propagating, sometimes

---

[26] Robert B. Edgerton, *Mau Mau: An African Crucible* (London: Tauris, 1990), p. 48.

[27] 'As Lord Delamore, the acknowledged leader of these first settlers, made plain, their goal was to recreate the Virginia plantocracy in which white gentlemen of breeding and leisure oversaw vast plantations worked by black men … Lord Delamere's Rift Valley ranch was so large that 1,000 miles of barbed wire were needed to enclose it.' Edgerton, *Mau Mau*, pp. 12, 25.

on the literal transplantation of different plant and spice species from one part of the world to another. Her essay begins with the rather benign image of horticulture and of the development of the botanical gardens of the Caribbean. However, these gardens, she reminds us, have their origins in economic botany, when new plants, ferns and palms were being rigorously studied by nineteenth-century horticulturalists in an effort to determine whether they could be used by western medicine or utilized as food, timber or dye. The attitude displayed towards nature by European colonists, then, was radically different from that developed by African-American and Caribbean authorities. For the European, garden landscapes work to confirm universalist or eurocentric models and values, whereas the diasporic view of the garden is more a matter of reconnection to an earlier history, a means of memorialization and continuity with another time. Political, yet also thoughtful about complex environmental matters, the writers discussed by Davis argue that although the landscape was altered, sometimes irrevocably, by colonialism, it is nevertheless still useful to see it as a site of contestation, and as an historical narrative that documents, in its own way, diasporic identity. In an overview of several of the works of Hurston, Rhys, Kincaid, Walker and others, Davis reveals the affirmative experience of reclaiming the landscape, and in particular how an alternative attitude to the garden may be posited against the European model, where the emphasis is frequently on productivity, classification and knowledge.

In the final essay in this volume we read not so much of ravaged, transformed or de-territorialized landscapes, or of productivity or aesthetics, but of spatial and cultural antagonisms within the 'states' of Ireland. Beginning with an examination of Colm Toibin's border travelogue, Conor McCarthy argues that the Irish border functions in Toibin's writing as a way of articulating a political stance towards both jurisdictions, but a stance carefully modulated, and operating, on several levels. Although the border is a focus for much contemporary Irish life, however politically constructed, legally defended and militarily guarded it may be, it is granted little historical understanding in the work of Toibin. As a significant legacy of empire, the border, McCarthy argues, simply wastes away as a source of historical and ideological difficulty, becoming, instead, a focus for ironic, stylized detachment. So, by emphasizing its physical reality – Toibin walks its length – and then choosing to ignore it in any meaningful way other than to comment wryly about occasional community stresses, he manages, McCarthy suggests, to have it both ways: to desensitize its significance, while accepting, indeed insisting upon, its sense of fixity. Although the social anthropologists Wilson and Donnan suggest that it 'is precisely at borders that state power is most keenly marked and felt, in ways that ethnographic research can be particularly effective at uncovering', such an experience is curiously absent in the work of Toibin.[28] Indeed, from McCarthy's reading of Toibin we sense that whatever else was likely to be considered during that long walk from Lough Foyle to Carlingford Lough, it was certainly not going to be a recognition of the border as

---

[28] Thomas M. Wilson and Hastings Donnan, *Border Identities: Nation and State at International Frontiers* (Cambridge: Cambridge University Press, 1998), p. 17.

an emotive, powerfully felt presence in peoples' lives, but rather a systematic cataloguing of it as a fixed and indisputable 'fact'. Like his novel set along the Dublin–Wexford axis, Toibin employs Irish geographical co-ordinates and references to disturb, though at other times simply to confirm and reinforce, the politics and legacies of empire.

The intention of this volume is to explore how landscapes have been changed, and sometimes re-imagined, in the wake of colonial contact. It is not intended as an endpoint, but rather a consideration of how our lived environments have been historically and politically conditioned. Just as there have been many imperial systems, so too have there been various ways of reading and responding to landscape, and these essayists chart the implications of writing about very different cultures and locales. However, the emphasis, clearly, is on those places most affected by the British colonial experience – in New Zealand, Canada, Dominica, Ireland, India, South Africa, Kenya and Jamaica – although the traffic is not all one way, and the effect on Britain of movement *from* the Caribbean is discussed, while the specificities of 'postcolonial' America are also touched upon. A comparative structure, in other words, examining how British responses to landscape differed from other colonial and imperial systems, is not one of our concerns, although implicit comparisons throughout the empire, showing how it responded to regional variation, is certainly intended. As suggested from the outset, the determination here is to secure a sense of how imperial energies, so often taken in the direction of establishing a base and then making that base amenable to metropolitan authority, were deployed across several territories. The idea, also, is that the interaction between landscape and empire may be read from a variety of sources: from historical documents, from maps and other elements stemming from a visual culture, from the notes and memorandums of those who worked at the chalkface of colonial administration, but especially from novels and poems and travelogues, the sort of material which arguably disseminated impressions about empire most effectively. Drawing on over two hundred years of contact, alert to historical fluctuations along the way, these essays write of an especially volatile interface: between the presence of an imperial authority and the physical reality of the landscape.

Chapter One

Planning Control: Cartouches, Maps and the Irish Landscape, 1770–1840

Glenn Hooper

Throughout the 1980s, especially in the work of J. B. Harley, we begin to see a scientifically entrenched history of cartography become less and less secure. In the first place, Harley insisted on the historical context of a map, thereby switching the focus from one of 'technical' to 'political' appreciation, arguing that the map was not something to be evaluated solely in terms of its mathematical accuracy, but regarded, rather, as a 'thick text', a layered and potentially multiple form of representation. In *Concepts in the History of Cartography* (1980), jointly written with M. J. Blakemore, for example, the *cultural* meaning of a map was declared to be crucial, a line of reasoning that set its authors on a collision course with many of their colleagues ('Historians of cartography have tended to neglect metaphorical, poetic or symbolic meanings within their maps').[1] Harley drew on the work of the Polish theorist, Irwin Panofsky ('In essence iconography takes a linguistic or structuralist view of images'), although this was soon toned down in favour of more historicist models.[2] For example, in his contribution to Sarah Tyacke's essay collection *English Map-Making 1500–1650* (1983) he still insisted on a rigorous application of Panofsky's ideas, and searched for iconographical parallels in art and cartography, yet the emphasis steadily shifted towards a more 'semiotic approach', with the historical and political contexts for maps increasingly emphasized.[3] Indeed, a break of sorts would appear to have taken place within Harley's thinking throughout these years, with essays from the later 1980s beginning to depart significantly from earlier efforts. For instance, in 'Maps, Knowledge and Power' (1988) Harley engaged with empire and nation building, employed a broadly Foucauldian line, and made Panofsky still useful to his arguments, but he also situated his analyses of the map and map-making within a decidedly historical

---

[1] M. J. Blakemore and J. B. Harley, *Concepts in the History of Cartography*, vol. 17, no. 4 (Toronto: University of Toronto Press, Monograph 26, 1980), p. 76.

[2] Blakemore and Harley, *Concepts*, p. 77.

[3] J. B. Harley, 'Meaning and Ambiguity in Tudor Cartography', in Sarah Tyacke, ed., *English Map-Making 1500–1650* (London: The British Library, 1983), p. 23.

framework.[4] In 'Silences and Secrecy' (1988) an even more emphatic position appeared to have been adopted ('My reading of the map is not a technical one … but a political one')[5], while in 'Deconstructing the Map' (1989) and 'Historical Geography and the Cartographic Illusion' (1989) Harley appeared increasingly committed to a reading of the map that borrowed heavily from models within literary studies, but was sufficiently elastic to be useful to the cartographic historian.

It is difficult to know what exactly triggered Harley's thinking on the ideal model for cartographic analysis, but that he moved from structuralist to à la carte post-structuralism is fairly evident. He was certainly impressed by Peter Hulme's work, citing Hulme's definition of colonial discourse approvingly,[6] although he missed an opportunity to discuss Hulme's comments on high theory that go towards explaining, I believe, his own, subsequent developments. Explaining in the introduction to *Colonial Encounters* (1986) the general theoretical thrust of his study on the Caribbean ('generally Marxist … socioeconomic and political'), Hulme acknowledged the appeal and potential authority of high theory, but cautioned against its wholesale appropriation.[7] He wrote of the persuasive strength of post-structuralism and argued that despite the reservations of many, in 'purely philosophical terms [it] is difficult, perhaps impossible to counter'.[8] However, the downside to such high theorizing, he shrewdly observed, was that 'such a position can lead only to quietism, since no action at all can be validated from its theoretical endpoint, or to a false radicalism which engages in constant but ultimately meaningless transgression of all defended viewpoints'.[9] And this, I believe, published midway through Harley's own re-evaluation of the history of cartography, was just the sort of exit-route out of the thicket of hard post-structuralism that Harley needed. In other words, Harley found himself in agreement with Hulme, took Foucault at his word and approached literary theory very much like a 'tool-box', and thereby devised the freedom to subsequently develop a deconstructionist reading of the map that was political and theoretically grounded, yet humanist.[10]

---

[4]   J. B. Harley, 'Map, Knowledge and Power', in Denis Cosgrove and Stephen Daniels, eds, *The Iconography of Landscape: Essays on the Symbolic Representation, Design and Use of Past Environments* (Cambridge: Cambridge University Press, 1988).

[5]   J. B. Harley, 'Silences and Secrecy: The Hidden Agenda of Cartography in Early Modern Europe', *Imago Mundi*, 40 (1988), p. 57.

[6]   Harley refers to Hulme in a lengthy footnote (no. 5), stating, the 'word discourse has so many interpretations in linguistic and literary studies that it is necessary to define it here. I take the sense nearest to my own from Hulme.' Harley, 'Silences and Secrecy', p. 71.

[7]   Peter Hulme, *Colonial Encounters: Europe and the Native Caribbean, 1492–1797* (London: Methuen, 1986), p. 5.

[8]   Hulme, *Colonial Encounters*, p. 6.

[9]   Hulme, *Colonial Encounters*, p. 6.

[10] Barbara Belyea acknowledges the 'strong social conscience [that prompted Harley] to see maps as instruments by which modern nation-states acquired territory and maintained a political status quo', but argues that he 'refuses to accept the implication of the poststructuralist positions he claims to espouse'. Barbara Belyea, 'Images of Power: Derrida/Foucault/Harley',

Harley tore up the way we read maps then, and how we continue to approach them now.

Throughout the 1980s, then, until his early death in 1991, J. B. Harley revolutionized the history of cartography.[11] And although not all of his work had been completed, the excitement of these new ideas, which Harley shared generously with his readers, is still evident. He wrote of state secrecy and map distortion, argued for a less technical approach to cartography and repeatedly drew attention to what he saw as the lack of anything like a political and historical context governing much cartographic discussion. He was also – and this will be the subject of my essay – one of the first to write, not only of map symbolism, but of the political import of much map decoration and of how it needed to be assessed in terms of its ideological significance. His discussion of Tudor cartography, for example, involved arguing, first, that maps be seen for the frequently political documents they are: 'Maps were one of a number of instruments of control by landlords and governments; they were spatial emblems of power in society; they were artefacts in the creation of myth; and they influenced perceptions of place and space at a variety of geographical scales.'[12] But more than this, Harley argued that the *totality* of the map must be fully assessed, and that those historians of cartography who have ignored the 'decorative content [of the map] in favour of concentration on the central geographical image' were seriously misguided.[13] So captions, cartouches, even the type of lettering used by engravers were all part of the message and meaning of a map, argued Harley:

> It is surely high time that this superficial, 'ornamental' view of decoration on Tudor maps is superannuated. It is an attitude based on the notion that decoration is a marginal exercise in aesthetics in contradistinction to the central map image, which is in the proper business of communicating 'hard' information ... A more satisfactory interpretation, however, which has hitherto slipped through our fingers, is to regard both decorative and geographical images on a map as unified parts of a total image.[14]

Cartographica, 29:2 (Summer 1992), pp. 1–3. Notwithstanding Belyea's critique, it is not difficult – despite Harley's allegedly weak grasp of theory – to see why orthodox post-structuralism would have had little appeal for the humanist scholar.

[11] Of the many obituaries, see David Woodward, 'Obituary: J. B. Harley (1932–1991)', *Imago Mundi*, 44 (1992), pp. 120–25 ('Harley's attack on the technical study of maps appears somewhat enigmatic on the surface. He had a deep knowledge and interest in the technical *minutiae* of early maps ... It was, however, not the *techniques* per se that were being attacked; the criticism was aimed at his colleagues' tendency to focus on these technical matters without understanding what they meant to society in a broader context. It was not that technical knowledge should be *replaced* by broad contextual studies, but that the latter should enlarge and extend it', p. 122).

[12] Harley, 'Meaning and Ambiguity', p. 22.

[13] Harley, 'Meaning and Ambiguity', p. 36.

[14] Harley, 'Meaning and Ambiguity', p. 36. A somewhat different, though nevertheless useful, focus – with the emphasis laid on the hitherto under-researched 'explanatory writing' of maps – is discussed by Catherine Delano Smith, in 'Cartographic Signs on European Maps and their Explanation before 1700', *Imago Mundi*, 37 (1985).

Although historians of British cartography relative to Ireland have frequently written of the historical dimension to Irish maps, they have confined much of their discussion to that area which seems most likely to yield results: the early modern era. For example, John Andrews has written of the work of Robert Lythe, one of the 'better-known Elizabethan surveyors [who] approached regional cartography as a military engineer and fortifications expert', and who mapped parts of Ulster and Leinster in the late 1560s and early 1570s.[15] Indeed, Ulster features in several maps of this period, although accuracy occasionally gave way to rough estimations of scale and terrain as map-makers struggled with hasty impressions drawn from inhospitable and dangerous territory. One such map, a copy of which is in the Royal Irish Academy, includes the following legend:

> This plat not drawn owt by order of skayll for want of tym to survey upon it, to do it so axackely as I would have done yf I had had that tym to have done it in that order ... but this and in this order the contrey seyeth erland ofe of skotland from glanarme to loughfoyll.[16]

The emphasis here is on making as quick an estimation of the major features of the Ulster shoreline as possible, the purpose of which is to satisfy military and naval rather than strictly cartographic requirements. The map itself – part promotional and ideological narrative, part fearful fantasy – visualizes Britain (or more specifically, England) in expeditionary mode, as ships surge towards the Irish coast, heavily manned, with cannons and clearly displaying the St George's Cross, while the land itself is only weakly documented; rabbits and deer pockmark the 'plat' alongside the natives of 'Ākānes contre' (O'Kane's country), long-haired Irish drawn only from the chest up and buried in – or erupting from – the undulating landscape.

David Baker has argued, as 'English colonialism strove to impose itself on Ireland's recalcitrant terrain – and *because* it thus strove to impose itself – it found itself in (literally) uncharted space, drawn beyond the limits of its own plausibility.'[17] Despite this, G. A. Hayes-McCoy has described the linkage made in many an Elizabethan mind between maps and power, and specifically how Ulster – the least known of all the Irish provinces at the end of the sixteenth century – was regarded

---

[15] J. H. Andrews, 'The Irish Surveys of Robert Lythe', *Imago Mundi*, 19 (1965), p. 22.

[16] '16th century map of Ulster', copy of PRO 551, MPF 88, Royal Irish Academy. Later maps, especially those drawn after the surrender of O'Neill (1603), when plans to colonize Ulster were properly underway, were only a partial improvement: 'The allotment could not proceed without maps. So another commission, headed by Lord Deputy Chichester, went round the region ... "so as the more obscure part of the king's dominions is now as well-known [as] ... any part of England". This was a flattering description; the maps were beautifully drawn and coloured, but were not based on actual measurements and were without a scale.' J. G. Simms, 'Donegal in the Ulster Plantation', *Irish Geography*, 5 (1972), p. 388.

[17] David J. Baker, 'Off the Map: Charting Uncertainty in Renaissance Ireland', in Brendan Bradshaw, Andrew Hadfield and Willy Maley, eds, *Representing Ireland: Literature and the Origins of Conflict, 1534–1660* (Cambridge: Cambridge University Press, 1993), p. 78.

not just as intractable, but intractable because unmapped and therefore unknown ('Ulster, and particularly the interior of that province, was for long *terra incognita* to the English').[18] In Ulster, a boggy and notoriously wooded area that favoured the insurgent, native Irish, resistance was related directly to a lack of knowledge ('The English government in Ireland was fully conscious of this geographical *lacuna*'), a deficiency in serious need of attention.[19] The resulting decision to appoint Richard Bartlett as an embed within the ranks of Lord Mountjoy's soldiery helped, but for only a short while:

> Bartlett was ... killed during his survey work in Donegal in 1603. He had been 'appointed ... to draw a true and perfect map of the north parts of Ulster (the old maps being false and defective)', but some of the inhabitants, 'because they would not have their country discovered' – and with (it may be advanced in extenuation of their deed) a prophetic vision of the land confiscations which were to follow such discovery – 'took off his head'.[20]

Image Conscious

While it is relatively easy to identify certain developments within cartography as related to emergent nationalism, and/or to the territorial conflicts between certain European powers in the early modern period, an examination of later maps can be just as fruitful, revealing the extent to which cartography was enmeshed in sometimes quite sophisticated ideological struggles over space, place and landscape. Although peripheral to Europe, and occasionally marginal even to British interests, it is perhaps unsurprising that it is at the very limit of the 'Irish' map itself that we find political and territorial ambitions sometimes fitfully played out. Indeed, when John Rocque moved to Dublin in 1754 he arrived to something of a hero's welcome, as a figure 'already well known for having surveyed London, Paris and Rome ... [but who now] at the suggestion of a number of Irish noblemen and gentlemen ... undertook to do the same for Dublin'.[21] Rocque was taking up, in other words, the invitation of several who saw the mapping of Ireland as a patriotic duty as much as anything else, a role

---

[18] G. A. Hayes-McCoy, 'Contemporary Maps as an Aid to Irish History, 1593–1603', *Imago Mundi*, 19 (1965), p. 33. For an updated view, with an especial appreciation of the geo-political significance of Cork city, see Mark McCarthy, 'Historical Geographies of a Colonized World: The Renegotiation of New English Colonialism in Early Modern Urban Ireland, c. 1600–10', *Irish Geography*, 36:1 (2003). The role of the map within early modern culture is also usefully discussed in Bruce Avery, 'Mapping the Irish Other: Spenser's *A View of the Present State of Ireland*,' *English Literary History*, 57:2 (1990).

[19] Hayes-McCoy, 'Contemporary Maps', p. 33.

[20] Hayes-McCoy, 'Contemporary Maps', p. 36.

[21] J. H. Andrews, 'The French School of Dublin Land Surveyors', *Irish Geography*, 5 (1967), p. 278.

they believed him adequately fitted for. And by 1760, when he returned to London, he had not merely drawn a city map of Dublin, but also a county map of Armagh and city maps of Kilkenny, Cork and Thurles, among several others. A highly regarded surveyor, engraver and cartographer, 'between 1734 and 1762 ... [Rocque] published more than one hundred maps, plans, road books and indexes ... [and established] himself as one of the most prolific and interesting map-makers of the first half of the eighteenth century'.[22] In the work of John Rocque, map-maker, and ultimately chorographer to the King, then, we confront a major force. Moreover, although his style was to present exact and accurate maps, he wished to do so in a fashion that made of the map a decorative, but also highly impressive feat; his staggeringly proportioned 'City and Suburbs of Dublin' map – two hundred feet to an inch – so impressed George II, for example, that 'he ordered it to be hung in his own apartment'.[23]

But it is how the 'decorative' and aesthetic elements of Rocque's maps worked, what they suggested and evoked for those who contemplated them, that is of interest here. Rocque's style was certainly impressive, building, as it did, on already established cartographic tradition. James Welu suggests that:

> For roughly a century, from 1570 to 1670, mapmakers working in the Low Countries brought about unprecedented advances in the art of cartography. The maps, charts, and globes issued during this period, at first mainly in Antwerp and later in Amsterdam, are distinguished not only by their accuracy according to the knowledge of the time, but also by their richness of ornamentation, a combination of science and art that has rarely been surpassed in the history of mapmaking.[24]

In addition to what they may have signified in the sixteenth or seventeenth centuries, the ornamentions of several eighteenth- and nineteenth-century maps of Ireland are a useful source for reading the political and historical anxieties of the period. In Fig. 1.1, for example, taken from Rocque's 'A Plan of the City and Suburbs of Dublin' map (1773), we are presented with a cartouche in which the very idea of cartographic activity itself has been ritualized and desensitized. Engrossed and absorbed by the task in hand, the putti in this particular tableau enhance the image and reputation of mapping, presenting their surveying equipment, texts and even a blank map of Ireland against a backdrop of soft, slightly pre-pubescent flesh, a gesture designed to downplay, if not displace, the cartographic exercise itself.[25] Aided by the classical

---

[22] John Varley, 'John Rocque. Engraver, Surveyor, Cartographer and Map-Seller', *Imago Mundi*, 5 (1965), p. 83.

[23] Andrews, 'The French School', p. 279.

[24] James A. Welu, 'The Sources and Development of Cartographic Ornamentation in the Netherlands', in David Woodward, ed., *Art and Cartography: Six Historical Essays* (Chicago: University of Chicago Press, 1987), p. 147.

[25] The role of the putto had a long shelf life within 'Irish' cartography. See the prancing, chain-measuring creatures who feature on the cartouche from Charles Vallancey's 'Map of Ireland' (1795).

1.1   John Rocque, cartouche, 'A Plan of the City and Suburbs of Dublin' map (1773). Courtesy of the Royal Irish Academy.

ornamentation (always a sign of respectability) and the coastal setting, here mapping itself becomes something of a depoliticized activity, with even the scales – in which the inhospitable Irish landscape is Anglicized and made therefore more manageable – appearing somewhat less than real. Moreover, although the surveying equipment and the almost tutorial arrangement of the figures gives a certain substance to the cartographic act, the relaxed posture and invitational look of the most foregrounded putto disarms us of any sceptical notions we might harbour.[26]

Although any overt political statements of the sort produced later in Ireland, or indeed in parts of America, are omitted from Rocque's cartouche, it nevertheless images Ireland in terms of a series of absences: the 'real' Irish landscape is made peripheral – the putto offers only the most tentative of footholds – while an empty canvas awaits instruction. It is true that the presentation of cartographic activity is diffused somewhat by being framed within a romantic and rather idealized locale, but the presence of books, globe, dividers and other measuring equipment heightens the sense of potential, and very real, change. Regarding several of Rocque's Kildare estate maps, produced in the late 1750s, Arnold Horner has written of the 'extravagance of the baroque' style, and of how the cartouches may be 'loosely described as belonging to a rustic/romantic genre found in much of the map decoration of the period'.[27] Horner celebrates the 'high level of accuracy and comprehensiveness' of Rocque's work, suggesting that he stands far ahead of any of his colleagues, not just in terms of the detail of the work produced, but 'on account of [the] artistic quality' of the maps themselves.[28] Although Horner rightly draws our attention to the sophistication of Rocque's estate maps, he fails to attribute any political importance to the images themselves. For Horner, the cartouches are decorative, sometimes emblematic, spaces to the side of the main cartographic image, which 'give an insight, albeit fragmentary, into the better class rural housing of the early Georgian period'.[29] Nevertheless, one wonders if there is not rather more to it than this. We might also argue that while Fig. 1.1 may appear as a classically influenced aspect of map imagery, it also diverts the reality of eighteenth-century mapping away from a particular type of landscape appreciation, showing it to be a co-operative, agreeable and inoffensive cherubic impulse, rather than the political activity it arguably is.[30]

---

[26] The metamorphosis of surveying with aesthetic pleasure is enacted more emphatically in an earlier Rocque map, 'An Exact Survey of the City and Suburbs of Dublin' (1756), where the putti literally read and inscribe the Irish landscape.

[27] Arnold Horner, 'Cartouches and Vignettes on the Kildare Estate Maps of John Rocque', *Quarterly Bulletin of the Irish Georgian Society*, XIV: 4 (Oct.–Dec. 1971), p. 60.

[28] Horner, 'Cartouches and Vignettes', pp. 58–9.

[29] Horner, 'Cartouches and Vignettes', p. 71.

[30] Other maps from the period take a more direct approach to the reconfiguration of Irish space. See, for example, Bernard Scalé's 'A Survey of the Barony of Upper Ossory' (1776) which celebrates the work being undertaken on the lands of the Rt. Hon. Earl of Upper Ossory. It details new walls, gates, recently planted trees and orchards, and gives a sense of

Sign Writing

In Richard Helgerson's much cited article 'The Land Speaks: Cartography, Chorography, and Subversion in Renaissance England' (1986), the author writes of how Saxton's book of county maps, published in 1597, allowed 'Englishmen … [for] the first time … [to take] effective visual and conceptual possession of the physical kingdom in which they lived'.[31] These county maps, argues Helgerson, synthesized, but also made theoretically coherent, the very notion of 'England'. And like the maps that were to follow – by William Camden and John Speed, for example – they used decorative or symbolic aspects of the map to articulate various political positions and sympathies. Like Harley and others, Helgerson regards a range of map imagery – cartouche, frontispiece, emblem or symbol – as enabling the cartographer to realize fully his view of the land. However, although Helgerson's appraisal of internal British politics, with its sometimes anti-monarchical strains, adds significantly to the history of early modern cartography, the readings produced from an examination of later maps can be just as rich. G. N. Clarke's work on late eighteenth-century maps of North America, for instance, shows how cartographers used the cartouche to effectively capture, at a single glance, the 'message' of the map. Working from a range of maps of New England, Maryland and South Carolina, all from the 1770s, Clarke argues that 'map and cartouche, as word and image, are fused into equivalent representations of a single unity: a single text'.[32] The cartouches describe and evaluate the land, hint at its abundance, and offer hope and reassurance to potential settlers. In this manner these apparently innocuous decorations help to underpin the prevailing colonial discourse.

In Figs. 1.2 and 1.3, the two cartouches taken from Alexander Taylor's 'A New Map of Ireland' (1783), an overt political note is struck. In Fig. 1.2 we are informed of the purpose of the map – to help travellers and tourists, who were then embarking on increasing forays to all parts of the Celtic fringe, to travel more knowledgeably around the country. The elaborately lettered title produced by Taylor, a Lieutenant in his Majesty's Royal Engineers, hints at nothing more than the map as an aid to leisure tourism, an antiquities-aware effort designed simply to promote the country

---

contentment and ease across the landscape as our eye is drawn to the 'View of Kylegurtrean House'. Scalé's celebration is taken further with the publication of his 'An Hibernian Atlas; or General Description of the Kingdom of Ireland' (1777), in which lavishly engraved title pages are accompanied by written justification of his craft: 'Amongst the first and most necessary of Liberal Arts is Geography; by it we may form a better Idea of any Country than it is possible for us to conceive without its Assistance, but how strange is it to reflect that no Man has ever exhibited an actual Survey of this Ancient and of late cultivated fertile Kingdom' (Preface).

[31] Richard Helgerson, 'The Land Speaks: Cartography, Chorography, and Subversion in Renaissance England', *Representations*, 16 (Fall 1986), p. 51. See, for further discussion of Saxton, Dee and Speed, Jerry Brotton, 'Mapping the Early Modern Nation: Cartography along the English Margins', *Paragraph*, 19:2 (July 1996).

[32] G. N. Clarke, 'Taking Possession: The Cartouche as Cultural Text in Eighteenth-century American Maps', *Word & Image*, 4:2 (April–June 1988), p. 459.

and its more noticeable natural features to scenically inclined visitors. Indeed, the fact that Taylor's 'Map of Ireland' has not one, but two cartouches – reinforcing for some the 'decorative' and thus apolitical nature of the map – suggests an even greater emphasis upon the visual impact of the cartouche and its relationship to the broader meaning of the map. Moreover, the allegorical content establishes a binary message that helps underpin the essence of the map; both cartouches have the same centrally inscribed sections, with figures to either side, plus associative decoration below. But in Fig. 1.2, to the top, and arguably the lead-in image, we have two figures, here engrossed in a visual discussion of that most central of all colonial encounters: trade.[33] 'Ireland', depicted here with cornucopia of untold wealth, is a picture of vulnerability, articulated most specifically by her partially clothed state, while 'Britannia', seated, and keeping a watchful eye on Ireland, represents economic value and exportable worth. Moreover, in lifting her skirt to one side to allow the packing case on which she sits to be seen, she not only establishes the idea of British commercial acumen, but invites the reader to 'buy' into the message itself, to collude with the ideological narrative being loudly stated from the map's margins. The loyal reader, then, is allowed access (unbeknown to Ireland, of course) to the reality of this particular encounter, while Ireland, hair bedecked in flowers and 'netted' to the right of the scene, acts as unsuspecting dupe to fortified English ability.

In Fig. 1.3 we have two further feminized representations of 'England' and 'Ireland', to the left and right respectively, providing an image that says much about both cultures, as well as about the relationship between them: English self-dependence and military might, and Irish narcissism and sinful, unprovoked vanity. Britannia, like the feminized figure in Fig. 1.2, is assured and self-confident, a figure leaning in a posture of possession, arm resting on a combination of two shields (the outer one clearly showing the Irish harp). Attired in a military fashion with protective headgear and spear, and looking outwards and *at* the feminized picture that is Ireland, she presents a forbidding sight: confident, self-contained and at ease. By contrast, the figure to the right is a combination of self-doubt and apprehension. Holding a mirror in her left hand she exudes a multiplicity of vices or undesirable qualities: vanity and narcissistic self-indulgence or an immature and disquieting search for the national self-image. If John Berger is right to suggest that the mirror has often been used as 'a symbol of the vanity of woman', then the vanity evoked here refers less to a gendered view of the world than to the latent expectations of a barely suppressed Irish nationalism.[34] Seen in this way, Ireland, because of the image of fickle and potentially convulsed national self-determination she portrays, must be presented as an observed

---

[33] Trade was a key theme among many map-makers of the period, with alterations to the landscape visually stressed and exalted. See the cartouche on John Brownrigg's 'Survey of the Grand Canal' (1788), dedicated to 'those PATRIOTICK Promoters of the TRADE of Ireland', in which the canal registers itself as both an exemplary engineering triumph and a tasteful distraction for day-tripping tourists.

[34] John Berger, *Ways of Seeing* (London: Pelican, 1984), p. 51.

1.2 **Alexander Taylor, cartouche, 'A New Map of Ireland' (1783). Courtesy of the Royal Irish Academy.**

figure, a figure watched over by a militarily prepared and cautious Britannia.[35]

Alexander Taylor's 'A New Map of Ireland' symbolizes, and at the same time celebrates, the acquisition of Irish land. And it does this largely by delineating the benefits of commercial trade and then consolidating those benefits by recourse to militaristic imagery, as suggested by the abundant and unambiguous hardware that situates itself along the breadth of the foreground in Fig. 1.3. Moreover, it makes the relationship between both countries a curious one of interconnectedness, intimacy almost, yet one also riven by notions of doubt, unease and potential disloyalty; the cartouche on 'trade' in the top left hand corner of the map, and the one on 'national

---

[35] Military representation, however, was not always thus depicted. For example, in a cartouche on John Senex's 'A New Map of Ireland' (1720), a native Irishman – possibly a hunter – is shown with spear and shield.

1.3   Alexander Taylor, cartouche, 'A New Map of Ireland' (1783). Courtesy of the Royal Irish Academy.

self-interest' in the bottom right hand corner present a complex political picture. Organized to be read downwards, the cartouches may be said to articulate, first, celebratory and productive abundance and, second, militaristic self-protection. They work in conjunction with one another, offer a note of caution, but ultimately display, as we move from a foreground of fruit and fish to one of cannon and pike, an image of uneasy territorial ownership. Ireland, observed, unclothed, self-obsessed and presented as, at once, provider of all that is good *and* potential deviant, serves as a troubling symbol of alterity. Indeed, in choosing to present Ireland in such a conflictual mode, a political reading of the cartouche is easily established – the snake and mirror, as symbols of potential revolutionary fervour, see to that. The combined visual and ideological purpose of the cartouches, then, is clear: to alert and caution, and to inform the viewer that the moment of Irish national self-contact – the mirror – is imminent. They suggest that the country continues to be a place of geo-political worth and potential, but a place, also, that requires constant surveillance.

'Cartography', suggests Stephanie Pratt, 'is more than a verbal discourse; the concepts it deploys are encoded in a system of signs inscribed on a flat surface or a globe and, as such, it offers a suitable subject for semiotic analysis.'[36] In a discussion of Daniel Augustus Beaufort's 'A New Map of Ireland' (1792), John Hargreaves makes a passing reference to the cartouche on Beaufort's map, describing it as 'the only part of the map attributable to another hand ... designed by his daughter Frances to embody a number of family allusions, including a dunce's cap, though no doubt a dedicated semioticist could find some ideological significance in it as well'.[37] In these two statements we find entirely opposed views of the value of interpreting cartouche imagery from cartographic sources. From Pratt, whose work on images of Native Americans on British maps suggests that cartouches are one of the most important cultural and political aspects upon which to focus, to Andrews, the most respected historical geographer working on British cartography relevant to Ireland, stretches a widening and deepening gulf. For Andrews, what is most important about a map such as the one produced by Beaufort is its detail, the fact that Beaufort 'depicted relief by hachures' and 'distinguished the bogs by a reed-and-water symbol'.[38] For Pratt, who argues for a 'less than strict Derridean deconstructive analysis of the cartouche', the point is simply this: that 'we might wish to claim that far from being marginal the cartouche constitutes the map'.[39]

Although Andrews's rejection of such analysis remains firm and clear, it is difficult to see how a cartouche as visually arresting and vibrant as the one that accompanies Beaufort's map could have been regarded at the end of the eighteenth

---

[36] Stephanie Pratt, 'From the Margins: The Native American Personage in the Cartouche and Decorative Borders of Maps', *Word & Image*, 12:4 (Oct.–Dec. 1996), p. 349.

[37] J. H. Andrews, *Shapes of Ireland: Maps and their Makers, 1564–1839* (Dublin: Geography Publications, 1997), p. 233.

[38] Andrews, *Shapes of Ireland*, p. 237.

[39] Pratt, 'From the Margins', p. 362.

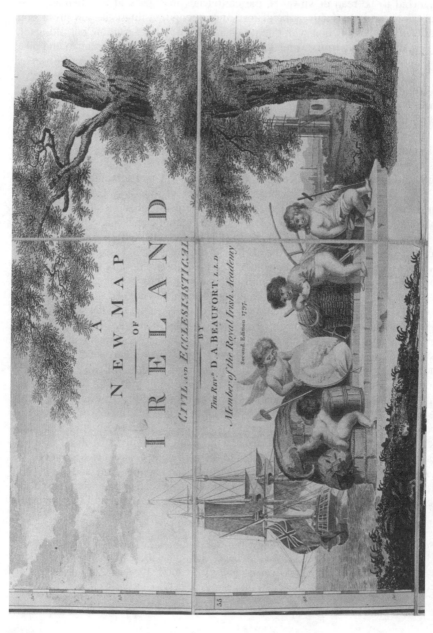

1.4   Daniel Augustus Beaufort, cartouche, 'A New Map of Ireland' (1797). Courtesy of the Royal Irish Academy.

century – in the immediate aftermath of the French revolution and at a time of increasing political agitation in Ireland – as anything less than a commentary on the then parlous state of Anglo-Irish relations. Born in England, though educated and long resident in Ireland, Beaufort was a member of the Anglo-Irish gentry, a founding member of the Royal Irish Academy and a Church of Ireland clergyman. A complex and hyphenated figure, Beaufort was also steeped in Irish history, genealogy and antiquities, and a more than able candidate for the cartographic test he set (and privately funded) for himself at the end of the eighteenth century.[40]

But what might be said about the cartouche that so visually dominates Beaufort's map? In my view, Fig. 1.4, not unlike Taylor's cartouches, articulates a somewhat conflicted position. Ireland appears, on the one hand, as a dangerous and potentially volatile environment, but on the other hand – and this would have been especially necessary for a figure writing from within the ranks of the Anglo-Irish ascendancy – as a place of stability. Again, trade seems to largely dominate the scene as well as the message of the map, with cherubic figures working to establish the place as attractive, lucrative and inviting. Packing cases, barrels and woven baskets of corn – immediately recognizable images of exportable worth – await transport from the quayside, and there is a general sense of activity and bustle. But trade may be read – at least within the context of Anglo-Irish relations – in at least two ways: as an entirely factual statement about the economic and contractual relationship between the two countries, but also as a very specific metaphor for co-operation and harmony. And this, I would argue, is where we find Beaufort's cartouche, straining to articulate something of the agreeable nature of Anglo-Irish politics, only to find itself hedging its bets; using signs of worth and productivity to suggest mutual interest and well-being, but also employing the flag-flying galleon as a way of imposing order and authority. The land appears fertile and bountiful, its inhabitants co-operative and helpful (the cherubic, infantilized Irish?), and the church (given a particulary robust and fortified appearance in this instance) presented in improved and expansive form. It is true that the signs of a culturally displaced Other are also included, but the Gaelic abbey and round tower that are jettisoned (and made politically as well as literally miniaturized) to the rear of the frame tell a different story. The abbey and tower are part of the past, not of the present. They are fine as archaeological or antiquarian artefacts and relics, but they have no role in an Ireland increasingly linked to a superior trading economy.

Date Sensitive

In J. B. Harley's essay 'Silences and Secrecy' the argument is made that when faced with the unique and strange surroundings of the American landscape European

---

[40] For a thoughtful appreciation of Daniel Augustus Beaufort, see Canon C. C. Ellison, 'Remembering Dr. Beaufort', *Quarterly Bulletin of the Irish Georgian Society*, XVIII: 1 (Jan.–March 1975).

engravers engaged in a 'deliberate act of colonial promotion', by stereotyping
their new landscape, thereby making it 'more attractive to settlers ... proprietors
and potential investors'.[41] Although colonial promotion of the sort referred to by
Harley had dwindled somewhat by the early nineteenth century, the Act of Union
of 1800 managed to focus many minds on the benefits of Union, as well as on
the idea that Ireland was now a faithful and loyal partner bound within a newly
established constitutional arrangement. Given that Union was brought about partly
by the revolutionary activities of the Irish themselves, however, the ideology of
Unionism was always going to be difficult to sell. Ireland was a loyal partner, but a
possible source of insurrection; Ireland was the 'Sister Isle', but also a willing ally
of France who saw continental intervention as a way of furthering demands for self-
government.

In James Williamson's 'A Map of the County of Down' (1810) we find something
of the double-think that might be said to have characterized Beaufort's cartouche,
but displayed with even greater emphasis. To begin with, Williamson's map
comprises two cartouches, which like several of the other examples in this essay
are meant to be read in conjunction with one another. However, since greater spatial
prominence is given to the landscape of County Down, we shall again begin with the
lead-in image. On immediate examination, Fig. 1.5 reveals a landscape of serene and
unsullied beauty. It has, admittedly, about its edges – particularly in the foreground
– a certain rusticity, especially as it sits hemmed between the perfectly interlocked
brickwork in the middle distance (no dry stone walls for them) and the undulating
township in the background. It is an image of self-confidence, productivity and
husbandry, as can be seen by the fine two and three storey houses in the distance,
the attire of the gentlemen to the left, and the various animals used either for their
labour or as translatable beef and dairy produce. It is, in other words, a very specific
view of Downpatrick, *circa* 1810.

So what Williamson's first cartouche is largely concerned with is promotion:
promoting the quality of life, the improvements made to the land, the sense of a
harmonious community at ease with itself and its surroundings.[42] Moreover, if we
examine some of the finer detail of the image we can see this most clearly in the

---

[41]   Harley, 'Silences and Secrecy', p. 68.

[42]   Promotional cartography has a rich and complex history; see, by way of comparison,
Louis De Vorsey, 'Maps in Colonial Promotion: James Edward Oglethorpe's Use of Maps
in "Selling" the Georgia Scheme', *Imago Mundi*, 38 (1986); William Wyckoff, 'Mapping
the "New" El Dorado: Pikes Peak Promotional Cartography, 1859–1861', *Imago Mundi*, 40
(1988); David Bosse, 'Dartmouth on the Mississippi: Speculators and Surveyors in British
North America in the Eighteenth century', *Imago Mundi*, 41 (1989). For a discussion of
'persuasive cartography' and specifically the function of the propaganda map, see John
Pickles, 'Texts, Hermeneutics and Propaganda Maps', in Trevor Barnes and James Duncan,
eds, *Writing Worlds: Discourse, Text and Metaphor in the Representation of Landscape*
(London: Routledge, 1992).

1.5   James Williamson, cartouche, 'A Map of the County of Down' (1810). Courtesy of the Royal Irish Academy.

positioning of the two figures to the left of the scene. Standing in the immediate vicinity of what has all the appearance of an oak tree, our two figures, attired in frock coat and top hat, and gesturing symbolically to the utopian prospect ahead, say much about their attitude to the land.[43] This is a picture of environmental concord, but a concord brought about, we know, by the transformation of the land, the quelling of dissent, the suppression of unruly nativism. Undoubtedly, there is a desire here to simply celebrate hard-won achievements and accomplishments, but the manner in which this has been done evokes Cosgrove and Daniels's view of landscape as an opportunity to 'symbolise surroundings'.[44]

If we move to Williamson's accompanying cartouche – Fig. 1.6 – we see that where the scene of Downpatrick suggested gentrification and solidity, as it underscored its newly domesticated environment (see the geometrically pleasing orchard to the right of the church), this scene, set around the port of Belfast, suggests a more determined, military spectacle. A sailing ship, centrally placed to the scene, marks the midway point between the foregrounded dockworkers and their town in the far distance. But given the overly political message of the piece, this would appear as so much filler, a visual contrast to that which sits anchored and forbidding to the left: the warship. For added effect, the town and the workers are miniaturized, made peripheral and unimportant, while the real emphasis is kept for the way in which the cartouche presents itself as a statement about territoriality and possession. Recognizing that the ship flies four flags, two of which are clearly British, and that the corner stone of the pier flies another, one is left in little doubt as to the message of the piece. If we were expecting of a dock scene a picture of vibrancy and human activity, what we discover in Williamson's map is a rather different view, with the eye instinctively drawn to the plethora of flags and emblems to the left of the tableau. The wilderness has been replaced by a cultivated and domesticated world order made political by the clearly militarized ship in the bottom right-hand corner of the map, which looks suspiciously as though ensconced behind a stockade.

The combined effect of reading the cartouches on James Williamson's map of 1810, then, is to produce a picture of apparently apolitical bucolic splendour enmeshed within a larger narrative of assertive territoriality.[45] As the nearest of the

---

[43] William Shenstone referred to the oak as 'the perfect image of the manly character: in former times I should have said, and in present times I think I am authorized to say, the British one'. Cited in Tom Williamson, *Polite Landscapes: Gardens and Society in Eighteenth-Century England* (Baltimore: Johns Hopkins University Press, 1995), p. 128.

[44] Denis Cosgrove and Stephen Daniels, eds, *The Iconography of Landscape: Essays on the Symbolic Representation, Design and Use of Past Environments* (Cambridge: Cambridge University Press, 1988), p. 1.

[45] A later example of coastal unease may be detected in the cartouche on William Duncan's 'County of Dublin' map (1821) where the sense of cultivation, new roads and 'cleanly habitations' – all signs of order upon the landscape – are undercut by the presence of the Martello tower: the 'bulldog' awaiting Franco-Irish invasion.

1.6 James Williamson, cartouche, 'A Map of the County of Down' (1810). Courtesy of the Royal Irish Academy.

two men in Fig. 1.5 gestures with outstretched arm to the improved landscape in the distance, one is reminded, in other words, that while the tone of the scene may loosely be described as pastoral, it shies away from statements of an arcadian nature. Work, we will have noticed, is suggested by the horse that pulls hay across to the centre of the scene, thereby presenting the town as a place of respectability and decency, but also a place of human habitation and labour. In this sense the homes of the townsfolk in the distance, unlike other pastoral scenes, are a constant reminder of settlement and fixity. They have cleared the land, and they now live on the land; they have taken possession, and they now cartographically celebrate that possession.

Fringe Benefits

In an essay on the work of the Ordnance Survey of Ireland, Mary Hamer suggests that maps, 'no less than any other text, are the agents of change'. Hamer's analysis of the work of those involved in the Survey of Ireland (authorized in 1824, the survey was complete by 1846) is one in which maps are regarded as contestatory sites that produce representations, rather than the physical realities with which they deal:

> Mapping conventions, their signifying practices, though apparently rigorously co-ordinated with material reality, cannot deliver cartographers from their inherent commitment to the creation of a new fiction.[46]

Despite this, such representations, she argues, are allotted a central role in the control and manipulation of space. Regardless of their 'fictional' status, or the epistemological limitations within which they work, they conveniently structure our sense of the world. To be sure, Richard Muir is correct when he argues that early modern maps show landscape geographers how an 'understanding of [a] locality [can be] suddenly catapulted from a rather fuzzy and gap-ridden vision of the medieval landscape, which is based on earthworks, fragmentary documentary references and air photographs, to a situation of intimate acquaintanceship'.[47] Nevertheless, maps also deal in a form of knowledge that is frequently partial, sometimes politically encoded, and to a certain extent fictional. They are not just transparent and mathematically accomplished works, but texts upon which different readings may, and must, be layered.

In Alexander Bath's 'Map of Cork' (1811) we are presented with, once again, the sight of trade as the answer to all of Ireland's problems. Fig. 1.7 speaks out as an image of possession and control, but that message has been translated into an active representation of commercial success. Ships loom up in the background, festooned in sails and bobbing heads, while in the centre foreground a new order

---

[46]   Mary Hamer, 'Putting Ireland on the Map', *Textual Practice*, 3:2 (Summer 1989), p. 184.
[47]   Richard Muir, *Approaches to Landscape* (Basingstoke: Macmillan, 1999), p. 67.

1.7 Alexander Bath, cartouche, 'Map of Cork' (1811). Courtesy of the Royal Irish Academy.

– of commerce and trade – is keenly established. Judging from the expressions on the faces of the workers to the left and right of the picture, there is no shortage of work. Barrels and packing cases are everywhere; so much so that the figure on the extreme left has to rest on one, and the top-hatted gentleman in the centre must, to complete his inventory, use another as a table. Indeed, the arrangement of the figures in the scene has been very carefully judged. For example, we are also reminded, as the men to the centre left move off into the distance, weighted down with the country's exports, of the sense of social and labour disparity that also exists here. The gentlemen in the centre are positioned differently; they are central in life, and central to it. Their clothes and demeanour, their literate and numerate abilities, and the ease with which they situate themselves in what is an intensely busy scene are clearly defined signs of their social position vis-à-vis the workers who surround them. For them, this brave new world of ladders, pulleys and weighing machines is one in which they have control, authority and legitimacy.

By contrast, our other cartouche – Fig. 1.8 – relates an image of Celtic iconography so complete that were it not for its inclusion here it would go largely unnoticed. Venturing all but the Irish wolfhound, it is a representation of such studied 'Irishness' that we at first feel its inclusion must be purely decorative. However, within the message of Bath's map it has an entirely different purpose; it forms part of an overall message about commercial success, and how best to ensure that that success is maintained. In other words, because the church is in a state of decay – its roof has fallen in and all that remains of its windows is its handsome tracery – it manages to appear uninhabited, overgrown, but also unthreatening. Not unlike the inclusion of such Irish symbolism within Beaufort's cartouche, the positioning of both of Bath's cartouches – and this is exactly what he had in mind, a contrastive, binary reading back and forth between the two – sets 'Irish' antiquarianism against 'British' modernity, ivy-strewn relics against commercial activity, the past against the present, stasis against activity, and the old Gaelic order against the new. Indeed, in this context the ruined church and uninhabited round tower take on added significance, for they are not just emblems of an old, now defunct Irish system, but rather very specific examples of decayed military and church might. In other words, they speak out, and in this situate the cartouche as central to the 'look' of the map, as failed aspects of a once threatening Gaelic way of life.

Denis Cosgrove suggests that 'to map is in one way or another to take the measure of a world, and more than merely take it, to figure the measure so taken in such a way that it may be communicated between people, places or times'.[48] When we examine a sample of cartouches from late eighteenth- and early nineteenth-century Ireland, such as here, we might wonder how it was that map symbolism could ever have been divorced from its political context. Indeed, Cosgrove's argument that

---

[48] Denis Cosgrove, 'Introduction', in Denis Cosgrove, ed., *Mappings* (London: Reaktion Press, 1999), pp. 1–2.

1.8 Alexander Bath, cartouche, 'Map of Cork' (1811). Courtesy of the Royal Irish Academy.

maps not only picture our world, but present it in a variety of ways, and for different purposes, appears to be borne out especially well in the case of Ireland, where maps were used less to determine precise locations – no British maps of Ireland that I know of situate the country with regard to lines of longitude and latitude – than for purposes of understanding Ireland in other ways. For example, we saw earlier how the cartographic efforts of Richard Bartlett, working in the inhospitable and ultimately fatal terrain of Ulster, were conducted alongside the soldiery who were seeking with some determination to subdue the Gaelic chieftain Hugh O'Neill. In Sir William Petty's 'The Down Survey' of the 1650s, 'the unprecedentedly extensive land survey that followed the Cromwellian confiscations', we see land, cartography and ownership wedded into a single vision, a unified idea of what the country signified for its British and loyal victors.[49] And even within the relatively intellectual enterprise that was the Ordnance Survey, conducted from the 1820-1840s, we are enmeshed within a web of detail concerning how cartographers worked alongside sappers, and the extra-curricular role of the surveyors, as well as the rather more controversial business of the naming, owning and reconfiguration of the landscape that was conducted within the first trigonometrical survey carried out in Britain and Ireland. John Andrews is surely correct when he writes of the 'depressingly cyclical character to Irish history as seen through English eyes. Each uprising leads to a conquest, each conquest to an uprising.'[50] But he is so much more accurate when he suggests how 'colonial cartography followed a similar course, progressing from regional sketches to fort plans, and thence to plantation surveys and estate maps'.[51] Mapping the Irish landscape, in other words, meant more than the attempt to come to terms with its topographical variety and detail, much more than a mathematical understanding of how it all fitted and worked together, but rather a frequently ad hoc, opportunistic response to the changing political circumstances of the day.

In Jacques Derrida's *The Truth in Painting* the cartouche is described as having an 'elliptical ring' about it, a term that refers to 'a place of exile on the map [carte] [cartuccio], on a card [carte] played, given out to chance or to necessity, the encrypted geography of an *imperium*, another family, another tribe, very familiar and very foreign'.[52] And we know how J. B. Harley absorbed something of these sentiments in his analysis of cartographic symbolism, seeing an 'encrypted geography' in the various decorative 'title pages, lettering, cartouches, vignettes, dedications, compass roses, and borders', all of which 'helped to strengthen and focus the political meanings of the maps on which they appeared'.[53] Located beyond the ostensible meaning of the map, the cartouche, Derrida rightly observes, appears

---

[49] Andrews, *Shapes of Ireland*, p. 121.

[50] Andrews, *Shapes of Ireland*, p. 118.

[51] Andrews, *Shapes of Ireland*, p. 118.

[52] Jacques Derrida, *The Truth in Painting*, trans. Geoff Bennington and Ian McLeod (Chicago: University of Chicago Press, 1987), p. 190.

[53] Harley, 'Maps, Knowledge and Power', pp. 296–7.

London.

1.9   Samuel Lewis, title page, *Atlas of Ireland* (1837). Courtesy of the Royal Irish Academy.

as something banished, deported or ostracized from its central purpose. Elliptical, difficult to pin down, the cartouche remains both distant and localized, a part of the map, but abroad, decorative but also central to its overall message. Whether Derrida supposed that something as provocatively playful as the cartouche should simply remain where it was, tempting us from the margins, continuing as a thing of elusive and shrouded mischief, is unclear. But for J. B. Harley, the matter of bringing something of such political significance to the forefront of cartographic discussion was vital:

> The frontispieces and titlepages of many atlases, for example, explicitly define by means of widely understood emblems both the ideological significance and the practical scope of the maps they contain.[54]

In Harley's view, these symbols were there to be uncoded, discussed and comprehended. And in wall maps, atlases, charts and sketches it was a matter of simply attending to such 'decoration' as a necessary act of recovery.

On the title page of Samuel Lewis's *Atlas of Ireland* (1837) – Fig. 1.9 – we see an attractively engraved image that fits well with the tone and impulse behind several of the cartouches already discussed. Presenting itself as an extraordinary picture of Anglo-Irish concord, through the depiction of large-scale exportation, Lewis's image moves away from the more overt message of territoriality explicit in, say, the cartouches used by James Williamson. By aligning itself with an allegorical representation in which Britannia complacently surveys the produce of Ireland, Lewis's title page once again chooses trade as the way in which to strengthen the notion of sisterly concord. However, although the image lays celebratory emphasis on Ireland's economic potential and employs allegorical figures to soften the vulgar and potentially unsettling aspect of commercial activity, in the background are miniaturist reminders of just what that commercial activity entails: numerous ships in various stages of nautical encounter, most of which represent human and mechanical industry, remind us of a broader picture, while smoke issues from busy, fuel-devouring chimneys at a number of points across the landscape.

So what narrative, only a few years after Catholic Emancipation (1829), is being conveyed here? Only that the relationship between Britain and Ireland, played out fitfully along a series of Irish coastlines, is one of harmony and mutual understanding, with trade and industry stressed as the key to ongoing commercial and economic development. Britannia may well be seated, with her right arm protectively placed around the shoulders of one of the young 'boys', but her left arm remains resting on the Irish harp. She displays, in other words, a double hold on the country to which she lays claim. Indeed, whatever else may be said about the image of concord she evokes, we are more reminded, I think, of a quality control

---

[54] Harley, 'Maps, Knowledge and Power', p. 298.

inspector, as the ritualized procession of Irish goods – wheat, linen, alcohol, fish and so on, – is presented for her pleasure and satisfaction before being trussed by the small boy, to the left of the scene, for export. In short, Lewis's title-page, used to introduce a full catalogue of maps of the country, presents us with a representation of demilitarized harmony in which Mother England and the children of Ireland work congenially together. By declaring a closer, almost familial, relationship between the two countries, this picture shifts the emphasis of the piece onto a more palatable plane, evoking guardianship and goodwill. Yet it is a benevolence in which paternalism and proprietorship are carefully blended and positioned. In this way Lewis's work stands as a developed example of the rich interpretive potential of cartouche imagery. A map can depict changes and improvements, offer reassurance to settlers and investors, and even image the land in the most literal of ways, but it is with the cartouche that the 'message' of the map most emphatically resides.

Chapter Two

African Land for the American Empire: The Proto-imperialism of Benjamin Stout

David Johnson

On 16 June 1796, the ship *Hercules* under the American Captain Benjamin Stout was transporting rice from Bengal to Britain, under charter to the British East India Company, when it ran aground between the Begha and Keiskamma rivers on the eastern shores of Southern Africa. Washed up with most of the crew intact, the survivors walked the 500 mile journey to Cape Town, helped along the way by sympathetic native inhabitants and Dutch settlers. When Stout returned to England in November 1796, he wrote a glowing 112 page account of his journey, which was published in 1798 together with a 58 page introductory dedication to American president John Adams, exhorting Adams to colonize the eastern Cape for America.[1] In this essay, I examine the detail of Stout's writing, especially the emphasis on land and land cultivation, and argue that Stout's descriptions of the eastern Cape utilize eighteenth-century notions of landscape appreciation – the picturesque, the sublime and the romantic – in order to encode contradictory imperial ambitions. Further, I argue that although Stout's writings made little initial impact, and were in fact mobilized in ways he himself never anticipated, his travel writings express an enduring form of American imperial discourse in which landscape figures as a key element.

---

[1] Stout's Dedication to Adams is in keeping with the post-1776 revolutionary mood. The Connecticut Wit, Joel Barlow, for example, wrote at the time, 'Soon shall our [American] sails, in commerce unconfin'd,/ Whiten each sea and swell every wind', and, in like spirit, David Humphreys wrote, 'Bid from the [American] shore a philanthropic band,/ The torch of science glowing in their hand,/ O'e trackless waves extend their daring toils,/ To find and bless a thousand peopled isles …/ Bid them to wilder'd men new lights impart,/ Heav'n's noblest gifts, with every useful art.' Quoted in A. R. Booth, *The United States Experience in South Africa, 1784–1870* (Cape Town: A. A. Balkema, 1976), pp. 3–4.

Land into Landscape

At the beginning of his Dedication to Adams, Stout provides a contorted explanation of the violent changes in land ownership on Southern Africa's colonial frontier:

> As these colonists advance, they hunt the unfortunate natives as they do the lion and the panther, dispossess them of their lands by force, rob them of their cattle, and, by every possible means, endeavour to effect a total extirpation of the original and unoffending inhabitants. This inhuman conduct must surely meet the execration of every man not totally lost to the feelings of humanity; but still it may be alledged [*sic*], that, having once possession of these lands, no matter how obtained, their right is established, and they cannot be dispossessed by a foreigner, as such conduct is not warranted by the law of nations. I will admit (but for the purpose only of elucidating the matter in question), that successful violence gives a title to the possessor, and that the colonists, as far as they have penetrated, are lawfully entitled to these estates; still this argument does not apply so as to exclude an American, or any other foreigner, who settles at a distance (suppose a 100 miles) from the most advanced colony belonging to the government of the Cape.[2]

In summary, successful violence against Africans, however inhuman, gives legal tenure to European colonial (dis)possessors, and the law of nations prescribes that subsequent colonists are obliged to observe such tenure. Stout's logic conforms with the dominant European jurisprudential consensus as to how the law of nations and the law of nature function in colonial contexts.[3] Africans might qualify as objects of pity, but they can never qualify as legitimate claimants for land restitution. Only land owned as private property by citizens of European nations enjoys legal protection. Stout introduces a further proviso toward the end of the same paragraph when he suggests that 'the people of any nation have an unquestionable right, provided the natives give their assent, to settle on such parts of the southern continent of Africa, as do not interpose with the lands already in possession of the colonists'.[4] Stout is not entirely clear here as to which carries the greater weight: the law of nations, which

---

[2]   B. Stout, *Narrative of the loss of the ship 'Hercules', commanded by Captain Benjamin Stout, on the coast of Caffraria, the 16th of June, 1796; also a circumstantial detail of his travels through the southern deserts of Africa, and the colonies, to the Cape of Good Hope. With an introductory address to the Rt. Honourable John Adams, President of the Continental Congress of America* (London: J. Johnson, 1798), p. v.

[3]   Richard Waswo explains: 'the "law of nature" ... [produces] a universal principle, claiming its grounds in Roman law, and finding its precedents in myth, that will ... justify the dispossession of the indigenes ... What ... [the natural law theorists Victoria and Grotius] are theorizing and justifying is the continuing territorial expansion of Europe around the world.' R. Waswo, 'The Formation of Natural Law to Justify Colonialism, 1539–1689', *New Literary History*, 27:4 (1996), p. 746.

[4]   Stout, *Narrative*, p. vi.

endorses the colonial acquisition of African land by successful violence, or the moral consideration that allows the colonial acquisition of land on condition that the natives give their assent. The implication is that the latter route to land acquisition might be preferable, but that native assent was not a legal prerequisite for Americans to acquire African land as yet unclaimed by other colonial possessors.

Stout's *Narrative* combines two forms of travel narrative: the maritime survival genre (chapters 1–2), which had dominated travel writing up to the eighteenth century, and the emergent genre of continental exploration (chapters 3–8). It is also complicated by the fact that it is addressed to two imagined audiences: President John Adams of the United States and the wider reading public. These imagined readers exert different pressures, as Stout strives to convince the former of the economic attractions of Southern Africa and to thrill the latter with tales of the exotic and the dangerous. These contradictory pressures mark Stout's descriptions of the land and the people he encounters, as the economic and the exotic tropes alternate throughout the text. Indeed, the tension is nicely captured in a passage from Francois Le Vaillant (1753–1824), quoted with approval by Stout in the Dedication to Adams.[5] Reflecting on his travels to the eastern Cape, Le Vaillant draws the following contrast with Cape Town's Table Bay:

> [In the eastern Cape] nature appeared in all her majesty; the lofty mountains offering from every side the most delightful and romantic views I have ever seen. This prospect, contrasted with the idea of the parched and barren lands about the Cape, made me think myself at a thousand miles distance ... What a being is the sordid speculator, whose views, bounded by commerce, port fees and customs, can prefer the storms and dangers of Table-Bay, to the safe riding, or natural and charming ports, that are so common on the oriental coasts of Africa.[6]

Le Vaillant's enthusiasm for the natural beauty of the Cape's eastern coast serves well Stout's goal of selling Adams this section of African land. However, Stout is careful to refuse Le Vaillant's contrast between the commercial advantages of the western Cape as opposed to the 'romantic views' of the eastern Cape by insisting that the latter is not only pleasing to the eye, but *also* has immense potential for economic exploitation. Just after Le Vaillant's contrasting descriptions, for example, Stout emphasizes that the land of the eastern Cape 'abounds in timber of the best quality; possesses many excellent harbours; is blessed with the richest pasturage that feeds innumerable heads of the finest cattle ... and their shores are frequented by fish of every quality'.[7]

---

[5]   Le Vaillant's journeys in the Cape had just been translated into English and published: *Travels into the Interior Parts of Africa* (London: William Lane, 1790) and *New Travels into the Interior Parts of Africa* (London: G. G. and J. Robinson, 1796).

[6]   Stout, *Narrative*, pp. x–xi.

[7]   Stout, *Narrative*, pp. xx–xxi.

In the *Narrative* itself, Stout's first descriptions of the landscape are of the countryside where the *Hercules* ran aground, and he again describes in detail both its exotic and economic attractions:

> During our miserable abode under the sand-hills, we frequently contemplated the scene before us. Nearly as far as the eye could travel, we beheld a country finely wooded, and considering the season, which was their winter, producing a most bountiful vegetation. Their cattle appear in such prodigious numbers as to baffle calculation; and their condition, which was equal to the best fed oxen in Great Britain, clearly demonstrated the richness of their pasturage. Sheep were not to be discovered, nor could we perceive the most distance traces of agricultural labour.
>
> The country in our view was of an immense extent, yet surrounded by a chain of hills that appeared to contain the fountains of those numerous rivulets which glided through the plain in a variety of directions. The *mimosa tree* appeared native to the soil, and the woods were so beautifully interspersed, as to give the lands all the appearance of a plantation originally defined by art, and afterwards perfected by the hand of elegance. In my opinion, the whole wanted nothing but villages, corn and inhabitants, to render this spot an enviable abode for the most enlightened and luxurious of our countrymen.[8]

The weight of Stout's descriptions of the landscape rests on its potential for commercial farming on the western model. These attractions, in combination with an absence of indigenous agricultural labour *and* an aspect pleasing to western aesthetic preferences, positively invite cultivation of this land by North American colonists.

In claiming that the landscapes of the eastern Cape are pleasing to the artistic sensibilities of the European or North American viewer, Stout (like Le Vaillant) uses the adjective 'romantic' to describe the aesthetic appeal of the landscape. However, in each of the two instances Stout uses the term, he refers to somewhat different landscapes. In the first instance, Stout declares:

> The countries through which we passed were alternatively hill and dale, and often afforded the most romantic prospects. We frequently perceived vast quantities of wolves, and often such droves of that species of deer which the farmers call *spring buck*, that we supposed one flock alone could not contain less than from *twelve* to *fourteen thousand*.[9]

What Stout stresses in this description is the wildness of the landscape, with the sheer numbers of wild animals attesting to the absence of human agency. In the second instance, the term romantic has slightly different connotations:

> It is called by the settlers *Long Cluff*, and affords, perhaps, as many romantic scenes as can be found in any spot of the same extent on the face of the earth. The hills for seventy or eighty miles run parallel to each other. The lands between are wonderfully rich, and produce vast

---

8   Stout, *Narrative*, pp. 44–5.
9   Stout, *Narrative*, p. 82.

The Loss of the Hercules.

2.1 Shipwreck. Engraving in G. W. Barrington, *Remarkable Voyages and Shipwrecks. Being a popular collection of extraordinary and authentic sea narratives relating to all parts of the Globe* (London: Simpkin, Marshall, Hamilton, Kent and Co., n.d. – c.1880), facing p. 123.

quantities of a plant similar in its smell and taste to our thyme. On this fragrant herb are fed immense quantities of sheep and cattle; they devour it with great eagerness, and it gives the mutton a flavour like our venison, that an epicure might be deceived in the taste.[10]

'Romantic' here *is* associated with human cultivation, as it is not the numbers of wild animals, but the numbers of sheep and cattle that are emphasized. However, what the descriptions of the two landscapes have in common is that in neither description is there acknowledgement of human agency in the landscape and, second, both passages describe vistas of great natural abundance from an elevated viewpoint.[11] Both these aspects require further elaboration.

Stout emphasizes repeatedly the emptiness of the land.[12] Shortly after leaving the site of the shipwreck, he notes that 'in the course we pursued, not a human footstep could be traced; no cattle, no sign of cultivation could be observed'.[13] A couple of weeks further into the journey to Cape Town, he still encounters vacant land: 'We likewise traveled this day through delightful country ... but not a sign of agriculture was to be observed.'[14] Only as Stout and his fellow-travellers near the western Cape are there signs of human habitation. In a sequence with biblical echoes,[15] they pass first with trepidation through 'a dismal valley of about three miles in length ... called Boshisman's path', where they anxiously anticipate a Bushman attack, before entering 'upon a champaign country'[16] populated with increasing numbers of Dutch farmsteads. Stout enthuses about how successfully the settler farms have taken advantage of the bountiful landscape: 'The country, as we advanced, increased in population; and the farmhouses were, in several places, not more than two hours distant from each other. Many of them were beautifully situated, and their land produced grain, oranges, figs and lemons in abundance.'[17] Stout's descriptions of the Dutch farmsteads here reproduce a colonial version of William Gilpin's idea of the picturesque in that

---

[10] Stout, *Narrative*, p. 90.

[11] M. L. Pratt invents the term 'the monarch-of all-I survey' (*Imperial Writing: Travel Writing and Transculturation*, London: Routledge, 1992, pp. 201–8) to describe the use of the elevated viewpoint, and claims it to be a pre-eminently mid-Victorian travel narrative convention. Stout's use of the elevated viewpoint precedes the examples Pratt discusses, and he displays rather less mastery over the landscape than subsequent travellers.

[12] On the deployment of the myth of empty land in the eastern Cape in the eighteenth and nineteenth centuries, see C. Crais, 'The Vacant Land: The Mythology of British Expansion in the Eastern Cape, South Africa', *Journal of Historical Sociology,* 25:2 (1991).

[13] Stout, *Narrative*, p. 53.

[14] Stout, *Narrative*, p. 63.

[15] Before setting out from the wreck of the *Hercules*, Stout asks the Xhosa chief to 'send a guide with us through the deserts to the first christian settlement' (Stout, *Narrative*, p. 31), and both Old and New Testament allusions to testing journeys through deserts and wilderness recur in the text.

[16] Stout, *Narrative*, pp. 85–6.

[17] Stout, *Narrative*, p. 95.

they present the settler presence as a happy complement to the natural beauty.[18] Furthermore, as Gilpin's British picturesque suppresses evidence of enclosures and rural poverty,[19] so too does Stout's Cape picturesque suppress the economic and military violence of colonialism. The final conclusion Stout offers is simple: with the addition of American settlers, the vacant land of the eastern Cape can emulate the happy agricultural achievement of the Dutch settlers in the western Cape.

There are, however, many other descriptions of the landscape that emphasize not the land's potential for cultivation, but rather its dangers and terrors. Soon after having crossed the Fish River, a spectacular view greets Stout and his party:

> We had scarcely put ourselves in motion, when a scene of the most extensive and luxuriant beauties burst in a moment on our view. The danger we had just escaped, engaged our attention so entirely, when we gained the summit, that we did not immediately perceive the world of beauties that now lay spread before us. All stood for some time in a state of rapture and amazement. The country was mostly a level, yet pleasingly diversified with gentle elevations, on the tops of which we could perceive clumps of the *mimosa tree*, and the sides clothed with shrubs of various denominations. A thousand rivulets seemed to meander though this *second Eden*; frequently skirting or appearing to encircle a plantation of wood … As we stood gazing on this sylvan scene, we perceived innumerable herds of animals, particularly of the species of the gazelle, scouring over the plains; some darting through the woods, others feeding, or drinking at the rivulets. As far as the eye traveled in pursuit of new beauties, it was most amply gratified, until at length the whole gradually faded on the view, and became lost in the horizon.
> —We were so wrapt in extacy [*sic*] at this landscape, that we forgot our danger, and remained too long upon the mountain. We at length descended, and proceeded on our journey.[20]

Whereas Stout's descriptions of the Dutch farmsteads near the western Cape suggest the picturesque, passages like these, describing the vast and intimidating landscapes of the eastern Cape, satisfy the requirements of Edmund Burke's 'sublime'. According to Burke, the '[a]stonishment … is the effect of the sublime in its highest degree; the inferior effects are admiration, reverence and respect'.[21] The expansive views that leave Stout and his party 'wrapt in extacy' certainly provoke astonishment, and the impact is enhanced by the fact of their own vulnerability within the landscape.

---

[18] William Gilpin argues that 'A cottage, a mill, or a hamlet among trees, may often add beauty to a rural scene: but when houses are scattered through every part, the moral sense can never make a convert of the picturesque eye.' W. Gilpin, *Observations on the River Wye, and Several Parts of South Wales, etc. relative Chiefly to Picturesque Beauty* (London: R. Blamire, 1782), p. 4. The two-hour distances between the Dutch farms Stout observes would seem to conform to Gilpin's requirement of the picturesque.

[19] For the argument that Gilpin's picturesque excludes the economic and political, see M. Andrews, *Landscape and Western Art* (Oxford: Oxford University Press, 1999), pp. 166–7.

[20] Stout, *Narrative*, pp. 61–2.

[21] Edmund Burke, *A Philosophical Enquiry into the Origin of our Ideas of the Sublime and Beautiful* (Oxford: University Press, 1990), p. 53.

As regards the use of an elevated viewpoint, Stout's various descriptions of the landscape – those he terms 'romantic', as well as those we might designate 'picturesque' or 'sublime' – are all viewed from above.[22] To provide two more examples. About two weeks after leaving the *Hercules*, Stout recounts: 'We reached at length some highlands, from the tops of which we discovered several beautiful vales clothed with long dry grass, small clusters of trees, and in other places, forests of considerable extent, skirting mountains of different elevations.'[23] And as Stout moves from the wild scenery of the eastern Cape to the cultivated west of the country, so he maintains his elevated perspective: 'From the seventeenth to the twenty-first [July 1796] we traveled a mountainous country; but the valleys constantly presented farms and habitations where the industry of the husbandman was amply rewarded.'[24]

John Barrell has argued persuasively that in Britain in the late eighteenth century the capacity to appreciate panoramic landscapes in art was tied both to a facility with abstract thought and a mastery of the public sphere.[25] According to Barrell, an opposition tying landscape appreciation to politics is constructed during this period:

> Those who can comprehend the order of society and nature are observers of a prospect, in which others are merely objects. Some comprehend, others are comprehended; some are fit to survey the extensive panorama, some are confined within one or other of the micro-prospects which, to the comprehensive observer, are parts of a wider landscape, but which, to those confined within them, are all they see.[26]

---

[22] Stout's use of the panoramic viewpoint was shared by travellers to North America too. For example, William Bartram, who had the same London publishers as Stout, in his *Travels through North and South Carolina...*(1792) describes North Carolina as follows: 'Having now attained the summit of this very elevated ridge, we enjoyed a fine prospect indeed; the enchanting valley of Keowe, perhaps as celebrated for fertility, fruitfulness and beautiful prospects as the Fields of Pharsalia and Vale of Tempe' (repr. in T. Fulford and C. Bolton, eds, *Travels, Explorations and Empires* (London: Pickering and Chatto, 2001), vol.1, p. 156.

[23] Stout, *Narrative*, pp. 55–6.

[24] Stout, *Narrative*, p. 96.

[25] David Bunn extends Barrell's arguments about the relation between landscape and the public sphere to a colonial context in his discussion of Thomas Pringle in the Cape Colony of the 1820s. Bunn argues convincingly that Pringle's version of the Eastern Cape landscape 'helps to naturalize the settler subject and establish a local version of the bourgeois public sphere'. David Bunn '"Our Wattled Cot": Mercantile and Domestic Space in Thomas Pringle's African landscape', in W. J. T. Mitchell, ed., *Landscape and Power* (Chicago and London: University of Chicago Press, 1994), p. 138. Stout's writings, of course, precede the appearance of any kind of colonial public sphere in the Eastern Cape, but his descriptions of landscape nevertheless anticipate those of Pringle.

[26] J. Barrell, 'The Public Prospect and the Private View: The Politics of Taste in Eighteenth-century Britain', in S. Pugh, ed., *Reading Landscape: Country – City – Capital* (Manchester: Manchester University Press, 1990), pp. 27–8.

In Stout's descriptions of the colonial landscape, he is the one who observes and comprehends the extensive panoramas of the Cape; the inhabitants themselves are either absent or – as we shall see – bounded by the landscape, in that they are incapable of seeing its full (economic) potential. As an American observer of African landscapes, Stout's assumption of this observer-position has a further resonance. By demonstrating repeatedly his capacity to appreciate panoramic perspectives, Stout lays claim to the related political status of citizen, a claim clearly invigorated by the post-1776 separation from Britain. The power associated with the capacity to appreciate panoramic landscapes, located in eighteenth-century Britain with 'the lords or the meritocratic bourgeoisie',[27] is thus claimed by a confident New World adventurer competing with recently defeated colonial masters for imperial land. The crucial continuity, of course, is that those who work the land, in Britain and the colonies alike, are denied this panoramic perspective, and the elevated outside viewer diminishes, and often effaces, their labour from the landscape.[28]

Inhabiting the Land

What of the people already inhabiting this landscape? Stout's repeated point is that the native inhabitants of Southern Africa have been grossly misrepresented in settler writings. In concluding his address to Adams, he declares:

> I have been encouraged to publish [this narrative] ... from a belief that some useful information may be derived from a genuine description of the natives and their country ... To remove, therefore, such prejudices as have arisen from the extravagant and deceptive tales of those travellers who have represented the natives as monsters, that delight only in human slaughter, becomes a duty, as it may encourage future adventurers in their pursuits, and relieve the unfortunate from unnecessary apprehensions.[29]

In the narrative itself, he repeats this argument several times, noting for example that descriptions of the Tambouchis (a Xhosa clan) as 'the most *ferocious*, *vindictive* and *detestable* class of beings that inhabit the vast and fertile territory of Cafraria' amount to 'a calumny so undeserved, so atrocious, and possibly so mischievous in its tendency, I can not suffer to pass without censure and contradiction'.[30] Stout cites

---

[27] Barrell, 'The Public Prospect', p. 33.

[28] The geographer Denis Cosgrove argues that the rise of the concept of landscape is coterminous with early modern capitalism that consigns those working the land to the position of 'insiders' who can never see their land as landscape: 'The insider does not enjoy the privilege of being able to walk away from a scene as we can walk away from a framed picture or from a tourist viewpoint.' Denis Cosgrove, *Social Formation and Symbolic Landscape* (Madison: University of Wisconsin Press, 1998 [1984]), p. 19.

[29] Stout, *Narrative*, p. xlvi.

[30] Stout, *Narrative*, p. 46.

the great kindnesses shown to him and his men by the native inhabitants, describing them as 'possessed of all those compassionate feelings, that alone give a lustre to, and adorn humanity', and, further, that they are 'people of great natural sagacity, and of an active and enterprising disposition'.[31] Any perceived deficiencies on their part he attributes to climate and lack of educational opportunities:

> *Man* is only a *savage* from *habit*; he is ever capable of receiving instruction, and analysing in his own mind by the powers of his reason. Possessing the organs of speech, he can communicate his ideas; and when moulded by education, the *savage* is seen no more, but he enters into society with all those advantages which other men experience from instruction. To say, therefore, that any race of mortals are *naturally savage*, and of course not capable of enjoying the blessings of civilisation, is a dogma arising from ignorance, or a want of due consideration.[32]

To reinforce this notion of cultural relativism, Stout juxtaposes on a number of occasions the alleged 'savagery' of the Africans and the 'civilisation' of Europeans. Right at the outset, for example, he contrasts the hospitality and protection afforded by the natives with the unfriendliness he had encountered in the 'polished nations of Europe'.[33]

However, there are two exceptions to Stout's generous attitudes towards the native inhabitants. The first relates to a particular Xhosa clan 'distinguished, by their countrymen, as a *bad tribe*'.[34] Stout's encounter with this 'bad tribe' concludes with the following description of one of their number:

> At the moment he stood in this attitude, a more finished picture of horror, or what we understand of the *infernals*, was perhaps never seen before. The savage wore a leopard's skin; his black countenance bedaubed with red ochre; his eyes, inflamed with rage, appeared as if starting from their sockets; his mouth expanded, and his teeth *gnashing* and *grinning* with all the fury of an exasperated demon. At this instant, the *tout-ensemble* of the figure would have been a subject highly deserving the pencil of *Raphael*.[35]

What is perhaps most interesting about Stout's description is that authority for this negative portrait is the designation of this particular tribe of natives as 'bad' by their more friendly countrymen.

The second exception is Stout's descriptions of the Bushmen, which alternate between acknowledging their potential for improvement and compassion for their cruel treatment, to the uncritical repetition of settler tales of Bushmen savagery. In the address to Adams, he introduces the Bushmen as quite terrifying – they 'wage

---

[31] Stout, *Narrative*, pp. iii, xxxiv.
[32] Stout, *Narrative*, p. xxxviii.
[33] Stout, *Narrative*, p. ii.
[34] Stout, *Narrative*, pp. 58–9.
[35] Stout, *Narrative*, p. 60.

perpetual war with every horde, and plunder wherever they come'[36] – and reinforces this impression when he describes settler relations with the Bushmen in the narrative itself. Given his earlier criticisms of settler hostility towards the native inhabitants, Stout's silence about the treatment of the Bushmen is striking:

> The *Bushmen*, when they are sufficiently strong in number, attack and kill the *Hottentots* and *Caffres* wherever they find them; and the *colonists* hunt the *Bushmen* as they do the *lion* and the *tiger* – A farmer never thinks of giving quarter to these people; but slay[s] them the very instant they are in their power.[37]

After describing further experiences of settler hospitality, and the dangers posed by Bushmen arrows to travellers on a particular mountain pass, Stout appears at least tacitly to endorse the genocidal behaviour of the settlers towards the Bushmen:

> The farmers told us, they frequently assemble to the number of *forty* or *fifty*, and then go in quest of the *Bushmen*, whom they destroy without mercy if they come upon them.[38]

These lines suggest the Bushmen, so integral to the pre-colonial landscape, should be violently purged in order that the land might be transformed for commercial agriculture.

In addition to providing lavish descriptions of the terrain and, for the most part, generous portraits of the native inhabitants, Stout's concern is to assess Kaffraria's potential as a colonial enterprise. To this end, he gives substantial attention to the different nations who have colonised Africa, with the ultimate aim of setting out the best means for American settlement of the region to proceed. Of the Dutch, Stout is contemptuous for at least two reasons. Their treatment of the native inhabitants is barbarous and Stout refers to them with heavy irony as 'those *enlightened savages*, who, under the appellations of *Christians* and *Dutchmen*, settled themselves by violence on the southern promontory'.[39] He describes their seizing of the Cape in extremely critical terms: 'As these colonists advance, they hunt the unfortunate natives as they do the lion and the panther, dispossess them of their lands by force, rob them of their cattle, and, by every possible means, endeavour to effect a total extirpation of the original and unoffending inhabitants.'[40] At least as offensive to Stout as the Dutch treatment of the native inhabitants is their ineptitude as colonial administrators. Given the remarkable natural resources at their disposal, their failure to pursue a vigorous policy of free trade appals Stout. He quotes with approval the angry complaints of an unnamed settler, who describes the punitive protectionist

---

[36] Stout, *Narrative*, p. xxxvii.
[37] Stout, *Narrative*, p. 84.
[38] Stout, *Narrative*, p. 86.
[39] Stout, *Narrative*, p. ii.
[40] Stout, *Narrative*, p. v.

policies of the VOC (Dutch East India Company) and appeals for more enlightened colonial governance:

> We are, (said these people) although living on the confines of the deserts, so barbarously treated by our rulers, that we are unable to proceed … We have the finest timber in the world; and although it could be conveyed to the Cape by sea at the most trifling charge, yet our government supplies their settlement with that valuable commodity from Europe, and as you may suppose, at an expense which must be enormous. We live in the hope however, (continued these colonists) that some nation more liberal than ours, will form a settlement on the eastern or western coast, that we may get supplied with such articles as are necessary to our situation, and will trade with us on principles of mutual advantage.[41]

The only glimmer of hope for the Dutch Empire, according to Stout, lies in the impact of the 'late revolution … on the national character', as it might have the effect of 'expanding their minds, teach them to found their commerce on the principles of *humanity* and *justice*'.[42]

As regards the English, Stout's views are more forgiving.[43] In the address to Adams, he concedes that 'the inhabitants of the Cape, and the colonists in general, entertain a strong predilection in favour of the British, and the sagacity of the English government will soon point out the means of perpetuating their friendships'.[44] Both in terms of their treatment of the native inhabitants and in terms of their sympathy for promoting free trade, the British exceed the Dutch handsomely. Aware that England's struggle with France remains in the balance, Stout declares his sympathies for the English in the conclusion of his address to Adams: 'as I have been apprehensive that you would consider a settlement of this description as a measure which American policy forbids, I have likewise directed my observations to the

---

[41] Stout, *Narrative*, pp. xvii–xviii.

[42] Stout, *Narrative*, p. xxxix.

[43] It is worth noting that contemporaneous British accounts of the Cape registered with some anxiety the competitive threat posed by American traders. Based on visits to the Cape in the second half of 1796 (the same time as Stout's walk to Cape Town) and then in 1801, Captain Robert Percival, for example, published *An Account of the Cape of Good Hope, exhorting the British government to regain, at all costs, control of the Cape*. In his conclusion, Percival observes: Other nations, Americans in particular, have already begun to share our trade in the East-Indies, and our fisheries in the South-Seas. Every circumstance that tends to obstruct our commerce in that quarter, must in the same proportion increase that of our rivals; and in this manner a door may be opened to undermine one of the most valuable branches of our resources. If, on the other hand, the Cape of Good Hope were in our possession, the facility of carrying on the East-India trade, and the South-Sea fishery, would greatly preponderate on our side; and our established commerce, supported by the vast capital of this country, might then set all competition at defiance. (London: C. and R. Baldwin, 1804, p. 334)

[44] Stout, *Narrative*, p. xxvii.

English nation, whose prosperity has ever had a second place in my affections'.[45] He emphasizes the enormous benefits that would accrue to Britain should it develop the Cape along the lines he suggests, and on the final page of the travelogue concludes that 'if in the present work I have furnished a single hint that eventually may be found useful to the BRITISH NATION, I shall not hereafter repine at the calamities I have suffered'.[46]

Having identified the failings of the Dutch and English, Stout concludes by extolling the Americans, and he imagines the relation between America and Africa to be mediated in a non-coercive fashion by the means of free trade. In promoting the humane treatment of the native inhabitants and policies of free trade, Stout casts America in a benign role. He appeals in the first instance to what he assumes to be the humane sensibilities of John Adams: 'The untutored tribes of America have already experienced the beneficence of your nature, and I am desirous to arrest your attention and interest your feelings, on behalf of those wandering children of nature, who are scattered over the deserts of the African world.'[47] However, he is swift to emphasize that American generosity to Africans has substantial economic benefits for America:

> After having attempted thus to pay the debt of gratitude to my liberal benefactors on the continent of Africa, I shall now endeavour to draw your attention to those commercial benefits which I conceive may be obtained by establishing a colony from America, on that part of the coast where the ship I commanded was unfortunately wrecked.[48]

Given the harsh treatment both native inhabitants and settlers have suffered at the hands of Dutch rulers, the Americans are likely to receive a warm welcome:

> I speak of these people as I found them; and from this knowledge I form an opinion, that so far from interrupting any settlement of the nature I have before alluded to, they would hail the American, when they were convinced of his justice, as their friend, their protector, and deliverer.[49]

As to the appropriate strategy for containing any remote possibility of native resistance, Stout recommends free (if unequal) trade and liberal governance:

> This portion of Africa is fairly open to the government of the Cape, provided the natives can be induced to consent to the establishment of European colonists, and their acquiescence could be soon obtained, by gifts of little value to the donor, and their allegiance secured by a kind and liberal treatment in the course of their negotiations.[50]

---

[45] Stout, *Narrative*, p. xlv.
[46] Stout, *Narrative*, p. 112.
[47] Stout, *Narrative*, p. ii.
[48] Stout, *Narrative*, p. iv.
[49] Stout, *Narrative*, p. xxvi.
[50] Stout, *Narrative*, pp. xxx–xxxi.

With all these advantages, Stout has little difficulty in imagining a happy future for American colonists settling in the southern Cape:

> [The colonists] all expressed a wish to have [tobacco] seed from America, and to have people from that continent established in their neighbourhood. An American well acquainted with the growth and manufacture of this plant, must, in a few years, if settled in these parts, become not only independent, but opulent.[51]

Stout's *Narrative* therefore combines a number of distinct elements into a powerful case for American imperial intervention in Southern Africa: (1) prime land, particularly for commercial agriculture, but also as exotic spectacle; (2) friendly (or absent) local inhabitants, made up of indigenous African communities and Dutch settlers, with both groups amenable to integration into an American economy; (3) weakened imperial rivals, with the Dutch mired in antiquated forms of mercantile protectionism and the English pre-occupied with France; and (4) an ideology of free trade, guaranteed to invigorate the economies of America and Africa alike.

Reception

How was Stout's *Narrative* received? I have been unable to find any evidence that John Adams ever read Stout's *Narrative*. There is no mention of Stout in the indices of the ten volumes of Adams's *Selected Writings*, and Stout's book does not appear in the catalogue of Adams's personal library. The years of Adams's presidency (1797–1801) were busy ones, and it is perhaps unsurprising that Adams failed to find the time to colonize the southern Cape, or indeed even respond in any way to Stout's appeal. Stout constructs Adams as an American president opposed to slavery and in sympathy with native Americans, a champion of democracy in all quarters of public life, hostile to economic protectionism and unequivocally in favour of free trade. In every respect, the historical figure of Adams differed from Stout's idealized presidential reader. To take but two of these imagined qualities, Adams might have voiced his opposition to slavery, but under pressure always bowed to the slave-owning politicians of the South,[52] and his commitment to democracy was always substantially qualified.[53] Furthermore, as regards his foreign policy, Adams was

---

[51] Stout, *Narrative*, p. 88.

[52] In 1821, after the Missouri Compromise allowed the extension of slavery in the western states, Adams declared, 'Slavery in the country I have seen hanging over it for half a century ... I have been so terrified of the Phenomenon that I constantly said in former times to the Southern Gentlemen, I cannot comprehend the object; I must leave it to you. I will vote for forcing no measure against your judgments.' Quoted in J. J. Ellis, *Passionate Sage: The Character and Legacy of John Adams* (New York: W. W. Norton, 1993), p. 138.

[53] Adams was, for example, very critical of Tom Paine's *Common Sense* (1776), arguing that his proposals were 'so democratical, without any restraint or even an attempt at any

consistently opposed to any involvement in anti-Spanish struggles in Spain's South American colonies. It is also worth adding that Adams's indifference to Stout's book was more than a single failure of communication; subsequent nineteenth-century American travellers seeking to encourage American investment in Africa experienced similar neglect.[54]

As regards his popular audience, Stout's travelogue would appear to have succeeded in thrilling his readers, as a number of further editions followed. The only full-length edition that included the dedication, however, was published again in 1820, specifically for the English settlers to the eastern Cape, with a foreword emphasizing the positives in Stout's account of the region.[55] The unnamed editors declare:

> The measure now so actively and wisely undertaken by our government, that of colonizing those delightful regions, 500 miles northward of the Cape of Good Hope ... has lately engaged much of the public attention; and as it is highly approved by all those who are acquainted with the important subject, we feel a very earnest desire to accelerate so glorious an undertaking by every means in our power. The immediate consequence to be expected from the adoption of this measure is of no less importance than happily providing for a numerous and distressed population, and at the same time laying the foundation of a commerce with the parent state, which cannot, perhaps, be appreciated too highly.[56]

---

equilibrium or counter-poise, that it must produce confusion and every evil work'. Quoted in H. Zinn, *A People's History of the United States, 1492– the Present* (New York: HarperCollins, 1995), p. 70.

[54] Stout's failure to stimulate American interest in Southern Africa was repeated in 1828 when another American seaman, Captain Benjamin Morrell, also wrote glowingly – but ineffectually – about Africa's potential for American investment. Morrell's editor, P. Petrie, records the captain's exasperation at the indifference his proposals encountered in America: 'I have been fated to sustain an unequal combat with the giants of prejudice and the hydras of malice and jealousy.' P. Petrie, ed., *Morrell's narrative of a voyage to the south and west coast of Africa...* (London: Whittaker, 1844), p. iv.

[55] The new title and lengthy title page of this 1820 edition express clearly the propaganda motives for re-publishing Stout's *Narrative*. The title page reads: *Cape of Good Hope and its dependencies. An accurate and truly interesting description of those delightful regions, situated five hundred miles north of the Cape, formerly in possession of the Dutch, but lately ceded to the Crown of England; and which are to be colonized, with every possible dispatch, under the authority of the British Government, by agriculturalists and artificers of every denomination from the United Kingdom of Great Britain and Ireland. By Captain Benjamin Stout, late commander of the American East-Indiaman named the 'Hercules', lost on the coast of Caffraria, within a few miles of the River Infanta, where the 'Grosvenor' perished in 1782. Likewise A luminous and affecting detail of Captain Stout's travels through the deserts of Caffraria and the Christian settlements, to the Cape* (London: Edwards and Knibb, 1820).

[56] Stout, *Cape*, pp. ix–x.

That Stout's *Narrative* suits this purpose precisely is warmly acknowledged by the editors:

> we found it written in a style of uncommon conciseness and elegance; but what rendered it truly valuable to us was, that it contained a most faithful and minute description of the very country which our government are now determined to colonize ... [Stout] has delivered his opinions with so much candour, fidelity, and ability, that we cannot too strongly recommend his narrative to public attention at this critical and important moment.[57]

However, the 1820 edition was exceptional, as all other editions of Stout's tale in the nineteenth century ignored the dedication to Adams, drastically cut the stories of the overland journey, focused on the shipwreck and published the *Hercules* tale along with a number of other shipwreck yarns. There was a condensed version of Stout's tale included in volume two of Archibald Duncan's 1805 *The Mariner's Chronicle*,[58] together with many more shipwreck stories. In 1809, Stout's *Narrative* was published in two cheap London editions by Thomas Tegg: one edition, costing just a sixpence, was a 28 page summary of the 1798 edition, with Stout's tale recounted in the third person and the terrors of the sea and shipwreck given prominence.[59] Tegg also published this same version of the wreck of the *Hercules* in a kind of nautical adventure compendium, together with condensed tales of *The Guardian* (wrecked in 1789) and the *Account of an Indian Woman* discovered on Hudson Bay in 1772. In 1822, a cheap Dublin edition was published, also accompanied with other shipwreck tales,[60] where the editors singled out for praise Stout's generous descriptions of the native inhabitants. In 1842, a condensed French translation of Stout's journey was published in Volume XVI of C. A. Walckenaer's *Collection de voyages en Afrique*.[61]

---

[57] Stout, *Cape*, pp. xiii–xiv.

[58] A. Duncan, *The Mariner's Chronicle; or Interesting Narratives of Shipwrecks* (London: James Cundee, 1805), vol. 2, pp. 244–82. This collection includes the stories of many shipwrecks from around the world, with an average of about 15 tales per volume.

[59] Tegg's edition was published as *Interesting particulars of the loss of the American ship 'Hercules', Capt. William [sic] Stout, on the coast of Caffraria, June 16, 1796; the consequent sufferings and subsequent adventures of the crew, during a long and painful journey over the southern regions of Africa, to the Cape of Good Hope* (London: Thomas Tegg, 1809). The compendium edition has the same title page.

[60] The full title of the Dublin edition was: *Wonderful escapes! Containing the narrative of the shipwreck of the 'Antelope Packet'; the loss of the' Lady Hobart Packet' on an island of ice; the shipwreck of the 'Hercules' on the coast of Africa; an extraordinary escape from the effects of a storm in a journey over a frozen sea in North America* (Dublin: Richard Grace, 1822).

[61] C. A. Walckenaer, *Collection des relations de voyages par mer et par terre, en differentes parties de l'Afrique*, Vol. XVI (Paris : Walckenaer, 1842). In addition to Stout, volume XVI also includes the travel narratives of Sparrman (1775), Thunberg (1772–73, 1775), Patterson (1777, 1779), Le Vaillant (1780-85) and Degrandpre (1787).

The popular fascination with shipwrecks was undiminished in the second half of the nineteenth century, and George Winslow Barrington included his own summarized version of Stout's journey, together with 31 other tales of shipwreck, in *Remarkable Voyages*.[62]

In the twentieth century, interest in Stout's journey has been principally of a journalistic and antiquarian nature, with several accounts of his story in newspapers,[63] magazines[64] and popular books.[65] A more scholarly exchange took place in the pages of *Africana Notes and News* in 1966, when contributor E. C. Tabler suggested that the British had invented Stout's tale as part of their strategy to encourage British settlers to move to the eastern Cape. Tabler lists the many implausible aspects of Stout's *Narrative* – his account of the native inhabitants, the ease with which they traversed such difficult terrain, the fact that neither Stout nor the *Hercules* are mentioned in other public accounts of the period – and concludes: 'The book seems to be propaganda aimed at ensuring that the British keep the Cape of Good Hope and extend the settled area as a safety and commercial measure ... It is doubtful if the author was ever closer to South Africa than Grub Street ... and it is suspicious that Stout was resurrected at the time of the 1820 Settlement.'[66] Two issues later, Vernon S. Forbes answered Tabler's doubts by citing two authoritative sources confirming the veracity of Stout's tale, namely an article by John Barrow and a reference to Stout in Andrew Steedman's travel writings.[67] The debate about authenticity is

---

[62] G. W. Barrington, *Remarkable Voyages and Shipwrecks. Being a popular collection of extraordinary and authentic sea narratives relating to all parts of the globe* (London: Simpkin, 1880).

[63] See, for example, 'In Days of Old. From Kaffraria to the Cape', *Cape Mercury*, 9 December 1918, p. 4 and N. Howell, 'South Africa might have been an American Colony', *Cape Times*, 3 September 1938, p. 3.

[64] See, for example, 'Some Old-time Shipwrecks. The Toll of our Coast in the Eighteenth and Nineteenth Centuries', *South African Railways and Harbours Magazine*, May 1930, pp. 774–8. This account of Stout's journey emphasizes the kindnesses of the Dutch farmers, but not those of the Xhosa and Khoi guides.

[65] E. Rosenthal, *Stars and Stripes in Africa*, 2nd edn (Cape Town: National Books, 1968).

[66] E. C. Tabler, 'Notes and Queries', *Africana Notes and News*, 17:2 (June 1966), p. 88.

[67] V. S. Forbes, 'Notes and Queries', *Africana Notes and News*, 17:4 (December 1966), p. 188. Barrow's account of Stout in *Quarterly Review*, 20 (1819–20), p. 246 is worth quoting: 'Now we know something of Captain Stout. He was, to be sure, very illiterate, not to say ignorant, and wonderfully apt to wander into those "beautiful obliquities" in point of fact, for which the mercantile marine of his country is so justly celebrated; but he certainly did not deserve to be altogether annihilated. We can assure our skeptical brethren, that we not only witnessed the appearance of Captain Stout and some of his crew at the Cape, but that we saw, with our own eyes, the wreck of *Hercules* on the coast of Caffraria, and on the precise spot indicated by the Captain: his testimony, therefore, to the general appearance of the country, and to the humanity of the Caffres, is beyond the possibility of question.'

taken further in a 1975 edition of Stout's *Narrative*, where A. Porter convincingly discredits Barrow's account of Stout, but at the same time reveals several further sources that confirm his existence and the bare facts of Stout's journey.[68]

African Economic Lions

The published reception history of Stout's *Narrative*, however, tells only part of the story. At the level of ideological history, Stout's arguments have had a rather more enduring impact. After a boom period in the early part of the late eighteenth and early nineteenth century, American trade in the Cape slumped dramatically under pressure from, first, the American Embargo Act of 1807 and subsequently from strictly enforced British trade protection policies.[69] Britain prevailed as the dominant imperial presence in the Cape in the nineteenth century and American traders had only a peripheral place in the colonial economy. However, a brief examination of the current rhetoric of US engagement with Southern Africa reveals that Stout's arguments for the American colonization of the Cape, a doomed fantasy in the nineteenth century, have had a resurgence at the dawn of the twenty-first century.

On 26 March 1998, US President Bill Clinton addressed the South African Parliament as follows:

> I am convinced we agree on most things and on the important things because we share the same basic values: a commitment to democracy, a commitment to open markets, a commitment to give our people all they need to succeed in the modern world... Yes, Africa remains the world's greatest development challenge, still plagued by poverty, malnutrition, disease, illiteracy and unemployment. Yes, terrible conflicts continue to tear at the heart of the continent, but from Cape Town to Kampala, from Dar es Salaam to Dakar, democracy is gaining strength, business is growing, peace is making progress. As Africa grows strong, America grows stronger through prosperous consumers in the continent and new African products brought to our markets, through partners to seek and find solutions to our common problems, and most of all, through the invaluable benefit of new ideas, new energy, new passion from the minds and hearts of the people charting their own future on this continent.[70]

---

[68] A. Porter, ed., *The Loss of the Ship 'Hercules', 16 June 1796* (Port Elizabeth: Historical Society of Port Elizabeth, 1975). Porter also provides evidence that Stout might have been a nom de plume, and that Stout's real name was more probably Benjamin Carpenter.

[69] A. R. Booth records that in 1806, of 235 arrivals in Cape Town harbour, 143 ships were English, 61 American, 20 Danish and 6 Portuguese, with the balance made up of single ships from German states (*The United States*, p. 14). In financial terms, American exports to the Cape rose from $46 582 in 1792 to $473 345 in 1806 (Booth, *The United States*, pp. 18–19). Booth records that by the 1820s, however, American trade to the Cape had diminished dramatically, with the $13 495 for American Cape exports in 1822 a typical annual figure (*The United States*, p. 23).

[70] J. Rantao, '"Let's be partners," says Clinton', *Star*, 27 March 1998.

The emphasis on economic 'partnership' was also well to the fore in the words of Susan Rice, the US assistant secretary of state for African affairs, who claimed that 'Africans are taking their seats at the economic table and arriving with hearty appetites for lucrative commercial dealings.'[71] In a similar vein, Clinton's envoy, Vernon Jordan, proclaimed that by means of free trade agreements the Clinton administration's economic partnership with Africa would see the emergence of 'African economic lions' that would surpass 'the Asian tigers'.[72]

In certain quarters, Clinton's 1998 approach to Africa was hailed as a fresh departure, as a substantial advance on the combination of neo-colonial paternalism and Cold War opportunism that had dominated US relations with Africa in the past. However, what I want to stress is the continuities in US ideas of Africa from the eighteenth to the twentieth centuries. If Britain replaced the tentative US presence in the eastern Cape of the early nineteenth century, the imperial pecking order was emphatically reversed in the latter half of the twentieth century. Although clearly Clinton was not agreeing to colonize South Africa, the nature and form of contemporary engagement in the region repeats all the key elements of Stout's appeal. Both Stout's 1798 appeal and Clinton's 1998 speech embrace free trade as the key to a successful economic partnership, with Stout's trinkets-for-land exchange updated in Clinton's North American Free Trade Agreement for Africa. Alternative trading partners for Africa are dismissed, explicitly by Stout, in denigrating the Dutch and (less emphatically) the English, and implicitly by Clinton, whose visit to Africa was substantially motivated by US business pressure to out-manoeuvre European Union and Japanese trading blocs. Africans themselves are defended against negative stereotypes – Stout rejects the view of Africans as savages and Clinton defends them from the media clichés of poverty and conflict – and they both construct, instead, an image of Africans as potential workers and consumers. Finally, as regards African land, Stout's *Narrative* transformed the African land of the eastern Cape into a landscape both rich in agricultural potential for servicing American economic needs and exotic in providing escapist fantasies for British and North American readers. For Clinton, the exotic appeal of Africa's landscape was not neglected – the obligatory game reserve tour was included in his itinerary and the routine gestures as to the importance of tourism observed.[73] However, a far more important aim for Clinton was that agricultural resources produced on Southern African land should no longer be protected from US economic imperatives; instead

---

[71] Quoted in A. Duval Smith, 'Markets shape Clinton's Itinerary', *Mail and Guardian*, 20 March 1998.

[72] Quoted in D. A. Toler, 'Clinton goes Big-game Hunting in Africa', *Mail and Guardian*, 20 March 1998.

[73] A previous US president visiting Africa, Theodore Roosevelt in 1909, took the exotic appeal of Africa rather more to heart, shooting over 500 species of wildlife during his visit (see Toler, 'Clinton goes').

Southern African land should produce cheap exports for American markets. Deborah Toler argues to the contrary:

> African nations should be allowed to protect their fragile agricultural resources from subsidised US and other First World competitors. In the absence of such meaningful steps, Clinton's African safari becomes nothing more than a recolonization of Africa by the West under the auspices of 'free trade'.[74]

In the light of Stout's eighteenth-century blueprint for American intervention in Africa, Clinton's safari reads not so much as an instance of 'recolonization' than as the long-delayed culmination of American free trade policies dedicated to re-configuring African land use to serve the needs of the US market.

---

[74] Toler, 'Clinton goes'.

Chapter Three

Landscape, Empire and the Creation of Modern New Zealand

Cheleen Ann-Catherine Mahar

This essay examines the British diaspora with reference to the colonial experience that created New Zealand as a British colony out of the Maori land of Aotearoa – two bush-covered islands in the southern Pacific Ocean. Specifically examined is the cultural role that land played in the domination of a Pacific country and its native inhabitants by Euro-ideologies. Writers, painters, businessmen, politicians and newly arrived immigrants viewed New Zealand within a nineteenth-century Arcadian tradition.[1] This vision, combined with the material interests of farmers, land speculators and government, created a landscape, both ideologically and materially, within three powerful fields of social forces, each of which expressed nineteenth-century bourgeois British culture: the field of the aesthetic gaze, which includes painting and literature; the field of economic and political structures; and the field of social relations within new colonial communities, which dotted the country from the mid-1800s. In this essay I discuss particular aspects of these larger fields. I include a short discussion on landscape painting and New Zealand as an example of what I term the field of the aesthetic gaze; an overview of farm production, business and Arcadian imagery as an example of the field of economic and political structures; and, finally, a discussion of the early immigrants to New Zealand, their transformation of the land and their rural communities. I use these three social spaces as reflective of the larger field of social relations.

---

[1] Early British literature about New Zealand (1840–1909) characterized the country as an Arcadia, set in opposition to the social problems of Victorian Britain. Arcadia is characterized as a place of abundant resources and a population who exemplify the hard-working, moderate and moral life of nineteenth-century values. See Miles Fairburn, *The Ideal Society and Its Enemies: The Foundations of Modern New Zealand Society, 1850–1900* (Auckland: Auckland University Press, 1989) p. 29; Bernard Smith, *European Vision and the South Pacific* (New Haven: Yale University Press, 1985); Nicholas Thomas, *Colonialism's Culture: Anthropology, Travel and Government* (Princeton: Princeton University Press, 1994).

While the European colonists could in no way be said to have created the New Zealand countryside in what is sometimes referred to as its 'natural' state, one could argue that a second-order landscape was constructed by the new arrivals insofar as it was defined as having a particular relationship to the Europeans, in a system of production and reproduction. This relationship took place at two levels: one, as an idealized and symbolic 'gaze' which constructed the land as landscape and, two, in the material construction of land as a foundation for the social relations of production in New Zealand. Historical and contemporary rural communities in New Zealand were created as a social space in which to produce agricultural wealth, to sustain growth in newly developed towns and to provide the basis (materially and symbolically) for the transformation of social classes from their British antecedents. Land was the basis of wealth, power, prestige and profits. While the earliest European inhabitants (the whalers, sealers and traders) did attempt to take control of large tracks of land, New Zealand rural communities and the effective control of land in agriculture began in earnest with the arrival of the Wakefield settlements during the 1840s, and with other immigrants who made their lives in farming and pastoralism: 'From the late eighteenth century, natural history was the intellectual framework of exploration and settlement, the way to knowledge about unknown lands ... In Australia and New Zealand, it was at the base of settlement.'[2]

The structure of these communities can be analyzed as a series of social fields (aesthetic, politico-economic and social relations) within which the powerful and ambitious residents used various strategies in the reproduction and transformation of their own interests.[3] The defining social forces and capitals which constructed these fields, I suggest, are the following: the notion of New Zealand as an ideal landscape able to sustain visions of an Arcadian dream; the development and domination of nature through particular types of agriculture; and, given the group of immigrants who arrived, the emergence of a particular form of New Zealand class structure. The physical and symbolic creation of pastoral New Zealand was directly informed by nineteenth-century Britain and infused, at least on an ideal level, with a sense of moral purpose and virtue. In contemporary rural communities, social values and events that make up rural life are not only a transformation of this history, but contain old patterns that are still in evidence today and exist as social markers of class distinction.[4]

New Zealand agricultural life is structured by competing groups of people whose identity is situated within relationships between specific capitals. Land, homes,

---

[2]   Thomas Dunlap, *Nature and the English Diaspora: Environment and History in the United States, Canada, Australia and New Zealand* (Cambridge: Cambridge University Press, 1999), pp. 35–6.

[3]   See Pierre Bourdieu, *The Logic of Practice* (Cambridge: Polity Press, 1990); Richard Harker, Cheleen Mahar, Chris Wilkes, eds, *An Introduction to the Work of Pierre Bourdieu: The Practice of Theory* (New York: St. Martin's Press, 1990).

[4]   Cheleen Mahar, 'On the Moral Economy of Country Life', *Journal of Rural Studies*, 7:4 (1991).

gardens, livestock, agricultural and horticultural production, wealth, schooling, marriage alliances and dress can all be defined as manifestations of types of capital. Capital provides the foundation for particular social relationships. The power and meaning that such capital has is embedded in the land, with the land itself regarded as a type of capital, and defined and used in the lives and personal histories of rural people. The landscape, as a field of forces, and the structural positions that exist within it reflect the strategies and capital of its inhabitants, as well as providing material wealth and products for the sustenance of the entire country.

The Field of the Aesthetic Gaze: Painting

Early New Zealand painting expresses nineteenth-century bourgeois British culture and reveals itself as a constructed reproduction of the individual's imagined relationship to the means of production. These paintings can be historically and sociologically read as a particular class view of the land, which embodied a set of socially and economically determined values. Thus, there is a profound and corresponding (homologous) connection between the creation of the landscape and the social space. The process of reconceptualizing land into a landscape depicted nature within an Arcadian framework, in which the new country was ready and waiting to be used in productive ways by hard-working *British* people. One of the requirements in the creation of a new Britain from Aotearoa was a change to land, as well as the importation of animals. In addition, the growth of agricultural domains was constrained by the need for farmers and business to be sensitive to overseas markets (then as now). British picturesque artists in the early 1800s, such as Gainsborough, were committed to revealing this 'essence' of the countryside. Moreover, in New Zealand, one could say that early paintings also discovered the countryside. The colonial gaze, founded as it was on a doxic understanding of nineteenth-century nature, already knew what it was that would be discovered in New Zealand; the predetermined perceptions were shaped by artistic convention which, in part, determined nature itself. In fact, one could argue that nature is invisible outside of the conventional genres of seeing. Such conventions, which were imported from Europe, such as the Topographic, the Ideal, the Sublime and the Picturesque, determined New Zealand's idea of landscape. Indeed, the notion of landscape itself is a European import.[5] Francis Pound argues that there is no English word for a piece of land that is perceived visually but not pictorially.[6] Before the European arrived the Maori did not paint landscape nor did they see the 'land as

---

[5] 'Landscape' is a word borrowed from the Dutch in the sixteenth century to mean a pictorial representation of countryside. This representation evolved to mean the countryside itself.

[6] Francis Pound, *Frames on The Land: Early Landscape Painting in New Zealand* (Auckland: Collins, 1983), p. 23.

picture'.[7] The process of 'seeing' the landscape is thus a conventional act which is learned. Nature as pictorial representation was expressed by early painters of New Zealand, and in these paintings one finds an expression of European codes of behaviour, conventions and, above all, the promise of agricultural wealth.

Landscape painting and its Eurocentric interpretation of the indigenous world were not innocent of ideology. In the creation and painting of New Zealand, land was symbolically, as well as materially, appropriated from the Maori inhabitants. Painting fulfilled certain requirements of land exploration in early New Zealand map-making, planning improvements and exploration, which in turn led to land speculation. Some scholars have argued that landscape paintings predominated during this early period simply because the land was there, calling upon a kind of geographic determinism: 'The landscape is, in the first place, an unavoidable presence in this country. New Zealand's population was, and still is, sparsely spread over the land of constant variety and presence. It is there and dominates our lives.'[8]

Other scholars have argued for a more historically based analysis of New Zealand landscape painting, and they point to the fact that landscape was the most popular genre in Europe at the time of early New Zealand settlement. While the overwhelming force and dominating presence of the land in such a thinly populated country is unavoidable, there are historical, cultural and ideological antecedents to this tradition. It is clear that both accounts give us some insight into the early preferences of landscape painting. However, the important question is not *why* landscape painting, but *how* such paintings reflect the vision that the British immigrants had of New Zealand as a land of pastoral plenty, as evidenced in letters, travel books, academic manuscripts and advertisements for land and labour: 'Settlement was less an escape from civilization into the wilderness than a way to take nature to the market.'[9]

While there are New Zealand examples of all nineteenth-century landscape genres the topographical and the ideal are common in New Zealand. Figs 3.1 and 3.2 are two examples which are reproduced from Francis Pound's book *Frames on The Land: Early Landscape Painting in New Zealand*. Topographical landscapes were more of a recording of 'that's how it is', but they also implied the use-value of the land through pictorial description. The aim was to provide a portrait of a specific place as conceived in eighteenth-century travel books, which had, at this time, become a popular literary genre. Topographical landscapes were included among surveyors' or geologists' charts. The ideal communicated the message of 'God in nature', of 'God the Great Artist' who travelled with the European to New Zealand. Indeed, 'God in nature' was one of the more pervasive European frames of mind in landscape painting and appeared everywhere the European went.[10] Those paintings that we characterize as 'ideal' were images set within a

---

7   Pound, *Frames*, p. 49.
8   Pound, *Frames*, p. 50.
9   Dunlap, *Nature*, p. 49.
10 Pound, *Frames*, pp. 17–18.

3.1   Arthur Sharpe, *A View of Wenderholme, Auckland*, 1880. Watercolour on paper, 635 × 946 mm. Fletcher Holdings collection, Auckland (reproduced by kind permission of Collins Publishers, Auckland).

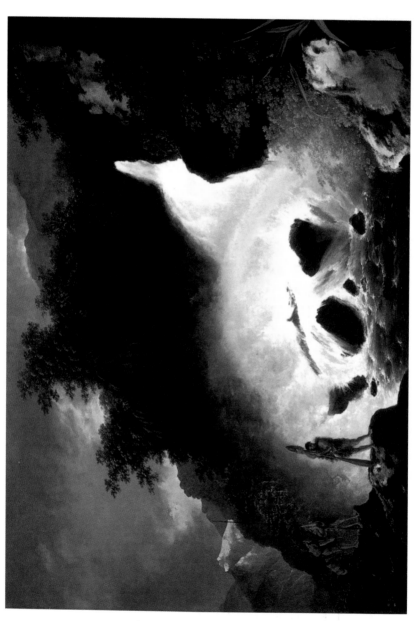

3.2   William Hodges, Water fall in Dusky Bay, New Zealand, 1775. Oil on canvas, 1524 × 2108 mm. Admiralty House, Whitehall, London (reproduced by kind permission of Collins Publishers, Auckland).

biblical, historical or mythological framework, and both ideal and topographical genres offered a code of expectations as well as a code by which to *recognize* the country:

> So landscape painting, for the first settlers in New Zealand as for us, was a way of inventing the land we live in, of modifying and reconstructing it in pictorial terms, in terms of the codes of the genres. No visual experience of nature – whether in New Zealand or elsewhere – can exist outside the frames of the genres: there is no innocent eye, no possible access to a 'real' and pre-existing New Zealand nature.[11]

Alfred Sharpe worked in the topographical style. A painter trained in art and architecture, he arrived in Auckland in 1859. He farmed, exhibited his artwork and was also a prolific writer about watercolour landscape painting. Figure 3.1, *A View of Wenderholm*, records the disappearance of the native forest. Note the trees and stumps which, as Pound says, are the signs of destruction being softened and civilized; he uses the term *civilizing destruction*.[12] Sharp recorded the changes to the landscape but in such a way (using the light of evening to unite the picture) that the result is European and reminiscent of a parkland setting with the framing of trees, grasses, hills and water. Sharpe finally left New Zealand for Australia in 1887 where he worked as an architect.

William Hodges, on the other hand, was the official artist of Cook's second voyage to the Pacific, and exemplifies the idealist tradition (1772–74). Hodges was trained by Richard Wilson (the main English representative of the Claudian Ideal) and by Salvator Rosa, master of the sublime. To his landscapes he added classical adaptations of what he perceived to be native exotica: to signify Polynesia he incorporates an exotic carving and tattoo. Otherwise the models were classically draped and Nature was depicted in a Claudian tradition. The landscape reproduced in Fig. 3.2, *Waterfall in Dusky Bay*, could have been painted anywhere, following the sublime tradition of Salvator Rosa. Pound writes, 'And yet even in this "far, far away", what was sought for and found was what the Grand Tourist might seek in Italy: the Beautiful … stock picturesque items as waterfalls, natural grottoes, etc … For the travelling Englishman carried with him everywhere he went the mode, style and language available to him from the traditions of tourism.'[13]

The landscape paintings of New Zealand were not so much distinguished as art, but rather valued as records of natural history. Moreover, such paintings implied a use of land consistent with the ideology of an empire's notion of Arcadia. The situation in New Zealand was one that grew from the milieu of the artists as recorders of the environment.

The environment, then, was seen to present possibilities for future achievements

---

[11] Pound, *Frames*, p. 14.
[12] Pound, *Frames*, p. 94.
[13] Pound, *Frames*, p. 60.

as opposed to one (such as the European environment which was beset by problems of work, land ownership and production) that was constrained and limited. Britain in the mid-1800s was the era of the deliberate production of social institutions, of morality externalized and of education-moulding respectable habits. This was also the era of 'nature as evolution' and 'culture as man's production of himself'.[14] In this spirit of what Smith calls heroic humanism, the 'natives' of the Pacific recalled the manners and customs of the early Europeans, being 'exemplars of hard primitivism'. And so, for these early adventurers, the development of civilization in the Pacific was a simple step: the New World duplicating the progress of the old.

The Field of Economic and Political Structures: The Agricultural Base

[T]hey could speak of creating a 'new England' – a dream as marked in New Zealand, founded on the Wakefieldian vision of a transplanted and purified British society in the South Seas ... Read through their literature, newspapers, legislative debates, and speeches. They were new nations populated by new men. (Women were physically present but rhetorically almost invisible). Everywhere there were the same appeals to the 'conquest of nature', 'progress', a particular kind of civilization, and until recently the virtues of an agricultural life and a society of independent farmers.[15]

Such was the imagination of the greater populace about the possibilities for new nations and new men. In the fields of politics and business this popular imagination was further fuelled by Edward Gibbon Wakefield and Mr H. G. Ward, the chairman for the Committee on Colonial Lands, both of whom had a vested interest in colonizing and selling land. But such depictions of the rural countryside were also, partly, the justifications of capital's transformation of nature. The owners of capital and land were not only the local landed Europeans, but those businesses and businessmen in Britain upon whom the development and commercialization of New Zealand agriculture was so dependent. The co-operation between business (industry) and the countryside (rural production) was critical.

The view of New Zealand as Arcadia was the ideological gloss or apparatus whereby institutions and social relations were misrecognized. In reality, life in Arcadia was all about land, power and the control of resources, all of which were social fields dominated by the great landowners and the import-export businessmen. However, New Zealand as Arcadia was not without its critics, as recorded by Fairburn. A notorious example comes from Nelson in 1843 when its 'workingmen' went on strike, and petitioned the New Zealand Company, saying that they came to

---

[14] Marilyn Strathern, *After Nature: English Kinship in the late Twentieth Century* (Cambridge: Cambridge University Press, 1992), p. 119.
[15] Dunlap, *Nature*, pp. 1–2.

New Zealand under the deception that it was a 'Splendid country', one of 'Elysian fields and Groves adorned with every beauty of Nature ... [but] instead of the bread fruit tree there is the flax tree in a Swampy piece of Ground'.[16]

In this view of New Zealand we see a country developed by the British as an economic venture. As Wilkes has suggested:

> there had been a concerted attempt to ensure an adequate supply of laborers to complement members of the capitalist class, as they were then called. If there were utopian plans for New Zealand, many took the view that it might be an ideal place to get capitalism right, to plan and order the new settlement so that mistakes in the old country were not repeated. Rather than an eradication of class, therefore, the purpose was to make a system of social classes work more effectively.[17]

Many settlements turned to sheep rearing, and often grazing land was leased rather than sold as freehold land.[18] Such extensive pastoralism was successful because in many locations, particularly in the South Island, local grass and scrub were used during the first decades as pasture. Further, the international market for wool was very strong. Not all land was bought from the Crown; some was taken by squatters and was therefore outside the control of local government, a problem put to rights in 1854 as Provincial Councils gained control of all land and squatters became leaseholders. After the fall of wool prices and the depression of the 1860s the system of runholding (of leasing land and grazing stock) moved to a system of estate production; land ownership became concentrated in the hands of fewer families whose interests were merged with the interests of urban banks and merchants, including land dealers and speculators.[19]

The entirety of New Zealand colonial development was a consequence of British migration, capital and market opportunities. In the 1870s, the country borrowed £20 million to construct a railway, telegraph lines, roads, public buildings and bridges to give the public in Britain confidence in the New Zealand economy, but also to facilitate the marketing of primary goods; the population was concentrated in the many rural hamlets and townships, rather than in the larger cities. The businesses that flourished were those connected to rural produce exports: in the 1880s, 72 per cent of exports were sent to Britain, while 65 per cent of New Zealand imports

---

[16] Miles Fairburn, *Ideal Society*, p. 21. See also Ton Otto and Nicholas Thomas, eds, *Narratives of Nation in the South Pacific* (Amsterdam: Harwood, 1997).

[17] Christopher Wilkes, *Reinventing Capitalism: History, Structure and Practice in the Formation of Social Classes in New Zealand* (Palmerston North: Massey University, 1993), p. 14.

[18] David Kenneth Fieldhouse, *The Colonial Empires: A Comparative Survey from the Eighteenth Century* (London: Macmillan, 1982), p. 253.

[19] John R. Fairweather, 'White-Settler Colonial Development: Early New Zealand Pastoralism and the Formation of Estates', *ANZJS*, 21:2 (1985).

arrived from Britain. The New Zealand economy rested upon primary production, particularly wool, which by 1890 constituted two-thirds of all exports.[20] During this decade, the New Zealand economy again faced difficulties due to the decline of wool prices. The response to this decline was market-led. First, technical advances such as refrigerated shipping and improvement in dairy production, as well as new breeds of sheep, helped production into the 1900s. Second, more land was brought into commercial production (for export), which increased meat, wool, dairy and wheat exports. The redistribution of land was a policy of the new Liberal government of the 1890s.[21] Generally, large holdings were sold off willingly by their owners, rather than through government intervention. More than half of all privately owned land was held in blocks of 5000 acres or more, by not more than 584 owners. Also, the amount of Maori land in commercial production grew. Denoon notes that in some areas Maoris became honorary settlers or rural labourers, even though in those same areas some forms of tribal organization survived. This meant that some were embedded in both European and indigenous modes of production which were themselves connected at particular conjunctures.[22]

Equally crucial to the growth of production into the 1900s was the credit allowed to small farmers under the Land Settlement Finance Act (1909). This allowed small landholders the necessary capital to buy a family farm. The leasehold system, introduced in 1882 and extended by the Liberal Party over the next 10 years, was used to settle small farmers on land, and allowed for long-term leases (from the government) and a tenure known as lease-in-perpetuity. The government, in order to hold and conserve Crown land, and to break the land monopoly of large landholders, also used such a system. However, soon after its inception, Crown tenants argued for a change to a freehold policy, arguing that the Crown would benefit financially, that there would be fewer restrictions to cropping, as well as beneficial changes to the taxation policy.[23] While leaseholders focused upon the benefits that the Crown would accrue in allowing them freehold land, the leaseholders as freeholders could realize rising values of land through land speculation, which began to dominate farming in New Zealand after the turn of the century.

To briefly summarize, it is clear that two major factors contributed to the economic and political structures of New Zealand as a British dominion and as part of the Commonwealth. One, the dispositions and vision of a future prosperity that the British population brought to the new country and, two, the surplus of capital and labour in Britain which flowed into New Zealand and created a reliance on British capital, markets and the government. Leaving the Arcadian gaze aside, the

---

[20] Donald Denoon, *Settler Capitalism: The Dynamics of Independent Development in the Southern Hemisphere* (Oxford: Oxford University Press, 1983), p. 72.

[21] William James Gardner, 'A Colonial Economy', in W. H. Oliver and B. R. Williams, eds, *Oxford History of New Zealand* (Wellington: Oxford University Press, 1981), pp. 84–6.

[22] Denoon, *Settler Capitalism*, p. 224.

[23] Denoon, *Settler Capitalism*, p. 259.

fundamental value of New Zealand to its new settlers was the control of resources through, initially, the control of land and its products. The colonization of New Zealand was based on the initial domination of landed interests and the various skilled workers in crafts, trades, farm workers, servants and shopkeepers who were part of that economy's constellation. It is quite clear that not all settlers lived a British county life; neither did they become the small owners or petty capitalists of Wakefield's plan. After the depression of the 1860s, fewer families owned land, and those that did owned large tracts whose interests merged with those of banks and merchants. The economy rested upon primary production and was heavily dependent upon British imports. The later break-up of large holdings (which did not completely disappear) was due to government land redistribution under the Liberal government of the 1890s, which offered Crown land as long-term leases, some of which were later converted to freehold parcels. However, leasehold or freehold, this primary layer of production in New Zealand's settler-capitalist economy was consistently dominated and bounded by the interests of international finance and industrial capital, a situation that still exists in the first decade of the twenty-first century.[24]

The Field of Social Relations: Immigrants, Land and Community

At the time that the early settlers left Britain (1840–80) British agriculture had been reshaped and reorganized through the Enclosure Movement. Part of this reorganization included innovations in agriculture, as well as the landlord–tenant relationship, which was called the English System, and which led to a rise in production in the output of grain or what was called high farming. During the late 1800s, the bulk of English farming land was under the landlord–tenant system and there existed a persistent and longing sentiment for the family farm, which is reflected in the Arcadian image so often used to describe New Zealand.[25]

The paucity of opportunities in Britain combined with the idealized potential for land ownership in New Zealand inspired a particular group of immigrants, many of whom accounted for their move within narrative tropes that discussed how hard they were working, how well the land was producing, and generally how exciting life in New Zealand was. A typical sentiment is expressed by a Mrs Sarah Greenwood, who wrote of:

> the extreme difficulty of finding employment in England even for single men; but how much more for a numerous family. Then again, in a few years we shall have sons to place

---

[24] Wilkes, *Reinventing*, pp. 62–4.
[25] According to E. P. Thompson in *The Making of the English Working Class* (London: Gollancz, 1963), the majority of British farmers emigrated to the United States.

out, and only think of the many anxieties experienced even by parents with money ... you will feel what a comfort it must be to reside in a country where every young person of good conduct is sure to meet with profitable and useful employment.[26]

British dreams of Arcadia were primarily carried out through the hard and diligent work of clearing forests, which made way for grazing pasture, as well as the importation of seeds, trees, birds, grazing animals and other fauna. These changes helped to meet some of the immigrant expectations for agricultural production:

> It is interesting that observers were already beginning to emphasize the antique look of places in the South Island. The old world had certainly been reproduced in fairly convincing facsimile. Everything, from the farmhouses in the countryside to the street names in the towns, indicated a society which was at once hierarchical and self-conscious.[27]

However, the pockets of British country life were few and far between, and the actual situation at the time was that most settlers owned neither farmhouses nor houses in town. Most passengers who arrived in Nelson during the 1840s, for instance, were servants, labourers or artisans who did not have the skills or capital to obtain a comfortable life from farming.[28] A look at the records of daily life contradicts the Arcadian notion of yeoman farmers and a gentrified countryside. Life, in fact, was grubby, hard, completely without services, schools or roads, and lacked any depth of social life in terms of the arts, religious tradition and education. Moreover, within early settlements there was a surplus of men to women. For instance, in 1851 there were only 776 European women for every 1000 European men.[29] The rural working population was largely composed of unmarried men with few obligations, who looked to other men for company in the bush and in the pubs. In such company there was an emphasis on physical strength and capabilities; this, as Philips has argued, is where male culture in New Zealand has its origins.

The optimism of immigrants, however, was not that of innocent Arcadian dreams. Aspiring landowners, for example, were searching for a prestigious way of life, which duplicated an older image of the English gentry:

> The owning of freehold acres and hence styling oneself 'esquire'; it was being seen in possession of fine saddle and harness horses; it was having grounds about one's house, perhaps not just a garden, but also a drive, and the beginnings of a park; it was joining

---

[26] J. S. Marais, *The Colonisation of New Zealand* (London: Oxford University Press, 1927), p. 5.

[27] Stevan Eldred-Grigg, *A Southern Gentry: New Zealanders who inherited the Earth* (Christchurch: Reed, 1980), p. 18.

[28] Eldred-Grigg, *A Southern Gentry*, p. 18.

[29] Jock Phillips, *A Man's Country? The Image of the Pakeha Male: A History* (Auckland: Penguin, 1987), p. 6.

in prestigious country sports and recreations ... it was the chance to be a person of consequence ... a man of property, able to launch one's children on a similar career and provide comfort for one's old age.[30]

There are two additional ways of dividing and describing early New Zealand settlers: first, by distinguishing between those who paid their own passage and those who would pay off their passage through their wages. Upward mobility was easier in the new country, and there was an egalitarian cast (or *méconnaissance* confusing Arcadian dream with reality) in social relations and social patterns, which was contrary to the patterns of social deference in Britain. This was, again, the result of the deep rural Arcadian myth of New Zealand, which was facilitated by official policy for political, economic and social reasons. By the 1880s there was a clear 'farming ladder', according to Wakefield, although one imagines that this would be a biased report given Wakefield's interest in New Zealand's settlers.[31]

A second method of distinguishing settlers is according to their place of origin and religious affiliation – this is particularly interesting in the case of the South Island settlements. In the South Island, the rough weather-beaten coast of Otago, where the city of Dunedin was founded, was the site for a large group of settlers from the Free Church of Scotland in 1848, whereas the expansive, warmer plain of Canterbury was the chosen site for English Anglicans. The South Island runholders consisted of two distinguishable categories: one group consisted of those who had established themselves in Australia and who then moved to New Zealand, bringing their economic capital and agricultural knowledge with them. A second group were the 'Canterbury Pilgrims', who had brought enough money from Britain to establish their own runs.[32] In Otago, the settlers had much fewer economic resources than did those in Canterbury, and so very few of the early runholders were from the original settlers.[33] Thus, while the decision to emigrate to New Zealand was undertaken in the hope of establishing different social relations between classes, upon arrival there was a clear contradiction between the Arcadian dream of yeoman farms and gentry, and the experience of the majority of working people who were mostly servants, labourers and artisans, and who stayed in this condition for their lifetimes.

---

[30] Phillips, *A Man's Country?*, p. 35.

[31] Edward Gibbon Wakefield, *New Zealand After Fifty Years* (London: Longman, 1889).

[32] Elvin Hatch, *Respectable Lives: Social Standing in Rural New Zealand* (Berkeley: University of California Press, 1992), p. 30. See also Gardner, 'A Colonial Economy' and Alfred Hamish Reed, *The Story of Canterbury; The Last Wakefield Settlement* (Wellington: Reed, 1949).

[33] Elvin Hatch, *Respectable Lives*, p. 31; Michele Dominy, *Calling the Station Home* (Lanham, Md. Rowman and Littlefield, 2002); Alexander Hare McLintock, *The History of Otago: The Origins and Growth of a Wakefield Class Settlement* (Dunedin: Otago Centennial Historical Publications, 1949).

Transforming the Land

While there was a class of impoverished people who lived with the help of charitable aid, small farmers and labourers were gradually prospering in rural New Zealand. By the mid-1860s the per capita annual income in New Zealand was £78, which was the highest in the world and was twice the average income in England, five times that of Ireland and much higher than that of Australia and the United States. By the early 1880s about one-quarter of all manual workers were owners of land.[34] In addition to their wages, working people from the 1860–1900 period would often own (by way of a mortgage) a home with a large garden, and would raise produce in order to supplement their wages.[35] From the perspective of new immigrants, working conditions in New Zealand, combined with the possibilities for land ownership, freed working people from the paternalistic and dependency relationships that existed in rural Britain. From the point of view of the gentry, workers were entirely dependent upon the estates for food, housing and wages, as well as organized 'fun'. In the South Island, in other words, class divisions along the lines of property ownership were strongly drawn. However, in the North Island gentry would often help yeoman farmers onto their own farms. This was not entirely altruistic, as the gentry did hold title and should the new farmer fall behind in his payments, the land would belong again to the gentry. Moreover, the large landowners could also control the type and size of surrounding farms, so their domination through symbolic and material capital grew into the surrounding countryside.

Not all land or indeed animals were intended for economic gain, but could be used as types of cultural capital. They enhanced surroundings, such as in the case of the landscape garden, or where used for sports, such as riding and hunting. Wealthy farmers constructed themselves into a rural gentry with large estate houses, servants, music rooms, libraries and private education, in addition to hunts, concerts and dances, as well as the church (largely Anglican or Presbyterian). In fact, large landowners began sending back to Europe for bloodstock as early as the 1840s; notable studs were set up in the 1850s and neighbouring gentlemen indulged in a friendly rivalry: 'by 1861 George Rich of Canterbury was actually selling pedigree stock to the Emperor Napoleon III. Lavish cattle and horse studs were founded too.'[36] In contrast were the poor who suffered by living in mud huts or even outside, who worked for wages or who were unemployed. One group in the town of Nelson faced starvation: 'They were so hungry that they dug up and ate their seed potatoes; others used to '"sit and cry" for lack of food.'[37]

Any survey of early pastoral farming gives a similar picture. The colonization of New Zealand and the domestication of the thick bush that covered the islands often

[34] Fairburn, *Ideal Society*, p. 45.
[35] Fairburn, *Ideal Society*, p. 102.
[36] Fairburn, *Ideal Society*, p. 55.
[37] Fairburn, *Ideal Society*, p. 19.

resulted in angry and violent exchanges with the local Maori, who suffered the loss of land, the loss of life and the loss of Maoritanga. European immigration had a devastating effect on the Maori population, which by 1890 was reduced to as few as 40 000. After the Land Wars in the North Island the Maori lost some 3.5 million acres of land. While the various Maori tribes retained 11 million acres, some land was sold by individual Maori. Furthermore, Maori agriculture was disadvantaged by a racist European population and governmental structure through the systematic destruction by those structures of the Maori kin-based mode of production, by a lack of rural credit and the growth of dairy farming over pastoralism and agriculture.

European immigration also led to the destruction of ancient native forests. In contrast with an earlier, imagined version of a New Zealand Arcadia as depicted in paintings and in writing, early land 'management' was a brutal struggle against the natural landscape and the local indigenous populations. In the end, the natural habitat of the North and South Islands was reconstructed with the importation of English grasses, western domesticated animals, English flora (that is, oak trees, elms, poplars and a variety of flowers), English birds, rabbits and fertilizer. The colonial assault on the land and on the Maori people was not only vicious but unrelenting.

The creation of New Zealand as imagined by the British was an effort of extreme determination, personal greed and hard work: huts were constructed of mud and branches; tracks were pushed through any clearing, and if the ground was muddy the horses often sank in it up to their flanks; huge tracts of bush were burned off; sheep, driven along hillsides, made their own terraced pathways, which contributed to erosion and land slips during heavy rains; men dug railway tracks with picks and shovels, and sluiced the gravel with pans. There was an all-out assault on the local bird life, which was killed for food and died out due to the elimination of its natural habitat. Men who came into town from weeks in the bush had often lost their ability to fraternize peaceably in company and when they went berserk, which they commonly did, were put into a wooded wool press – surrounded by wool like a minute padded cell – until they could be trusted to behave.

Conclusions

In summary, working the land in order to establish an agricultural base for the country's economy meant that the land had to be extensively reshaped and re-imagined, with imported flora and fauna, so that wheat, sheep, cattle and dairy farms could be created. The new immigrants used European plants and animals and the 'tools of industrial civilization – axes, rifles, plows, poisons and railroads – to transform the countryside with a speed and thoroughness never seen before, and on a scale that will never be repeated'.[38] The ideal of such pastoral farms was not an

---

[38]   Dunlap, *Nature*, p. 20.

unadulterated success. The social relations of production were embedded in the land and the work that large and small farms necessitate: from the servants and shepherds on large South Island estates, to the liaison work between farmers and business by stock agents and dairy managers. In addition, the cost to the natural landscape of Aotearoa was enormous. The cost to the indigenous population to whom Aotearoa, now New Zealand, belonged was even greater as they suffered through a series of wars and government (British) and business (British) manoeuvres, and were subjugated by treaties to expropriate their land. The sense of Maoritanga, of identity and entitlement, of belonging to a culture and a language, was re-shaped, or rather mis-shaped, into a form of sub-proletarian life whose participants were treated as sub-human by the British in their colonial vision.[39]

European New Zealand is best conceived as a process of social construction, created through the sheer determination of its foremothers and forefathers. Flora, fauna and other natural resources (including the labour and culture of local Maori people) were used to further personal ambitions within the context of what was viewed as the manifest destiny of British colonists. Their future was inspired by images of English and Scottish country life and, simultaneously, constrained by local circumstances. Vast portions of the 'naturally' heavily forested hills were destroyed by fire and in the charred remains of this vegetation the soil was enriched with imported fertilizer and imported grass seed. It was planted with English trees and grazed by English and Australian sheep and beef, but these immigrants were both destroyers and creators, seeking to bring the land closer to their own ideal. They brought not only European household goods and social expectations, but European birds and deer, as well as horses, hounds and rabbits for their social hunts. The created landscape was a mode of expression for a web of social relations, then as now. Not only early agricultural production, but also cultural production, such as landscape painting, writing and personal letters, gives us some insight into these processes of creation and transformation. The created landscape gave form and purpose to migration, and provided justification for the imperial impulse in Aotearoa.

---

[39] It is not the purpose of this easy to review Maori/colonial relationships. These were complicated, occurred at many levels and differed between tribal groups and geographical area. The following references are helpful for anyone beginning to explore this topic: Patricia Burns, *Fatal Success: A History of the New Zealand Company* (Auckland: Heinemann Reed, 1989) and Anne Salmond, *Two Worlds: First Meetings Between Maori and Europeans, 1642–1772* (Honolulu: University of Hawaii Press, 1991).

Chapter Four

Ireland in Ruins: The Figure of Ruin in Early Nineteenth-Century Irish Poetry

Sean Ryder

Ruined abbeys and castles are stock elements of topographical poetry in the early nineteenth century. An important part of their function was to provide an interpretation of national history, both in England and Ireland. Of course, in doing so, Irish and English poems tended to reflect the diverging histories of the two nations. Anne Janowitz has argued that in English poetry a ruined castle tended to represent the naturalization of the post-1688 political dispensation in England, and was used to justify the positive achievements of 'British' imperial nationhood.[1] If this is so, then the Irish ruined castle served to illustrate the opposite: the failure to arrive at a similar political settlement in Ireland, and the destructive legacy of English and British rule. In the English ruin poem the dust of national history has settled, while in the Irish ruin poem national history is very much unfinished business.

These political meanings are registered in the relationship between the ruins and the natural landscape that surrounds them. The more 'naturalized' the ruin appears, the less politically radical its meaning tends to be. Luke Gibbons has argued that in mainstream romanticism 'ruins represented the triumph of natural forces over human endeavour, and if at one level this was a process of destruction and decay, at another level it was redeemed at a higher totalizing, in the form of a trans-historical communion with nature'.[2] Janowitz links this totalizing process with nation-building, remarking that in English ruin poems of the late eighteenth and early nineteenth century:

> The ruin serves as the visible guarantor of the antiquity of the nation, but as ivy climbs up and claims the stonework, it also binds culture to nature, presenting the nation under the aspect of nature, and so suggesting national permanence ... One can interpret the growing taste for the picturesque as part of the literal groundwork of building a nationalist consciousness which paradoxically presents itself as being natural, not cultural.[3]

---

[1]   Anne Janowitz, *England's Ruins: Poetic Purpose and the National Landscape* (Oxford: Blackwell, 1990).

[2]   Luke Gibbons, 'Race Against Time: Racial Discourse and Irish History', *Transformations in Irish Culture* (Cork: Cork University Press, 1996), p. 159.

[3]   Janowitz, *England's Ruins*, p. 55.

Janowitz links this taste for picturesque representations of ruin with the political developments of the eighteenth century, specifically the Acts of Union with Scotland (1707) and with Ireland (1801). The creation of a British national identity 'demanded images of a coherent British polity'.[4] In this process, the genre of the 'chronicle history poem' of earlier times, which detailed the distinct events and personalities associated with a ruin's past, was superseded by the genre of the 'ruin poem', whose 'focus was the ideological homogenization of the nation, prompting a coincident mythologization of the past'. In these latter poems ruins tend to be evacuated of their specific historical meanings, especially the political causes and consequences of their destruction. The violent and divisive upheavals that accompanied the Reformation and the Civil War, and which led directly to physical ruin of many abbeys, houses and castles, are seldom mentioned. Ruins become objects of aesthetic appreciation rather than historical memory, with the result that the unsettling record of internecine violence is suppressed. Also suppressed are the ideological debates and conflicts that led to such wars, and the vista of alternative political paths that English history might have taken. When the political causes and consequences of real events associated with the building disappear, the ruin becomes merely a source of aesthetic and sentimental pleasure. As Rose Macauley remarks, ruined castles only become 'beautiful' when they have ceased to serve their original purposes of defence and intimidation.[5] It is a process that parallels the aestheticization of ruins in eighteenth-century painting, and indeed the aestheticization of the English landscape itself in the same period. For the ruling classes, the manufactured ruins, architectural follies and pastiches of eighteenth-century landscape gardening supplied ruins as they 'ought to be'; that is, pleasing to the eye, domesticated and detached from the messy and disturbing actualities of historical record. All of this proved useful in supporting the newly minted ideology of British nationhood based on peace, national unity and the sanction of 'nature'.

The case in Ireland is somewhat different. Luke Gibbons has noted that the figure of ruin became a significant trope in Irish nationalist iconography, just as it had in England, but the representation of Irish ruins was characterized less by a sense of order and stability than by a sense of unresolved disjunction and conflict.[6] Irish history could not so easily be converted into a narrative of past wounds being healed by a new dispensation. The political, economic, cultural and religious divisions in Ireland were still raw, and the meaning of the nation itself and its relation to a larger British state was still in contention. For many Irish poets and artists of the early

---

[4]   Janowitz, *England's Ruins*, p. 59.

[5]   Rose Macauley, *Pleasure of Ruins* (New York: Barnes and Noble, 1953), p. 441.

[6]   See Luke Gibbons's two articles, 'Between Captain Rock and a Hard Place: Art and Agrarian Insurgency', in T. Foley and S. Ryder, eds, *Ideology and Ireland in the Nineteenth Century* (Dublin: Four Courts, 1998), p. 31, and 'Romanticism in Ruins: Developments in Recent Irish Cinema', *Irish Review*, 2 (1987), p. 62.

nineteenth century, ruins bore witness not only to struggles and losses in the past, but to continuing trauma and an obvious lack of closure in the present.

As a consequence, the Irish ruin was not simply an aesthetic feature, integrated into the landscape as a tranquil sign of natural process and order. Instead it tended to serve as a site of continuing historical and ideological activity. Sometimes, as we shall see, that activity might be of a supernatural rather than a historical kind – it might have its source in the ghosts of the previous inhabitants, for instance – but in either case, the ruin was remarkable in its refusal to stay quiet. It is interesting to consider the paintings of nineteenth-century Irish artists like Daniel Maclise, Joseph Peacock and Henry MacManus in this regard, since they similarly depict Irish antiquities or ruins as locations for intense and vibrant social and political activity. Maclise's famous canvas *Marriage of Strongbow and Aoife* (1851) depicts the cataclysmic consequences of the twelfth-century Norman-Gaelic conflict in terms of both architectural ruin and the ruin of human bodies. Works purporting to represent the actualities of nineteenth-century Irish life such as Maclise's *Installation of Captain Rock* (1834), Joseph Peacock's *Glendalough* (1828) or even Henry MacManus's *Reading the Nation* (1849) show contemporary social and political activities taking place within, or alongside, ancient ruins. This style of representing ruins is a strong contrast to the English and Irish topographical paintings of the same period that focus on the ruin as an object-in-itself, reducing any human presence to the lone figure of a detached observer with no organic or historical connection with the building or its past. In populating their ruins with communities living and dead, the narrative Irish paintings of Maclise and the others refuse to create the controlled and tranquillizing relationships upon which the ideological work of the English ruin depends.

The persistence of historical consciousness and the belief in the necessity of preserving exact historical records are prominent features of cultural nationalism generally. Historiography and antiquarian research become means of countering the alleged ignorance, errors and myths promulgated by imperialist versions of native history: 'In other countries the past is the neutral ground of the scholar and antiquary; with us it is a battlefield', as one writer in the *Nation* newspaper put it.[7] In a contrary motion to the English ruin poem, the Irish nationalist text sought to recover history in its material exactness and specificity, and to make historical detail vivid to contemporary readers. Historical knowledge was a crucial part of the assertion of unique cultural identity for the Irish, which was itself to be a necessary base for the establishment of a unique and independent political state. Thomas Davis, the principal nationalist ideologue of the 1840s, argued that such historical material ought to be presented to the people in a literary or artistic form, in order to ensure its efficacy as an instrument of cultural consciousness-raising. The nationalist ballad, for instance, should 'make Irish history familiar to the minds, pleasant to the

---

[7]   Cited in Gibbons, 'Race Against Time', p. 159.

ears, dear to the passions, and powerful over the taste and conduct of the Irish people in times to come'.[8] History was to be understood as a renewable resource rather than a vague or redundant past. For nationalism, even ancient history exists in a living and powerful continuum with the present and the future.

To illustrate some of these arguments, it is instructive to contrast two roughly contemporaneous poems from the Irish and English traditions: William Drennan's 'Glendalloch' (1802) and the anonymous English poem 'Conway Castle' (1809). Both poems deal with the legacy of violent political conflict, but where the English poem uses the figure of the ruined castle to signify a phase of violent history that has been thankfully superseded, the Irish poem's ruined monastery acts as a reminder of political violence that cannot be easily forgotten. 'Glendalloch' is a poem written shortly after two significant blows to Irish independence: the unsuccessful Irish rebellion of 1798 and the 1800 Act of Union. In Drennan's poem the ruined monastery of Glendalough in Co. Wicklow, with its remarkable round tower, becomes not merely a reminder of the inexorable passage of time and the vanity of human pride, as it might in a conventional ruin poem. Instead, Drennan's ruin is a much more disturbing thing, a literal grave of national hopes and identity:

> O COUNTRY, gain'd but to be lost! …
> Where shall her sad remains be laid?
> Where invocate her solemn shade?
> HERE be the mausoleum plac'd,
> In this vast vault, this silent waste; –
> Yon mouldering pillar, midst the gloom,
> Finger of Time! Shall point the tomb;
> While silence of the ev'ning hour
> Hangs o'er Glendalloch's ruined tow'r.[9]

The ruin has not been quietly assimilated into nature, nor can it be a sign of the healing of political wounds. The mausoleum metaphor suggests a state of permanent national grief, with little likelihood that the 'silent waste' observable here will be aestheticized or made fruitful by natural overgrowth. The violence of history in this case leaves these ruins as a memorial to unrelieved trauma.

The poem 'Conway Castle' takes a very different approach in its meditation on the ruins of the great medieval castle built by the English monarchy to subdue the Welsh. Originally, like an Irish ruin, the castle was a sign of violent invasion and the suppression of one culture by another. Now, however, in its ruinous state it is used to

---

[8] Thomas Davis, *Selections from his Prose and Poetry*, intro. T. W. Rolleston (Dublin: Talbot, n.d.), p. 96.

[9] William Drennan, *Fugitive Pieces, in Verse and Prose* (Belfast: Finlay, 1815), pp. 114–15.

remind the reader that the historical conflict between the Welsh and English has been replaced by a new harmonious relationship under the unified British state:

> … Conway! Then thy towers arose
> Mid thy bleeding country's woes!
> It was not pride, it was not state,
> That raised thee high and made thee great;
> But fell ambition, to control
> Cambria's brave and stubborn Soul!…
> Britain, now with freedom crown'd
> Leaves these proud turrets to decay;
> She wants no castle's strength, or high-rais'd mound,
> To check the battle's stern array,
> Secure in his benignant sway,
> Whose scepter'd virtues guard the throne,
> Who feels his people's happiness his own;
> And, when for war she doth prepare,
> Looks in each British heart, and sees a fortress there.[10]

This is a striking representation of the ideological manoeuvres through which the establishment of empire was made to seem natural and emancipatory. The military coercion necessary in the period of the castle's construction has been replaced in the present day by the even more effective ideological control in which the subject rationalizes and accepts his or her own coercion. Here the newly formed British subject has apparently internalized the rationale for Welsh subjugation which previously had to be militarily enforced. The acceptance of this situation can only be successful, however, if certain ideological contradictions pass unnoticed. One basic contradiction is the fact that the 'British' freedom celebrated by the poem has been achieved through the violent suppression of the freedom of the Welsh. This contradiction is masked, or made acceptable, by the poem's definition of the English violence as 'fell ambition', which appears to acknowledge the negative aspects of that imperial violence, while at the same time maintaining that the long-term result of violence has been the establishment of a 'benignant sway'. The decay of the ruins is thus not presented primarily as a sign of the loss of Welsh power and identity. Instead the decay ultimately appears to confirm the naturalness and validity of the political process that subsumed Wales into Britain. The sense of grief and loss that suffuses Drennan's Irish poem is entirely absent.

Irish ruins are usually haunted places, unable and unwilling to shake off the ghosts and memories that a poem like Conway Castle has apparently laid to rest. Thomas Moore's *Irish Melodies*, for instance, are full of ruins: ruined palaces, unstrung harps, broken hearts – all signs of destruction whose causes are identified as ultimately political, not natural. At the end of the famous lyric 'The Harp That

---

10 Janowitz, *England's Ruins*, p. 74.

Once through Tara's Halls' (1808), Moore describes a scene that begins as a conventional lament for the passing of a glorious moment of civilization:

> No more to chiefs and ladies bright
> The harp of Tara swells;
> The chord alone, that breaks at night,
> Its tale of ruin tells.
> Thus Freedom now so seldom wakes,
> The only throb she gives,
> Is when some heart indignant breaks,
> To show that still she lives.[11]

The scenario is one that at first seems to follow the conventions of the ruin poem as found in English writing since Anglo-Saxon times: a lament for the passing of the great and a wistful recognition of the effects of time and decay. In other words, it can be read as a meditation on the vanity of human pride and the transience of life. But the final lines of Moore's poem give this situation a political rather than just a moral or metaphysical meaning. The ruins are the home of a battered, but still living political spirit ('Freedom'). It is not just the loss of a past civilization that is being lamented by Moore; it is the unending assault on Irish freedom that moves him most.

A generation after Moore, haunted ruins continue to be found in nationalist verse. Like Moore's work, the poem 'The Old Castle' (1847), by 'Mary of the *Nation*', describes a ruin that has not yet collapsed into a state of nature. The 'soul in the ruin' – the spirit of freedom, again – has not died or disappeared, with the result that the castle is still in a sense inhabited. Because it has not died, the ruin remains a site of political possibility:

> There is an old Castle hangs over the sea –
> 'Tis living through ages, all wrecked though it be;
> There's a soul in the ruin that never shall die,
> And the ivy clings round it as fondly as I.
> [...]
> Right grand is the freedom that dwells on the spot,
> For the hand of the stranger can fetter it not;
> The strength of that Castle its day-spring has told,
> But the soul of the ruin looks out as of old;
> [...]
> How weird on those waters the shadows must seem,
> When the moonlight falls o'er them as still as a dream,
> And the star-beams awake at the close of the day,
> To gaze upon a river eternal as they!
> How the ghosts of dead ages must glide through the gloom,

---

[11] Thomas Moore, *Poetical Works* (New York: Appleton, 1854), p. 230.

And the forms of the mighty arise from the tomb,
And the dream of the past through the wailing winds moan,
For they twine round the ruin as if 'twere their own.

There is an old Castle hangs over the sea,
And ages of glory yet, yet shall it see,
And 'twill smile to the river, and smile to the sky,
And smile to the free land when long years go by.[12]

As in Moore, restless spirits flit about this ruin, but what most distinguishes this
from an English ruin poem is its association of the castle with a glorious future, in
which the values of the past will be reconstituted; when the glories of the past, if
not the castle itself, shall be restored. The spirits of the past cling tenaciously to the
ruins and will not be dislodged by the arrival of a new dispensation, such as the new
imperial British order that made Conway Castle redundant. Instead, the Irish future
is imagined in terms of revival rather than linear progress. The relation between past
and future is understood as a kind of repetition rather than a relegation of the past
into redundancy.

The invocation of ghosts is interesting in this type of poem. In the mainstream
gothic tradition, ghosts and spirits are associated with terror and mystery, as they are
in nineteenth-century Anglo-Irish gothic fiction. In the Irish nationalist ruin poem,
on the other hand, ghosts are usually noble victims with whom the reader is intended
to feel sympathy and solidarity. They are metaphors for a 'virtual' community that
once existed and now, as conditions become ripe, waits to be brought again to
life. The occasions when Irish ruins do appear terrifying in nationalist writing are
more often found in cases where the perceiver of the ruin is an outsider, such as an
English visitor. For example, Thomas Moore's *Captain Rock* (1824) is prefaced by a
narrative of the book's supposed 'editor', who is a stranger to the land he visits. In the
preface, the 'editor' describes a nocturnal visit to a ruined abbey in Roscrea, where
he has a terrifying encounter with an assembly of Rockite insurgents, all dressed in
ghostly white.[13] Once the narrator learns of the injustice that has driven Irish people
to support the Whiteboys, however, and becomes sympathetic to their cause, the
terror and mystery are dissipated. Ironically, in the conclusion of the memoir, it is
the forces of the British state who appear as sources of terror in the landscape: they
arrest Captain Rock while he is out for a romantic, nocturnal stroll and have him
sentenced to transportation for the offence of 'being out by moonlight', unable to
give a satisfactory account of himself.

The English ruin poem is more likely to avoid the issue of ghosts, spirits and
other gothic residues altogether. The poem 'Lines, Written at Kenilworth Castle,
Warwickshire' (1808) populates its ruin not with spirits of the past, but with living

---

12 Edward Hayes, ed., *Ballads of Ireland* (Dublin: Duffy, 1855), vol.1, p. 6.
13 [Thomas Moore], *Memoirs of Captain Rock*, 4th edn (London: Longman, 1824), p. xi.

flowers and children from the present. These denizens are free from the weight of history and care, are close to nature and are illuminated in sunlight. They have no connection at all to the historical past or political identity of the ruin:

> Many a ruined tower
> Gives kindly shelter to the struggling flower,
> And many a child, escaped from school to play,
> Pursues its gambols in the sunny ray.[14]

This poem constructs a temporal and political distance between the human figures and the physical ruin which allows the ruin to become merely picturesque, a pretty backdrop to a romantic vision of childhood innocence.

The tendency to imagine the human and physical restoration of the ruin in Irish nationalist poetry was not new to the nineteenth century. An early example in the Irish language tradition is a seventeenth-century poem, rendered into English in 1846 as 'To the Ruins of Donegal Castle', by James Clarence Mangan. This elegiac poem addresses the castle of Red Hugh O'Donnell (d. 1602), chieftain of the territory of Tirconnell, one of the leaders of the rebellion against Elizabeth in the 1590s. O'Donnell in fact destroyed his own castle in Donegal town rather than allow it to fall into the hands of his enemies. The poem concludes with an imagined restoration that is both architectural and political:

> By God's help, he who wrought thy fall
> Will reinstate thee yet in pride
> Thy variegated halls shall be rebuilded all,
> Thy lofty courts, thy chambers wide.
>
> Yes! thou shalt live again, and see
> Thine youth renewed! Thou shalt outshine
> Thy former self by far, and Hugh shall reign in thee,
> The Tirconnellian's king and thine![15]

The impulse to rebuild from the ruins of the past, rather then abandon those ruins, is characteristic of nineteenth-century nationalist discourse generally. In an essay entitled 'Irish Antiquities' (1843), Thomas Davis imagines a similar kind of process whereby the relics of the past may be made useful for the economic and cultural needs of the present. Expressing his horror at a proposal to demolish the prehistoric chamber tomb of Newgrange in Co. Meath in order to build a new road, Davis argues that Irish ruins should not merely be preserved but recycled:

> It would be politic and a noble emulation of the sects, restoring the temples wherein our sires worshipped for their children to pray in ... Nor do we see why some of these

---

[14] Cited in Janowitz, *England's Ruins*, p. 59.
[15] Hayes, *Ballads of Ireland*, p. 159.

hundreds of half-spoiled buildings might not be used for civil purposes – as almshouses, schools, lecture-rooms, town-halls.[16]

To re-use the past in this way is in a sense to arrest the processes of natural decay, again in contrast to the English ruin, for which the gradual disintegration of the building can be a source of pleasure.

While in the examples so far the distinction has been made between an English tradition that tends towards de-historicization and an Irish tradition that insists on maintaining historical consciousness, it is also possible to find nationalist ruin poems that perform a certain de-historicizing of their own. Denis Florence McCarthy's 'The Pillar Towers of Ireland' (1845) gives a register of historic invasions of Ireland, but then contrasts the ephemeral nature of these events with the much more permanent pillar tower that is somehow elevated out of history and whose historical origins are themselves obscured:

Around these walls have wandered the Briton and the Dane –
The captives of Armorica, the cavaliers of Spain –
Phoenician and Milesian, and the plundering Norman Peers –
And the swordsmen of brave Brian, and the chiefs of later years!

There may it stand for ever, while that symbol doth impart
To the mind one glorious vision, or one proud throb to the heart;
While the breast needeth rest may these gray old temples last,
Bright prophets of the future, as preachers of the past![17]

Like the old castle of Mary's poem, and much more optimistically than the tomb-like ruins of Moore and Drennan, these ruins represent Irishness itself, which must be imagined as a spirit or quality that transcends material form and therefore exists outside historical change. MacCarthy's poem embodies the bourgeois nationalist desire to find an essential 'spirit of the nation' that will define in a permanent way Ireland's difference to other cultures, especially England. In some ways this desire to find an object or space that transcends historical change is similar to the process of naturalization found in an English ruin poem like 'Conway Castle'. Yet for nineteenth-century nationalism, as in other decolonizing movements, it was imperative to define Ireland in terms of its *cultural* distinctiveness, which meant that transcendence of history could never be complete. The result is the paradoxical situation whereby MacCarthy's pillar towers are supposed to be both beyond history (they transcend all the historical waves of Irish invaders and settlers) and historical objects themselves (they are distinctively products of an *Irish* civilization). The contradiction here is never fully resolved in nationalist writing.

---

[16] Davis, *Selections*, p. 103.
[17] Hayes, *Ballads of Ireland*, p. 5.

John de Jean Frazer's nationalist poem 'The Holy Wells' (1847) represents a structurally similar situation, though like many of Frazer's poems it also brings an interesting awareness of class politics to the analysis of Ireland's plight. The ruins of Irish castles and abbeys remind the poet of the way that the poor are continually exploited by their rulers:

> ... knowledge has abused its powers, an empire to erect
> For tyrants, on the rights the poor had given them to protect;
> Till now the simple elements of nature are their *all*,
> That from the cabin is not filched, and lavished in the hall –

The poem goes on to argue that there is one thing that cannot be stolen from the poor. It is a phenomenon of nature; the water from the spring:

> And while night, noon, or morning meal no other plenty brings,
> No beverage than the water-draught from old, spontaneous springs;
> They, sure, may deem them holy wells, that yield from day to day,
> One blessing which no tyrant hand can taint, or take away.[18]

This might appear to challenge the idea that politics and culture can resist oppression. In some ways it is an invocation of the power of nature alone to sustain the poor. But Frazer insists on calling these springs 'holy wells', thus linking them to popular religious practice and making them cultural objects. In Frazer's Ireland, religion, politics and economics are inseparable, since political authority, the historical suppression of Catholicism and the control of the land are all by-products of English and later British rule. Holy wells are therefore not just places of spiritual sustenance; they are also sites of political resistance. The fact that holy wells are frequently found on ruined religious sites also links them to history and makes them symbolic of native Irish spirituality that is structurally cognate with Moore's and Mary's unquenched spirit of freedom.

Frazer was writing during the period of the Great Famine, an event which produced its own intense visions of ruin. One of the most famous nationalist poems to address the Famine was Aubrey de Vere's 'Ode: The Curse of Cromwell, or, The Desolation of the West' (1847). The poem opens with a vision of a deserted landscape that produces gothic effects of 'gloom and dread':

> In trance I roamed that Land forlorn,
> By battle first, then famine worn;
>   I walked in gloom and dread:
> The Land remained: the hills were there:
> The vales: but few remained to share
>   That realm untenanted.

---

[18] Hayes, *Ballads of Ireland*, p. 6.

Having described the bleak consequences of British misrule allied to natural misfortune, de Vere takes up the tomb metaphor already deployed by Moore and Drennan to symbolize Ireland under the Empire. But de Vere then diverts the metaphor away from the political towards the metaphysical, finding consolation in the possibility that such a tomb may in fact be a form of Christian altar. Instead of political or cultural resurrection, de Vere's ruin inspires visions of a spiritual one:

> A Land became a Monument!
> Man works; but God's concealed intent
>   Converts his worst to best:
> The first of Altars was a Tomb –
> Ireland! thy grave-stone shall become
>   God's Altar in the West![19]

Such religious interpretations of the causes and consequences of the famine were common in the 1840s and, in a structural sense, de Vere's devotional perspective closely replicates the qualified optimism of the other poems we have seen.

Yet belief in the possibilities of revival, resistance or salvation are not found in all Irish ruin poems from the nationalist tradition. A poem like James Clarence Mangan's well-known translation 'Lament over the Ruins of the Abbey of Teach Mologa' (1846) challenges the positive conclusions of both British poems of imperial pride and Irish poems of revivalist optimism. The abbey of Timoleague referred to in Mangan's poem had been suppressed, like all Irish and English monasteries, by Henry VIII, and was finally burned by English forces in 1642. Mangan's poem is a rough translation of a late eighteenth-century Gaelic poem by Seághan Ó Coileáin, in which the speaker is moved by the sight of the abbey ruins to contemplate both the persecution of Catholicism and the transience of his own life. The original poem concludes with the poet comparing the decline of the monastery to his own physical decline. Ó Coileáin's poem was first translated (very loosely) by Thomas Furlong for Hardiman's bilingual anthology *Irish Minstrelsy* in 1831. Samuel Ferguson published a more literal translation of the poem in 1834. Mangan's translation, published 12 years later, follows the general spirit of the original elegy, but relies on Furlong's English phrasing in many places and makes some significant changes in vocabulary. It also makes the political implications of the poem much more explicit than Ferguson had done, or indeed than the original Gaelic poem had done.[20] Imagining the destruction of the monastery, Mangan's poet asks:

> Where wert thou, Justice, in that hour?
> Where was thy smiting sword? What had those good men done,

---

[19] Aubrey de Vere, *The Poetical Works of Aubrey De Vere* (London: Kegan Paul, 1884), pp. 108–10.
[20] See James Hardiman, *Irish Minstrelsy, or Bardic Remains of Ireland*, 2 vols (London: Joseph Robins, 1831), vol. 2, pp. 234–42.

That thou shouldst tamely see them trampled on
By brutal England's Power?[21]

These lines had been translated by Ferguson as:

Oh! the hardship, oh! the hatred,
Tyranny, and cruel war,
Persecution and oppression,
That have left you as you are![22]

It is Mangan who introduces the very specific reference to 'brutal England', thus
ensuring that the reader is in no doubt as to the political causes of the abbey's ruin.
He does not leave the poem at this point of political critique, however. The poem is
steered back to the theme of individual ageing and personal decay:

        … If Change is here,
Is it not o'er the land? Is it not too in me?
Yes! I am changed even more than what I see.
Now is my last goal near!

and Mangan adds a concluding stanza entirely of his own invention:

I turned away, as toward my grave,
And, all my dark way homeward by the Atlantic's verge,
Resounded in mine ears like to a dirge
The roaring of the wave.

In this poem, the ruins offer no possibility of renewal or restoration. The devastation
visited upon the abbey is not healed by nature or time. Most importantly, its prospect
of desolation and death have been internalized by the speaker, so that the political and
religious ruin of Teach Molaga becomes a metaphor for his own personal fate. Much
like the speaker in Mangan's famous short lyric 'Siberia', published in the same year,
the speaker here is not merely an observer, but a sufferer whose own psychological
condition reflects or is reflected by the physical landscape. The poem is deeply
pessimistic, since the speaker, the national subject, sees no chance of revival, literal
or metaphorical. There is no spirit of freedom still flitting about these ruins, nor is
hope to be found in the heart of the speaker. Nor is there a Wordsworthian sublime –
a 'spirit that rolls through all things' – to mitigate the speaker's apprehension of loss.

---

[21] James Clarence Mangan, 'Lament over the Ruins of the Abbey of Teach Mologa', *Nation*
(8 August 1846), p. 681.
[22] Samuel Ferguson, *Lays of the Western Gael, and Other Poems* (Dublin: Sealy, Bryers &
Walker, 1888), p. 146.

Nature, in the form of the sea, provides only the sound of a dirge. In a way Mangan provides a more complex version of Drennan's mausoleum from a generation before, unable to see a way forward from the ruined past to a bright future. Mangan's note of despair is somewhat atypical in the nationalist verse of the 1840s, and in fact draws attention to the fragility of his contemporaries' more optimistic visions. In Mangan, the figure of ruin is internalized without being depoliticized, in a way that reflects the colonized condition even more dramatically than depictions of the physical ruins in the landscape. Mangan gives us a bleak version of the Romantic psychological landscape, an inverted 'Tintern Abbey', where instead of a naturalized ruin associated with uplifting thoughts, we have a traumatized landscape that reflects colonial paralysis. And like the less complicated work of his contemporaries, Mangan's work still refuses to allow history to slip under the forgetful ivy cladding of nature.

Chapter Five

'A hot place, belonging to Us': The West Indies in Nineteenth-century Travel Writing by Women

Evelyn O' Callaghan

For British 'lady travellers' to the West Indies in the nineteenth century, defining the place they expected to find did not present much of a problem. A useful example comes from an upper-class English woman called Winifred James: about to embark on a voyage to the Caribbean, she admits – in the self-deprecating manner common to women travel writers – her complete ignorance of the colonies beyond 'little ideas of Jamaica as a hot place and belonging to Us'.[1] 'A hot place' is shorthand for an *exotic* landscape which, in the case of the West Indies, translates into certain iconic images: sun, sea, colourful and lush vegetation, and dusky natives. In short, 'the tropics' signify a pre-scribed postcard scene onto which is projected desire for the sometimes dangerously exciting, strange and other. 'Belonging to Us', on the other hand, counterbalances this strangeness by translating it in terms of familiar prescriptions, making it *safe* because ultimately framed within the categories of European knowledge-building (hence travel writing's inclusion of scientific 'facts', the details of flora and fauna, ethnographic manners and customs) and European rule. The exotic familiarized (for Us), the tropics textually appropriated and made safe (for Us): this was an underlying formula in many nineteenth-century travelogues of the West Indies.

Accordingly, critics like Sarah Mills and Mary Louise Pratt have stressed the intimate connection between travel writing and colonialist discourse. Pratt sees travel writers as part of 'the capitalist vanguard', thematizing European expansionist designs: travel writing participates in 'the rhetoric of discovery' and 'a goal-oriented rhetoric of conquest and achievement'. Destinations, in place of kingdoms, are conquered textually; native society and landscape are encoded as 'obstacles to the forward movement of the Europeans';[2] and these logistical, rather than military, challenges are overcome by the narrator.

---

[1] Winifred James, *The Mulberry Tree* (London: Chapman, 1913), p. 7.
[2] Mary Louise Pratt, *Imperial Eyes: Travel Writing and Transculturation* (London: Routledge, 1992), p. 148.

In this essay I examine constructions of the West Indies as a problematically inhabited landscape in a selection of later nineteenth- and early twentieth-century travel narratives by women of creole (native-born white) as well as English, Irish and Australian origin. Accordingly, it is useful to begin by asking, with Susan Blake, 'What difference does gender make?'[3] After all, colonialism was generally imaged as a 'masculine' project. Hence, Mills argues that:

> In the colonial context, British women were only allowed to figure as symbols of home and purity; women as active participants can barely be conceived of. This is because of social conventions for conceptualizing imperialism, which seem to be as much about constructing a *masculine* British identity as constructing a national identity *per se* ... [so that] women's writing and involvement in colonialism was markedly different from men's ... women travel writers were unable to adopt the imperialist voice with the ease which male writers did. The writing which they produced tended to be more tentative than male writing, less able to assert 'truths' of British rule without qualification.[4]

Because of women's marginal position in relation to the imperial record – in terms of assuming an 'official' voice – Mills notes that female travel writers were often considered eccentric, abnormal, even slightly ridiculous, and the 'truthfulness' of their narratives cast in doubt as exaggerated 'women's' tales.[5] This is, of course, not to claim that a woman writer's awareness of her own marginal status automatically entails sympathy with other oppressed groups. As Pratt suggests, even those female-authored accounts that affirm feminocentric values by writing women into a male-dominated genre simultaneously take European privilege for granted. Mills, too, registers awareness of 'the clash of feminine and colonial discourses [that] constructs texts which are at one and the same time presenting a self which transgresses and which conforms both to patriarchal and imperial discourses'.[6] What I want to attend to, then, are the complex interconnections between discourses of feminism, femininity, colonialist ideology and an embryonic West Indian nationalist impulse in a selection of women's travel narratives of the period.

The Texts

The works discussed constitute a varied but representative sample and, given their unfamiliarity, a brief description of each is appropriate here. *The Mountain Pastor*

---

[3] Susan L. Blake, 'A Woman's Trek: What Difference Does Gender Make?', in Nupur Chaudhuri and Margaret Strobel, eds, *Western Women and Imperialism: Complicity and Resistance* (Bloomington: Indiana University Press, 1992), p. 19.

[4] Sara Mills, *Discourses of Difference: An Analysis of Women's Travel Writing and Colonialism* (London: Routledge, 1991), p. 3.

[5] Mills, *Discourses of Difference*, p. 112.

[6] Mills, *Discourses of Difference*, p. 106.

(1852), a collection of moral tales by a white Jamaican woman of English descent, Mrs Henry Lynch, only qualifies as a travel narrative in its introductory section. A prefatory letter exhorts 'my young friends' to turn their minds from the crowded streets of London and take an imaginary trip: to 'search with me in a far distant island of the West' for the beautiful tropical highlands where the eponymous Mountain Pastor has his home.[7] The invitation is an excuse for a descriptive account of the Jamaican highlands in a style that shifts between lyrical rhapsody, natural history and a Romantic predilection to intuit the divine in nature's magnificence. Lynch's later text, *The Wonders of the West Indies* (1861), is prefaced by a letter that betrays a similar temptation into 'poetic' excess ('The tropical dews, resting like heavy rain on the morning world') and a propensity to apprehend her Maker in this contemplation of jewelled beauty.[8] There follows a sketch of the 'official' narrative of West Indian settlement, with customary natural history details from each territory, together with notes on folklore, crops, manners and customs. Somewhat uneasily, Lynch's introductory narratives shift between an informed, not to say expert third-person account and a receptive first-person plural persona: an 'us' to whom this beauteous tropical world is strange and new.

Ethel Maud Symmonett (a Jamaican creole), in *Jamaica: Queen of the Carib Sea* (1895), purports to deliver the same package: prefatory remarks indicate that it will be 'a synopsis of the actual manners, customs and appearance of the natives, with a few of the most prominent sceneric features of attraction'.[9] But what follows, to the initial bewilderment of the reader, is a story: a shipboard dialogue between travellers, some of whom are Jamaica-bound and others who try to convince the former that the 'Isle of Springs' (Jamaica) is a 'God-forsaken hole', full of cannibals, drunken savages, disease, alligators and wild hogs.[10] On arrival in Jamaica, these horror stories – a pre-scripting of the more dangerous side of the 'hot place' – are instantly revealed to have been a hoax, and the narrative ends with a lengthy letter combining the requisite practical information alongside hyperbolic praise for the natural beauty and resources of the island.

Glimpses of Life in Bermuda and the Tropics (1897) opens with the English Margaret Newton's evocative categorizing of her work as a record of 'wanderings in the regions of unending summer', purportedly to encourage other visitors to follow suit. This translates into a colourless but ladylike first-person narrator affording us 'glimpses' of several West Indian islands and liberally illustrating the composite of 'manners and customs', natural history and 'painterly' descriptions with her own black and white sketches. Her methodology is to describe 'rambles' taken in pursuit of 'subjects' which are then painted or sketched, with various facts and

---

[7] Mrs. Henry Lynch, *The Mountain Pastor* (London: Darton, 1852), p. 5.

[8] Mrs. Henry Lynch, *The Wonders of the West Indies* (London: Seeley, 1861), p. 3.

[9] Ethel Maud Symmonett, *Jamaica: Queen of the Carib Sea* (Kingston: Mortimer, 1895), p. 4.

[10] Symmonett, *Jamaica*, p. 6.

subjective impressions of the place and its people thrown in. In common with the other narratives discussed, *Glimpses* waxes lyrical about the natural beauty of the region. Newton's vision is always 'artistic', though her aesthetic is deeply invested in a colonial world view. For example, describing an area in Bermuda, her painterly eye observes that some:

> dark-hued natives, graceful and picturesque, at work upon the red brown clay nearby, or anon marching lightly, bare-footed or straw-hatted, with sometimes a bundle on their heads like bronze caryatides ... [give] just the touch of humanity and colour to the peaceful scene which it needs.[11]

People are consistently depicted in terms of the visual field, so that peasant women 'are very imposing ... when attired in their fresh print dresses with the trains tucked up on one side and with colours harmonised bewitchingly with their bronze skins'.[12]

Irish-born May Crommelin's brief and breathless memoir of a week's holiday in the Blue Mountains shortly after her arrival in 'the dream-island' is aptly titled 'The Mountain-Heart of Jamaica' (1898).[13] The impassioned first-person narrator drags the reader along on a (frequently hair-raising) whirlwind tour of this ravishing landscape. The account of bewitching scenery is peppered with asides on the (sensationalized) history of the island, subjective impressions of encountered natives – often seen through the semi-fictional filter of historical romances – and concludes with an apparently sincere if overblown celebration of the 'other worldly' terrain of the Blue Mountains, prosaically illustrated with several photographs.

Reflection – in Jamaica (1932) by Mary Gaunt, an Australian, is the longest of the texts. It is prefaced by an introductory account of the first-person narrator's lifelong wish to travel to 'wild' and romantic places, which – as Gillian Whitlock discusses – is exactly how she constructs the island of Jamaica.[14] Gaunt foregrounds her gender, and her intention to depart from the format of her hero (a male travel writer, Captain Speke), in writing 'about trivial things'. Like several of the narrators mentioned, she also insists on her own authority, promising to impart a 'tale of Jamaica' that 'is not a tale of what the ordinary tourist sees'.[15] Her travel narrative is as much a trawl through Mary Gaunt's somewhat fevered imagination as it is a tour

---

[11] Margaret Newton, *Glimpses of Life in Bermuda and the Tropics* (London: Digby, 1897), pp. 12–13.

[12] Newton, *Glimpses*, p. 114.

[13] May Crommelin, 'The Mountain-Heart of Jamaica', *The Ludgate,* VI (October 1898), pp. 525–32.

[14] Gillian Whitlock, '"A Most Improper Desire": Mary Gaunt's Journey to Jamaica', paper presented to the Ninth International ACLALS Conference, University of the West Indies, Mona, Jamaica (13–20 August 1992).

[15] Mary Gaunt, *Reflection – in Jamaica* (London: Ernest Benn, 1932), p. viii.

of the island she is visiting: the rambling, anecdotal style seizes upon places and people and uses them as springboards for imaginative forays into a melodramatic, romanticized version of the island's historical past. The veracity of her lyrical celebrations of Jamaica's natural beauty is supported by visual testimony in the way of photographs.

Using these narratives as case studies, I now want to return to the 'difference that gender makes'. Mills's argument, in *Discourses of Difference*, is that women writers who inserted themselves into the 'masculinist' constraints of the nineteenth-century travel narrative had difficulty with a number of generic conventions, including the adoption of the voice of the adventurous male hero. After all, the woman writer's need to fulfil cultural expectations of the 'feminine' (properly concerned with domestic and interpersonal relations) clashed with her deliberate entry into a world of novelty, difficulty and even danger abroad. And, of course, she could hardly claim to have either a place within or inside knowledge of colonial conquest and administration, which might have justified her attempts to add to the written record. Negotiating between the powerful discourses of colonialism and femininity, women had to modify and manipulate the genre of the travel narrative in order to use it. For example, Blake cites male travel writers following a pattern whereby the hero overcomes obstacles (the intractable landscape or native) and proves his manhood by 'getting things done' through using either force or superior knowledge.[16] For the female author, such options are closed; thus women's travel writing tends to be more concerned with interpersonal relations, acknowledging the value of judicious reciprocity on the trail, and in the text. Female travellers assert the 'superiority of courtesy to force and the corrective power of experience over myth'.[17] The traveller, in other words, is always a *lady*, even as she transgressively assumes an authoritative voice in representing the strange new land.

Inevitably the intersection of discourses of femininity and colonialism led to certain interesting departures in the genre. For instance, Gaunt's explicit desire to record 'trivial things', 'trivial daily happenings' as against the 'serious matter' of male writers, results in a new focus on the domestic, the everyday, in the textual construction of the colony, and it would be interesting to conduct a close study of how such a focus interrogates official accounts by juxtaposing the 'trivial' quotidian with the apparently authoritative monolithic record. Attention to this 'tampering' with the conventions of the genre have led some critics to isolate a number of features common to female-authored travel narratives. Three such features, which I will explore in West Indian travelogues, are use of the 'spontaneous', confessional form, ambivalence about the 'truth value' of the works, and a complex relationship to tropes of discovery and possession, long part of the colonial representation of tropical landscapes.

---

[16] Blake, 'A Woman's Trek', p. 20.
[17] Blake, 'A Woman's Trek', p. 31.

The 'Confessional', Truth Value and the Narrative Relationship to Landscape

Women travel writers' construction of the West Indian landscape, as evident in the brief synopses above, tends towards the 'sentimental' rather than the 'scientific', the 'literary' or poetic rather than the factual, and frequently assumes a spontaneous, personal, confessional style. Researchers like Pratt, Mills and Eva-Marie Kröller note the predominance of this mode in female-authored travel narratives generally, reinforced by the nineteenth-century European consideration of letters, journals, diaries or other 'confessional' vehicles as singularly appropriate to women writers.[18] They were suitable for women because they favoured intimacy, and did not demand strict accuracy or organization given that the accretive epistolary/anecdotal form was, as Mills points out, perceived to be 'loose enough to contain [women's] unstructured narratives'.[19] The confessional did not stretch credibility either by demanding the use of specialized knowledge and language (for example statistical data), but passed itself off as a collection of jotted-down notes almost casually pulled together. Many writers went along with these expectations. Hence Newton's assertion that her scenic 'glimpses' were 'written at the time [more] with a view to keep the memory fresh for me than with any distinct idea of publication',[20] which disguises the fact that her text is a consciously worked, selective document. Kröller observes that the 'confessional' form allows for a certain discursiveness, redundancy and spontaneous response, which have much in common with literary narratives and which serve as cues inviting a literary, if not fictional, reading of the text. A 'spontaneous', subjective amalgam of responses to exotic landscapes, women's travel writing was inevitably discussed in terms of its relationship to fiction, and much was made of the employment of novelistic devices such as dramatized dialogue, poetic language and the like; clearly, the texts of Symmonett and Gaunt can profitably be read as utilizing such techniques.

But the trouble with the choice of such 'feminine' forms as the confessional or novelistic narrative is that they often put into question the 'truth value' of women's travel writing. Ethnographical 'facts' in this writing often appear to be informed by a preconceived poetic template. So, for example, when Gaunt 'objectively' observes that 'Blood is hot in the Tropics', she illustrates this assertion by way of a fabricated scenario from her imagination, in which 'two men set their hearts on the same woman ... The hussy very likely doesn't play fair ... A wild burst of temper and a deed is done that many a man has expiated on the gallows.'[21] Here stereotypes from popular romance are used to substantiate observations normally conveyed in a more

---

[18] Eva-Marie Kröller, 'First Impressions: Rhetorical Strategies in Travel Writing by Victorian Women', *Ariel*, 21:4 (October 1990), pp. 87–99.

[19] Mills, *Discourses of Difference*, p. 104.

[20] Newton, *Glimpses*, p. 2.

[21] Gaunt, *Reflection*, pp. 109–10.

dispassionate 'manners and customs' account of native behaviour. It is worth noting, by the way, that the two men and the hussy are not race-specific; 'hot' tropical blood plagues *all* creoles, it seems, whether black, mulatto or white.

Mills points out that the accounts of travellers, like women's tales, had long been subject to the charge of poetic licence, if not downright deceit. In many ways, then, 'truth value' depended on the strength of the *narrative figure*, 'which in turn poses problems of credibility because strong women narrator figures conflict with the cultural norms for women' in the nineteenth century.[22] Writers who narrate 'like a woman', who adopt the discourse of femininity (using the confessional mode, opting for the 'sentimental' or poetic style), are subject to charges of exaggeration; writers who draw on other discourses, such as that of imperialism (using a brave questing hero or a scientific account of discovery) are also suspect, since such narrative strategies, Mills explains, were considered foreign to a female sensibility. Perhaps preconceptions about licence within women's travel narratives explains the defensive strategy of including maps, photographs and drawings in order to document the 'objective' truth of observations made 'subjectively'. I will return to this issue of the ambivalent 'truth claims' of women's travel writing and the corollary tendency to read their texts for contradictions. First, however, I want to focus on the narrative relationship to landscape in their writing.

'Inspirational Landscapes'

Women in nineteenth-century, middle-class Europe were constructed as more sensitive to nature, and to spiritual matters, than their male counterparts, and it became increasingly common to see depictions of landscape in women's travel writing in terms of 'the sublime', and/or linked with religious sentiment. This marginalized their texts to some extent since such depictions, of course, had no place in 'scientific' accounts of travel. But despite the apparently 'natural' aesthetic or devout celebration of the foreign terrain – part of what Pratt terms the rhetoric of 'anti-conquest', where a narrative speaks from a position of unaccountability and innocence – this kind of relationship to landscape nonetheless demonstrates certain ideological underpinnings. For one thing, as Mills reminds us, mapping a specific colonial topography with reference to a universalizing Romantic model erases 'the specificity of the country'.[23] Newton found the 'Arcadian' aspect of several islands led naturally to the contemplation of 'the Author of such perfection', and her debt to the Romantic poets is evident: 'Truly has Wordsworth said, "For in the mountains he did feel his faith."'[24] Symmonett is also moved by an evening seascape – 'the pale

---

[22] Mills, *Discourses of Difference*, p. 112.

[23] Mills, *Discourses of Difference*, p. 183.

[24] Newton, *Glimpses*, p. 216.

moon majestically rising ... spreading her pure silvery sheen in a quivering nervous moonlit kiss on the placid visage of the sea of calm' – to praise God:

> 'Tis there! where the tale of old romance is so oft again and again whispered. 'Tis there the artist wends his footsteps at eventide. 'Tis there the author reads the volumes written by nature. 'Tis there the atheist denies no longer the existence of a Supreme Being.[25]

But 'tis *here* that attention is deliberately shifted away from the particulars of the Jamaican landscape towards a transcendent spiritual meditation, as also happens when Lynch invites us to 'Look down the tremendous steep into that ravine – the river-course below. In His hands are the deep places of the earth.'[26] What we *do not* see is what the ravine and the river course actually look like.

Even where the 'sublime' is eschewed for another type of aesthetic depiction – as when Newton writes about the Bathsheba coast of Barbados in terms of Matthew Arnold and the Greek myth of Andromeda and Perseus[27] – literary possession of land, by imposing upon its specificity a generalized aesthetic value and system of referencing from another culture, is still notable. Gaunt's *Reflection* and Crommelin's 'Mountain-Heart' take a slightly different tack in that they overlay sensationalized versions of Caribbean history on to the landscape. Crommelin projects onto the mountain scene an atmosphere of flux and danger, a place 'always on the verge of an air-world, vapours with mists, into which, if our steeds stumbled, or there chanced an earth-slip of the crumbling track, we should be inevitably hurld'.[28] For her, it is somehow a short step to intuit in (or more accurately, to overlay onto) such a 'fictional' space the presence of a fearsome 'history', tales of 'terrible negro risings of old, when the fetish oath was taken at dead of night, under a sacred cotton-tree, the vow pledged in a cup of rum and blood'.[29] Again, the countryside is not seen and described as it appears but rather as 'naturally' serving, by virtue of its *exoticism*, its unfamiliarity, as a canvas for screening familiar historical vignettes. In *Reflection*, Gaunt inhabits particular Jamaican spaces – for example, a Great House called 'Knockalva' in the district of Ramble – but constantly filters them through a 'remembered' fiction of the past:

> When the tropical darkness fell, the candles were lighted and they were still at their feasting ... The ladies in their hoops and high head-dresses retired. The gentlemen loosened their lace vests; perhaps took off their wigs, for the weather was sure to be hot, and gave themselves up to the pleasures of the table.[30]

---

[25] Symmonett, *Jamaica*, p. 26.
[26] Lynch, *The Mountain*, p. ix.
[27] Newton, *Glimpses*, pp. 160–61.
[28] Crommelin, 'The Mountain-Heart', p. 529.
[29] Crommelin, 'The Mountain-Heart', p. 528.
[30] Gaunt, *Reflection*, p. 204.

No. 4. Road to Bog Walk.

5.1 Bog Road. Postcard, from the collection of Dr Karl Watson, University of the West Indies, Cave Hill, Barbados. Reproduced by kind permission.

Gaunt is, at least, relatively honest about what she is doing. 'I don't know really if it was a bit like that,' she confesses, after narrating a dramatized scene, complete with dialogue, of Cristoval Yssassi's last days in Jamaica.[31] The island, its landscape and villages and people are, in a sense, simply 'material' for her literary imaginings, as for Newton's artwork. The district of Harmony, just the sound of its name, inspires her: 'I am going to try to write a book about Harmony.'[32] She did so, soon after: *Harmony, a Tale of the Old Slave Days in Jamaica* (1933) is, true to form, a sensational period drama that has little to do with the place itself.

Whitlock argues that it is only through imaginatively representing the landscape in terms of discourses of historical adventure, romance and 'the sublime' that the female narrator can share in 'the wilds' she desires to enter. The point remains that her relationship with landscape is no innocent artist's appreciation. For colonialist writers the aesthetic qualities of the scenes they view constitute (metaphorically, anyway) the *value* of their discovery for the explorer's home culture. The more lovely the description, the worthier the prize seems, and the more one can anticipate improving and developing it. What you see *is*, in a sense, what you get. Since Columbus's journal, of course, the lines between the region's value as aesthetic/material wealth have been blurred in narratives. Mrs Lynch's depiction of the Jamaican landscape in terms of precious jewels ('emerald and amethyst, with touches of ruby light ... transparent veil of gold ... arrayed in diamonds ... crystal treasure ... pearl-drops')[33] clearly translates natural beauty into the region's treasure or capital, a similar construction of the West Indies to that of Jean Rhys's novel *Wide Sargasso Sea* (1968), also set in the nineteenth century. Like a frustrated conquistador, the English husband acknowledges the beauty of the island, which is associated with his creole wife – 'wild, untouched, above all untouched, with an alien, disturbing, secret loveliness' – but desires what lies below the surface: 'What I see is nothing – I want what it *hides*.'[34] Ultimately, what he wants is the wealth represented by the island, metonymic of the region; like Antoinette's stepfather, 'He didn't come to the West Indies to dance – he came to make money as they all do.'[35]

One of the most sustained elaborations of the construction of the West Indies in terms of an Eden, a promised land, occurs in the 'Victorian Memoirs' of Yseult Bridges, published by her nephew as *Child of the Tropics* in 1988. Bridges recounts the story of her English paternal grandfather who, on an official visit to Trinidad just after Emancipation, is smitten by the island's natural charms. On his return, his evocation of the paradisal scenery – 'luxuriant fertility ... pellucid stream ... rare

---

[31] Gaunt, *Reflection*, p. 73.
[32] Gaunt, *Reflection*, p. 153.
[33] Lynch, *Wonders*, p. 3.
[34] Jean Rhys, *Wide Sargasso Sea* (London: Penguin, 1968), p. 73.
[35] Rhys, *Sargasso*, p. 25.

orchids ... exotic birds'[36] – seduces his wife, and the couple immediately purchase and settle on an estate in Diego Martin. Her plan is to rebuild the plantation house 'and to surround it with a park-like pleasance, to enclose which she ordered from England an elaborate wrought-iron fence'.[37] But tropical rains, the collapse of country roads, the dishonesty of overseers and the failure of crops put an end to such ambitions; the disillusioned young couple abandon the dream 'and by the time the innumerable sections of the wrought-iron fence had at last been laboriously conveyed to the estate, they were left to rust where they lay for everything was already up for sale to liquidate as many debts as possible'.[38] They stay on in Trinidad, but Bridges describes her artistic grandmother's frustration in the society 'of people whose interests and outlook were severely limited', choosing to wander the countryside in search of subjects to paint instead of building her dream or, indeed, of doing the expected: 'relaxing into the genteel indolence proper to a lady'.[39] Still pursuing adventure and enchantment, at the age of 63, she 'conceived the notion of exploring the upper reaches of the Orinoco river in Venezuela, into which no white man, let alone woman, had ever ventured for any distance'[40] and *does* so, going missing for over a year! Clearly, the imaginative lure of El Dorado, the magical territory of untold riches, survives her earlier disappointment in the West Indies.

Given the interconnection of aesthetics and ideology then, one can see the West Indies constructed for a variety of purposes in these women's travel narratives: as a collage of 'picturesque' painterly scenes and 'subjects' to be captured on paper in Newton's sketches; as a beautiful backdrop against which melodramatic historical tableaux are played out in the fertile imaginations of Crommelin and Gaunt; as an other-worldly Eden in which it is easier to apprehend God/the sublime in the homiletic writings of Lynch and (some of) Newton. All of these strategies, to some extent, appropriate the landscape as 'already known' and construct it within a number of already charted aesthetic categories of 'exotic'.

'Complicatedly Creole': The Local Angle

I have said very little about *Jamaica: Queen of the Carib Sea*. Symmonett's narrative is an interesting amalgam of several of the constructions noted above, but rather than simply illustrating these features, I want to conclude by discussing this work within the context of the concept of women's travel writing as inherently multiple, if not contradictory, in terms of its production and reception. As noted, such writing was

---

[36] Yseult Bridges, *Child of the Tropics: Victorian Memoirs*, ed. Nicholas Guppy (Port-of-Spain: Aquarela Galleries, 1988), p. 72.

[37] Bridges, *Child*, p. 73.

[38] Bridges, *Child*, p. 74.

[39] Bridges, *Child*, pp. 75–6.

[40] Bridges, *Child*, p. 76.

dubiously received in terms of its factual nature because the 'feminine' narrative forms (confessional, poetic, subjective, 'sentimental') were perceived to undercut the objective truth of content. Again, the authors had to negotiate between contradictory 'feminine' (decorous, decent, modest, caring) and 'imperial' (brave, courageous, adventurous, superior) discourses in positioning themselves as narrators.

Kröller makes an interesting observation about the supposedly 'spontaneous' confessional forms favoured by women travel writers, charging that such accounts are examples of self-referentially split, or multiple, discourse. Her contention is that the first-person travel diarist is both protagonist *and* narrator, and doubly self-conscious in both roles: as protagonist in an alien environment and as narrator in the unsettling, potentially embarrassing (for a woman) public textual environment. Kröller sees a shifting, shuttling movement in this writing between the public and private, where protagonist effaces narrator and vice versa.

It seems to me that the texts of *creole* women like Lynch and Symmonett further amplify this paradigm of contradictory, spilt, ambivalent narrators, in respect of their relationships to their own West Indian subject matter. Pratt, too, feels that '[m]uch remains to be learned about the extent to which creoles, from the Americas, Africa or Asia, participated in the dialogues that gave rise to both colonialist and anti-colonialist doctrines.'[41] Given that these political ideologies are intimately related to aesthetic productions, it may be useful to examine Symmonett as an example of such dialogue. Indeed, Pratt reminds us that while the tendency has normally been to see European culture emanating out to the periphery from a self-generating centre, this has obscured the movement of people and ideas *from* the colony to the centre. Thus, while several texts depict West Indian natural phenomena in terms of the discourse of European Romanticism, Pratt would maintain that to an extent Romanticism was a *product* of the contact zone, a consequence of the encounter with 'primal landscape' in the eighteenth- and nineteenth-century imagination. But for Pratt the creole woman writer of the mid-nineteenth century would find it problematic to apply this trope of 'primal landscape' to her familiar *home* territory.[42] Pratt's focus is on South and Central America, where white creoles reinvented America for Europe using the trope of the New World as 'primal landscape', but also used it as a point of departure for their goal of an independent, decolonized continent that yet retained European values and white supremacy. Nonetheless her point about the 'transculturation' of European material in creole representations is also relevant to West Indian narratives.

To an extent, one can see Symmonett's novella 'transculturating' European pre-scriptions of the West Indies as a place of savagery, death and disease by allowing colonial prejudice such rhetorical excess in its articulation that the ridiculous and comic undermine its 'truth'. For example, poor Mrs Chandler is warned about

---

[41] Pratt, *Imperial Eyes*, p. 90.
[42] Pratt, *Imperial Eyes*, p. 193.

aspects of life in Jamaica such as:

> every few yards encountering with a cesspool of black stagnant water, swarmed with mosquitoes, out of which pop up the heads of those hideous batrachian reptiles – toads; and foul malaria also arising: or coming in contact with a rut, or gully – regular breaknecks.[43]

The reality, she discovers on arrival, could not be more different. In Symmonett's account, there is a positively nationalistic fervour, which accounts for the almost *idealized* portrayal of the island which follows exposure of the hoax. In a letter to England after a year in the colony, Mrs Chandler emphasizes that the health and welfare systems are properly run; 'colleges for boys and girls ... are so satisfactory, that we are rendered quite independent of sending home our children for that object';[44] professionals of all kinds are in practice, as well qualified as anywhere else; polite divisions of society obtain, as do all forms of amusement. Although 'the negro peasantry of the interior country districts present in themselves a very forbidding, repulsive appearance' they are hardworking;[45] the towns are well-laid out and have architectural merits, although she reserves the highest praise for the beauty of the countryside and particularly the mountains. The parish of St Ann enchants her ('I was transported with delight – I was involuntarily thrown into ecstasy by the prospect and beauty in the novelties of nature')[46] and Blue Mountain Peak draws forth an awed reflection on:

> the melancholy piping of the wind in the naked wood, in a low minor key, at another time in the chromatic, and sometimes supplemented by a loud vociferous clap of thunder causing the peak to tremble and shake, and the bravest heart to quake. Which eyes of an admirer of nature would not fain be centred thereon, on this elysium of earth! on this El Dorado of the 'Queen of the Carib Sea'?[47]

Another nineteenth-century text, written by a white Antiguan woman, although a novel rather than travel narrative, demonstrates in places the same kind of West Indian proto-nationalism that informs Symmonett's rhapsody. In Frieda Cassin's *With Silent Tread; A West Indian Novel* (c.1890), the young creole girl Morea impresses a visiting English cousin with her passionate attachment to, and identification with, her beautiful tropical landscape.[48] Yet when Morea pays a visit to England, she refers to 'going *home*'.[49] Alas, however much they insisted upon their European ancestry,

43 Symmonett, *Jamaica*, p. 11.
44 Symmonett, *Jamaica*, p. 21.
45 Symmonett, *Jamaica*, p. 22.
46 Symmonett, *Jamaica*, p. 31.
47 Symmonett, *Jamaica*, pp. 33–4.
48 Frieda Cassin, *With Silent Tread; A West Indian Novel* (St John's, Antigua: G. A. Uphill, 1890), p. 110. Reprinted with a new introduction (London: Macmillan, 2002).
49 Cassin, *Silent Tread*, p. 106.

or attempted to assimilate the manners and customs of the Mother Country, white West Indian creoles never quite made it in British eyes, either at home or abroad. Hence, Morea meets with English prescriptions of herself as a stereotypical creole, a *different* creature. The English Selwyn expects the Antiguan Morea to be short and yellow, 'utterly incapable of helping herself' without 'six or seven black maids lolling about', indolent, drawling and fond of giving orders.[50] After all, as far as he is concerned, she is identified with her exotic homeland, the 'hot' place which, though it belongs to 'Us', is still alien: for him, she comes from a 'topsy-turvey land with fishes that fly, and crazy cashews growing their seeds outside instead of in'.[51] Morea, however, 'refuses to fit into that niche'. She continually compares West Indian and English customs, to the detriment of the latter, and takes pleasure in comparing the 'sun at home' with its English equivalent, a 'poor watery thing'.[52] She insists that she will continue to love her West Indian friends, including her black nurse, 'quite as much as anybody in this muddy England',[53] and even mocks preconstructed notions of English manhood, that ideal of 'strength, vigour and athletic ability. I hope I am not doomed to prove him a mere delusion and a fraud.'[54] Indeed, she advises Selwyn, 'You are sadly in need of a little travel to enlarge your mind',[55] neatly turning the tables on the superior Englishman, and perhaps squaring accounts with colonialist propaganda.

For a notable feature of travelogues by creole women are their strong promotional intentions. Like Symmonett and Cassin, Lynch demonstrates pride in her West Indian landscape. One of her texts is introduced by the 'Right Rev. the Lord Bishop of Jamaica' (Aubrey G., Jamaica, 1856) who describes the narrative as a vindication of these 'enchanting islands', 'these magnificent islands', of which thus far 'very little has been investigated and less made known'.[56] So Lynch boasts:

> what is the oak-tree of our England when compared with the cedar or mahogany; the gigantic cotton-tree, whose very stem has produced a boat capable of containing more than a hundred persons; or the wild fig-tree, in itself almost a forest, of which Milton thus writes.[57]

But here one pauses. The Caribbean cedar and mahogany are valorized in comparison to the English oak; but the English oak is 'ours'. The cotton-tree and the wild fig-tree, native vegetation, are magnificent, but it is to an *English* poet that the narrator

---

[50] Cassin, *Silent Tread*, p. 116.
[51] Cassin, *Silent Tread*, p. 125.
[52] Cassin, *Silent Tread*, p. 121.
[53] Cassin, *Silent Tread*, p. 137.
[54] Cassin, *Silent Tread*, p. 120.
[55] Cassin, *Silent Tread*, p. 125.
[56] Lynch, *Wonders*, pp. i–ii.
[57] Lynch, *Wonders*, p. 2.

turns for an apt description. One could argue that Lynch uses 'our' only as a device to invite reader participation, but this only underscores the fact that her texts are directed at, and shaped by the expectations of, a British audience: 'Birds, flowers, insects', of the West Indies, she tells the reader, 'all are strangers to us.'[58] Why strange to the Jamaican born and bred writer? Similarly, when Symmonett praises the town of Mandeville – and this may be a clue to the fondness of several writers for the mountains of the region – she praises it for its bracing *English* climate. Lynch ends her account with a rousing hymn to Jamaica:

> She's a daughter of Old England,
> Tho' her sons be of diverse hue,
> And she loves her noble mother,
> Her church, and her sovereign too,
> And while the blue sea washes
> Her sands in her hundred bays;
> She trusts to her Queen's protection,
> And all her laws obeys.
>
> Then here's to Old Jamaica,
> 'Queen of the Carib Sea!'
> Dear island home, where'er we roam,
> We'll aye remember thee!

While clearly attempting to suggest that the colony's loyalty to Mother England makes it a comfortably safe (if 'hot') place 'belonging to Us', the poem's sentiments also include loyalty to her 'dear island home' which provides its inspiration; ironically, these verses turn out to be the composition of a 'tourist, a naturalist, who but a few months ago visited this island home'.[59] Ultimately, the final authorial stamp of approval on Jamaica's attractions (the local product) comes not from the native author, but in the observations of an anonymous foreigner. The multiple signification of the terms 'us' and 'home' indicates the complex definition of the colony for the *creole* writer.

Leaving aside the other types of split/contradictory/polyphonic features noted earlier in women's travel writing, I suggest that we see here an undermining of the patriotic, even proto-nationalistic impulse (which seeks to negate Eurocentric constructions of the West Indies and, as it were, 'redress the balance') by an implicitly colonial need to present 'us' for Europe. It is tempting to deduce that the text confirms, as Pratt claims, the rendering of landscape as spectacle, a panorama in which is implicitly coded its potential commodification for foreign visitors. Promoting the local, Lynch and Symmonett yet share with other Victorian women

---

58 Lynch, *Wonders*, p. 2.
59 Lynch, *Wonders*, p. 34.

travel writers the rhetoric of discovery for a (British) 'home' audience,[60] a textual 'discovery' of what the locals know in another way, a far less romantic way. This is a point made with devastating satire in Jamaica Kincaid's modern day travelogue *A Small Place* (1988). Pratt links 'discovery' with seeing and telling[61]: narrative 'telling' is equated with a certain mastery over the panorama which the traveller sees, paints *and* evaluates for a specific audience. While Gaunt, Newton and Crommelin project onto the West Indian landscape their own desires – for romance, for the sublime, for painterly inspiration, for adventure – Symmonett and, to an extent, Lynch construct their home as an exotic paradise which they 'discover' *for* others. Apparently, the white West Indian creole had too much invested in alliance with the Mother Country to confidently insist on an 'Other' perspective. After all, focusing on aspects of the island home which did not quite fit the template, which departed from the safe/exotic stereotypes, might draw attention to that difference which 'real' English people were quick to observe in creoles,[62] thus calling into question the somewhat tenuous basis of her privileged position: her *apparent* racial and cultural similarity to the masters in an ex-slave colony.

These deeply insecure responses of white creole writers to their indeterminate position vis-à-vis colony and centre result in the textual production of the West Indies in a manner that distances the native authors from the very material they claim to know intimately. Such complicity in the dissemination of stereotypes and the projection of fantasies and desires onto the tropical landscape is uncannily echoed in some aspects of modern day tourist promotions. For example, a slogan recently used by the Barbados Tourism Association to market the island is 'Barbados: just beyond your imagination', and the glossy brochures detailing local attractions can be read as contemporary reinscriptions of both the exotic (the 'hot place' with its invitation to sensual pleasure and romance) and the 'safe' (no longer 'belonging to Us' perhaps, but sufficiently civilized by 'Us' to provide 'a British flavour', friendly natives and a reassuring political and financial stability). The double self-consciousness of the nineteenth-century creole woman writer in constructing her exotic home by familiarizing and thus rendering it acceptable to a 'home' audience – by producing Self for Other – surfaces as a preoccupation in current Caribbean women's writing and invites further comparative studies across chronological boundaries.

---

[60] Pratt, *Imperial Eyes*, p. 201.

[61] Pratt, *Imperial Eyes*, pp. 204–5.

[62] In Jean Rhys's *Wide Sargasso Sea*, the English husband reflects on his creole wife's 'sad, dark alien eyes': 'Creole of pure English descent she may be', he decides, 'but they are not English or European either' (p. 56).

"Home Sweet Home," Jamaica, W.I.

5.2   Home Sweet Home. Jamaica. Postcard, from the collection of Dr Karl Watson, University of the West Indies, Cave Hill, Barbados. Reproduced by kind permission.

Chapter Six

Undeveloped Estates: Dominica and the Landscape of the New Imperialism[1]

Peter Hulme

After the ending of the institution of slavery in the 1830s, the imperial centre showed scarce interest in the fate of the islands of the British West Indies, once regarded as the heart of the Empire. On only one occasion, right at the end of the nineteenth century, while Joseph Chamberlain was Colonial Secretary, did this attitude change: so much so that, for a few brief years, there were new white settlers drawn to the islands. However, the tropics were still seen as a dangerous part of the world for whites – associated with the physical and moral degeneration displayed by the West Indian creole figure Bertha Mason, Rochester's first wife in *Jane Eyre* (1848) – so significant efforts were needed to remake the image of the islands' tropical landscape and climate. This essay starts by focusing on one such effort, a long letter written by the new Administrator of the island of Dominica, Henry Hesketh Bell, in 1899. In this text, as so often when landscape is viewed through an imperial optic, the georgic mode dominates its sublime partner, with work and productivity having to triumph over the magnificent scenery and breathtaking views. The ideal landscape Bell sculpts out of the Dominican mountains carries some of the same moral connotations – to do with climate, altitude and health – as its British equivalent; but being an imperial landscape in 1899, the West Indian version also speaks implicitly of issues of colour, race and sexuality. Nine years old when Bell wrote this letter, the Dominican-born writer Jean Rhys would, a full 70 years later, publish a tellingly ironic postscript to the ill-fated effort to renew white settlement in the Caribbean in her story 'Pioneers, Oh, Pioneers', which highlights those implicit issues, clarifying the extent to which that colonial landscape was a site for masculine enterprise. If white masculinity is represented as a 'product of enterprise and imperialism ... always already predicated on racial difference',[2] then Rhys wants to explore the anxieties that surround that predicate.

[1] For invitations to deliver earlier versions of this essay as lectures and conference papers I would like to thank especially Helen Tiffin, Glenn Hooper, Tim Youngs, Angela Smith, Catherine Hall and Deborah Cherry. I would like to acknowledge Sue Thomas's extremely helpful response to a first draft. The essay was written while I was on a British Academy Research Readership, so thanks are also due to the British Academy.
[2] Richard Dyer, *White* (London: Routledge, 1997), p. 13.

From an economic point of view Dominica had never been particularly important in the imperial scheme. But the rugged terrain that prevented the construction of large sugar plantations had given it the reputation as the most beautiful of the West Indian islands, a reputation enhanced by its primacy in the travel book published in 1887 by the Victorian historian and imperial ideologue James Anthony Froude, *The English in the West Indies: The Bow of Ulysses*. Froude himself demonstrates something of the range of writing possible about imperial landscapes in the tropics. He stayed in the Administrator's Residence on the outskirts of Roseau:

> The views from the drawing room windows were enchantingly beautiful. It is not the form only in these West Indian landscapes, or the colour only, but form and colour seen through an atmosphere of very peculiar transparency. On one side we looked up a mountain gorge, the slopes covered with forest; a bold lofty crag jutting out from them brown and bare, and the mountain ridge behind half buried in mist.[3]

Here, in this moment just after his arrival, the drawing room windows are allowed to frame the landscapes in classically picturesque fashion, the spectacular scenery reduced to a play of form and colour, the viewer insulated by the window from any danger or difficulty the terrain itself might afford.

With his host, Captain Churchill, out of commission with an injured foot, Froude takes a long walk up the Roseau valley with a Mr F–. There, like earlier visitors, Froude is deeply impressed by Dominica's wild beauty, but he is also eager to see it put to useful ends:

> The valley grew deeper, or rather there were a series of valleys, gorges dense with forest, which had been torn out by the cataracts ... Here was all this profusion of nature, lavish beyond example, and the enterprising youth of England were neglecting a colony which might yield them wealth beyond the treasures of the old sugar planters, going to Florida, to Texas, to South America, taking their energy and their capital to the land of the foreigner, leaving Dominica, which might be the garden of the world, a precious emerald set in the ring of their own Antilles, enriched by the sacred memories of glorious English achievements, as if such a place had no existence. Dominica would surrender herself to-morrow with a light heart to France, to America, to any country which would accept the charge of her destinies. Why should she care any more for England, which has so little care for her? Beauties conscious of their charms do not like to be so thrown aside.[4]

Froude certainly uses the language of the sublime in his descriptions here: phrases like 'gorges dense with forest' had, since the heyday of Romanticism, provided the standard vocabulary to describe mountainous grandeur. In imperial contexts,

---

[3] James A. Froude, *The English in the West Indies: or The Bow of Ulysses* (London: Longmans, 1909), p. 131.

[4] Froude, *The English*, pp. 141–2.

6.1   A Dominican Valley. Engraved from a sketch by Froude. In James A. Froude, *The English in the West Indies: or The Bow of Ulysses* [1887] (London: Longmans, 1909), facing p. 136.

however, that sublimity is often more susceptible to some form of human control than in its original Burkean sense. The indicative word here is 'treasure', an old word in the discourse of the Caribbean, but now given an agricultural turn. So Dominica is 'a precious *emerald*' – suggesting the usual metallic dimension of treasure – but that word is qualifying 'the garden of the world': the treasure lies in natural productivity, with emerald the colour of the landscape. Froude naturally moved in the social milieu of the old white plantocracy, but the language of the imperial sublime had become part of a wider island self-image, shared by the coloured landowners as well as the white, a language which by the second half of the nineteenth century had taken its place as an element in the discourse of economic modernization where primeval forest and virgin soil could – with new scientific and engineering possibilities – be transformed into wealth and prosperity.[5] As always, though, the place described in this language is feminized by the description: 'a beauty conscious of her charms', according to Froude, but passive and helpless on her own. The island's natural productivity needs the energy of English husbandmen to make it flourish: 'Skill and capital and labour have only to be brought together, and the land might be a Garden of Eden.'[6]

In 1895 a change of British government saw the introduction of Joseph Chamberlain as Colonial Secretary, the first in a long while with a deep commitment to the Empire and some strong ideas about how to make it viable again. Froude – who had died in the previous year – had been a friend of Chamberlain's and one of his main sources of information and ideas about the need to renew the Empire. Chamberlain soon stated his ideological position with respect to the colonies in a speech to the House of Commons. Britain had neglected its duty, he said, and if the British people were not willing to invest some of their superfluous wealth in the colonies, then it would have been better never to have gone there in the first place. He referred to the West Indian islands as 'undeveloped estates' in need of 'Imperial assistance'.[7]

Then, in 1897, in a speech to the Colonial Institute, Chamberlain announced what he called 'the true conception of our Empire' – what is usually referred to as the 'New Imperialism'. Within this Empire there is an openly racial distinction between the 'self-governing colonies', no longer thought of as dependencies, and the 'tropical colonies', which are still dependent. In the self-governing colonies such as Australia and Canada, Chamberlain said, the sense of possession had given way to a sense of kinship, while in the tropical colonies such as the West Indies it had given way to a sense of obligation.[8]

For Chamberlain, 'obligation' meant keeping up the number of white colonists in the West Indies 'with a view', he wrote in a private letter, 'to preventing the islands

---

[5]   This is what Rob Wilson describes as the 'American sublime': *The American Sublime: The Genealogy of a Poetic Genre* (Madison: University of Wisconsin Press, 1991).

[6]   Froude, *The English*, p. 140.

[7]   *The Parliamentary Debates*, fourth series, vol. XXXVI, cols 641–2 (22 Aug.1895).

[8]   Joseph Chamberlain, *Mr Chamberlain's Speeches*, ed. Charles W. Boyd, 2 vols (London: Constable, 1914), vol. ii, pp. 2–3.

from sinking to the level to which other negro communities have sunk'.[9] And it was Dominica that became the test case of this new imperial policy, for in Chamberlain's eyes it offered the worst case of previous neglect and yet was supposedly 'one of the very richest islands in the possession of the Crown in the West Indies in the natural productiveness of the soil'.[10]

Chamberlain appointed a new Administrator to Dominica, Hesketh Bell, a young colonial official who became the key figure in Dominica's modernization, embodying Chamberlain's imperial aims. He was to set about recruiting a new white planter class from Britain, to be assisted by modern agricultural methods and by the building of a new road, the Imperial Road, the first stretch of which would be duly opened at the beginning of the new century, in a ceremony which Jean Rhys later recalled in her posthumously published memoir, *Smile Please*.[11]

It was during his early reconnaissances of Dominica, made in part to decide on the route of the Imperial Road, that Hesketh Bell wrote the letter I want to analyse here. Formally, it is a 'Scheme for Expenditure', dated 26 October 1899 and addressed to his superior in Antigua, although there is no doubt that it was meant ultimately for Chamberlain's eyes.[12] The letter was written to assure Chamberlain that his scheme for Dominica was in good hands, and to ask for money to finance the building of a road to open up the interior of the island. One of the main reasons for the route Bell had chosen for the Imperial Road was the existence of a coffee plantation recently developed by a man called Gordon Fowler, who had already made his fortune in Ceylon. Bell's letter certainly has Fowler as its hero. Fowler had evidently taken something of a risk – perhaps not without some official reassurance – since he had embarked on this large plantation, renamed Middleham, which was not close to any roads. However, Bell's 'Scheme for Expenditure' makes it clear that means of communication will soon be provided for his pioneer.

The ideological topography which Bell spells out in his 'Scheme' depends on a broad distinction between coast and interior. According to Bell the coastal areas of Dominica are heavily settled and divided between large 'estates' and small

---

[9]   Minute from Joseph Chamberlain to Hicks Beach, 26 November 1895 (The Chamberlain Papers, Special Collections, University of Birmingham, 14/3/10).

[10]   *The Parliamentary Debates*, fourth series, vol. XXXVII, col. 1409 (28.ii.1896).

[11]   Jean Rhys, *Smile Please: An Unfinished Autobiography* (London: Penguin, 1981), pp. 89–92. For more on Chamberlain, Bell and Rhys, see Peter Hulme, *Remnants of Conquest: The Island Caribs and Their Visitors, 1877–1998* (Oxford: Oxford University Press, 2000), pp. 106–18 and 204–43. I have explored further the resonance of the Imperial Road for Jean Rhys in 'Islands and Roads: Hesketh Bell, Jean Rhys and Dominica's Imperial Road', *The Jean Rhys Review*, 11:2 (2000) pp.23–51.

[12]   Henry Hesketh Bell, 'Imperial Grant to Dominica: Scheme for Expenditure', C.O. 152/249 (Letter to the Governor of the Leeward Islands, 26.x.1899).

'settlements', a distinction which is racially coded. Economically speaking, the estate owners – white or coloured Dominicans – are characterized as pre-modern: 'satisfied with a slow rate of progress', lacking the 'energy' which Bell wants to introduce.[13] The interior is 'luxuriant waste', 'virgin country'[14] waiting for development. However, Bell has to dispel the traditional view that the Dominican interior is sublime and therefore uncultivable. In order to do this, he places himself at Middleham, Fowler's estate high in the Antrim Valley, where he can enjoy a view *over* the island, rather than the more usual official view from the administrative centre of the island (where the letter was actually composed), which looks up the island's main valley towards its mountains – the view which had so enchanted Froude on the day of his arrival in Dominica. The literal and metaphorical height from which Bell speaks is a crucial element in what he has to say, allowing him to adopt a position of masculine dominance over the sexualized island landscape: 'From a point on this estate, some 2400 feet above the sea, I was able to enjoy a magnificent view over a great part of the island ... almost the whole of the centre of Dominica lay spread out below me'.[15] From Middleham Bell can look around him at the hills and rivers, which bring the abundant rainfall to the lower slopes: 'Nearer me, and at my feet, lay a magnificent stretch of gently undulating land, comprising many thousands of acres covered with virgin forest-growth. The plateaux just below ... sometimes known collectively as the "Layou Flats" appeared particularly promising'.[16] 'Magnificent' belongs to the vocabulary of the sublime, but here it is deployed to describe gentle undulations, land which, though inland and high above the coast, is reassuringly known in the local toponymy as 'flats', a levelling word which reduces the threats implicit to planters in the usual landscape of the sublime. Bell's own offering is to call the whole centre of the island 'a vast punch bowl',[17] a term nicely chosen to domesticate the mountains – making the effort of climbing the outside rewarded by their contents, and associating the cornucopia of fruit and garden produce with a life of leisure and relaxation. 'I cannot', Bell continues, 'too strongly represent the advantages of opening up this "undeveloped estate" in Dominica',[18] picking up here, as a quotation he does not even need to source, Chamberlain's phrase about certain colonies as 'undeveloped estates', a phrase that draws on that Lockean imperative to make land as productive as possible.

The potential productivity of the land is one thing, however; the tropical climate is an altogether more ticklish subject. Bell's letter was written at a key moment in the

---

[13] Hesketh Bell, 'Imperial Grant', pp. 3, 11. 'Energy', a word also used by Froude and appearing several times in Bell's letter, is exactly what is lacking in the tropics, mired as they are in a 'climate so conducive to *dolce far niente*' (p. 22).

[14] Hesketh Bell, 'Imperial Grant', pp. 7, 11.

[15] Hesketh Bell, 'Imperial Grant', p. 9.

[16] Hesketh Bell, 'Imperial Grant', p. 10.

[17] Hesketh Bell, 'Imperial Grant', p. 10.

[18] Hesketh Bell, 'Imperial Grant', p. 11.

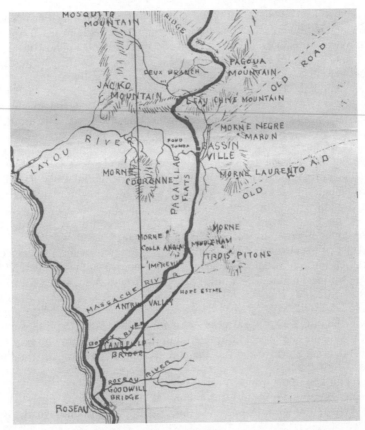

6.2 **Dominica. Showing route taken by survey for proposed interior main road. In Henry Hesketh Bell, 'Imperial Grant to Dominica: Scheme for Expenditure', C.O. 152/249 (Letter to the Governor of the Leeward Islands, 26.x.1899).**

debate about tropical diseases, long considered 'incidental to Europeans'.[19] Patrick Manson's influential textbook *Tropical Diseases* was published the same year as Bell's letter, one sign – along with the foundation of the London and Liverpool

---

[19] Many of the key eighteenth-century texts on the subject, including James Lind's *Essay on Diseases Incidental to Europeans in Hot Climates* (1768), are now usefully collected in Alan Bewell, ed., *Slavery, Abolition and Emancipation: Writings in the British Romantic Period*, Vol. 7: *Medicine and the West Indian Slave Trade* (London: Pickering & Chatto, 1999).

Schools of Tropical Medicine – that the subject had become a legitimate speciality, with new scientific evidence constantly emerging and being tested.[20] But just the previous year, in response to the US invasion of Cuba and Puerto Rico, a British civil servant, Benjamin Kidd, had written *The Control of the Tropics*, restating the long-held idea that white people were physically and morally unsuited to living in the tropics. Chamberlain had even written a favourable review of Kidd's book.[21] Against this fraught background, Bell began to develop the moral connotations of his landscape, basing them firmly on empirical science. To begin with, the difference in temperature between seaboard and plateaux is, says Bell, 'extraordinary'.[22] The manager of Middleham has, he reports, taken a record over the previous 12 months, revealing that the average temperature is 68 °, with the highest 82 ° and the lowest 54 °. Bell's more subjective report is that '[t]here is a delightful sense of exhilaration in the mountain air, and one can walk and work, even in the middle of the day, without turning a hair. In spite of the heavy rainfall, there is very little of the dampness that is so general in the tropics, and the natural drainage of the gradual slopes removes all possibility of malaria.'[23] The final piece of evidence in favour of the salubrity of the climate comes from the living example of the appearance of the manager's children at Middleham: 'While those who live on the sea coast, 2000 feet below, are wan and pallid like all little ones in the tropics, Mr Elliott's boys and girls are rosy and fresh as English children.'[24] 'White' is strictly the *absence* of colour, but ideologically the sign of true whiteness, at least by the end of the nineteenth century, is the pinkness of the cheeks – sometimes the ability to blush, sometimes, as here, the rosiness apparent in healthy children (the rose being the very emblem of Englishness).[25] Since rosiness is the true ideological whiteness, it is therefore possible – Bell implies – to be dermatologically *too* white: wan and pallid like European children in the tropics.

Climatic zones have always carried moral baggage, as is suggested by the connotations of the term 'temperate', long seen – at least through British eyes

---

[20] Dane Kennedy, 'The Perils of the Midday Sun: Climatic Anxieties in the Colonial Tropics', in John M. MacKenzie, ed. *Imperialism and the Natural World* (Manchester: Manchester University Press, 1990), pp. 120–21; David Arnold, *Colonizing the Body: State Medicine and Epidemic Disease in Nineteenth-century India* (Berkeley: University of California Press, 1993), pp. 23–43; and, more generally, see Nancy Leys Stepan, *Picturing Tropical Nature* (London: Reaktion, 2001).

[21] D. P. Crook, *Benjamin Kidd: Portrait of a Social Darwinist* (Cambridge: Cambridge University Press, 1984), pp. 115–25.

[22] Hesketh Bell, 'Imperial Grant', p. 11.

[23] Hesketh Bell, 'Imperial Grant', p. 11. In stressing the health benefits of mountain air, even in the tropics, Bell is following the familiar examples of the Indian hill stations and the tea valleys of Ceylon.

[24] Hesketh Bell, 'Imperial Grant', p. 11.

[25] See Mary Ann O'Farrell, *Telling Complexions: The Nineteenth-century English Novel and the Blush* (Durham, NC: Duke University Press, 1997).

– as offering a model for ideal behaviour: moderate, mild, self-controlled, between extremes. Although western thought is notoriously marked by persistent dualisms, climate and landscape have always operated in threes: an 'ideal' temperature is always somewhere between too hot and too cold, and an ideal climate is usually seen as existing only in the temperate zone, which is given its definition by its place between the zones of the polar regions and the tropics. This notion of 'ideal' was, of course, developed by geographers who inhabited the northern temperate zone, which included most of Europe.[26]

Internal British distinctions based on landscape and climate developed in the late eighteenth century when writers such as Wordsworth began to emphasize the *moral* superiority of certain areas, such as the Lake District, associated with particular moral economies. Aesthetic criteria might play a part in this superiority, as theorists of the picturesque would suggest when they explored northwards and westwards from England's major cities, but for moralists like Wordsworth and Charlotte Brontë – as for colonial promoters such as Bell – health was more dependent on work than on beauty, which is why the vocabulary of the georgic returned to prominence in Romantic writing.[27]

Jane Eyre is still relevant here. Rochester's story of his West Indian marriage tells of how Bertha's creole vices 'sprang up fast and rank' like tropical weeds[28] – suggesting a landscape in which personal growth is always a difficult challenge. Rochester's account of his moment of truth drips with the implied immorality of the coastal tropical landscape from which Bell would have to distance his Dominica so carefully: 'The air was like sulphur-steams – I could find no refreshment anywhere. Mosquitoes came buzzing in and hummed sullenly around the room ... I was physically influenced by the atmosphere and scene.'[29] Rochester himself nearly succumbs to the degenerative force of this climate, with its moral equivalents of vice and madness, before he is rescued from the danger of suicide by 'a wind fresh from Europe', which purifies the air and shows him the right path to follow[30] – only for him to find that there are further distinctions to be made. Still unconsciously tainted

---

[26] See David N. Livingstone, 'The Moral Discourse of Climate: Historical Considerations on Race, Place and Virtue', *Journal of Historical Geography*, 17:4 (1991), pp. 423–34.

[27] Recent work in this area includes Catherine Bruce, 'Finding England Everywhere: Regional Identity and the Construction of National Identity, 1890–1940', *Ecumene*, 6:1 (1999); Denis Cosgrove, 'Landscapes and Myths, Gods and Humans', in Barbara Bender, ed., *Landscape: Politics and Perspectives* (Oxford: Berg, 1993); and Marjorie Morgan, *National Identities and Travel in Victorian Britain* (London: Palgrave, 2001).

[28] Charlotte Brontë, *Jane Eyre*, ed. Richard J. Dunn (New York: Norton, 1987), p. 269. Bertha's brother Richard Mason's skin is described as 'singularly sallow', offering that same combination of ill-health and off-colour as Bell's 'wan' – there is an absence of proper whiteness here: see Sue Thomas, 'The Tropical Extravagance of Bertha Mason', *Victorian Literature and Culture*, 27:1 (1999), pp. 1–17.

[29] Brontë, *Jane Eyre*, p. 271.

[30] Brontë, *Jane Eyre*, p. 271.

by his experience, Rochester offers Jane a life as, in her words, 'a slave in a fool's paradise at Marseilles' – coastal, very hot and dangerously close to Africa – which Jane rejects in order to become, again in her words, 'a village schoolmistress, free and honest, in a breezy mountain nook in the healthy heart of England'.[31] What *Jane Eyre* can be taken as offering here is a moral mapping of the British Isles in which the 'healthy heart' is to be found in the hills and dales of the north-centre of England, an open landscape which Brontë famously contrasted with the overcultivated gardens of Jane Austen and the south-east of England, but which is equally different from the wild and dangerous mountains of Britain's extremities.

Hesketh Bell is, as it were, mapping this map onto Dominica and, in the process, creating for Dominica a new landscape of moderation: the high flats that lie beyond the precipitous mountains and that offer an *intermediate* landscape in which can be raised not only crops but – even more tellingly – healthy English children. Between the sublime, which can only be looked at in awe, and the coastal areas, which are mired by their inhabitants' lack of energy, there is a middle ground previously seen only as 'luxuriant waste', but which Bell now redescribes in terms of 'flats' and 'punchbowl', associating its climate with physical and moral health. Naming and renaming are always crucial dimensions of the imperial relationship to landscape. Fowler himself has done some of Bell's work for him by naming the estate 'Middleham', which carries the appropriate suggestion of moderation, and – through its reference to the town in the Yorkshire Dales – even manages to evoke the open Brontëan landscape.

One potential drawback to Bell's grand scheme is implicit in the picture of the ideal settler he sketched in the publicity leaflet he had printed after Chamberlain had approved his plans:

> Any man fond of an open-air life and interested in agriculture would probably make a successful planter in Dominica. He should also be healthy, active, and temperate. Good temper is required in dealing with the labourers, likewise patience. A man very keen on social pleasures and 'functions' will rarely make a good planter. He should stick to his estate so long as it requires attention ... An intending settler, if young, should endeavour to get a friend to accompany him to Dominica ... They will be glad of each other's society when the day's work is done, and can compare notes of progress to their mutual advantage.[32]

If the extent of young settlers' social lives was comparing notes of progress to their mutual advantage, then each new generation would need bringing out from Britain, hardly a satisfactory arrangement. Bell was aware of the problem, though he did not

---

[31] Brontë, *Jane Eyre*, p. 316.
[32] Henry Hesketh Bell, *Dominica: Notes and Hints to Intending Settlers* (n.p., 1903), pp. 13–14.

have a solution. There was a practical difficulty: the point of the Imperial Road was to open up the interior of the island, but a plantation several miles from Roseau was several miles from any kind of approved social life and therefore at risk. So the ideal planter – represented by Gordon Fowler – has its counter-image in Bell's letter. In making out a case for a kind of training institution for young planters, Bell outlines what could easily happen to someone arriving with little previous experience:

> He is entirely dependent on the opinion of more or less qualified persons as to the suitability of his land for the cultivation of the product he has decided upon, and he frequently loses a large amount of money in buying knowledge. Furthermore he has probably been obliged to locate himself in a somewhat isolated district, and finds himself far removed from any congenial society. If he is a bachelor, solitude will doubtless pall upon him, and in many cases, he will seek a native companion. His habits of life will deteriorate, he may become discouraged by the losses he suffers through inexperience, take to drink, and 'go to the Devil' generally.[33]

The young planter might be drawn to seek sexual company across the racial divide, Bell suggests, if solitude 'palls' on him: another interesting use of a colour term to suggest, unconsciously, that there can be too much whiteness, that whiteness might lead to death or at least to a failure to reproduce. Bell's promotion of a mixed landscape and a mixed economy did not extend to a mixed population. So, to the extent to which the Imperial Road would open up new and productive lands in the interior of Dominica to new white planters from England, those planters were faced with a choice between a racial exclusivity that was basically homosocial – the company of their male peers – and sexual company that crossed the racial divide, a crossing seen as leading to drink and the devil. The landscape of the tropics can be redefined as temperate, but a temperate planter, it seems, has no way of reproducing himself without falling into dissipation.

The dangers associated with a tropical climate remained a staple ingredient of colonial discussions right into the era of decolonization: the subject was, for example, formally debated by 42 scholars at the International Geographical Congress in 1938, two years after Jean Rhys's single return visit to the island of her birth and around the time she probably wrote some of the early drafts of her story 'Pioneers, Oh, Pioneers'. Dane Kennedy's account of the state of play in the first part of the twentieth century provides an invaluable background against which to read both Bell's warning and Rhys's story:

> Decline, decadence, deterioration, degeneration – these were the codewords repeatedly invoked to suggest the fate that awaited the unwary white settler in the tropics. The early warning signs were depression, indolence, and lack of initiative, a disregard for the specialised rules of personal hygiene and social conduct in the colonial tropics, and

---

[33] Hesketh Bell, 'Imperial Grant', p. 25.

a drift into alcoholic and sexual profligacy (particularly the latter, with its prospect of miscegenation), all of which led slowly but inexorably to a terminal status of depravity. In effect, the process of degeneration was the process of dissolving the boundaries that distinguished 'civilized' from 'barbarous' behaviour and the physical boundaries that distinguished 'white' from 'coloured' race.[34]

Bell's letter was written in October 1899. Jean Rhys's story, 'Pioneers, Oh, Pioneers' begins 'It was still the nineteenth century, November 1899', though that date marks the end of the story it tells, the story of Ramage the pioneer, which had begun two years earlier.[35] The close proximity of the dates must be a coincidence, although Rhys did remember Bell and associated the Imperial Road and the new planters with him ('pioneer cultivators' Bell had called them[36]), and so in all probability she deliberately placed her story in the period that Bell spent in Dominica. Ramage becomes in effect one of the Englishmen attracted by Bell's publicity campaign, even though Rhys backdates the story of the pioneers a few years to the end of the nineteenth century. Ramage was a real person, an eccentric white planter from this period, well-known on Dominica for building a very big hole in the ground, which he would tell people was a personal underground road which would come out at the other side of the world in China. Rhys gives him a rather different story.

Jean Rhys's childhood years on Dominica had seen her family deeply involved in issues of land and national identity. The Captain Churchill who hosted Froude married one of Jean's mother's sisters, and the Mr F– who accompanied Froude on his walks was reputed in the local press to be Acton Don Lockhart, one of her mother's brothers.[37] But, in addition, a prominent coloured Lockhart family spelled out the consequences of 'intemperate' behaviour,[38] and may have helped broaden Rhys's perspectives. In any case 'Pioneers' was written much later, perhaps originally in the late 1930s before being revised for publication in 1969.

'Pioneers' opens and closes with the effect of Ramage's death on a young girl, Rosalie, aged 9 (the same age as Rhys in 1899), whose father is the local doctor (as Rhys's was). In between, the narrator recalls Ramage's story. Rosalie had first met him when he had visited her father in search of advice about buying a small

---

[34] Kennedy, 'Perils of the Midday Sun', p. 131.

[35] Jean Rhys, 'Pioneers, Oh, Pioneers', in her *The Collected Short Stories* (New York: Norton, 1987), pp. 275–84. It was first published as 'My Dear Darling Mr Ramage', *The Times*, no. 57598 (28 June 1969), p. 19. Early drafts are found in the 'Black Exercise Book' (Jean Rhys Collection, McFarlin Library, University of Tulsa) and in manuscripts held at The British Library (Additional MS 57859, Jean Rhys papers, vol. IV). There is an incisive analysis, on which I draw here, in Thorunn Lonsdale, 'Reconstructing Dominica: Jean Rhys's "Pioneers, Oh, Pioneers"', *Journal of the Short Story in English*, 26 (1996), pp. 75–86.

[36] Hesketh Bell, 'Imperial Grant', p. 36.

[37] See Hulme, *Remnants of Conquest*, p. 99, n.3.

[38] See Hulme, *Remnants of Conquest*, pp. 234–5.

and remote estate: 'I was told that there were several places going along this new Imperial Road you've got here,' Ramage had said.[39]

Ramage in fact went on to buy one of the older plantations called Spanish Castle and disappeared from view. It emerged that he had married a coloured girl 'who called herself Isla Harrison, though she had no right to the name of Harrison'. Isla had been brought up by her godmother in Roseau and 'was very well known in the town – too well known … "It's not as though she was a nice coloured girl," everybody said. So the Ramages were lost to white society.'[40] However, the real trouble started with an incident in which Ramage was caught by his neighbours wandering around naked, and the doctor's wife started pestering her husband with the local gossip:

> It was Mr Eliot, the owner of Twickenham, who started the trouble. He was out with his wife, he related, looking at some young nutmeg trees near the boundary. They had a boy with them who had lighted a fire and put water on for tea. They looked up and saw Ramage coming out from under the trees. He was burnt a deep brown, his hair fell to his shoulders, his beard to his chest. He was wearing sandals and a leather belt, on one side of which hung a cutlass, on the other a large pouch. Nothing else.[41]

The doctor tried to warn Ramage, but could not quite bring himself to say anything. Then a rumour started that Ramage's wife had mysteriously disappeared; and the local newspaper stepped in with a vitriolic article about the failure of 'the so-called "Imperial Road"', singling out one of these 'gentlemen planters' for seeing himself as 'the king of the cannibal islands' and ending with the provocative statement: 'Black people bear much; must they also bear beastly murder and nothing be done about it?'[42] A riot soon followed when a small crowd started to throw stones at Ramage's house and he came out onto the verandah with a shotgun. However, when the police went to investigate the following morning, they found that Ramage had turned the gun on himself. At which point his wife returned from a visit to relatives in Guadeloupe.

Hesketh Bell's picture of the inexperienced pioneer seems to foreshadow Ramage in several respects – his ignorance of what is involved in planting, his purchase of a rundown plantation, his isolation, his seeking out of a 'native companion', his deterioration and discouragement. Yet within the broader discursive framework provided by Froude, Chamberlain and Bell, 'Pioneers' might be read as a satire or critique of – or at least a counterpoint to – imperial ideology, and especially to the implicit ideal of Englishness which the earlier texts share and which they try to lend, by extension, to Dominica's tropical landscape.

---

[39] Rhys, 'Pioneers', p. 277.
[40] Rhys, 'Pioneers', p. 278.
[41] Rhys, 'Pioneers', p. 279.
[42] Rhys, 'Pioneers', p. 282.

For a start, Ramage does not come as an enthusiastic planter and then degenerate. He comes looking for an estate which is 'small and remote' – precisely the opposite of Bell's promoted ideals, which are based on accessibility. He is *looking* for isolation, not accepting it as the unfortunate concomitant of an otherwise profitable venture: there is a hint of some psychological complexity there, possibly some desired escape from Britain, for whatever reason. From the beginning Ramage wants nothing to do with the colonial dances and the tennis parties – everything associated with 'the club', which in Dominican terms means the whites-only club set up by Hesketh Bell.

Rosalie's father is the most sympathetic of the white adults whom Ramage meets, but even the doctor has second thoughts after Ramage's death, questioning his own denial that Ramage was certifiable: 'All wrong, Ramage, probably a lunatic, was now as dead as a doornail',[43] finally aligning his views with popular white opinion as voiced by 'one lady': 'He was evidently mad, poor man – sitting in the sun with no clothes on – much worse might have happened.'[44] Failure to conform is pronounced as evidence of madness; but, as elsewhere, the narrator uses the resources of tone to take her distance from this popular view.

As so often, the themes that carry the narrative configurations of Englishness are sexuality and colour. As mentioned earlier, Ramage was the name of a planter on Dominica renowned for his eccentricity. In most of the early versions of the story, Rhys changed the name, but she eventually went back to it, possibly because of its connotations: 'ramage' means an untrained hawk and has an obselete meaning in English as 'wildness, high spirit, courage' – characteristics which are the opposite of temperance. Indeed, given that the moment when Rosalie falls in love with Ramage is when he sings 'Baa baa black sheep' to her, Rhys presumably was not immune to the even stronger implications of the Ram in *Ram*age – particularly since one of his admirers on the island is a Miss *Lamb*ton. The cutlass and pouch, which shock the Eliots, may also have sexual connotations. Be all that as it may, one of the story's telling moments sees Ramage set himself up with Isla Harrison, 'a coloured girl' – 'very well-known … too well-known' – so becoming 'lost' to the white community. Yet the narrative voice is noticeably less condemnatory than that of the white community. The use of direct quotation, rather than indirect speech, comes across as quietly satirical, as if *exactly* those words were coming out of everybody's mouth; as does the 'everybody' itself – referring to about 100 people out of a population of 30 000. In the Dominican context, 'no right to use the name of Harrison' means that Isla's white father, Harrison, had not recognized his coloured daughter. Her given name, Isla, the Spanish for island, may suggest that Ramage has embraced the island itself, not just in the usual way of taking a mistress, but by *marrying* Isla, his truly unacceptable move from the respectable point of view.

---

43   Rhys, 'Pioneers', p. 276.
44   Rhys, 'Pioneers', p. 284.

When Ramage's encounter with Mr and Mrs Eliot is reported, the narrative voice is again at least ambivalent, if not fully sympathetic to Ramage. His appearance is immediately preceded by the Eliots having afternoon tea in the middle of a tropical estate they have renamed Twickenham – with its literary resonance from Alexander Pope's grotto – in place of its creole name, Malgré Tout. There is a hint – not least in the wild inappropriateness of Twickenham to the topography of Dominica – that the Eliots' behaviour is just as odd as Ramage's. (They have the same name as the managers of Middleham in Bell's letter, which may not be coincidental since the Middleham Elliotts would be part of Rhys's childhood memories. Indeed, in the early drafts of the story the name is spelled Elliott.) The offence caused is by no means straightforward. Ramage insults Mrs Eliot's clothes ('What an uncomfortable dress – and how ugly!'[45]), to which her response, after politely offering Ramage tea, is to lock herself in her room, admit that Ramage was right and accuse her husband of being 'mean'. In other words she reads Ramage's insult as a comment on the quality of Eliot's love for her expressed in the way he clothes and keeps her, that is to say on his temperate indifference towards her appearance, with temperance recoded as stinginess from the female side of an older imperial settlement.

As in Bell's letter, matters of climate connote issues of colour. Middleham's temperate climate is associated with a colour poised between the pallor of the coast and the blackness of beyond, but the ideological constraints of 'whiteness' determine that that colour should be 'rosy' rather than the more obvious brown – the latter being a colour associated at best with indigeneity, at worst with miscegenation. Ramage's public appearance as naked, with long hair and deep brown skin, seems to indicate a serious, if flawed, attempt to go native.[46] Ramage looks – with the exception of the beard – just like depictions of the real natives of Dominica, the Caribs, who gave their name to cannibalism. The local newspaper picks up this resonance when it says that Ramage has thought of himself as 'the king of the cannibal islands', referring to a popular Victorian nursery rhyme.

How to adapt to a tropical climate is a question that troubles Ramage from the start. He turns up on Dominica in full tropical kit, including solar topee, and even after abandoning the topee in the face of admiring interest from local children, he retains his white suits, 'though most of the men wore dark trousers even when the temperature was ninety in the shade'.[47] In seeking accommodation to the island, he stands in stark contrast to the defiant maintenance of English norms and nomenclatures for which Rhys's narrator demonstrates little sympathy. His abandonment of all clothes but sandals and belt suggest a healthy, if troubled, embrace of his adopted home, fully – perhaps too fully – in keeping with Walt Whitman's resonant

---

[45] Rhys, 'Pioneers', p. 279.
[46] This phrase has been widely used in discussions of the story: see Lonsdale, 'Reconstructing Dominica', pp. 82–3.
[47] Rhys, 'Pioneers', p. 276.

line in the pioneer poem from which Rhys gets her title: 'All the past we leave behind'.[48] However, it is the sexual embrace that puts Ramage beyond the pale. Here his newly acquired brownness threatens to erase the distinction between Ramage and Isla, just as their marriage threatens to lend respectability to their union.

All land and landscape tends to be coded as female, but in different ways. Froude had referred pastorally to the island as a beauty conscious of its charms, Bell georgically to its virgin land in need of energetic English husbandmen to make it fertile. The official discourse has Dominica itself feminized and therefore playing the part of the woman, with the pioneer planters left to form a purely homosocial community, disastrously unable to reproduce themselves as a class.

'Pioneers, Oh, Pioneers' offers an ambiguous but wryly satirical view of this project, seeming to tell a story of colonial degeneration, but instead offering a subtle portrait both of an eccentric 'pioneer' in social relationships and of an imperial culture at what was presented as a turning point, but proved to be a cul-de-sac. Hesketh Bell has the final words:

> It is grievous to have to relate that my scheme for opening up the interior of Dominica resulted in failure ... The local Government, hampered by decreasing revenues and the consequent lack of funds, found itself unable, not only to improve the new roads, but even to maintain them properly. The difficulties of transport greatly discouraged and handicapped the planters in the interior and gave them a grievance. A severe disease, which decimated the lime trees, together with a ruinous fall in the price of cocoa, completed the misfortunes of the settlers and exhausted their resources. One by one they gave up the struggle, and there are few who were not obliged either to abandon their plantations or sell them for a song.[49]

---

[48] Walt Whitman, 'Pioneers! O Pioneers!' [1865/1881], in his *Complete Poetry & Selected Prose and Letters*, ed. Emory Holloway (London: Nonesuch Press, 1938), p. 212.

[49] Henry Hesketh Bell, *Glimpses of a Governor's Life: From Diaries, Letters, and Memoranda* (London: Sampson, Low & Marston, 1946), pp. 94–5.

Chapter Seven

Reading Romance, Reading Landscape: Empires of Fiction

Mary Condé

An attention to landscape has always been a staple of fiction set in India and Africa: the summary of the ninth chapter of Mrs R. Lee's *The African Wanderers* (1850) opens laconically: 'Beautiful Scenery. – Elephants. – Pelicans. – Creek. – Mangroves. – Lizards. – Butterflies. – Birds. – Parrots. – Monkeys. – Forest in a swamp.'[1] More specifically, landscape was used by several nineteenth- and early twentieth-century women writers of romance as both a rival of and metaphor for the heroine, as well as an internal criticism of the novel form itself. Typical in this way is K. M. Edge's *The Shuttles of the Loom* (1909), which opens by following the sweeping glance across a south Indian forest by the Deputy-Conservator of Forests, John Grange, and then explaining that what informs this glance is a comprehensive and accurate knowledge of every tree, which entails a heavy responsibility. Grange must make himself active in this landscape, and inscribe himself in it, by building bridges and demarcating boundaries. However, he is also an impassive presence within it, in the best tradition of the strong, silent hero, and even when standing 'in the midst of forests he loved, no muscle of his face moved, and his expression was hard',[2] so that his face effectively becomes a landscape of its own for the reader to decode as he decodes the forest. Face as landscape also appears in Ethel M. Dell's best-selling *The Way of an Eagle* (1912), in which Nick Ratcliffe's physiognomy is desperately searched by the soldier who must confide his daughter to him 'as a man who views through field-glasses a region distant and unexplored'.[3] Ratcliffe, however, ends happily married to the heroine, while Grange dies of cholera almost immediately after he marries and is buried in the landscape he has helped to shape, eliciting the verdict that: 'His body was fitly given to the land for which he had spent his manhood, and in which his influence must remain long after he himself

---

[1] Mrs. R. Lee, *The African Wanderers: or, The Adventures of Carlos and Antonio. Embracing Interesting Descriptions of the Manners and Customs of the Western Tribes, and the Natural Productions of the Country*, 2nd edn (London: Grant, 1850) p. 132.

[2] K. M. Edge, *The Shuttles of the Loom* (London: John Murray, 1909), p. 4.

[3] Ethel M. Dell, *The Way of an Eagle* (London: Ernest Benn, 1912), p. 11.

was forgotten.'[4] Landscape here is not just an indicator of a man's masterful and loving attitude to a woman, but represents a rival romantic embrace.

A variation on this theme is the fate of Jan in Nora Stevenson's *African Harvest* (1928), whose love for his Boer homestead, Burghersrust, on the veld, is his one redeeming feature. He receives his only satisfactory embrace from 'the hug of the mountain' as he lies reflecting on his love for the English Trixie, 'daughter of the conquering race; with her face set, as the faces of islanders are, away from the veld towards the sea ... waiting in vain for the salt breezes to kiss her lips'.[5] Like John Grange, Jan is buried in the landscape he has helped to shape, but, since he is a Boer, it is 'with his broken heart, among the ruins of Burghersrust'.[6] Trixie is here equated with conquering sea and Jan with vanquished veld, but the lure of the latter is very frequently compared with the lure of a woman. Jack, in Thirza Nash's *The Ex-Gentleman* (1925), falls in love with the veld and finds to his cost that she 'was a most sweet mistress when one was young, most adventurous, alluring, but how hard, how jealous when wedded to her!'[7] Anthony Kinsella, the maverick hero of Cynthia Stockley's *The Claw* (1911), makes the heroine Deirdre say ruefully of her rival, the landscape that has enslaved him, that, 'a moment later he was talking of the veldt as tenderly as a lover might talk of the woman he loves ... For I had not a word to say, I could only listen to him talking about Africa like a lover. At least I felt that was the way I should like my lover to speak of me.'[8]

In Richard Dehan's *The Dop Doctor* (1910), a chorus-girl, impulsively married by a young viscount, is conflated with a South African landscape in a sequence in which he and a friend, who had hoped that South Africa might save him 'by the skin of his teeth',[9] together imagine the chorus-girl and her blandishments:

There is another short interval of silence in which the two men on Nixey's verandah see the same vision – limelights of varying shades and colours thrown from different angles across a darkened garden-scene where impossible tropical flowers expand giant petals, and a spangled waterfall tumbles over the edge of a blue precipice in sparkling foam. The nucleus of a cobweb of quivering rays, crossing and intersecting, is a dazzling human butterfly, circling, spinning, waving white arms like quivering antennae, flashing back the coloured lights from the diamonds that are in her hair and on her bosom, are clasped about her rounded waist and wrists, gleam like fireflies from the folds of her diaphanous skirts, and sparkle on her fingers.[10]

---

[4]   Edge, *The Shuttles*, p. 339.
[5]   Nora Stevenson, *African Harvest* (London: Butterworth, 1928), pp. 35–6.
[6]   Stevenson, *African Harvest*, p. 320.
[7]   Thirza Nash, *The Ex-Gentleman* (London: Jarrolds, 1925), pp. 21–2.
[8]   Cynthia Stockley, *The Claw* (London: Hurst & Blackett, 1911), pp. 6–7.
[9]   Richard Dehan, *The Dop Doctor* (London: William Heinemann, 1910), p. 314.
[10] Dehan, *The Dop Doctor*, pp. 315–16.

This tawdry, meretricious temptress, a woman masquerading as landscape, actually functions as a very close parody of South Africa as temptress, even down to the diamond fields of Kimberley, here routinely deprecated as a hellish aspect of her appeal;[11] theatrical display and exotic vegetation combine to suggest the alien and the dangerous. The reverse of this was an analogy between Africa and desired woman, which suggested freshness and innocence, and even the sacred. Cynthia Stockley's Dalla 'had her virgin look of undiscovered country upon her ... like rose-petals and dew',[12] a 'warm and living piece of Africa',[13] while her Linnet, in *Kraal Baby* (1933), is described rapturously by her husband as 'a field of amaranths that the lord hath blessed ... something immortal, too lovely for this world ... and yet, thank God, a living bit of spring earth.'[14] Charlotte Mansfield feels bound to make it clear that the heroine of *Gloria: A Girl of the South African Veld* (1916), with her dazzling 'complexion of cream and roses' does not express the whole truth about her country. Her deformed younger brother, Johannes, Mansfield argues, makes it seem 'as though nature had sent him as a contrast to Gloria; the two children might be said to represent South Africa, the land of surprises and contrasts'.[15]

Another heroine, Madeleine in Mrs Alexander's *A Missing Hero* (1901), like South Africa in containing 'a vein of undiscovered gold',[16] also herself personifies the landscape by saying of her favourite spot, 'I hate to see my fairy dell all disfigured, as though it had been in a tearing passion and then a flood of tears!'[17] This girlish conceit, of a safe and sexless haven functioning both in a real and a psychological landscape, may be compared with the convenient plot device, reminiscent of *The Mill on the Floss*, of Annabella Bruce Marchand's *Dirk: A South African* (1913), where the hero and heroine die together in a flood. Marchand writes that the 'sweet scent of the *keurboom* trees whose scattered blossoms like massacred virgins lay ravished and muddied in thousands at their feet, the loud plashing of the waterfall, the familiar feel of the place, rolled from Dirk's mind the growth and accretions of twenty-five years'.[18] She here manages to combine the chaste and the erotic in a scene which is essentially the hero's reconstructed childhood; as a South African Dirk does not possess, but is rather possessed by, and dissolved into, the landscape with his lover.

---

[11] See, for example, Cynthia Stockley, *Pink Gods and Blue Demons* (London: Cassell, 1920), p. 18; A. Elizabeth Douglas, *The End of the Trek: A Story of South Africa* (London: Andrew Melrose, 1923), p. 241.

[12] Cynthia Stockley, *Dalla the Lion-Cub* (London: Hutchinson, 1924), p. 286.

[13] Cynthia Stockley, *The Leopard in the Bush: A Sequel to Dalla the Lion-Cub* (London: Putnam, 1928), p. 14.

[14] Cynthia Stockley, *Kraal Baby* (London: Cassell, 1933), p. 313.

[15] Charlotte Mansfield, *Gloria: A Girl of the South African Veld* (London: Holden & Hardingham, 1916), pp. 6–7.

[16] Mrs. Alexander, *A Missing Hero* (London: Chatto & Windus, 1901), p. 34.

[17] Alexander, *Missing Hero*, p. 145.

[18] Annabella Bruce Marchand, *Dirk: A South African* (London: Longmans, Green, 1913), p. 372.

Landscape as adversary can be emotionally ambiguous, as it is in *The End of the Trek: A Story of South Africa* (1923). The devoted couple of the first generation, Ken and Cecil (her name perhaps a tribute to Rhodes), exult in the beauty of South Africa and report triumphantly back to England: 'You talk of Turner Sunsets! We have the real thing.'[19] The ascent of a mountain actually culminates in a divine vision, a shape with wings and a glorious face,[20] but both Ken and Cecil expire tragically and prematurely, Ken struck by lightning and Cecil dying in childbirth. There is a sense that the landscape has spiritually overpowered them, uplifting them above their ordinary lives and yet nullifying these lives in the process. In other novels, landscape is more conventionally paired with antagonists like war and disease, to thwart or threaten the hero. In Annie S. Swan's *Love Grown Cold* (1902), the story of a Boer War correspondent and his tragic love story, a grim struggle for survival is dramatically enacted: 'About eight o'clock on a wet, blustering evening a horseman rode wearily into the little town of Newcastle in Natal. He had traversed since daybreak the awful track of alternative swamp and boulders which lies between Maritzburg and Newcastle. Exposed all day to torrents of rain, he was now soaked to the skin.'[21] Anna Howarth's *Katrina: A Tale of the Karoo* (1898) had opened four years earlier in a way seemingly very similar, with a solitary horseman who 'rode, somewhat slowly and wearily, along a sandy and ill-made waggon road which traversed a part of one of those wild and arid portions of South Africa called Karoos'.[22] This horseman is pitted not against a human enemy (tactfully, since this novel is very sympathetic to the Boers) but against smallpox; although 'a solitary and feeble Don Quixote',[23] he manages to rescue a little girl from the disease, and Howarth has much to say about the magically reviving effects of rain on the Karoo, 'which never dies, however long it may be without the means of life'.[24] The landscape here becomes both accomplice and symbolic affirmation of the cycle of life which makes the little girl, eventually, the romantic heroine.

The male narrator of Elizabeth Charlotte Webster's *Pot Holes: An Adventure of the Diamond Fields* (1928), instinctively pits himself against the landscape he sees from the train to Johannesburg. He admits that there:

> was, to me, something terrifying about the immensity of the wilderness. The lines of the hills of home are soft and undulating, a series of graceful sweeps and curves upon the horizon. But the kopjes of the karroo are fierce, jagged, and primeval; they cut the skyline with a serrated edge, and are all angles … I was impressed with the scenery, but I was

---

[19] A. Elizabeth Douglas, *The End of the Trek: A Story of South Africa* (London and New York: Andrew Melrose, 1923), p. 40.

[20] Douglas, *The End of the Trek*, pp. 41–2.

[21] Annie S. Swan, *Love Grown Cold* (London: Methuen, 1902), p. 244.

[22] Anna Howarth, *Katrina: A Tale of the Karoo* (London: Smith, Elder, 1898), p. 1.

[23] Howarth, *Katrina*, p. 15.

[24] Howarth, *Katrina*, p. 235.

also a little afraid – afraid of the stark, naked grandeur of seemingly never-ending miles of barren peaks and plains.[25]

Here again the individual triumphs, and again in a way that echoes the landscape. The narrator takes back to his home in Edinburgh not only several thousand pounds from the diamond fields, but a beautiful young wife who is regarded as another threat to his superiority: her father tells him, 'She has a temper, the minx! But you seem to be able to fight, Lewis. You'll subdue her.'[26] This, however, is an unusually clear-cut outcome, just as Lewis is an unusually vain, mercenary and aggressive hero. In much of this romantic fiction, the alien landscape, at first 'strangely desolate to unaccustomed eyes',[27] does become home, and yet a home in which the heroine struggles to assert her importance, so that the dual impulse is to exult in the 'vast tracts of virgin soil',[28] the 'grand sweep of the hills',[29] and the 'wide open empty world',[30] but simultaneously to also acknowledge that within it a girl is 'a bright and alien little figure in the middle of so much strangeness'.[31]

In other novels, the challenge for the heroine, often flagged in the subtitles, is that despite the establishment of England as the norm, England is not home, and that a mixed heritage is often a mixed blessing. A. Werner says of her South Africa heroine, Meinwen, daughter of a Welsh Calvinist and a 'colonial woman', that 'Puritan though she might be, by fibre and training, she had been born in this land of sunshine, and had grown up drawing in light and freedom at every pore';[32] Meinwen, despite the power she absorbs from the landscape, is powerless to capture or even communicate with the Englishman she loves. This failure of romance is not unusual in this fiction. In so far as they are subsumed into landscape the heroines often lose their identity as free individuals. And in so far as they come out of an alien landscape they often lose their chance to win the hero, despite the superficially attractive juxtaposition of alien land and strong male.

One troubling aspect for many writers seems to have been a perceived mismatch between female fantasy, represented by the novel itself, and male empire-building

---

[25] Elizabeth Charlotte Webster, *Pot Holes: An Adventure of the Diamond Fields* (London: Chapman and Hall, 1928), p. 19.

[26] Webster, *Pot Holes*, p. 273.

[27] Ethel M. Dell, *The Top of the World* (London: Cassell, 1920), p. 35.

[28] Elizabeth Charlotte Webster, *Bullion: A Tale of Buried Treasure and the Bush* (London: Eldon Press, 1933), p. 42.

[29] Anna Howarth, *Sword and Assegai* (London: Smith, Elder, 1899), p. 1.

[30] Cynthia Stockley, *Poppy: The Story of a South African Girl*, 5th edn (London: Hurst and Blackett 1910), pp. 40–1.

[31] L. C. M. Lockhart, *Fire of Life: A Domestic Chronicle* (Edinburgh: William Blackwood, 1924), p. 241.

[32] A. Werner, 'Her Ride', in *The Captain of the Locusts* (London: Fisher Unwin, 1899), p. 105.

[33] Many writers concealed their sex: Charlotte Despard and Mrs Monkland wrote

reality, which may account in part both for the number of 'male' female authors and for the decided hostility towards imaginative writing in the novels themselves.[33] It is certainly a fact that some authors had no real knowledge of the landscapes about which they wrote. I. A. R. Wylie left Mills & Boon when the firm deprecated her dropping of Indian settings; as she tartly recorded in her memoirs, 'On no account was I to write about anything about which I knew anything.'[34] Nor had Ethel M. Dell ever been to India, although generations of readers formed their ideas of India from her work. Publishers, however, were at pains to present their writers as authoritative, and various guarantees of authenticity were often placed at the beginning of the narrative, ranging from the dedication to a maharajah 'in memory of a very happy visit' (Alice Eustace's *Flame of the Forest*, another Mills & Boon),[35] to the assurance that the author had 'represented the *Lady's Pictorial* and several other periodicals at the Imperial Durbar' (Charlotte Cameron's *A Durbar Bride*).[36] The latter is rather a fragile assurance in view of the fact that ladies' magazines were seen as epitomizing female vanity and folly. When the heroine, Peggy, writes to two of them before leaving for India in May Crommelin's *Pink Lotus*, Lady Ermyntrude of the *Dame's Delight* recommends a cork helmet with blue or green veiling for garden parties, and Godmother Prue of *Teapot Twaddle* recommends a portable bath and 'lots of books on India'.[37] This last is clearly regarded as just as absurd as the cork helmet.

---

anonymously and Edith E. Cuthbell wrote as 'An Idle Exile'; Bithia Mary Croker started writing as 'B. M. Croker', Alice Perrin as 'A. Perrin', Fanny Emily Penny as 'F. E. Penny' and Olivia Douglas as 'O. Douglas'; J. E. Muddock, Sydney Carlyon Grier, Maxwell Gray, John Travers, Richard Dehan, Ray Merton, L. C. M. Lockhart, A. Werner, E. Everett-Green, I. A. R. Wylie, C. M. K. Phipps, J. M. Graham, M. J. Colquhoun, H. M. Cadell and E. W. Savi all had deceptively masculine names. E. W. Savi's novels even included deliberately misleading reviews with remarks like 'Mr. Savi knows his India well' (*Standard*) and 'Mr. Savi knows his India very well' (*Aberdeen Journal*). This was partly because there does seem to have been a prejudice against female authors: the *Daily Mail* was quoted in Cynthia Stockley's *Poppy: The Story of a South African Girl* (1910) as saying of her *Virginia of the Rhodesians* (1903) (which was actually a collection of short stories), that 'It is rarely possible to offer a lady an honest congratulation on her first novel, but Miss Cynthia Stockley deserves more than moderate praise.' Rudyard Kipling, specifically, was constantly used as a standard against whom female writers were measured, and indeed these writers quoted and borrowed from him very liberally. The publishers of the 1905 edition of Flora Annie Steel's *On the Face of the Waters*, who elevated to the front cover the *Spectator's* comment that 'there is many an officer who would give his sword to write military history as Mrs Steel has written it in this great novel of the Indian Mutiny', were, in addition, implicitly acknowledging the perceived inferiority of the 'lady' to the man of action.

[34] Quoted in Joseph McAleer, *Passion's Fortune: The Story of Mills & Boon* (Oxford: Oxford University Press, 1999), p. 44.

[35] Alice Eustace, *Flame of the Forest* (London: Mills & Boon, 1927).

[36] Charlotte Cameron, *A Durbar Bride* (London: Stanley Paul, 1912).

[37] Mary Crommelin, *Pink Lotus: A Comedy in Kashmir* (London: Hurst and Blackett, 1914), pp. 30–33.

There is a strong impulse within the novels to present their landscapes as having an integrity that would be compromised either by 'the foot of the globe-trotter'[38] or by the would-be lady novelist, as we are told the wilder scenery round Simla would be in *A Pinchbeck Goddess* (1897) by Alice M. Kipling, Rudyard Kipling's sister.[39] In B. M. Croker's *Her Own People* (1903), Captain Malcolm Haig tells a lady at dinner that a novel called *Thrills from the Hills, or the Curse of the Khitmagar* seems to have its facts taken from fiction and its local colour taken from Earl's Court, which is tactless, as the lady is the (lady) author's sister. He, who has been in India for seven years, significantly declares that, 'the truth is that India – real India – is to the European a closed book!' in the face of his dining companion's confidence that although she has never been there, she has read about it, 'which amounts to almost the same thing'.[40] Croker is of course trading on exactly this confidence in her reader, that the closed book may be opened by the novelist, yet within novels, novels were routinely scorned. In Anna Howarth's *Nora Lester* (1902), when a very sympathetic character is advised to read, he replies, 'the only novel I ever read seemed to me great nonsense. Why should people want novels when they have real life?'[41] Later, when the hero Noel goes out to South Africa, he admiringly tells a heroic old Englishman that he talks like a book. Mr Mayer responds,

'Nay, I have never read many books. My books have been just my own life, and the lives of my neighbours. They have taught me all I know.'
'And all you need to know, I think,' replied Noel, smiling.[42]

Nella, in Mrs G. Bowden's *Nella of Pretoria* (1907), the daughter of a Dutchman from the Transvaal and an Englishwoman, surprises her English friends by her refinement, and comes from a home that visually reflects her cultivation, with its avenue of orange trees and its beautiful circular garden,[43] but does not need to impress her friends, or the reader, with her literary appetites. When she is asked,

---

[38] Bithia Mary Croker, *A Bird of Passage*, 3 vols (London: Sampson Low, 1886), vol. I, pp. 1–2. The extent to which the tourist experience was governed by the printed word in the form of the guidebook is discussed in Inderpal Grewal, *Home and Harem: Nation, Gender, Empire and the Culture of Travel* (London: Leicester University Press, 1996), pp. 95–6.

[39] Alice M. Kipling (writing as Beatrice Grange), *The Heart of a Maid* (Allahabad: A. H. Wheeler, 1890), p. 200.

[40] Bithia Mary Croker, *Her Own People* (London: Hurst and Blackett, 1903), pp. 25–6.

[41] Anna Howarth, *Nora Lester* (London: Smith, Elder 1902) p. 42. Although in fact the popularity of imperialist fiction was closely linked to a real-life enthusiasm for imperialist action. See, for example, Martin Green, *Dreams of Adventure, Deeds of Empire* (London: Routledge, 1980) and Joseph Bristow, *Empire Boys: Adventures in a Man's World* (London: HarperCollins, 1991).

[42] Anna Howarth, *Nora Lester*, p. 282.

[43] Mrs. G. Bowden, *Nella of Pretoria* (London: Digby, Long, 1907), pp. 101–2.

in Bayswater, whether she would like any particular author, she replies, 'Oh, no; as long as it's not a very large book'[44]

What particularly vexed these women writers was what they saw as a contemporary avalanche of women's writing. In Charlotte Mansfield's *Red Pearls* (1914), Sir Reginald, in Durban, asks Mrs Clayton, whom he will eventually marry:

> 'Most women write now-a-days, do you?' 'Oh no, why should I? I am far too lazy, and why do a thing that has been in all its branches so well done? If no more books were written there would still be enough for future generations to read for centuries to come. No! I prefer to be unique and remain simply a woman, don't smile, I assure you I am serious; now-a-days to be only that is unique; women seem to have at present a strange thirst for ink, they simply wallow in it, and write whether they have ability or not.'[45]

It is a male writer, however, who wafts through the pages of Mrs Alexander's *A Missing Hero* (1901), set in 'still savage South Africa'[46] – except that the Hon. Tom St. Mawr omits the actual writing. He blithely tells the heroine Madeleine that, 'You know, I'm writing a book, Miss Erle – a book about South Africa. We have got a lovely title for it – can't remember it for the moment: all about elephant-shooting and lion-hunting, and politics, and society, and the future, and a lot more. I do the observations, and Mark Forrester writes them all down.'[47] This genial idiot demonstrates his ineptitude by his indifference to South Africa's wild landscapes, dawdling for seven or eight weeks in Cape Town, 'enjoying the blandishments of the colonial belles!',[48] as Mark Forrester puts it, and thereby demonstrating what is clearly regarded as a foolish and corrupt preference. Conversely, the novel Cynthia Stockley's heroine, Poppy, is planning to write is enthusiastically approved by her friend Clementine precisely because of Poppy's love for the wide open spaces of South Africa: 'I *know* it will be good … I can feel that it will have big bits of open space like the veldt in it, with new sorts of trees growing by the wayside as one passes along … I hate the modern woman's book, because it always makes me gasp for air.'[49] What these protestations taken in conjunction suggest is that the romantic heroine should preserve her womanliness, and her chance of winning a man, by setting her face against the form that has produced her, a form seen as typically at odds with a respect for landscape.

An aspect of this antagonism between fiction and landscape was the sheer scale of the latter in India and Africa, always insisted upon, which made many heroines regard their own romantic stories as trivial. It reduces Fay, in Perrin's *The Anglo-Indians*, to 'this little girl, this atom of life',[50] and makes May, in Alice Kipling's

44 Bowden, *Nella of Pretoria*, p. 22.
45 Charlotte Mansfield, *Red Pearls* (London: Holden & Hardingham, 1914), p. 65.
46 Alexander, *Missing Hero*, p. 23.
47 Alexander, *Missing Hero*, p. 67.
48 Alexander, *Missing Hero*, p. 90.
49 Stockley, *Poppy*, p. 153.
50 Alice Perrin, *The Anglo-Indians* (London: Methuen, 1912), p. 4.

The Heart of a Maid, accept a man she does not love because 'The great grey hills were very vast and solemn in the dim light; looking at them she felt dwarfed, and of no importance: they had stood and would stand for centuries. What did her insignificant little life matter, after all, how spent, or with whom? It was all so small and contemptible.'[51] A truly grand and mysterious landscape, in addition, explicitly resists a reading as a romance does not. Gertrude Page's *The Rhodesian* (1912) opens with the Zimbabwe ruins, which 'continue to baffle the ingenuity and ravish the curiosity of all who would read their story', even though they are now no longer 'alone and unheeded', and 'left solely to the idle pleasure of a careless black people'.[52] Imperial inscriptions on Africa, for their part, are read by female characters in obviously idiosyncratic ways. One young woman who sees 'battalions' of trees on the veld, and the beams of the 'spiked and glinting warrior' sun throwing 'lances of gold' across it, is significantly and, it has to be said, improbably disguised as a man as she travels through Rhodesia.[53] In a novel of 1925, *Shadowed Blood*, Dulcie looks out from a train and realizes with beating heart that she is travelling through the landscape of the Boer War, in which her father had fought. This is set against the sight of Majuba, appearing in a kind of ahistorical vacuum:

> in striking solitude, defiant of the ages, or time, or man. Grim, absolute, it towered over the silent veld as immovable and inscrutable as the Sphinx. Not a sound broke the silence, not the whirr of a bird's wing or the chirp of a sparrow, or any sign of life. It was desolation personified, but a desolation that impressed by its very magnitude.[54]

The contrast here between battlefields and mountain encapsulates Dulcie's conflicted parentage. Her English father enables her to pass for white in London, but the disclosure of her Zulu mother impels her to become a kind of native goddess hunting down white men in Rhodesia, until she kills herself in remorseful despair, a struggle prefigured in the third element of the landscape: two vultures tearing at a sheep.

In Charlotte Mansfield's *"For Satan Finds ...."* (1917), it is the writer who consciously takes control of the reading of landscape. Mary, who must learn through the course of the novel to love her sometimes errant husband Frank and his farm in the Orange Free State (the two being emotionally inseparable), has a tender moment with him as they hold hands at the Cecil Rhodes monument at Groote Schuur. Mansfield, here using 'we' and 'us' for the only time in her novel, is anxious to emphasize that:

> the landscape round seems a part of the laudation as it was indeed a part of the inspiration of the Empire Maker. The view of verdant plains that lie beneath us and the Indian Ocean and the Atlantic there shimmering in the distance, all seem part of the tribute to the spirit

---

[51] Kipling, *Heart of a Maid*, p. 6.
[52] Gertrude Page, *The Rhodesian* (London: Hurst and Blackett, 1912), pp. 1–2.
[53] Cynthia Stockley, *Ponjola* (London: Constable, 1923), p. 58.
[54] A. Elizabeth Douglas, *Shadowed Blood* (London: Andrew Melrose, 1925), pp. 128–9.

of the man in honour of whom the monument whereon we stand was built. Nature herself is offering her wealth of aspect in respect due to one of Nature's children.[55]

Here, the landscape both asserts the moral purity of Rhodes' imperial ambitions, which Mansfield defends at length, and confers by proxy a romantic aura on the hero. Building a church, however, although also in the best imperial tradition, is not romantic. Jack, in Ray Merton's *My Cousin's Wife* (1892), gazes out over an African landscape and wants to see a stone-built church in the middle of it;[56] Stephen in Mary E. Palgrave's *A Promise Kept* (1887) boasts of his wooden church 'rising in the midst' of 'the vast howling wilderness of heathen tropical Africa'.[57] Neither man, however, in either of these rather ambiguous love stories, ends up with a woman.

The ability at least to respond to a landscape, if not read it, is consistently an important moral register for characters, which is why landscape is rarely treated brusquely by authors, although M. J. Colquhoun in *Every Inch a Soldier* does impatiently conclude one description, 'But to return to our story.'[58] When an admirable character is indifferent to a landscape, his creator is liable to leap in to defend him. An Englishman looking out over the River Ganges 'looked at it all, and saw nothing, principally because he was thinking of his work – he very seldom thought of anything else – and also because he was so accustomed to the scene',[59] explains Alice Perrin. Only the most empty-headed of flirts, like Ursula à Beckett's Sybella, remain completely indifferent to Indian scenery;[60] more common is the experience of Frances M. Peard's Patty when she sees the broad treeless plain and mountains near Peshawar: 'A new dumb awe struck Patty which she could not have explained, but which kept her silent.'[61] The narrator of May Edwood's *The Autobiography of a Spin* (i.e. a flirt) is explicit in congratulating herself on her delighted response to the landscapes around the hill station of Murree, commenting that, 'It must be a very hard nature indeed that is not affected in some way by all these wonders and beauties.'[62]

A sensitive response to landscape is an important register not only of moral fibre, but of race, especially in novels set in India. In Ethel Duff-Fyfe's *The Nine Points*, the mixed-race Bulbul, named after the Indian nightingale that features in

---

[55] Charlotte Mansfield, *"For Satan Finds ...."* (London: Holden, 1917), p. 39.

[56] Ray Merton, *My Cousin's Wife* (London: Digby, Long, 1892), p. 118.

[57] Mary E. Palgrave, *A Promise Kept* (London: National Society's Depository, 1887), p. 242.

[58] M. J. Colquhoun, *Every Inch a Soldier* 3 vols (London: Chatto & Windus, 1888), vol. I, p. 34.

[59] Alice Perrin, *East of Suez* (London: Anthony Treherne, 1901), p. 2.

[60] Ursula à Beckett, *In Extenuation of Sybella* (London: Stanley Paul, 1910), p. 277.

[61] Frances M. Peard, *The Ring from Jaipur* (London: Smith, Elder, 1904), p. 31.

[62] May Edwood, *The Autobiography of a Spin. A Story of Anglo-Indian Life* (Calcutta, Bombay and London: Thacker and Spink, 1893), p. 161.

so many descriptions of Indian landscapes, redeems himself morally and becomes 'an unconscious poet' as he describes the beautiful landscapes of his home in Mhudapur.[63] However, in F. E. Penny's *The Sanyasi*, the mixed-race Averine, born in India, reveals both her moral inferiority and her sexual rapacity at a party on the Thames, for while her companions are thinking sedately only of the sedges and the river, 'she sat dreaming of the passionate beat of the monsoon-driven surf upon the west coast of India'.[64] Conversely, in *A Bottle in the Smoke* (1912), Mrs Fellowes demonstrates her essential decency by enjoying the beauty of an Indian beach because it suggests to her 'one of the vanished haunts of my girlhood' – in England.[65] *A Bottle in the Smoke* is a convoluted narrative in which the good mixed-race character is discovered to be English, and the bad English character is discovered to be mixed-race, a doubly convenient outcome which we could have anticipated if we had tracked their respective attitudes to landscape – although even the evil Alfred, when gazing out over a beautiful starlit garden, does experience 'one of those moments of self-revelation which visit even the basest and shallowest of human hearts'.[66]

Gardens, and particularly their management, are especially important as moral touchstones; the huge and beautifully designed gardens of the Moghul Emperors, featured in Flora Annie Steel's quartet (*King-Errant, A Prince of Dreamers, A Mistress of Men, The Builder*), are proof of the high level of their civilization, whereas in the India of 1911 the political and sexual waywardness of a rajah is demonstrated by the 'wild profusion' of the flowers in his palace garden, 'without the restraining influence of the pruning knife'.[67] English gardens in India and Africa, with their mixture of exotic blooms and suburban order, are, as a metaphor for harmonious imperial rule, often meticulously described, the individual flowers carefully enumerated. In *Tagati (Magic)* (1930), although suburban English names in Rhodesia, like Staines, Chertsey, Sunnyside, Sandwich, Ally Sloper and Belle Vue, are mocked as particularly unsuitable for 'a country reeking with poetical native expressions, as well as heroic episodes of the Pioneers and early settlers',[68] in the same novel, the heroine 'delved furiously in the dark earth that gave out fresh ravishing odours, feverishly flinging in handfuls of seed, mignonette, poppies, gaillardias, forget-me-nots, stocks, phlox, and pinks, all the sweet English things that bring back "home" to the exile'.[69] The urgency here is an echo of her sexual

---

[63] Ethel Duff-Fyfe, *The Nine Points* (London: John Long, 1908), p. 255.

[64] F. E. Penny, *The Sanyasi* (London: Chatto & Windus, 1904), p. 15.

[65] Mrs. Milne Rae, *A Bottle in the Smoke: A Tale of Anglo-Indian Life* (London: Hodder & Stoughton, 1912), p. 220.

[66] Milne Rae, *Bottle in the Smoke*, p. 199.

[67] F. E. Penny, *The Rajah* (London: Chatto & Windus, 1911), p. 45.

[68] Cynthia Stockley, *Tagati* (Magic) (London: Constable, 1930), p. 54.

[69] Stockley, *Tagati*, p. 210. The many connotations of women as gardeners are extensively explored in Annette Kolodny, *The Land Before Her: Fantasy and Experience of the American*

ardour; Indian gardens too are often suggestive of the heroine's sexuality, frequently in what they surprisingly contain. In E. W. Savi's *Baba and the Black Sheep* (1914), the idyllic scene on the west bank of the Ganges is shattered by the irruption of the English girl who lives in the bungalow; to the horror of the Englishman who looks on, she shoots a mad dog.[70] There is a very similar sequence in F. E. Penny's *Love in the Hills* (1913), in which a visiting Englishman is first soothed by the mixture of 'homely' and 'humble' English and 'flaming' Indian flowers in the heroine's garden in the Nilgiri Hills,[71] and then alarmed by the appearance of 'Teddy', a pet bear belonging to the heroine which attempts to maul him. Elsewhere in the novel the garden is more conventionally a personification of the heroine, for example in *A Mixed Marriage* (1903), where the new blossoms opening their petals after a night's destructive rain and the 'unsullied' butterflies hovering over the flowers represent Lorina, rescued from a harem;[72] here, however, the bear, like the mad dog, appears to be a trope of erotic power, all the more powerful for appearing unexpectedly amid the flowers (although Honor, in Maud Diver's *Captain Desmond, V.C.* (1931), also impresses the hero by shooting a mad dog in a more prosaic compound).[73]

The Englishman the bear attempts to maul, a captain in the Royal Engineers, stationed near Ootacamund, has just been wandering in the jungle, where he has been taking pains to monitor and collate its different sounds: 'More than once he seated himself on a wayside boulder to watch and listen; and each time he discovered in the chorus a new voice that had escaped him before.'[74] The birds, frogs, lizards, bees, water and foliage that people this beloved landscape are regarded here and in many other novels with just as much, if not more, affection as human figures, who are often no more than local colour, especially in novels with Indian settings.[75] Indeed, Indians can be seen as positively sullying an Indian landscape with their presence,[76]

Frontiers, 1630-1860 (Chapel Hill: University of North Carolina Press, 1984). See also Vera Norwood, *Made from this Earth: American Women and Nature* (Chapel Hill: University of North Carolina Press, 1993) and Stacy Alaimo, *Undomesticated Ground: Recasting Nature as Feminist Space* (Ithaca: Cornell University Press, 2000). Notions of British imperial identity are linked to notions of the English garden at home in Rebecca Preston, 'The Scenery of the Torrid Zone: Imagined Travels and the Culture of Exotics in Nineteenth-century British Gardens', in Felix Driver and David Gilbert, eds, *Imperial Cities: Landscape, Display and Identity* (Manchester: Manchester University Press, 1999) and Annette Kolodny, *The Land Before Her*.

[70] E. W. Savi, *Baba and the Black Sheep* (London: Hurst and Blackett, 1914), p. 2.

[71] F. E. Penny, *Love in the Hills* (London: Chatto & Windus, 1913), p. 9.

[72] F. E. Penny, *A Mixed Marriage* (London: Methuen, 1903), pp. 266–7.

[73] Maud Diver, *Captain Desmond, V.C.* (London: George Newnes, 1931), p. 401.

[74] Penny, *Love in the Hills*, p. 2.

[75] See, for example E. W. Savi, *A Blind Alley* (London: Digby, Long, 1911), p. 157; M. J. Colquhoun, *Primus in Indis: A Romance*, 2 vols (London: Chapman and Hall, 1885), vol. II, pp. 107–8; F. E. Penny, *Dark Corners* (London: Chatto & Windus, 1908), p. 300.

[76] Margaret Peterson, *Dust of Desire* (London: Andrew Melrose, 1922), p. 35.

and this is often reflected in the way that the scenery is interpreted, taking 'weird shapes of crouching beasts and mis-shapen men, ready to spring' on a hapless traveller.[77]

Closely connected with a sense of threat is what is described in one novel as the sheer untidiness of Indian landscapes,[78] whether it is 'a confused dream of feudalism and Gothic Middle Ages' in the case of a rajah's castle near Lucknow, among 'dark masses of unfamiliar foliage' (that is, unfamiliar to an English eye),[79] or (Lucknow again) 'a vast chaotic mass'.[80] And yet it is out of this vast chaotic mass that the novelist must construct her story. J. E. Muddock in *The Great White Hand* ('the great white hand' meaning British imperial rule), for example, offers this recipe for the construction of Cawnpore:

> you must take a big plain with lots of cocoa-palms about, and a broad river running through it. Then get many hundreds of bamboo and mud huts; a few marble palaces, some temples with gilded minarets, a few big public buildings, a hospital or two, a gaol, and a quantity of miscellaneous structures, such as an arsenal, barracks, etc., shake them all up together, and toss them out on the plain, and there you have your Cawnpore.[81]

Muddock is here surely not only referring to the incoherence, as she sees it, of the landscape, but writing about the creative imagination in which diverse elements are 'shaken all up together' to produce a fictional territory. *The White Dove of Amritzir*, *In the Heart of the Storm*, *Douglas Archdale* and *The Great White Hand* were all novels of the Indian Mutiny, in which there was a particularly conflicted assertion of the power of imperial might together with the power of romantic love,[82] which led to an especially acute consciousness on the part of the writer of the incompatibility of her materials. But in all of these romantic novels that relied upon an imperial setting, this incompatibility was felt to a greater or lesser degree, and was expressed through the writers' complex and varied negotiations with the landscape.

---

[77] Helen Bourchier, *The Ranee's Rubies* (London: Anthony Treherne, 1902), p. 114.

[78] Eliza F. Pollard, *The White Dove of Amritzir: A Romance of Anglo-India Life* (London: Partridge, 1897), p. 78.

[79] Maxwell Gray, *In the Heart of the Storm: A Tale of Modern Chivalry* (London: Newnes, 1903), p. 73.

[80] C. M. K. Phipps, *Douglas Archdale. A Tale of Lucknow* (London: London Literary Society, 1885), p. 89.

[81] J. E. Muddock, *The Great White Hand or The Tiger of Cawnpore: A Story of the Indian Mutiny* (London: Hutchinson, 1896), p. 136.

[82] Although Kate Teltscher feels that 'the imperial pen' generally wrote with more assurance after the Mutiny of 1857: Kate Teltscher, *India Inscribed: European and British Writing on India, 1600–1800* (New Delhi: Oxford University Press, 1995), p. 255. Other writers have remarked on the particular anxieties of the ending of empire, for example Phyllis Lassner, 'The Game is Up: British Women's Comic Novels of the End of Empire', in Graeme Harper, ed., *Comedy, Fantasy and Colonialism* (London: Continuum, 2002).

Chapter Eight

Landscape and the Foreigner Within: Katherine Mansfield and Emily Carr

Angela Smith

In this essay I focus on two colonized lands and the ways in which two women depict their landscapes in settler societies: British Columbia in Canada and the North Island of New Zealand. I use the Maori word 'pakeha' as it is used in New Zealand to indicate 'white' or 'European'. Emily Carr was born in Victoria, British Columbia, in 1871 and died there in 1945. She became Canada's best-known woman painter but she was also a writer; in her later years, when her health made painting physically difficult for her, she wrote a series of semi-autobiographical books, using a landscape image for the process: 'For writing is a strong easement for perplexity. My whole life is spread out like a map with all the rivers and hills showing'.[1] Katherine Mansfield was born in Wellington, New Zealand, in 1888, and so is roughly contemporary with Carr, though she died much earlier, of tuberculosis, in 1923. She too habitually sees her writing as a process of exploration of the literal and metaphoric landscape. She wants 'for one moment to make our undiscovered country leap into the eyes of the old world'[2] but also has a pioneering approach to fiction itself: 'People have never explored the lovely medium of prose. It is a hidden country still – I feel that so profoundly.'[3] Her short stories are at the cutting edge of thematic and formal modernist developments in fiction.

Using Carr's paintings as a visual record of the literal and metaphoric journey into the savage wilderness which has to be inhabited and cannot be perceived from a comfortable distance as a framed landscape, I would like to suggest that she and Mansfield reached a comparable awareness of what Julia Kristeva describes as the recognition of the stranger, the Other, not outside as alien and menacing but within the self: 'foreignness is within us: we are our own foreigners, we are divided.'[4] In

---

[1]   Emily Carr, Introduction to *The Complete Writings of Emily Carr* (Vancouver: Douglas & MacIntyre, 1997), p. 3.
[2]   Katherine Mansfield, *The Katherine Mansfield Notebooks*, ed. Margaret Scott (Canterbury: Lincoln University Press, 1997), vol. 2, p. 32.
[3]   Katherine Mansfield, *The Collected Letters of Katherine Mansfield* ed. Vincent O' Sullivan and Margaret Scott (Oxford: Oxford University Press, 1984–96), vol. 2, p. 343.
[4]   Julia Kristeva, *Strangers to Ourselves*, trans. Leon S. Roudiez (London: Harvester, 1991), p. 181.

this case, for both of them, it was a shift from seeing the Other within the familiar binary oppositions of colonial discourse, for example as a savage to be converted to civilization, to recognizing a disturbed and disturbing consciousness of inner disruption, paradox and contradiction. Both signal in their work their awareness that the colonized Other, who had been patronized by patriarchy as child-like, savage and uncivilized, is within the self; as Kristeva has it: 'when we flee from or struggle against the foreigner, we are fighting our unconscious – that "improper" facet of our impossible "own and proper"'.[5] The doubling of colonizer and colonized to signal the foreigner within the self is erratically suggested in Mansfield's early journals and fiction, and is articulated with increasing power in Carr's mature writing and painting. For both, internalizing landscape and finding a way to represent a non-European country are integral to recognition of the Other.

Emily Carr and Klee Wyck

From her infancy Emily Carr seems to have identified patriarchy with a civilizing project: 'Family prayers were uppish with big words on Sunday – reverend awe-ful words that only God and Father understood.'[6] Father even has the power to add to the Bible: 'In the middle of the Bible, between the "old" and the "new", were some blank pages, and all of us were written there. Sometimes Father let us look at ourselves'.[7] That idea of separation from the self, so that the patriarch controls the infant female subject's ability to perceive herself, is to be found throughout Mansfield's stories about children; in them the Law of the Father often produces little girls who stutter, as if they cannot get past the daunting figure of the father to enter the symbolic order. Similarly the colonized subject is often portrayed as child-like in relation to the paternal colonizer in the fiction of the period, able only to blurt out memorable but grammatically crude and infantile fragments, such as 'Mistah Kurtz – he dead' in Joseph Conrad's *Heart of Darkness*. Conrad's Marlow, however, sees what he defines as the primitive savage as an appalling revelation of what lurks within the 'civilized' self, maintaining a polarized perspective, whereas Carr and Mansfield imply that patriarchy's conception of civilization is blinkered by the rigid boundaries it sets.

From the beginning of *The Book of Small*, Small, a version of Carr as a child, resents the spiky hedges and fences she encounters, both literal and metaphorical, which parcel up the land and enclose the adventurous little girl with obstacles and prohibitions. Her British father's role in attempting to alter the landscape links patriarchy and empire; Small's childish and female view of his pioneering intervention is clearly articulated in the chapter called 'Sunday':

---

5   Kristeva, *Strangers*, p. 191.
6   Emily Carr, *The Book of Small*, in *The Complete Writings of Emily Carr*, p. 91.
7   Carr, *The Book of Small*, p. 96.

A twisty little path ran through the shrubbery. Father wanted his place to look exactly like England. He planted cowslips and primroses and hawthorn hedges and all the Englishy flowers. He had stiles and meadows and took away all the wild Canadian-ness and made it as meek and English as he could.[8]

In an attack on what she calls 'the cultivated mind', Mansfield articulates the symbolism implicit in Carr's childish dislike of her father's shrubbery:

The mind I love must still have wild places – a tangled orchard where dark damsons drop in the heavy grass, an overgrown little wood, the chance of a snake or two (real snakes), a pool that nobody's fathomed the depth of, and paths threaded with those little flowers planted by the wind.

It must also have real hiding places, not artificial ones – not gazebos and mazes. And I have never yet met the cultivated mind that has not had its shrubbery. I loathe & detest shrubberies.[9]

Patriarchy's attempt to civilize the landscape and to contain girls and women within it is recognized by both writers as constriction. It is no accident that Small feels happiest in the Cow Yard, where the cow herself provides a female landscape: 'The straight outline of the cow's back in front of Small was like a range of mountains with low hills and little valleys.'[10] Here Small can sing wordless songs to her mother's window, in a non-verbal, semiotic celebration of the fecund and female space of the yard. Bong, the Chinese servant whose foreignness is even more evident than Small's, also 'sang to the Cow – a Chinese song in a falsetto voice', as if he is feminized and accommodated by the ambient sounds and smells.[11]

Carr's account of her determined breaking of the boundaries as an adult is called *Klee Wyck*, the name, meaning 'Laughing One', that she was given by the First Nation Haida people whose way of life she depicted. Her acknowledgement of the renaming process signifies her awareness of the foreigner within, in colonial terms the improper facet of the bourgeois society's own and proper. Initially her paintings were decorative records of a way of life that she entered into by asking First Nation canoeists if she could travel with them and visit their villages. The paintings from that time are in watercolour or thinly applied oil paint, such as *Tanoo, Queen Charlotte Islands* (1912; Fig. 8.1). The expanse of sky in the picture gives the viewer a comfortably distanced familiar landscape; the village is framed in such a way that it is not threatening,[12] though Carr's memories of that time in her later writing reveal

---

[8] Carr, *The Book of Small*, p. 93.

[9] Mansfield, *The Notebooks*, vol. 2, p. 163.

[10] Carr, *The Book of Small*, p. 107.

[11] Carr, *The Book of Small*, p. 98.

[12] A subtly nuanced reading of this and other documentary paintings is offered in Gerta Moray's essay 'Emily Carr and the Traffic in Native Images', in Lynda Jessop, ed.,

8.1 Emily Carr, Tanoo, 1912. Watercolour, pencil on paper, 76.4 × 55.5 cm.
Vancouver Art Gallery, Emily Carr Trust, VAG 42.3.94 (Photo: Trevor Mills).

a darker perception. She juxtaposes the landscape and the Catholic church. The church is central but elderly or lifeless in her description, whereas the landscape and its elements, such as the wind, are alive and vigorous:

> The Village was centred by the Catholic Church – its doors were always wide. Wind entered to whisper among the rafters. The wooden footstools creaked beneath our knees ... The bell-rope dangled idly ... Behind the Indian Village, way up in the clouds stood 'The Lions.' [*sic*] twin mountain peaks, their crowns gleaming white against blue distance, supporting the sky on their heads.[13]

The monotheism of the church seems at odds with the animist landscape.

The tension in the village between what are experienced as two incompatible ways of life is expressed in the mortality of the children. The landscape flowers, with natural rather than church bells: 'In Spring the Village shimmered with millions of exquisite, tongueless bells of cherry-blossom (every Indian had his cherry-tree).'[14] Nonetheless, the babies in this fecund environment died: 'Indian babies were temporary creatures: behaviour half-white, half-Indian, was perplexing to them. Their dull, brown eyes grew vague, vaguer – gave up – a cradle was empty – there was one more shaggy little grave in the cemetery.'[15] The image of the cemetery, which appears in a later painting, *Indian Church* (1929), is distinctly invasive and is dominated by a controlling icon of patriarchy: 'Passing under a big wood cross spanning the gateway, we were in a rough, grassed field bristling with tipping crosses, stone, iron, wood crosses. In the centre stood a big, straight, steady cross raised on a platform, a calm, reassuring cross.'[16] The irony of this reassurance is immediately revealed as Carr's First Nation friend parts the brambles to show the 21 crosses of her own dead babies, victims of 'behaviour half-white, half-Indian'. The narrator comments obliquely on settler invasion and appropriation of a landscape inhabited by indigenous people when she remarks, again ironically, since she is referring to the peace of the tomb, that the 'blue waters of the Inlet separated the hurry and hurt of striving Vancouver from all this peace – stagnant heathenism, the city called it'.[17]

The doubling in her names, Emily Carr and Klee Wyck, signals Carr's consciousness of the foreigner within; she is not one of the First Nation people, but

---

Antimodernism and Artistic Experience: Policing the Boundaries of Modernity (Toronto: University of Toronto Press, 2001). Moray writes: 'convinced that the totem poles could not be understood outside their context within the community and the landscape, she painted views of the villages with their geographic settings', p 77.

[13] Emily Carr, *Growing Pains* in *The Complete Writings of Emily Carr*, p. 438.

[14] Carr, *Growing Pains*, p. 438.

[15] Carr, *Growing Pains*, p. 438.

[16] Carr, *Growing Pains*, p. 438.

[17] Carr, *Growing Pains*, p. 438.

she recognizes within herself their construction of femininity. The first time she encountered an image of the wild woman of the woods, Zonoqua, she was staying, significantly, in the deserted Mission House of what she calls a remote Indian village; the word 'remote' suggests, of course, that there is a centre elsewhere and that she has internalized concepts of measuring, mapping and defining from the metropolitan centre. Alone, but for her dog, she sees a creature, with the sea in front of her and the forest behind; the visit was in 1912, but the painting, *Guyasdom's Zonoqua*, dates from 1928. The memory remained vivid, but at this stage her painting technique was not adequate to embody the cultural impact of the encounter. What she saw was a statue soaring up from its natural pedestal; Carr's description of her first view of the figure, and its setting in the landscape, shows her awareness of the cultural constructions of femininity that it challenges:

> Her head and trunk were carved out of, or rather into, the bole of a great red cedar. She seemed to be part of the tree itself, as if she had grown there at its heart, and the carver had only chipped away the outer wood so that you could see her. Her arms were spliced and socketed to the trunk, and were flung wide in a circling, compelling movement. Her breasts were two eagle-heads, fiercely carved. That much, and the column of her great neck, and her strong chin, I had seen when I slithered to the ground beneath her. Now I saw her face.

The passage is complex, in that it recognizes both the wildness of the landscape and the indigenous sculptor's ability to meet it on its own terms, with a craft that is not dehistoricized as a mystic phenomenon in the passage, but particularized and located in colour and texture; one artist sees how another has constructed the figure, socketing the arms to the trunk:

> The eyes were two rounds of black, set in wider rounds of white, and placed in deep sockets under wide, black eyebrows. Their fixed stare bored into me as if the very life of the old cedar looked out, and it seemed that the voice of the tree itself might have burst from that great round cavity, with projecting lips, that was her mouth. Her ears were round, and stuck out to catch all sounds. The salt air had not dimmed the heavy red of her trunk and arms and thighs. Her hands were black, with blunt finger-tips painted a dazzling white. I stood looking at her for a long, long time.[18]

Carr's view of the figure's face reveals her own awareness of the indigenous artist's fusion of landscape and culture. The sculpture is not a block of stone imposed on a landscape but has been a living part of the coast and now has a different vitality. The sculptor has expressed female empowerment, choosing a tree that situates the statue at the edge of the forest facing the sea. This female figure, with its emphatic colours, is not marginalized, but it marks the margin. As Mary Douglas says, 'all

---

[18]   Emily Carr, *Klee Wyck*, in *The Complete Writings of Emily Carr*, pp. 40–41.

margins are dangerous',[19] but here the female totem pole combines the power of the landscape with the feminine to express 'some tremendous force … that the carver had believed in'.[20]

Though she recorded totemic figures in her field studies in the summer of 1912 and reproduced them in oils and watercolours after the journey north, Carr was not certain at this stage what she was doing with the pictures: 'This friction between Carr the artist and Carr the documentarian is never fully resolved in these 1912 images and certainly was one of the reasons for the refusal of the government to make a purchase of her Indian collection in 1913.'[21] She had been to Paris, reluctant though she was to leave Canada, and had been deeply impressed by the work of the Scottish Colourist J. D. Fergusson and the second wave of Fauves, of which he was a part. Ian Thom writes of Fergusson's impact on her:

> Fergusson was perhaps the most original of the British expatriates living in Paris. His landscapes are characterized by a strong use of drawing, in particular the use of a reddish-purple outline which is seen in some of Carr's French and 1912 Canadian landscapes, bright colour and simplified form … Fergusson combined strong colour with a secure sense of pattern and linear design which appealed to Carr.[22]

Her return home with paintings that had adopted a Fauvist aesthetic clarified her view of her position but she could not yet find a form that would embody the British Columbian landscape: 'My seeing had broadened. I was better equipped both for teaching and study because of my year and a half in France, but still mystified, baffled as to how to tackle our big West.'[23] Her new Fauvist style was rejected by her compatriots when she returned to Vancouver, as she explains: 'Perplexed, angry, they turned away, missing the old detail by which they had been able to find their way in painting. They couldn't see the forest for looking at the trees.'[24] The Post-Impressionist concern with deep structures rather than with a decorative surface realism repelled visitors to Carr's first exhibition in Vancouver after her return from France, and she resented what she saw as their provincialism: 'Why should simplification to express depth, breadth and volume appear to the West [of Canada] as indecent, as nakedness? People did not want to see beneath

---

[19] Mary Douglas, *Purity and Danger: An Analysis of Concepts of Pollution and Taboo* (London: Routledge, 1966), p. 121.

[20] Carr, *Klee Wyck,* p. 42.

[21] Ian M. Thom, *Emily Carr: Art and Process* (Vancouver: Vancouver Art Gallery, 1998), p. 7.

[22] Ian M. Thom, *Emily Carr in France* (Vancouver: Vancouver Art Gallery, 1991), pp. 14–15.

[23] Carr, *Growing Pains*, p. 436.

[24] Carr, *Growing Pains*, p. 437.

surfaces.'[25] She was sensitive to humiliation and mockery but vigorously defended her own position:

> Nevertheless, I was glad I had been to France. More than ever was I convinced that the old way of seeing was inadequate to express this big country of ours, her depth, her height, her unbounded wideness, silences too strong to be broken – nor could ten million cameras, through their mechanical boxes, ever show real Canada. It had to be sensed, passed through live minds, sensed and loved.[26]

Carr admired the pared-down directness of Fergusson's French and Scottish landscapes, but she was not uncritical of other Fauvist artists. The English painter Harry Phelan Gibb had befriended Carr; she writes of his work:

> Against the distortion of his nudes I felt revolt. Indians distorted both human and animal forms – but they distorted with meaning, for emphasis, and with great sincerity. Here I felt the distortion was often used for design or in an effort to shock rather than convince. Our Indians get down to stark reality.[27]

It is significant that she turned to her First Nation friends when, on her return from France, she was emphatically rejected by the Vancouver Ladies' Art Club and The Fine Arts Society in Vancouver. A Fauvist emphasis on stark outlines and clear design is implicit in her pleasure in First Nation crafts: 'The people were basket-weavers, beautiful, simple-shaped baskets, woven from split cedar roots, very strong, Indian designs veneered over the cedar-root base in brown and black cherry bark.'[28] As she returned to experience the First Nation art of the west coast of Canada after her time in France she was able to recognize its aesthetic cogency, without being able to produce more than a pale imitation of it in her own work. The colonizer attempting to mimic the colonized has an interesting postcolonial resonance, but at this stage, to adapt Homi Bhabha's phrase, it is not even nearly the same, but not quite.

Carr needed a further impetus that came when she was offered the support and recognition of a group of Canadian artists, the Group of Seven, who were interested in finding a form that would adequately represent the Canadian wilderness. Encouraged by them, Carr moved into a confidently Fauvist style that seems to represent a journey into the history of her own country, into its wilderness and into herself, not the quasi-anthropological project of the earlier paintings. She painted a series of pictures that are increasingly claustrophobic, all in densely applied oils; they are inside the landscape which wraps round the viewer, who feels entrapped and dwarfed by the swirling foliage and weather. Often a totem pole appears as a

---

25 Carr, *Growing Pains*, p. 437.
26 Carr, *Growing Pains*, p. 437.
27 Carr, *Growing Pains*, p. 430.
28 Carr, *Growing Pains*, p. 437.

dominant part of the forest, rearing out of it and seeming to root the ephemeral play of light, wind and cloud in its grounded quality. *Big Raven* (1931) is an example of this (Fig. 8.2). The foreigner within the self confronts its own Other in these pictures, and no longer tries to domesticate and tame aspects of the landscape that are terrifying, nor to imitate First Nation art. In Carr's writing and painting, the forest is gendered through its relationship with the wild woman of the woods, for instance in the painting of an inside-house carving, *Zunoqua of the Cat Village* (1931; Fig. 8.3). In this case, Carr's interpretation of what she saw is inaccurate; a First Nations authority, Chief J. J. Wallas, told the curator of the Carr collection at Vancouver Art Gallery that the original housepost figure is male.[29] Carr saw the figure as feminine, as Zunoqua, and painted it in the belief that it was another wild woman of the woods. From a negative perspective, this can certainly be viewed as an exaggerated example of her habitual colonial appropriation of indigenous art. Since 'the Cat Village' is not a geographical location, it can alternatively be interpreted as Carr's image of her own revelatory experience, which sees in First Nation culture attitudes to gender and the landscape that were lacking in the version of Canadian identity to which she was expected to conform. Carr writes in *Klee Wyck:*

> She appeared to be neither wooden nor stationary, but a singing spirit, young and fresh, passing through the jungle. No violence coarsened her; no power domineered to wither her. She was graciously feminine. Across her forehead her creator had fashioned the Sistheutl, or mythical two-headed sea-serpent. One of its heads fell to either shoulder, hiding the stuck-out ears, and framing her face from a central parting on her forehead which seemed to increase its womanliness.
>
> She caught your breath, this D'Sonoqua, alive in the dead bole of the cedar. She summed up the depth and charm of the whole forest, driving away its menace.
>
> I sat down to sketch. What was that noise of purring and rubbing going on about my feet? Cats.[30]

The painting observes the viewer as the cats' eyes look out and are also echoed in shapes in the foliage, which seems to be watching. The power of the figure is its indifference to the viewer as its shadowed eyes look both out to the left, towards something that the viewer cannot see, and inward to whatever makes it, like the sea-serpent on its head, both smile and grimace. Carr's attempts to capture the power of the indigenous carver's image in these paintings are a significant indicator of her own recognition of the colonial process. It is not mimicry, but an effort at attaining the ability to inhabit both the physical forest and the repressed but powerful feminine.

---

[29] Jay Stewart and Peter Macnair, *To the Totem Forests: Emily Carr and Contemporaries Interpret Coastal Villages* (Victoria: Art Gallery of Greater Victoria, 1999), p. 32.
[30] Carr, *Klee Wyck*, p. 44.

8.2 Emily Carr, Big Raven, 1931. Oil on canvas, 87.3 × 114.4 cm. Vancouver Art Gallery, Emily Carr Trust, VAG 42.3.11 (Photo: Trevor Mills).

8.3   Emily Carr, **Zunoqua of the Cat Village, 1931. Oil on canvas, 112.5 × 70.5 cm.
Vancouver Art Gallery, Emily Carr Trust, VAG 42.3.21 (Photo: Trevor Mills).**

Katherine Mansfield and Hinemoa

Mansfield did not live long enough to pass through the stages of artistic development that Carr experienced, and she was never able to return to her native New Zealand after she left it at the age of 20. The publication of all her notebooks and journals in 1997 revealed how persistently her imagination returned to a duality in the self; she constantly reiterates in different experimental fictional forms, and in a specifically colonial context, Kristeva's formulation that we are our own strangers. In an early poem, 'To Stanislaw Wyspiansky', she seems to accept the conventional view of New Zealand as having no history until its colonization by a power with a Grand Narrative of its own significance, but then she immediately undermines that perspective:

> From a little land with no history,
> (Making its own history, slowly and clumsily
> Piecing together this and that, finding the pattern, solving the problem,
> Like a child with a box of bricks),
> I, a woman, with the taint of the pioneer in my blood,
> Full of a youthful strength that wars with itself and is lawless,
> I sing your praises.[31]

The praise of a Polish patriot leads her to examine the complexity of any patriotism that she might feel, as someone who has the *taint* of the pioneer in her blood. The suggestion is that the position of the settler pioneer is compromised, even guilt-ridden, rather than heroic, and that this induces a war within the self.

One of Mansfield's earliest publications explores the question of national identity more fully. When she was 19, and still living in New Zealand, she published a vignette in a Melbourne magazine, *The Native Companion*. It begins by describing the Botanical Gardens in Wellington, which apparently mimic that unmissable destination for colonial travellers who want to return home with the right credentials, Kew Gardens. Having dutifully described the exotic plants that, like those in the shrubbery that Emily Carr grew up with, are 'meek and English' daffodils, forget-me-nots and cowslips, the narrator moves out of the 'new country' into something different:

> And, suddenly, it disappears, all the pretty, carefully-tended surface of gravel and sward and blossom, and there is bush, silent and splendid. On the green moss, on the brown earth, a wide splashing of yellow sunlight. And, everywhere that strange, indefinable scent. As I breathe it, it seems to absorb, to become part of me – and I am old with the age of centuries, strong with the strength of savagery.[32]

---

[31] Katherine Mansfield, *Poems of Katherine Mansfield*, ed. Vincent O' Sullivan (Oxford: Oxford University Press, 1988) p. 30.
[32] Mansfield, *The Notebooks*, vol. 1, p. 171.

The landscape itself is both familiar and foreign, with the irony that it is the foreign that seems most familiar to the speaker. What is alien, however, also becomes part of her, so that paradoxically the young woman becomes old and strong. The Maori are crassly defined as savage by the teenage author, though this is renegotiated in her later writing, and her awareness that colonization comes at a brutal cost to the first inhabitants of the country is pursued in the vignette, hinting at the guilt of being implicated in attempted genocide. As she attempts to become one with the bush she wonders:

> Shall I, looking intently, see vague forms lurking in the shadow staring at me malevolently, wildly, the thief of their birthright? Shall I, down the hillside, through the bush, ever in the shadow, see a great company moving towards me, their faces averted, wreathed with green garlands, passing, passing, following the little stream in silence until it is sucked into the wide sea …
> There is a sudden restless movement, a pressure of trees – they sway against one another … It is like the sound of weeping.[33]

Another western paradigm is implied in 'passing, passing'; social Darwinism proposed that the 'weaker' race and culture would die out or be subsumed by the 'stronger'. However, the indigenous trees and the people weep for what is seen as their own inevitable passing, which by implication kills a part of the speaker who has 'become one with it all'. She returns to the carpet bedding, and the Latin names for the flowers, conscious of loss; the speaker's strength 'wars with itself'. The transformation of the landscape and the displacement of its people are implied by the vignette to be acts of savagery.

A motif that recurs in Mansfield's writing can be seen in connection with the foreigner within. An uncanny doubling of little girls and young women in relation to landscape is reiterated. It occurs, for instance, in an early vignette, written when she was 19 and on a camping trip to the Urewera district of the North Island of New Zealand. She often writes of herself in the third person, and suggests the tension in her between the Europeanized aesthete and the New Zealander:

> Next morning – mist over the whole world. Lying, her arms over her head, she can see faintly like a grey thought the river & the mist – they are hardly distinct. She is not tired now – only happy. Goes to the door of the tent, all is very grey, there is no sun first thing, she can see the poplar tree mirrored in the water. The grass is wet, there is the familiar sound of buckets. As she brushes her hair a wave of cold air strikes her, clamps cold fingers about her heart – it is the wizard London.[34]

The liminal greyness catches her between places, in the bush, but lured by the metropolis. The following evening she imagines a mirror image of herself, also in

---

[33] Mansfield, *The Notebooks*, vol. 1, p. 171.
[34] Mansfield, *The Notebooks*, vol. 1, p. 145.

a grey mist; she watches ('I am alone. I am hidden') as a Maori girl climbs a hill and looks at the lake and the sunset as she herself is doing: 'She is very young. She sits silent, utterly motionless, her head thrown back. All the lines of her face are passionate, violent, crudely savage ... The sky changes, softens, the lake is all grey mist, the land in heavy shadow, silence broods among the trees.'[35] Though the description of the Maori girl reads as Othering, in fact Mansfield's journals at this time are obsessed with anxiety about 'that "improper" facet' of her own 'impossible "own and proper"', her sexual licentiousness, and in particular her lust for a Maori girl, Maata Mahupuku. She writes desperate ungrammatical injunctions to herself in her diaries, such as: 'with a rapidity unimaginable, you are going to the Devil. PULL UP NOW YOURSELF.'[36] The passion, violence and 'crude savagery' are within the self, though she wants to externalize them.

In drafts for stories in her journals these doubles recur, dismantling conventional boundaries between the pakeha and the Maori. In a fragment about Rachael and Tui, Rachael rebels against her violent father, wishing he were dead, but 'that sort of person seemed too real to die'.[37] Her consolation lies in her Maori friend Tui, and in her own grandmother, who is herself under the shadow of settler patriarchy: 'And her thoughts recalled again the image that kept such stern vigil with her – her husband lying in his coffin, with the grey hair brushed off his brow & his face pale & watchful, pressed between the banks of wet clay – and waiting for her.'[38] Tui, the Maori child, wants to live a glamorous life, marry an Englishman and escape New Zealand, whereas Rachael wants to stay where she is and keep bees.

A more significant complete story, which was never published until the notebooks appeared, is 'Summer Idylle', written in 1906. Here the doubling of pakeha and Maori is overt, and linked to a capacity to live with the land and sea. Marina, whose name is a reminder of Pericles' daughter in Shakespeare's play, is a Maori girl, whereas Hinemoa is pakeha, though her name invokes a Maori legend in which a girl swims to an island to join her lover as there are no canoes for her to use. Both names have mythic status within their own cultures, but in Mansfield's story it is Marina who shows her friend how to swim to an island, how to dive and how to read the landscape: 'the fern trees have beautiful green hair...should a warrior venture through the bush in the night they seize him & wrap him round in their hair & in the morning he is dead'.[39] Early as 'Summer Idylle' is in Mansfield's writing career, it plays with essentialist notions of the 'natural':

'Hinemoa eat a koumara [sweet potato].' 'No, I don't like them. They're blue – they're too unnatural. Give me some bread.' Marina handed her a piece, then helped herself

---

[35] Mansfield, *The Notebooks*, vol. 1, p. 148.
[36] Mansfield, *The Notebooks*, vol. 1, p. 111.
[37] Mansfield, *The Notebooks*, vol. 2, p 63.
[38] Mansfield, *The Notebooks*, vol. 1, p. 262.
[39] Mansfield, *The Notebooks*, vol. 1, p. 76.

to a koumara, which she ate delicately, looking at Hinemoa with a strange half-smile expanding over her face. 'I eat it for that reason' she said. 'I eat it because it is blue.' 'Yes.' said Hinemoa, breaking the bread in her white fingers.[40]

Koumaras are naturally blue when they are cooked and bread, homely as it is, does not occur naturally; its Christian symbolism is hinted at in the final line. Marina's apparently transgressive nature, which includes mesmerizing Hinemoa with homoerotic challenges, recognizes that definitions of the 'natural' are cultural constructs. While Hinemoa needs to look in a mirror to re-establish her sense of self, Marina inhabits her land and seascape and takes what it offers without reference to external authority, although she cannot simply be seen as the Maori in the story because of her name. The curious doubling invites the reader to question the essentialism of racial boundaries as terms of empire.

Mansfield moved to London when she was 20; she wanted to find a range of outlets for her stories and, in 1911, sent a story to a new little magazine, *Rhythm*. Its art editor was J. D. Fergusson and its illustrations were mostly Fauvist, by Fergusson, his partner Anne Estelle Rice and their circle. The magazine's Fauvist aesthetic was expressed in an editorial in its first edition: 'it is neo-barbarians, men and women who to the timid and unimaginative seem merely perverse and atavistic, that must familiarize us with our outcast selves'.[41] This resonated with Mansfield's preoccupation with the foreigner within the self; one of the first stories she published in *Rhythm*, 'How Pearl Button was Kidnapped', is the only one that engages directly with pakeha suspicion and fear of the Maori. The subtle manipulation of the narrator's voice keeps the reader in a position of uncertainty, in that the title suggests a stereotypical pakeha fantasy that is undermined by the story itself. The paradigm in which the Others of bourgeois respectability, gypsies, steal children and exploit their parents is signalled in the title, but the reader's experience of the story leads to a different interpretation.

As Pearl swings on her garden gate – always an indicator in Mansfield's fiction of a child who can cross the barriers that adults create for themselves – she sees two women coming towards her. They, unlike the house and street, are associated with strong, elemental colours: 'One was dressed in red and the other was dressed in yellow and green. They had pink handkerchiefs over their heads'.[42] They are not described as Maori, but because they are 'dark women' who 'talked to each other with funny words' they are intriguing to Pearl; the perspective is hers, and she seems

---

[40] Mansfield, *The Notebooks*, vol. 2, p. 77.

[41] *Rhythm*, 1:1 (Summer 1911), p. 3.

[42] Katherine Mansfield, *Katherine Mansfield: Selected Stories*, ed. Angela Smith (Oxford: Oxford University Press, 2002), p. 20. This text uses the version of the stories that appeared in Antony Alpers's 1984 edition of the stories, rather than the more usual Constable version edited by John Middleton Murry, because Alpers's text is more authentic than Murry's edition.

to be about 3, as she can speak, but is very small. The revelatory use of shifting from an adult narrator to an infant's point of view resembles Carr's in *The Book of Small*; Pearl says more than she knows when she tells the women that her mother is 'In the kitching, ironing-because-its-Tuesday.'[43] She is not coerced into accompanying the women; they seem as fascinated by her as she is by them: 'There was a cry from the other women and they crowded close and some of them ran a finger through Pearl's yellow curls, very gently, and one of them, a young one, lifted all Pearl's hair and kissed the back of her little white neck.'[44] Her name indicates the attraction of the Other.

Though she is so small, Pearl worries about her table manners, or in this case floor manners, but her companions laugh rather than scold; their feather mats and tikis make their ethnicity clear to the reader, but not to the seeing eye of the narrative. The physical affection and comfort of one of the big women, who 'breathed, just like purring', are new to Pearl: 'Pearl played with a green ornament [a Maori tiki, or greenstone pendant] round her neck and the woman took the little hand and kissed each of her fingers and then turned it over and kissed the dimples. Pearl had never been happy like this before.'[45] The colourist motif continues, linked only to the Maori and the landscape: 'Pink and red and blue washing hung over the fences and as they came near more people came out and five yellow dogs with long thin tails.'[46] Pearl does not experience this as kidnapping, and the reader shares her view; it is much closer to revelation. This culminates in her first view of the sea, which terrifies her, but for the Maori it is part of their environment that provides both pleasure and food. Two ways of life are juxtaposed when Pearl asks: 'Haven't you got any Houses in Boxes? ... Don't you all live in a row? Don't the men go to offices? Aren't there any nasty things?'[47]

As the women coax her into the sea she experiences a ritual baptism into the elements of her own place, but it comes to an abrupt conclusion when aliens appear and terrify her: 'Little men in blue coats – little blue men came running, running towards her with shouts and whistlings – a crowd of little blue men to carry her back to the House of Boxes.'[48] From the perspective of the story, the kidnapping is clearly the imminent snatching of Pearl by the little blue men and her impending incarceration.

The Maori women in the story have qualities that Emily Carr, who had a particular admiration for Mansfield's fiction, would have recognized. Her comment on sketching for her picture *Totem Mother, Kitwancool*, 1928, is: 'The mothers expressed all womanhood – the big wooden hands holding the child were so

---

[43] Mansfield, *Selected Stories*, p. 20.
[44] Mansfield, *Selected Stories*, p. 21.
[45] Mansfield, *Selected Stories*, p. 22.
[46] Mansfield, *Selected Stories*, p. 22.
[47] Mansfield, *Selected Stories*, p. 22.
[48] Mansfield, *Selected Stories*, p. 23.

full of tenderness they had to be distorted enormously in order to contain it all. Womanhood was strong in Kitwancool.'[49] Both painting and text explore the power that Mansfield evokes through Marina and the Maori women in 'How Pearl Button Was Kidnapped': femininity unconstrained by the gendering processes of patriarchy, those familiar terms of empire. This construction of women provides an implicit comment on an ideology that strove to outlaw and other the foreigner instead of acknowledging, as the image of *Zunoqua of the Cat Village* does, that the self is 'a strange land of borders and othernesses ceaselessly constructed and deconstructed ... The foreigner is within us.'[50]

---

[49] Carr, *Klee Wyck*, p. 80.
[50] Kristeva, *Strangers*, p. 191.

Chapter Nine

Streets, Rooms and Residents: The Urban Uncanny and the Poetics of Space in Harold Pinter, Sam Selvon, Colin MacInnes and George Lamming*

Gail Low

expressions and negotiations of imperialism do not just occur in space. This is a politics of identity and power that articulates itself through space and is fundamentally about space ... These place-based struggles are also the arena in which various coalitions express their sense of self and their desires for the spaces which constitute their 'home' – be it the local neighbourhood or nation, an indigenous home, or one recently adopted.[1]

What I want to do ... quite simply is to try and locate the context in which this arrival of writers from the Caribbean took place in London in the 1950s. Can you imagine waking up one morning and discovering a stranger asleep on the sofa of your living room? You wake this person up and ask them 'What are you doing here?' and the person replies 'I belong here' ... On the one hand, the sleeper on the sofa was absolutely sure through imperial tutelage that he was at home; on the other, the native European was completely mystified by the presence of this unknown interloper.[2]

The waves of migrations from the 'new' Commonwealth that provoked the introduction of the Commonwealth Immigrants Acts of 1962 and 1965 are commonly acknowledged to be a watershed in British history in all sorts of ways. These migrations made the process of postcolonial reckoning more immanent and less abstracted – 'you were there and so we are here' – and represent vital steps towards the making of a modern multicultural nation. This essay considers the social, cultural and symbolic uses space is put to in the narratives of Caribbean post-war migration in Britain. The literal movements of peoples, marked by the

---

* The research for this paper was undertaken with the help of a grant from the Leverhulme Foundation.

[1] Jane Jacobs, *Edge of Empire: Postcolonialism and the City* (London: Routledge, 1996), pp. 1–2.

[2] George Lamming, 'The Coldest Spring in Fifty Years: Thoughts on Sam Selvon and London', *Kunapipi*, 20:1 (1998), p. 4.

arrival of *Empire Windrush* in Tilbury in 1948, challenge us to think through the
problematics of space, identity and collectivities that inform the post-war narratives
of immigration, emigration, home and exile. Their impact is evidenced in recent
concepts of cultural identity, diaspora theory and 'new ethnicities', but the sheer
range and diversity of new writings that have followed in their wake have also
altered the very shape of English studies. Yet the excitement surrounding a more
cosmopolitan awareness of cultural difference should be tempered by a long hard
look at the racialization of immigration that is a product of this period, and an
enduring legacy in contemporary British politics. Racism is depressingly pervasive;
nowhere is this more clearly exhibited than in what Jane Jacobs has termed the
'place-based' battles over the local spaces that designate home, neighbourhood,
city and nation. If imperialism's territorization produced 'homely landscapes ...
evaluated and overlain with desire'[3] out of distant countries within a global map of
Empire, the hysteria over post-war migrations depicted the transformation of home
into a foreign land. George Lamming captures the high drama of this paranoia in his
vision of the uninvited stranger who is found asleep on the living room sofa. This
encroachment, described deliberately as an 'extraordinary predicament' that 'quite
ordinary English people found themselves in', is all the more acute as it is depicted
as taking place within the private and domestic spaces of home and hearth.

Streets

Wendy Webster's timely *Imagining Home: Gender, 'Race' and National Identity*
invites us to think about the social, cultural and political uses to which home is
put.[4] In particular, Webster highlights the importance of domestic landscapes
and explores the domestication of public spaces, such as neighbourhood and
workplace, in figurations of the national imaginary between 1945 and 1964. She
argues that crucial distinctions between white and black communities in media and
sociological literature of the time were made precisely on this terrain. Discourses
of Englishness insisted on the privacy of the national character; its recurrent pattern
of symbolism centred on domestic and familial life. Immigrants, in contrast, were
characterized precisely by their 'domestic barbarism' and 'incapacity for domestic
and familial life'.[5] But the spatial and aesthetic contours of this recurrent landscape
of national belonging, and its inverse – those estranging, yet familiar landscapes
of unbelonging – need further unpacking. In surveying the work of Harold Pinter,
Sam Selvon, Colin MacInnes and George Lamming, I want to show how their

---

[3]   Jacobs, *Edge of Empire*, p. 20.
[4]   Wendy Webster, *Imagining Home: Gender, 'Race' and National Identity, 1945–64*
(London: UCL Press, 1998).
[5]   Webster, *Imagining Home*, p. xii.

social and symbolic inscriptions of space inform, and are informed by, a vision of the 'urban uncanny' that engages with prevailing depictions of post-war migration as a dreaded colonization in reverse. In employing such a term, my aim is not to travel in the direction of a psychoanalytic palimpsest of unconscious desires, but to move towards an understanding of the textual and generic configurations of this construction within a discourse of landscape and space.

I take the term the 'urban uncanny' from the work of Phil Cohen and Anthony Vidler. Vidler's *The Architectural Uncanny* looks at contemporary architecture in the light of the estrangement, alienation and 'uncanny' in modern life.[6] Phil Cohen interrogates representations of the city in contemporary discourses of race and class.[7] Both begin with Freud's depiction of psychological and aesthetic estrangement in his theory of 'das unheimliche', as a particular fear, terror, 'dread and horror' that proceeds from what is (ostensibly) familiar. For Vidler, the 'multiple significations and affiliations' of the word 'unheimlich' allow Freud to describe the unhomely as the 'unconscious product of a family romance' and to ground his theory in the domain of the domestic.[8] Although the uncanny is a state of feeling, 'a mental state of projection' of ambivalent relation and not 'a property of space', Vidler argues for the importance of spaces that have been invested with 'uncanny qualities', inspiring feelings of dread, and of buildings that reflect a quintessentially urban modern estrangement. While the main concern of his monograph lies elsewhere, a supplementary aside calls attention to the necessary interface between aesthetic theories and social and political practices: 'questions of gender and subject might be linked to the continuing discourse of estrangement and the Other in the social and political context of racial, ethnic, and minority exclusion. The resurgent problem of homelessness ... lends, finally, a special urgency to any reflection on the modern unhomely.'[9]

Cohen's engagement with the uncanny is directed at those zones of exclusion and marginalization within the city. His uncanny begins with a walk with Freud's unconscious, his repeated return to a place of dubious repute despite Freud's avowed desire to stage a hurried departure. This scene of uncanny repetition prompts Cohen to ask, 'How does the urban *unheimlich*, with its characteriztic pattern of repeated interruption of social routine ... emerge in the interstices of everyday encounters? ... It directs our attention to a form of the dual city that is not much recognized or talked about.'[10] Cohen's dreamlike city exists as a psychic underbelly of the rational, ordered and visible. These are places where fantasies are textualized and inscribed

---

6   Anthony Vidler, *The Architectural Uncanny: Essays in the Modern Unhomely* (Cambridge, Mass.: MIT Press, 1992).

7   Phil Cohen, 'From the Other Side of the Tracks: Dual Cities, Third Spaces, and the Urban Uncanny in Contemporary Discourses of "Race" and Class', in Gary Bridge and Sophie Watson, eds, *A Companion to the City* (London: Blackwell, 2000).

8   Vidler, *The Architectural Uncanny*, p. 23.

9   Vidler, *The Architectural Uncanny*, p. 12.

10   Cohen, 'From the Other Side', p. 326.

onto public geographical spaces. These fantastical spaces make sense only with the 'aid of a special map whose keys are found in the subject's unconscious' – but this is an unconscious which is constructed not only psychically but also socially. A racist vision of the urban frontline in the London Dockland area affords Cohen an opportunity to address that crucial interface. His respondent's seemingly bizarre representation of black cultures, his social alienation and envy of the new cultures of consumption surrounding the Canary Wharf area are expressed as an uncanny vision of a 'flashy' black paradise across the Thames, and of being a stranger surrounded by zombies, foreigners and blacks. The urban uncanny, argues Cohen, offers a kind of 'symbolic displacement and disavowal', which affords racist discourse an opportunity to 'plunder' the social and cultural imaginary to establish its own strange version of the real.[11] Yet there is a real danger in simply reading aesthetic and rhetorical effects as psychoanalytic symptoms. As Robert Miles has warned in the case of the gothic, such a genre is not 'fantasy in need of psychoanalysis', but a self-conscious artefact with a coherent aesthetic code for representing the fragmented self.[12] Miles's cautions must be borne in mind in our excursions into the urban uncanny; in our brief look at the plethora of post-war social exploration narratives of West Indian immigration, several employ the 'unhomely' home as a symbol of dread. Here one notes how cannily the manipulation and management of space functions as the marker of identity and difference. Two well-known examples make my point succinctly.

Elspeth Huxley's populist *Back Streets, New Worlds* (1964) was published, first, as a newspaper column and then as a book detailing the various minority communities that have settled in Britain.[13] Huxley prefaces the book with the statement that unlike other sociological volumes, hers is written from 'the angle of that mythical creature, the man in the street'.[14] *Back Street, New Worlds* ranges across a variety of ethnicities, including the Irish, Italian, Polish, Jewish, Asian and West Indian communities, but her treatment of Asian and West Indian minorities is typically more animated than that of some of the earlier groups. Her solution to the 'colour problem' is not original: a demand for greater assimilation coupled with a marked reduction of numbers to integrate into the host community. Her depiction of foreigners as imagined pollutant to the hitherto unsullied white spaces of the nation, of course, leaves her with an ideal safety threshold of zero. But it is her tropic siting of these people as bodily and metaphoric aliens that offers us the clearest example of how the uncanny mode works as a spatialized metaphor of unhousing. Chapter titles like 'Blacks Next door', 'How to Buy Houses and Get Tenants Out', 'Coconuts in Ladbroke Grove', 'Poles to Dinner', 'Punjab in Middlesex' remind us that it is

---

[11] Cohen, 'From the Other Side', p. 326.
[12] Robert Miles, *Gothic Writing, 1750–1820: A Genealogy* (London: Routledge, 1993).
[13] Elspeth Huxley, *Back Streets, New Worlds* (London: Chatto & Windus, 1964).
[14] Huxley, *Back Streets*, p. 7.

in their proximity that these strangers turn a very British landscape inside out. Her implied reader and audience is the man in the street, who 'sees an ever increasing number of strange faces of all colours, casts of feature' and encounters 'unfamiliar clothing' and incomprehensible languages in his own back yard.[15] Stark contrasts are made between the domestic customs of the white natives at home and the new West Indian migrants that have recently arrived:

> Other Caribbean domestic habits and customs collide with our own. Most West Indians ... like loud music, noise in general, conviviality, visiting each other, keeping late hours at weekends, dancing and jiving, eating savoury stews and things like yams and cho-cho, frying fish in coconut oil, drinking rum if they can afford it, and generally having a high old time. Most English prefer to keep themselves to themselves and guard their privacy.[16]

Huxley's detailed scrutiny of – and objections to – how migrants live their lives flies in the face of her declaration that the English 'keep themselves to themselves'. Her transformation of race into culture is never far from the surface with her constant reminders about 'English housing standards', 'English needs' and 'English living patterns', which include such observations as houses in 'multiple occupation' are not 'part of our natural habit'. At one crucial point, Huxley admits in exasperation, 'at least the Wessex and the Irish peasants *looked* the same, even if they weren't; you couldn't tell them from their hosts in the street'.[17] Manipulating spatial metaphors into actual territorial battle zones and hostile encounters, Huxley works hard to reinscribe boundaries that have been eroded by the problem of 'a Negro [who] has bought the house next door'.[18] The representation of spaces and borders is consistently domesticized. At one point Huxley remarks, without any trace of irony, 'Ours is a land of the wall, the high fence, the privet hedge ... no other country has such an elaborate network of laws to stop people treading on each others' toes.'[19] West Indian migrants, of course, flout these cherished boundaries by their affinity for 'loud music, noise in general, conviviality', their domestic habits and their messy communal patterns of living. Huxley ends with a telling example of extreme unhousing. She likens the influx of strangers, finally, to a process of massive blood transfusion and asks whether one can describe the patient as being the same person as previously? For, Huxley argues, the body 'cannot absorb the alien blood so quickly'; 'each human body can take [only] so much of someone else's blood and no more'.[20] Not only are the consequences likely to prove fatal, but this literal bodily eviction of the resident transforms him into an alien. Significantly, Huxley's nightmare is

---

15 Huxley, *Back Streets*, p. 7.
16 Huxley, *Back Streets*, p. 46.
17 Huxley, *Back Streets*, pp. 55–6.
18 Huxley, *Back Streets*, p. 7.
19 Huxley, *Back Streets*, p. 47.
20 Huxley, *Back Streets*, p. 154.

the result not of miscegenation per se but of the collapse of the imperial idea that has left Britain a pale shadow of itself. The problems projected onto the presence of the immigrant are but a symptom of a deeper malaise. In a small paragraph on the penultimate page of her book, Huxley concedes:

> Immigrants have created few new problems, they have merely underscored those which already perplex our society. In this case it is a lack of national purpose, of self-confidence, of belief; the malaise of crusaders without a cross and youth without a cause; the end of an imperial purpose that, right or wrong, sustained and magnified us in the nineteenth century, collapsed in the twentieth, and has left us in a vacuum now.[21]

Compared with Huxley, with her imperial apologetics, Sheila Patterson presents an altogether different case.[22] As a social anthropologist, Patterson published academic work on matters of immigration and race relations, and also undertook studies of ethnic minority communities in Britain. Patterson's sociological treatise *Dark Strangers: A Study of West Indians in London*, first published in 1963, is a detailed study of immigrant–host relations over a five year span in Brixton, London.[23] Webster has observed that Patterson's monograph exemplifies the discursive shift in urban sociology from identifying working class within an imperial tropic structure of 'Darkest England' to redrawing that dividing line as one between residents and their dark interlopers.[24] Patterson's more scholarly rhetoric certainly regards immigration and settlement in less hysteric fashion than Huxley's study, but she is also not adverse to employing similar rhetorical and spatial codes to express what she terms the 'colour shock' of her experience of urban excursion in London. She begins her sociological treatise with an anecdote: a journey down a 'fairly typical' main shopping thoroughfare and a turn around a corner into a side street. Like Freud's sudden uneasy arrival in a place of ill repute, she describes herself in this Brixton side street as being 'overcome with a sense of strangeness, almost of shock', despite its normal, 'fairly typical South London' character. What produces the estrangement is that, apart from the few housewives and a group of teddy boys, 'almost everybody in sight had a coloured skin'. Looking around her, Patterson sees 'two dozen black men, mostly in the flimsy suits of exaggerated cut', infants '*café noir* or *café au lait* in colouring' and 'coloured men and women ... shopping, strolling or gossiping on the sunny street-corners with an animation that most Londoners lost long ago'.[25]

---

[21] Huxley, *Back Streets*, p. 162.

[22] For an assessment of Huxley's life and works see Wendy Webster, 'Elspeth Huxley: Gender, Empire and Narratives of the Nation, 1935–64', *Women's History Review*, 8:3 (1999).

[23] Sheila Patterson, *Dark Strangers: A Study of West Indians in London* (London: Penguin, 1965).

[24] Webster, *Imagining Home*, pp. 61–3.

[25] Patterson, *Dark Strangers*, p. 13.

Patterson explains that while such a scene would have been normal in her years in Africa and the West Indies, she did not expect to be confronted with such a 'strange and even out-of-place' picture 'in the heart of South London'. Described as 'a profound reaction to something unexpected and alien', Patterson's 'colour shock', is almost identical in its rhetorical and spatial coordinates to Freud's uncanny.[26] The careful steps by which an ordinary excursion is set up is followed by the deliberate way in which the innocuous *mis-en-scene* of the shopping street is contrasted paradigmatically with the presence of out-of-place, and dark, strangers.

Patterson's study is filled with anecdotes and interviews from white residents and council officers who become the structuring device for the study as a whole. Like her urban explorer/streetwalker, these expectations are normalized as 'our ways'. As Webster observes, a chain of identification operates between explorer, implied reader and white respondents. As a result, the cultural and social behaviour of the West Indian community is rendered uncanny or transgressive. For example, in a report by a Lambeth housing supervisor, West Indian-tenanted houses are characterized by multiple occupancy and the blatant flouting of the private/public divide crucial to the respectable working classes. 'Open doors, its friendly room to room visiting', the noise of music and conviviality, the 'quarrelsome voices from rooms in which gambling, ganja-smoking and drinking goes on' may be enough to drive out all but the elderly, lone 'white statutory tenant'.[27] Not unlike Huxley, 'our ways' evokes an organic, long-standing and essentially private community that has had to bear the consequences of alien settlement:

What, then do these respectable residents expect from their street and their neighbours? They expect a tolerable and at least superficial conformity to 'our ways', a conformity to certain standards of order, cleanliness, quietness, privacy, and propriety. Clean lace curtains are hung at clean windows, dustbins are kept tidy and out of sight, front steps are washed, front halls are like band-boxes, and house fronts are kept neat ... Except for the children, people do not fratenize nosily and for long periods in the street or on doorsteps. They 'keep themselves to themselves' and life is lived quietly within the house, often in front of the television set. Doors are kept shut, and wirelesses or radiograms are played discreetly ... Moral nonconformity is tolerated so long as it is discreet and causes no inconvenience to others. No immigrant group has in the mass so signally failed to conform to these expectations and patterns as have the West Indians.[28]

If Huxley's spectre of imperial decline offers a photographic negative of a glorious and triumphant nation, Harold Pinter's and Colin MacInnes's work puts the urban uncanny to good use by exploiting its ambivalences and turning the tables on the host culture. Both MacInnes and Pinter present a vision of white Britain that is hollow and empty of

---

[26] Patterson, *Dark Strangers*, p. 14.
[27] Patterson, *Dark Strangers*, p. 167.
[28] Patterson, *Dark Strangers*, p. 179.

life; Pinter, in particular, also shows how much dread and fear can be equally applied to both sides of the urban divide. But MacInnes might seem the better backdrop by which to start our explorations. MacInnes, a novelist and critic of some distinction in the 1950s and 1960s, is notable for being one of the very few 'English' post-war writers to deal with new black and youth subcultures in London. *City of Spades* oscillates, albeit somewhat mechanically, between the first person voices of the Nigerian student Johnny Fortune and Montgomery Pew, the English welfare officer.[29] They strike up a friendship that leads Montgomery into places he has never encountered. In a scene close to the beginning of the novel, the Englishman describes his journey as one into a subterranean world. This underworld is barely visible to the ordinary inhabitants of daytime London: 'It was the hour at which all honest Londoners have hurried to their beds and wisdom, and when the night owls, brave spirits in this nightless city emerge to gather in the suspect cellars that nourish the resistance movement to the day.'[30] At this point, Johnny turns to Montgomery and asks, 'Would you like to come in … where you've never set foot before, even though it's always existed underneath your nose?' What Montgomery is introduced to is the overlapping bohemian, seedy and criminal underworlds of pimps, prostitutes, bars, nightclubs, theatrical ventures, aesthetes and sexual shenanigans at 'dirty' parties with wealthy clients. Montgomery is but a sightseer in this 'city of spades', but he is also a figure that envies and craves what he thinks these 'spades' represent: 'They were wonderful, of course – exhilarating: the temperature of your life shot up when in their company. But if you stole some of their physical vitality, you found that the price was they began to invade your soul: or rather they did not, but your own idea of them did.'[31] After inviting two young black American dancers into his home, he finds his flat so transformed by their bonhomie and abandonment that he describes himself as being 'the interloper' in his own dwelling. To return to normality is to return to a drab and cloistered existence; but the novel ends with just such a separation of worlds. For Montgomery is a tourist rather than an inhabitant of this realism; just as Montgomery's homosexuality is plain for all to see, he himself remains an oddly chaste observer of his own desires.

In MacInnes's *Absolute Beginners* one finds an 'End of Empire' novel, with youth characteristically rebelling against the establishment and its values.[32] Like Jimmy Porter in *Look Back in Anger*, the novel's unnamed narrator pokes fun at the imperial aspirations of the elders. He remarks caustically to one of his wealthier clients, 'If they'd [the British] stick to their housekeeping, which is the only backyard they can move freely in to any purpose, and stopped playing Winston Churchill and the Great Armada when there's no tin soldiers left to play with any more, then no one would despise them because no one would even notice.'[33] MacInnes's hero

[29] Colin MacInnes, *City of Spades* (London: Allison, 1980).
[30] MacInnes, *City of Spades*, p. 64.
[31] MacInnes, *City of Spades*, pp. 152–3.
[32] Colin MacInnes, *Absolute Beginners* (London: Allison, 1980).
[33] MacInnes, *Absolute Beginners*, p. 25.

has very little time for both the power and parlour games adults play. The urban landscape of London with its class affiliations, local communities and leisure outlets is intimately detailed. Unlike the previous generation who have petrified within their class, MacInnes's 18-year-old narrator's physical mobility across the spaces of his city matches his ability to move between classes and groups: 'you're a teenage creation – if you have loot, and can look after yourself, they treat you as a man, which is what you are'.[34] However, in a novel that is acutely aware of the changing face of London, and conscious of the spatial dimensions of those class and racial affiliations, two scenes stand out in particular. In the first one, early in the novel, the narrator describes walking down Buckingham Palace Road towards Victoria coach station, where he sees different crowds of people milling at the terminals. His disavowal of his links with the new consumerism of the upwardly mobile middle classes with their 'mohair and line suits, white air-liner vanity bags, dark sun-spectacles and pages of tickets packed to paradise' is equalled by his distaste for the lower middle classes, 'shuffling along with their front-parlour curtain dresses and cut-price tweeds and plastic mackintoshes, all flat feet and fair shares and you-in-your-small-corner-and-I-in-mine' and the 'troop of toy tin soldiers'.[35] This crowd scene becomes the occasion of yet another complaint about the dreariness and lifelessness of Britain. However, immediately following his lamentations, we are taken to a park behind the coach station where we catch a glimpse of a West Indian gardener at work. MacInnes's narrator remarks on the problems of over-exuberant children at play, 'little horrors' who will in future capture 'the Bank of England and Buckingham Palace and the BBC'.[36] He also observes the easy charm with which the gardener engages with the adults and children who use the park, and remarks, with some surprise, 'in fact, this coloured character struck me as so bloody civilized'.[37] This early scene is worth remarking upon because it represents a strategic inversion of the more racist representation of race relations in the period; the passage takes place against the backdrop of a running commentary on the bankruptcy, emptiness and banality of a post-war Britain where the only signs of real life are to be found amongst the minority and youth subcultures of the city.

Yet the novel is mindful of what must, at times, seem like a romantic sentimentalism. It is an awareness that moves the novel towards its grim closing portrayal of the Notting Hill riots of 1958 and the fracturing of any easy alliance between white and black, and white and white. MacInnes's depiction of the riots is curiously restrained, and most of the action happens off-stage. What we do see falls mostly into one of two camps: the slow and eerie build up to the violent confrontations and then the after-effects of violence. This obliqueness is crucial in generating narrative tension and a feeling of dread as the narrator moves through

---

[34] MacInnes, *Absolute Beginners*, p. 48.
[35] MacInnes, *Absolute Beginners*, p. 44.
[36] MacInnes, *Absolute Beginners*, p. 45.
[37] MacInnes, *Absolute Beginners*, p. 45.

the landscape. Like Patterson's description of the 'colour shock', the journey through the street where the narrator lives is carefully handled for its evocation of the 'unhomely' home. MacInnes's narrator observes the usual Teddy boys outside their houses, the motorbikes and the delivery vans, girls and small children, but also notes that for each of these groupings something was out of kilter. If the street was 'quiet and ordinary', turning a corner brought one 'back once more in a part where the whole of Napoli seemed like it was *muttering*'.[38] The teenager's anxiety is heightened by the seeming calm of a place not quite right, and he equates this eerie silence to that of some kind of 'hole' that has allowed life to drain out of it, 'leaving a vacuum in the streets and terraces'. Significantly, the most unsettling aspect for the narrator is that 'as you looked around, you could see the people hadn't yet noticed the alteration, even though it was so startling to you'.[39] But it is precisely this lack of involvement that finally renders the urban rioting an uncanny experience. The narrator expresses a profound shock at the 'incredible' way in which English people 'just stood by, out of harm's way, these English people did, and *watched*. Just like at home at evening with their Ovaltine and slippers, at the telly.'[40] His attempts to round up support for the besieged black inhabitants of the city are met mostly with indifference. His friend and mentor Wizard is turned into a White Protection League 'zombie'. No more best friend and mentor, Wizard is now dangerous, body 'all clenched, and something … staring through his eyes that came from God knows where'.[41] If the novel ends on a hopelessly upbeat note, with MacInnes's narrator embracing more newly arrived 'spades' at the airport, the question of what kind of England and 'home' the nation will be for its new immigrants when its own 'natives' condone racial violence is allowed to hang in the air.

Rooms

Alan Sinfield's wide-ranging cultural history of the post-war period, *Literature, Politics and Culture in Postwar Britain*, observes of the playwright Harold Pinter that territory (and its defence) is the key to his early plays. Sinfield argues that in plays like *The Room*, *The Caretaker*, *A Slight Ache* and *The Dwarfs* characters 'fence aggressively for the possession of the room, the security of their boundaries'.[42] Pinter's early works are not often critiqued and examined for their topical or sociological references. Yet when read alongside the representation of West Indian migration, *The Room* and *The Caretaker* take up where MacInnes left off, by

---

[38] MacInnes, *Absolute Beginners*, p. 174.
[39] MacInnes, *Absolute Beginners*, p. 174.
[40] MacInnes, *Absolute Beginners*, p. 177.
[41] MacInnes, *Absolute Beginners*, p. 191.
[42] Alan Sinfield, *Literature, Politics and Culture in Postwar Britain* (London: Athlone, 1997), p. 144.

exploring the delineation of this new unhomely England.[43] In *The Room*, especially, we see a concerted attempt to address how race impacts on home, hearth and the discourses of the nation. Set in an unspecified urban area, the play centres on a couple, Rose and Bert Hudd. They rent a bedsit from a Mr Kidd who owns a large, if somewhat dilapidated, house. In the course of the play, the house's other inhabitants (or potential inhabitants) are introduced: Mr and Mrs Sands, another couple who are looking for a room to rent, and Riley, a black man who lives in the basement. The Sands seem to be lurking in the dark stairwell and Rose bumps into them outside her room. Once invited into her household, however, the couple behave as interlopers and remark repeatedly that they have been told that the Hudds's room is vacant, or about to be so. Such remarks generate an almost disproportionate fear on Rose's part. The audience is thus made to realize that Rose appears to be living under a cloud of generalized insecurity about her home. Her insecurity is evident in later scenes where she is seen to question her landlord again and again about his intentions: 'There were two people in here now. They said this room was going vacant. What were they talking about...? What was it all about? Did you see those people? How can this room be going? It's occupied. Did they get hold of you, Mr Kidd?'[44]

Mr Kidd's memories of the room when it was his add to the general sense that possession is not nine-tenths of the law. Simple occupancy of the room does not amount to much and is neither assured nor secure: Rose's present room was once someone else's home in the past, and may be some stranger's residence in the future. Earlier in the play, Rose is seen to contrast the security and comfort of her own dwelling with other damp and dark rooms in the house. Yet even these protestations of contentment are accompanied by anxious, repetitive references to unwelcomed others who may be sheltering in her building: 'Who is it? Who lives down there? I'll have to ask. I mean, you might as well know, Bert. But whoever it is, it can't be too cosy ... I wouldn't like to live in that basement.' Rose's dialogue exhibits a pathological obsession about who might be living in such dilapidated rooms:

> Did you ever see the walls? They were running. This is all right for me ... No this room's all right for me. I mean, you know where you are. When it's cold, for instance ... If they ever ask you Bert, I'm quite happy where I am. We're quiet, we're all right.[45]

Her speculation about people in such undesirable basements ends predictably: 'Maybe they're foreigners.' Indeed, Riley's appearance towards the end of the play simply confirms these fears, and Rose's response to his presence shows how the spaces of home and hearth have become racialized. Rose's xenophobic and racist

---

[43] Harold Pinter, *The Caretaker* (London: Methuen, 1978) and *The Room and the Dumb Waiter* (London: Methuen, 1979). I am indebted to Jon Cook for suggesting that I look at Harold Pinter's work.

[44] Pinter, *The Room*, p. 25.

[45] Pinter, *The Room*, pp. 8–9.

remarks are typical as she berates Riley with wild assertions about 'people like you' or 'creeps' who trespass on her territory, 'smelling up' her room. Riley is verbally harangued, accused of disturbing her evening and 'taking liberties'; he is accused of having 'barged in' and sat down uninvited, even when it was Rose who agreed to see him and who asked him to take a seat. While Riley's insistence that he has a message from her father is unnerving in the face of her repeated denials, his blindness and powerlessness negate her representation of Riley as a dangerous menace. That Riley brings to mind the more Irish-sounding name O'Reilly only calls attention to those racist boarding-house placards of the period that announced, 'No dogs, No Irish, No Blacks'. He is, of course, violently beaten up by Bert at the end of the play.

Pinter's depiction of the anxieties over housing and the proximity of strangers in one's homeland is rendered with some subtlety. Rose's repetitive speculations about the inhabitants of the basement are expressed when she is preoccupied with ordinary domestic rituals like cooking or cleaning. As a result, activities like brewing and serving tea, fussing over the strength of the 'cuppa', cooking bacon and eggs, and the smoothing of the net curtains are transformed into a ritualized marking of territory. If Webster has argued that the emblems of Englishness are strategically and defensively domesticized in this period, Pinter's plays turn them into a surreal piece of theatre, for these rituals are intimately bound up with a gendered construction of racialized boundaries of the nation. Ensconced in the protectiveness of her room, Rose comments, 'this room's all right for me. I mean, you know where you are … You can come home at night, if you go out, you can do your job, you can come home, you're all right.'[46] But Rose's remarks beg the question of a room 'where you [don't] know where you are', a home that you cannot return to and a place where you have no job. Despite the play's refusal to contextualize Rose's story, *The Room* calls out to be read as a political allegory of Britain at the end of empire.

I now want to turn my attention to West Indian narratives of post-war settlement by considering Sam Selvon's *The Lonely Londoners* (1956) and George Lamming's *The Emigrants* (1954).[47] Selvon and Lamming share common themes and preoccupations. Both address the cultural shock and alienation of Caribbean settlers and their strategies of survival within a hostile landscape. Both texts are, also, pre-eminently urban texts with a canny eye for how spatialized structures might be made to signify in textual form. Indeed, they cannot help but do so, given the context and language of immigration in this period. Not unlike Paul Gilroy, both writers have a sense of how space can be narrativized into something akin to a poetics of Caribbean identity. And both reveal (ironically) the formation and consolidation (more hope than consolidation in Lamming's case) of a pan-Caribbean West Indian identity in the metropolitan spaces of London itself. If Selvon's text has a much greater sense of the romance of London's public face – its icons, monuments

---

[46] Pinter, *The Room*, p. 11.

[47] Sam Selvon, *The Lonely Londoners* (London: Longman, 1994) and George Lamming, *The Emigrants* (Ann Arbor, Mich.: University of Michigan Press, 1994).

and glamorous thoroughfares – then Lamming's offers us a bleaker, claustrophobic and less visible account of a settler's London of hidden basement rooms and private housing. Indeed, at the close of *The Emigrants* these become a symbol of the deteriorating landscapes of the mind, and of how much colonialism and its legacy have persisted into the post-independence era. While not the main concern of this essay, both of these novels of migration should be read together, and against each other, as different accounts of how the process of migration is not simply a journey through space (the ship), an encounter with place (the city, the room), but also an exploration of how the language of space impacts on the very construction of identity and home (the resident).

Selvon's *The Lonely Londoners* humanizes the story of the Windrush migration away from the stark portraits that appear in the studies of black communities offered by Huxley or Patterson. Various readings of the novel have added to a rich body of criticism on Selvon. Ken Ramchand argues that the novel represents a journey from innocence to experience; it contrasts the excitement and buzz of being in a big city with the sense of alienation, stasis and entrapment that life in a big city – with poor wages and prospects – brings with it.[48] Susheila Nasta addresses the textuality of London city itself, in what she terms a 'romance of place-names' and a gradual creolization of the literary and social landscape.[49] More recently, James Procter remarks that Selvon portrays a diachronic narrative of adventure and mobility against a synchronic spatial topography of settlement and, crucially, of circularity and entrapment.[50] What I want to highlight in my own account of Selvon is the manner in which he signifies the urban uncanny as an explanation for the very act of narration itself.

Selvon's London is a place made up of small rooms and separate enclaves; London is 'divide up in little worlds, and you staying in the world you belong to and you don't know anything about what happening in the other ones except what you read in the papers'.[51] West Indian settlement in the cheap ghetto housing areas of London, multiple occupancy of deteriorating Victorian mansions subdivided into cramped rooms, dormitories in hostels and lodging houses that function as reception hostels for migrants are where Selvon's characters are mostly to be found. In *The Lonely Londoners*, these rooms function as the temporary and tentative spaces of community and communal feeling. Far from simply signifying a culture of fear and estrangement, the rooms of *Lonely Londoners* also offer human-interest stories. Gatherings in rooms offer some reprieve from the hostile world outside. More

---

[48] Ken Ramchand, 'The Lonely Londoners as a Literary Work', *World Literature Written in English* (Autumn 1982).

[49] Susheila Nasta, 'Setting up Home in a City of Words: Sam Selvon's London Novels', *Kunapipi* 18:1 (1991).

[50] James Procter, 'Descending the Stairwell: Dwelling Places and Doorways in Early Post-War Black British Writing', *Kunapipi*, 20:1 (1998).

[51] Selvon, *Londoners*, p. 74.

importantly, they literally enable an exchange of voices and stories. By so doing, rooms become the sites of identification occupied by various members of the group; these may be transitory and shifting, more temporary than the actualized spaces of home and settlement, but no less important for being so. Selvon's use of the second person interpellative invites the reader to share in that circle of stories. His use of nicknames for characters (who are raconteurs) and his steady focus on the comic aspect of their adventures create the illusion of an inclusive cultural community bound by gossip and intimate knowledge of each others' lives.[52] Structurally presided over by Moses, who acts as facilitator and social worker, the disparate stories enable the emergence of a narratorial and writerly space. Moses is a naive philosopher and also a writer in the making. It is his vision that holds the West Indian communities together in the long unpunctuated stream-of-consciousness segment of the closing section of the book. Much like Tireseas in Eliot's *The Waste Land*, Moses sees 'the black faces bobbing up and down in the millions of white, strained faces, everybody hustling along the Strand, the spades jostling in the crowd, bewildered and hopeless', and it is this vision that prompts him 'to wonder if he could ever write a book like that'.[53] The writer's alienation from the city, paradoxically sparking the beginnings of his writing and kinship with the city, has had a long and illustrious literary history.[54] Selvon should be read as coming out of this literary tradition: his vision of urban alienation is not only the subject matter of his writing but what enables the act itself. His version of an urban poetics is ultimately what enables his psychic and spiritual survival in London and is perhaps the only area of his life over which he can exercise control. For as the narrator of another of Selvon's short stories remarks, 'Each return to the city is loaded with thought … I move around in a world of words. Everything that happens is words.'[55]

Residents

If Selvon's London threads a fine line between romance and its disillusionment, Lamming's *Emigrants* offers a much bleaker vision of the metropolitan uncanny

---

[52] One sees how Selvon's novel might prefigure the conceptual terrain that Stuart Hall would later occupy: Stuart Hall, 'Cultural Identity and Diaspora', in Laura Chrisman and Patrick Williams eds, *Colonial Discourse and Post-Colonial Theory: A Reader* (Hemel Hempstead: Harvester, 1993). Hall theorizes identity as a position produced through the processes of identification that are offered in narratives and argues that Caribbean identities are necessarily hybrid and diasporic.

[53] Selvon, *Londoners*, p. 140.

[54] See, for example, Raymond Williams, *The Country and the City* (London: Hogarth, 1985).

[55] Sam Selvon, 'My Girl and the City', in *Ways of Sunlight* (London: MacGibbon and Kee, 1957), p. 188.

as colonialism's reproduction of hollow and estranged men. *The Emigrants* has a tripartite structure: the journey/arrival, settlement and the stocktaking of the future, two years down the line. The first section of the novel, entitled 'A Voyage', deals with the journey, from island to island and then to England, as well as the relationships that form in that passage of time. Its use of the ship is literal and figurative, or tropic. It not only indicates the physical journey on board the vessel, the friendship and communal links the emigrants form on board, but is also suggestive of how such a travelling space allows us to think of the history and legacy of slavery, a poetics of Caribbean identity crossing national boundaries (implicating both the Caribbean and Britain in a shared history) and memory (the kinds of identifications we forge with narratives of the past). As Gilroy argues, ships are 'mobile elements that stood for the shifting spaces in-between the fixed places that they connected'.[56] And it is on the ship that one encounters the most meditative and utopic sections of the novel – dramatic exchanges that look forward in time to the future and the connections that they may engender. In fact, the ship does the same kind of tropic work as Selvon's rooms. These offer a necessary space for the exchange of voices and stories and function as vital points of identification necessary for collective vision.

But the idealism connected to the ship's journeying rapidly gives way to the insecurity, disillusionment and alienation of arrival and settlement in London. The storm that greets the docking of the ship at Tilbury presages the violence and darkness that threatens to reduce these men to literally 'no-THING'. Higgins, a passenger on the ship whose confidence is all but destroyed by the knowledge of the sudden closure of the school for which he intends to enrol, is suddenly confronted by an existential abyss outside the security of the ship: 'Beyond their enclosure was no-Thing. Nothing mattered outside the cage, because there was no-Thing … It was unnatural and impossible to escape into something that didn't matter. Absolutely impossible, for within the cage where they were born and would die … Only where things mattered could they breathe, and suffer.'[57] For what prompts the West Indians' flight from the Caribbean islands has not gone away; the metaphor of the cage continues the earlier meditations on freedom and political independence in the Caribbean. The novel's bleak vision seems to suggest that, despite independence, culture and society is stagnant in the islands; everyone simply waits, 'sure that something would happen'. As Lamming says categorically elsewhere, 'the colonial structure' of the Caribbean 'has not been touched' in these post-war years.[58]

If the ship and the journey inscribe a traffic between periphery and centre that is characteristic of postcolonial and diasporic relations, arrival in Britain signals the abrupt termination of the mobility. As Procter notes, given the concerns of the period, the tropic trajectory is not towards the ship (diaspora), but towards the

---

[56] Paul Gilroy, *The Black Atlantic* (London: Verso, 1993), p. 16.

[57] George Lamming, *The Emigrants*, p. 105.

[58] George Lamming, *The Pleasures of Exile* (London: Michael Joseph, 1960), p. 47.

dwelling place (settlement).[59] And it is in the middle section of the novel, entitled 'Rooms and Residents', that we enter the territory of the urban uncanny, whether they be basement rooms, Fred Hill's barber shop, the obscure and secret location of Miss Dorking's hairdressing shop or the interiors of the hostel for immigrants and students. The world detailed in this, by far the longest section of the novel, is an underground London that little resembles its normal lineaments and remains invisible to the uninitiated. Lamming's novel offers very little sense of the outside world; with the exception of two short sequences, all the action takes place in confined and enclosed spaces. Hill's barber shop is located down a dark stairwell, 'the wounded face of a rock … dingy and damp, a hole which had lost its way in the earth; and … [where men] put their hands out along the wall and over the floor like crabs clawing for security'.[60] Miss Dorking's shop is also underground and at the end of a dark corridor; her basement rooms are situated between houses 'which came up like a wall between two foreign territories'. Hill's basement shop has only one narrow window and is 'railed perpendicularly with bars of iron', the door shut tight and the barber described as brandishing his scissors like 'a weapon in defence against some enemy'.[61]

Like Selvon's rooms, some of these spaces are bolt-holes as well as fortresses, providing security, support and respite from the world above. If Hill's barber shop is literally underground, the warmth of his shop contrasts with its surroundings. Similarly Miss Dorking's hairdressing salon is described as womb-like. The hostel promotes solidarity between its residents, and Tornado and Lillian's room, despite its run-down state, functions as a communal space. These spaces of the West Indian community are portrayed as subterranean and neglected by the outside world. The exclusive nature of these West Indian enclaves are evident from the way knowledge of their location is jealously guarded and only passed between friends. Outsiders are greeted with suspicion and white characters, like the policeman and Fredrick, are met with hostility. Battlelines between communities are drawn because of the racist animosity that greeted the migrants' arrival and settlement in Britain.

Rooms are purposely contrasted with houses in Lamming; the Pearsons' residence contains all the comforts of life, and Mr Pearson's power and wealth is confirmed by the way objects in his household become extensions of his self. His house is also envied by Collis, who describes it as a 'womb', as opposed to the 'rudimentary shelter' of his rooms in the hostel. Hence, despite their purpose as a place of refuge, Tornado and Lillian's bedsits and rooms are also depicted as a kind of prison:

> But this room was different. Its immediacy forced them to see that each [person] was caught in it. There was no escape from it until the morning came with its uncertain offer of

---

[59] Procter, 'Descending the Stairwell', p. 22.
[60] Lamming, *The Emigrants*, p. 129.
[61] Lamming, *The Emigrants*, p. 136.

another day's work. Alone, circumscribed by the night and the neutral staring walls, each felt himself pushed to the limits of his thinking. All life became an immediate situation from which action was the only escape.[62]

The difference between these rooms that Lamming describes and the rooms of the *Lonely Londoners* is that the exchange of stories and narratives within these spaces offer few points of identification that allow for the development of the community. Unlike the ship, exchanges in rooms are altogether more fragmented and disjointed. They express a desire to comprehend the experience, yet more often reflect bewilderment and lack of comprehension. Unlike the characters of *The Lonely Londoners*, who trade stories to generate laughter, knowledge and solidarity, Lamming's characters are often in the dark as to what others are doing and why. This is deliberately and forcefully implied by his choice of narration. For Lamming narrates against expectation and often surprises the reader with a character's actions (Lillian and the Governor's affair, Queenie's affair, and her relationship with Peggy and Una); he neither provides us with enough context to frame these unexpected actions nor full knowledge of the sequence of events. For example, it is only in the final section of the novel that we are able to reconstruct what troubles Dickson, why he slowly loses his sanity. It is only, in these closing pages, that we are able to place Fredrick as Una's former fiancé. Such a deliberate strategy has led some critics to call it a tactic of 'deferred disclosure'.[63]

Throughout the novel, in the narrative sabotage of time and progression, we are only ever offered partial knowledge, never a synoptic overview that would enable us to fit all the bits of the puzzle together. As a result, narratives and stories exhibit the very alienation of their characters. Under growing mental strain, for instance, Collis is bewildered about his inability to see people as anything but objects: 'I see faces without their attributes ... your face now, right now, might be just an object without any of the usual attributes.'[64] Collis's mental illness is prefigured in a curiously early passage by an extra-diegetic narrator who speculates that the sleeping sunbathers on board the deck might, due to an accident of light and perception, be taken for dead bodies: 'Would it matter if they didn't wake. The fact of their sleep seemed a reflection of the accident which would have been their failure to awake.'[65] This literal reduction of people to things is exemplified in Dickson's treatment as an exotic body for display, by Miss Bis's promiscuity and by Mr Pearson's treatment of Collis. Despite an initial façade of geniality, 'Collis understood that he did not then exist for Mr Pearson, and he understood that Mr Pearson didn't exist for himself. He was a fixed occasion, harmless as death until some urgency like the telephone call

---

[62] Lamming, *The Emigrants*, p. 192.

[63] See, for example, Nair Supriya, *Caliban's Curse* (Ann Arbor, Mich.: University of Michigan Press, 1996), for an exploration of Lamming's aesthetics.

[64] Lamming, *The Emigrants*, p. 275.

[65] Lamming, *The Emigrants*, p. 84.

informed it with danger.'[66] In this complete separation of worlds it is unsurprising that the West Indian experience remains invisible and subterranean.

Lamming's urban uncanny is more properly an extension of the effects of colonialism on an occupied culture, and offers an unrelentingly darker vision than Selvon's. Yet behind the kiff-kiff laughter and solidarity of Moses' rooms, the pathos of the migrants' situations are never far behind. Even in these rooms the sense of emptiness and aimlessness is never far away. The rooms simply punctuate the endless cycle of work and despair, but never provide a real home. The typographical metaphor of rooms, rather than houses, is apt; for houses connote security and solidity of habitation – witness their ironic (mis)use in Naipaul's work. Rooms, on the other hand, at least of the kind suggested by the habitations of Selvon's and Lamming's texts, connote a separation, an atomistic singularity and temporality of enclosure which might find completion only if set within the larger whole of a house. The novel opens into a brief glimpse of a street in the third section of *The Emigrants*, but ends, not with bedsits and basement rooms, but with the dance club jointly owned and managed by Azi, an African, and Governor, a West Indian we met earlier on the boat. The club is the scene of a tragic abortion, and the denial of the utopic vision of the ship's passage. The 'Strange Man' who appears at the club to remind Governor of his earlier, gentler idealism is rebuffed with some harsh words reminding him of the commercial functions of a nightclub. In the closing lines of this final section of the novel, Collis sits at a window 'watching the night slip by between the light and the trees'. This closing passage is identical to an earlier one where Collis (or an unnamed first person narrator) also sits at a window contemplating his future, believing that 'something would bound to happen'. Of course, very little happens during the course of the novel that is of positive, lasting value.

The world of bedsits and basement rooms expresses a desire and yearning to belong, which must be located in the wider history of black British rights, to render, finally, the unhomely home. In this brief journey through some narratives of migration, the textual and spatial matrix of the urban uncanny provides a quite startling and recurrent pattern as one of the privileged sites for expressing the anxieties of black/white encounters in post-war Britain.

---

[66] Lamming, *The Emigrants*, p. 142.

Chapter Ten

The Landscape of Insurgency: Mau Mau, Ngugi wa Thiong'o and Gender

Brendon Nicholls

There is a tendency to think of colonial discourse and its language of stereotype as instilling a monolithic system of power and perception that buttresses the imperialist project. But in the Kenyan Mau Mau Emergency (1952–60) we witness the full onslaught of colonial stereotype and racist iconography being brought to bear on a thing that did not exist, in order to conceptualize it in terms that did not apply, and to meet it with a brutality as overwhelmingly disproportionate as it was misdirected.[1] In an expanded definition, 'Mau Mau' – as settler fantasy, as colonial discourse or imperial military strategy – is only readable in terms of exaggeration or distortion, excess or oversight. The severity of the settlers' response to a threat that they themselves had largely *manufactured* ultimately rendered not only their counter-insurgency tactics but also the entire apparatus of Kenyan colonial rule utterly indefensible. Hence, far from shoring up white control of Kenya, or disciplining its unruly antagonists, the colonial discourses that produced 'Mau Mau' as an object of knowledge became hindrances in the war on the insurgents and ultimately proved fatal to the imperialist project in its Kenyan manifestation. In the Mau Mau period, British colonialism in Kenya was finally subdued by its own neurotic excesses.

Militarily, Mau Mau failed. Psychologically, Mau Mau was an incontestable force that continues to occupy an unsettling or disturbing place in the European and white African imagination. Significantly, the term 'Mau Mau' was a chimera, a pure figment of the settler imagination. Constituted by and existing only within colonial discourse,[2] 'Mau Mau' can not credibly be made to fit into the Gikuyu linguistic code. Indeed, the insurgents never called themselves 'Mau Mau'.[3] Hence, all attempts to

---

[1] Despite popular myth and colonial propaganda to the contrary, Mau Mau killed a mere 32 European civilians. The Emergency death toll for Gikuyu civilians may well be in excess of 1000 times that figure.

[2] David Maughan-Brown, *Land, Freedom and Fiction: History and Ideology in Kenya* (London: Zed, 1985), p. 260.

[3] For a list of some of the names used by the insurgents themselves, see Donald Barnett and Karari Njama, *Mau Mau from Within: An Analysis of Kenya's Peasant Revolt* (New York: Monthly Review Press, 1970), pp. 54–5.

translate or define 'Mau Mau' – and there have been many – are destined to fail. 'Mau Mau' refers to an intransigent absence since the term is symbolically indeterminate. It is remarkable that so many of the received etymologies of the term rely upon notions of linguistic slippage, in which 'Mau Mau' was a product of letter transposition, a settler misprision of Gikuyu onomatopoeia, an Anglicization of the Gikuyu for oath ('muma'), a Maasai's mispronunciation of 'muma', a Gikuyu term for non-specific objects (a 'thingamajig'), a Swahili acronym, an English acronym reversed, an allusion to Chairman Mao, a name derived from the Mau Forest in the Maasai region or a transcription of the last cries of a sacred wild cat killed by an unthinking white farmer.[4] This linguistic slippage, this referential vertigo, meant that it was impossible for the Kenyan settler to speak of 'Mau Mau' from a position of any authority. Every one of his attempts to master Mau Mau in discourse gave way to, or even instilled, the authority and mastery of the Other.[5] In 'Mau Mau', the settler became 'unsettled', and his relationship to place, space and landscape entered a phase of crisis.

Losing Ground

In response to Mau Mau's destabilization of the colonizer's relationship to colonial space, the British military introduced a programme aimed at the complete *re-ordering* of African space. The colonizer's production of the Kenyan landscape during the Emergency period evidences an attempt to isolate Mau Mau in the landscape, to contain it within certain boundaries or beyond impermeable barriers

---

[4]   The etymologies of 'Mau Mau' are listed by Carol Sicherman, *Ngugi wa Thiong'o: The Making of a Rebel* (London: Hans Zell, 1990), pp. 214–15; Robert Edgerton, *Mau Mau: An African Crucible* (New York: Ballantine, 1989), pp. 56–7; Credo Mutwa, *My People: The Writings of a Zulu Witchdoctor* (London: Penguin, 1977), p. 175; and Barnett and Njama, *Mau Mau from Within*, pp. 53–4.

[5]   Leading on from this point, the etymologies ascribed uncritically to 'Mau Mau' in historical accounts point towards the efforts of both colonial and African historians to appropriate the term for either the colonial or the Gikuyu nationalist constructions of the insurgency. These historians attempt to produce the Mau Mau insurgent as a homogeneous historical subject. As such, the Kenyan Land and Freedom Army, with its heterogeneous – and at times, divided or discontinuous – membership, aims and strategies, is almost invariably recuperated in terms of a colonial or nationalist narrative. The proper name, 'Mau Mau', is a site of contested desires and interests in the colonial social matrix. In addition, it is a term whose paleonomy – which Gayatri Spivak glosses as 'the charge which words carry on their shoulders', in Sarah Harasym, *The Post-Colonial Critic: Interviews, Strategies, Dialogues* (New York: Routledge, 1990), p. 25 – overwhelmingly locates and narrates the historian who uses it. In this essay, I have opted to retain the term 'Mau Mau', because I am overtly engaged with its discursive dimensions, but also because I believe that the insurgents themselves are better represented via a conscious misnomer ('Mau Mau') than an appropriated silence ('the Kenyan Land and Freedom Army').

– to define its dimensions in discourse, to locate it within spatial parameters and to thereby eliminate it. If the colonizer conceived of Mau Mau as an atavistic[6] and unpredictable insurgency, then his military strategies (of detection, containment, infiltration, detention, torture and the forced removals of vast swathes of the population from their homes) index an attempt by the colonizer to produce a spatial knowledge of Mau Mau, and to thereby restore to himself sovereign control of the landscape.[7]

In all of its aspects, this spatial knowledge relied fundamentally upon technologies of the visible to accomplish its aims. Unfortunately, colonial military strategy was premised upon stereotypical assumptions of 'the African', so that Mau Mau was typically associated in the settler mind with the bestial,[8] the occult, the primordial.[9] As a result, what the colonizer set out to find impeded was what he was actually able to see. Accordingly, the Kenyan administration sought to render Mau Mau visible by containing it within the 'wild spaces' of the forests, so that the civilian areas occupied by supposedly docile and loyal Gikuyu subjects could remain 'sanitised domestic spaces' uncontaminated by Mau Mau's pernicious influence. The colonial caricatures of the insurgency could only be emplotted on the landscape by imposing the most horrific brutality upon the Kenyan population. If the colonizer sought to produce a spatial taxonomy of Mau Mau, then the borders between the artificial categories he imposed had to be policed with brute force, with civilians bearing the brunt of military whim. In other words, the landscape had to be *inscribed* with the violence of the colonizer's narrative of self-legitimation.

---

6   See C. T. Stoneham, *Mau Mau* (London: Museum Press, 1953), pp. 61–2.

7   There were severe restrictions on the movement and employment of Gikuyu, Embu and Meru people. See Wunyabari O. Maloba, *Mau Mau and Kenya: An Analysis of a Peasant Revolt* (Bloomington: Indiana University Press, 1993), pp. 90–91.

8   Incidentally, during the Emergency, the settlers' 'pet' name for the Gikuyu was 'Nugu', or 'baboon'. See Edgerton, *Mau Mau*, p. 162. Edgerton also records that the term 'Mickeys' (from 'Mickey Mouse') was also used by British and Loyalist forces to describe Mau Mau (pp. 151–6). Edgerton comments on the British Army in Kenya, 'Most of these officers and men had left Britain with firm convictions about the racial superiority of whites. . . and their service overseas in places like Egypt, Cyprus, Palestine, and Malaya had only confirmed for them that "wogs" and "niggers" were a lower form of life' (p. 165). The ferocity of the British Army's attacks on and reprisals against Mau Mau (including civilians) suggests that these experienced soldiers were in no mood to humour uncooperative natives. Despite its overt resonances in Disney lore, the use of the term 'Mickeys' may also have displaced an unconscious animosity towards 'Micks' (the Irish) onto Mau Mau and the Gikuyu. Expanding on this theme, the Kenyan conflict may have concentrated a number of post-imperial resentments and its brutal moments may have provided psychological compensation for earlier imperial losses – such as Egyptian (1922), Irish (1922) and Indian independence (1947), and the establishment of the Irish Republic (1949).

9   For one example among many, see Stoneham, *Mau Mau*, p. 27.

Colonial military strategy was articulated throughout the 1952–60 period in five distinct phases. First, there was Operation Jock Scott (1952), in which the leaders of the Kenya African Union were arrested and detained. Second, the Rehabilitation programme was introduced (1953–59), in which Mau Mau suspects were detained in concentration camps until confessing the oath, after which they graduated through successive camps (the 'pipe-line') until they were considered to be innocuous enough for release. Confessions were believed to 'cure' the prisoner's pathological political sympathies and were extracted using inducements (such as prostitutes), brainwashing, propaganda, hard labour and, if all else failed, beatings and torture. Significantly, the treatment of prisoners in the camps by their guards and superintendents was as depraved as anything the settlers had claimed in regard to Mau Mau atrocities:

> Electric shock was widely used, and so was fire. Women were choked and held under water; gun barrels, beer bottles, and even knives were thrust into their vaginas. Men had beer bottles thrust into their rectums, were dragged behind Land Rovers, whipped, burned and bayoneted. Their fingers were chopped off, and sometimes their testicles were crushed with pliers.[10]

The severity of the prisoners' punishment regimes in the camps depended on whether they were classified 'black' (hardcore), 'grey' (Mau Mau supporters) or 'white' (clear or rehabilitated). Some 80 000 Gikuyu were detained in concentration camps, many without trial. Ultimately, the brutality of the Rehabilitation programme proved to be self-defeating. In Hola detention camp, 11 recalcitrant prisoners designated as 'hardcore' Mau Mau were beaten to death for refusing to work. After a settler cover-up was exposed and its political position in Kenya was revealed to be untenable, the British Parliament resolved to embark upon the path towards Kenyan independence.

The third phase of colonial military strategy was Operation Anvil (1954), in which 25 000 men of the government's forces surrounded Nairobi and searched it, sector by sector, for Mau Mau operatives. After being 'screened' by hooded informants and being interrogated by the authorities, approximately 30 000 Nairobi Gikuyu were sent to detention camps.[11] Fourth, the Villagization programme (forced removals; 1954–57) was implemented, which entailed the relocation of Gikuyu civilians to 'safe' villages (that is, surrounded by barbed wire and cut off from the forest by a trench 50 miles long, 10 feet deep and 16 feet wide, filled with barbed wire, sharpened stakes and booby traps), in order to minimize the contact between Mau Mau and its civilian wing. Almost all of the women in the villages were coerced into digging the trench that would limit Mau Mau's access to supplies, food and ammunition. The settler administration espoused the preposterous hope that the

---

[10] Edgerton, *Mau Mau*, p. 160.
[11] Maloba, *Mau Mau and Kenya*, p. 86.

Villagization and Land Consolidation programmes would 'produce a harmonious society of prosperous villages and sturdy yeoman farmers immune to the appeals of political radicalism. In the end, the Emergency became an attempt to re-create the administration's idealized image of the organic community of traditional England.'[12] In other words, the colonial administration sought to produce in the landscape a civilian population that was domesticated, easily subjected to surveillance and utterly visible, because community and landscape were essentially transcriptions of an English rural idyll. But 'Old England' was simulated at a terrible human cost, and over 250 000 people were removed from their homes in the forests or on the perimeters of the mountain ranges to villagized settlements.[13] By early 1955, 'over a million Gikuyu had been settled in these villages',[14] and Mau Mau operations in a given area led to communal punishments.[15] Since Mau Mau was alleged to be hiding in Gikuyu gardens, crops were destroyed. In conjunction with forced labour and curfews, the colonial administration effectively instituted widespread famine among the civilian population by keeping communities from their fields where they might assist Mau Mau fighters,[16] leading to an as yet unquantified civilian death toll.[17]

The fifth and final phase of colonial military strategy entailed Operations Hammer, Schlemozzle, Bullrush, Dante, Hannibal and First Flute (1955–56), in which the Aberdare forest was swept for insurgents. Some of the tactics employed against the forest fighters included using infra-red technology to scan the forests and then bombing heat sources,[18] or in the colonizer's more telling Conradian moments, shelling the edge of the forest randomly with light artillery at hourly intervals.[19]

The Villagization programme and the Rehabilitation programme fashioned the Emergency landscape in ways that reflected colonial constructions of Mau Mau. If Mau Mau issued from the adverse influence of the primordial and inscrutable African landscape, then the organization could be made visible by completely redefining space in the rural Kenyan countryside. If Mau Mau was a contaminant or a disease, then the body politic could be cured by quarantining the afflicted in concentration camps and removing the infection by tried and tested methods (torture, brutality). And if the good African was docile and domesticated, then this

---

[12] Bruce Berman and John Lonsdale, *Unhappy Valley: Conflict in Kenya and Africa – Violence and Ethnicity* (Book Two) (London: James Currey, 1992), p. 254.

[13] Barnett and Njama, *Mau Mau from Within*, p. 209.

[14] Maloba, *Mau Mau and Kenya*, p. 90.

[15] Marshall Clough, *Mau Mau Memoirs: History, Memory, Politics* (Boulder, Col.: Lynne Rienner, 1998), p. 156.

[16] Clough, *Mau Mau Memoirs*, p. 159.

[17] The food that was distributed was given in small quantities, to eliminate the sharing of rations with Mau Mau. See Tabitha Kanogo, *Squatters and the Roots of Mau Mau* (London: James Currey, 1987), p. 143.

[18] Animal fatalities are not recorded.

[19] Barnett and Njama, *Mau Mau from Within*, p. 223.

good African could be produced in the orderly space of the villagized settlements – and disciplined with industrious time-management and work regimes (curfews and forced labour). Of course, the boundaries that policed Kenyan subjectivities in the Emergency period could only be established by imposing overwhelming violence on a recalcitrant population. Much of this violence issued from legal and para-legal redefinitions of colonial space. For instance, a corridor 100 miles long and between 1 and 3 miles wide was established between the forests and the Gikuyu population. Huts, food stores and crops were burnt and the inhabitants were evicted. The corridor and parts of the forest were made 'Prohibited Areas', where unauthorized Africans could be shot on sight.[20] The majority of administrative districts in the Central and Rift Valley Provinces (the Gikuyu reserve) were made 'Special Areas', in which 'a person failing to halt when challenged could be shot'.[21] Under Emergency powers, this sanction also applied to 'military installations, prisons and power stations in danger areas' and thousands of African deaths resulted from this loophole in the law, along with the claims that the victims had been 'trying to escape'.[22] The topography of the Emergency period – with its restrictions on human movement, villagized settlements, fortifications, booby-trapped trenches, infra-red scanning, concentration camps, torture chambers, no-go areas – dramatized an afflicted colonial psyche in the theatre of war. In other words, the Emergency landscape evidenced the way in which the political imagination of the settler asserted itself upon space.

The Emergency period was marked by a colonial mythology of the domestic and the familiar giving way to the demonic and treacherous, the hospitable and habitable giving way to the unhomely, the trusted houseservant metamorphosing inexplicably into the treacherous or crazed fanatic[23] – as if the cultivated and civilized landscape of settler farms had been breached by the primordial landscape of the forests in which the insurgents sheltered,[24] as if anti-colonial resistance could only be explained by pathologizing the 'primitive or superstitious psychology' of the African.[25] For the settler, a primeval environment accounted for the African's unpromising political and socio-economic destiny. Unsurprisingly, given the instability of colonial space and the pathologizing of Mau Mau's political grievances, the colonial representation

---

[20] Barnett and Njama, *Mau Mau from Within*, p. 211.

[21] Maloba, *Mau Mau and Kenya*, p. 92; Barnett and Njama, *Mau Mau from Within*, p. 211.

[22] Maloba, *Mau Mau and Kenya*, pp. 92–3.

[23] This mythology fuelled settler hysteria: 'Farmers and their wives, even little children, were hacked to death by devils who up to the moment of their black treachery had been treated as loyal and trusted friends'. See Christopher Wilson, *Kenya's Warning: The Challenge to White Supremacy in our British Colony* (Nairobi: The English Press, 1954), p. 56.

[24] '[Eric Bowyer's farm] was no more than a mile from the forest, in whose depths wild beasts, and wilder men, might lurk.' Stoneham, *Mau Mau*, p. 70.

[25] 'The Nairobi houseboy or Government clerk . . . may even be a devout Christian, but still the superstitious terrors imbibed with his mother's milk will be lurking at the back of his consciousness, ready to creep forth for his undoing.' Stoneham, *Mau Mau*, p. 141.

of Mau Mau relied heavily upon a rhetoric of contamination.[26] To some extent, Mau Mau memoirs written by the insurgents themselves attest to the fact that the movement was able to infiltrate prohibited or sacrosanct spaces as part of its psychological weaponry and tactical capacity. For instance, when three of his men were captured, Brigadier Nyama Nduru (the *nom de guerre* of Paul Mahehu) 'arranged to sweep the remand toilets of the High Court on the trial day, working as a uniformed City Council employee'.[27] Nyama Nduru retained his broom and gave one of his three comrades, the principal defendant in the case, an overall and a bucket and the two men walked out of the court undetected, with the result that the trial collapsed. On other occasions, disguised as a policeman and with an accomplice disguised as a servant, Nyama Nduru stole weapons from the private armoury of Governor Evelyn Baring and organized the theft of 39 rounds of ammunition from the home of Mr Edward Windley, the Chief Native Commissioner.[28]

Mau Mau's relatively unhindered passage across the landscape and the ease with which it trespassed in the citadels of colonial power is a direct result of the discourse that yoked the insurgency to narratives of the crazed fanatic or the Gikuyu possessed by demonic tribal oaths.[29] In fact, Mau Mau's mobility – and in some cases, its continuing organizational survival – relied heavily upon covert support from a large, dormant civilian wing, and extensive collaboration by black colonial officials, 'loyal' houseservants, the King's African Rifles[30] and the loyalist, paramilitary Homeguards. Only the settler truly respected the battle-lines he had drawn. As the example of Nyama Nduru demonstrates, Mau Mau evaded detection by performing identities and subjectivities that went unchecked in the colonial landscape: it was only because the settler was on the lookout for a dangerous intruder that the Mau Mau raider was able to disguise himself as a compliant houseservant or a protective

---

[26] 'At an election meeting at Londiani, Hubert Buxton, a retired District Commissioner, warned that virtually the whole Kikuyu tribe had been "contaminated" with Mau Mau.' See David W. Throup, *Economic and Social Origins of Mau Mau* (London: James Currey, 1987), p. 226. Early on, Michael Blundell, the leader of the white elected members of Kenya's Legislative Council also warned of a 'subversive organization which is like a disease, spreading through the Colony'. See *Legislative Council Debates*, second series, vol. xlviii, 1952, first session, second sitting, 10 July 1952, cols 172–98 and 11 July 1952, cols 281–349. Also quoted in Throup, *Economic and Social Origins*, p. 225.

[27] Waruhiu Itote (General China), *'Mau Mau' General* (Nairobi: East African Publishing House, 1967), p. 114.

[28] Itote, *'Mau Mau' General*, pp. 112–13. I view this theft as an example of what I would call a 'rhetoric of hostile proximity' employed in Mau Mau's psychological warfare.

[29] Edgerton notes that, after the declaration of the Emergency, Michael Blundell gave Mau Mau fighters the derogatory label of 'debased creatures of the forest', but that as the war took its toll upon the remaining fighters in the latter stages of the conflict, the fighters truly became 'creatures of the forest' in their resourceful survival of hardship. See Edgerton, *Mau Mau*, pp. 107, 138.

[30] See Itote, *'Mau Mau' General*, p. 106.

policeman. It was only because the settler sought an unruly antagonist that the Mau Mau prisoner could walk unnoticed to his freedom, dressed as a prison warder.[31] Moreover, it was only because the Mau Mau operative was officially an ethnic Gikuyu that the Mau Mau escapee could perform Somali ethnicity (by donning a turban, robe and false beard) with impunity while running from the law[32] or the warrior pass undetected by braiding his hair in the fashion favoured by the Maasai.[33] In short, official colonial knowledges of *what* Mau Mau *was* – their reductive tableaux of the human figure in colonial space[34] – enabled many of the mutinous successes that Mau Mau achieved.

Gaining Ground

By contrast, Mau Mau's relationship to the landscape was strategically canny.[35] Insurgents used the forests for camouflage and for shelter – it was 'a home and a fortress as well as the provider of [their] most basic needs'.[36] They raided crops and livestock from nearby farms, hunted wild animals or located hives laid by honey harvesters in the forests when they were hungry.[37] They relied upon sympathetic civilian populations near the reserves to bury stores and supplies in pre-arranged caches. Some Mau Mau groups even adopted vegetarianism during the rainy season, when livestock raids would leave tracks betraying the way to their camps in the forest.[38] In addition, their childhood experiences as cattleherders equipped them to find water in inhospitable terrain.[39] The landscape was also a repository of significance for Mau Mau fighters, since it occasionally articulated their situation in times of difficulty. For recent Mau Mau escapees from the Manyani concentration camp, a nearby rhinoceros herd became a security cordon keeping watch over their sleep.[40] And for the injured fugitive left by his fellow escapees to fend for himself in an inhospitable landscape, a nearby anthill became a moral lesson in social co-operation and solidarity, so sadly lacking in the moment of his abandonment.[41]

---

[31] See Itote, *'Mau Mau' General*, p. 116.

[32] See Itote, *'Mau Mau' General*, p. 115.

[33] See Barnett and Njama, *Mau Mau from Within*, p. 174.

[34] C. T. Stoneham's account is saturated with ethnic stereotypes of Mau Mau.

[35] Since Mau Mau strategies and objectives varied between its component units, my version of Mau Mau is located less in the uniformity of its action than in the proliferation of its practices.

[36] Barnett and Njama, *Mau Mau from Within*, p. 146.

[37] See Joram Wamweya, *Freedom Fighter* (Nairobi: East African Publishing House, 1967), p. 151.

[38] See Wamweya, *Freedom Fighter*, p. 163.

[39] See Wamweya, *Freedom Fighter*, p. 93.

[40] See Wamweya, *Freedom Fighter*, pp. 91–2.

[41] See Wamweya, *Freedom Fighter*, p. 107.

Amongst the fighters, animals were a tactical resource. Elephant tracks guided them across rough terrain and showed the most direct route to water.[42] By listening attentively to forest sounds, such as bird calls or the erratic movements of frightened animals,[43] the insurgents produced a sympathetic sensory landscape in which the dangers of attack or discovery were signalled long before they became imminent and in which surveillance was delegated to omnipresent, non-human military 'allies', some of whom had become used to the insurgents' presence in the forests.[44] The co-operation and acceptance of animals and birds was taken to be a sign that *Ngai* (God) had given them power to assist the insurgents in thwarting the enemy.[45] Indeed, enemy soldiers were occasionally ambushed and chased deeper into the forest, where they could be picked off at will in hostile terrain or left to contend with marauding wildlife.[46]

In religious terms, many insurgents viewed their relationship to the landscape as a sacred one. Before embarking for the forests, they received instruction in forest lore from Gikuyu elders. These elders invested the landscape with spiritual significance, in which the slightest human action (such as cutting down trees, killing animals needlessly or shooting towards mountains in which spirits dwelled) interacted with a network of taboos and portents and could invoke adverse meteorological, military or even cosmological consequences.[47] Portent and prophecy occasionally informed Mau Mau's battle strategy, as when the appearance of a particularly bright star in the sky prompted the insurgents to conduct the raid on Naivasha Police Station (26 March 1953) without fear of capture or death.[48] Before and after important military operations, the fighters prayed facing the sacred landmark, Mount Kenya, frequently with a ball of earth held aloft.[49] The spiritual dimensions of Mau Mau led to the adoption of some unpredictable military tactics – as when the *mundu mugo* (religious practitioner) halted raids because a gazelle had crossed the fighters' path.[50]

In political terms, ownership of the land was one of the crucial aims of the movement that named itself, amongst other things, the 'Kenyan Land and Freedom Army'. One of the political grievances that facilitated Mau Mau's emergence was the colonial administration's policy of preventing soil erosion. The 'agricultural campaign, with its compulsory communal terracing two mornings per week, had provided the Nairobi militants with a ready-made constituency with which to

---

[42] See Itote, *'Mau Mau' General*, p. 76.

[43] See Itote, *'Mau Mau' General*, pp. 70–71.

[44] Among themselves, the fighters passed a law prohibiting the killing of 'friendly' wildlife. See Barnett and Njama, *Mau Mau from Within*, p. 146.

[45] Barnett and Njama, *Mau Mau from Within*, p. 167.

[46] Barnett and Njama, *Mau Mau from Within*, p. 207.

[47] See Itote, *'Mau Mau' General*, pp. 61–62. Although Itote dismisses the elders' admonitions on empirical grounds, he states that 'most of the men' believed these admonitions.

[48] Itote, *'Mau Mau' General*, pp. 82–3.

[49] See Barnett and Njama, *Mau Mau from Within*, p. 162.

[50] Barnett and Njama, *Mau Mau from Within*, p. 205.

challenge the African moderates' rural power base'.[51] In some instances, insurgents had an intimate relationship with the land on which, and for which, they fought. For example, Karari Njama became politicized when he realized (at a rally held by Jomo Kenyatta) that his family had been dispossessed of the land that bore his and his grandfather's name – Karari's Hill, alienated by the colonial government in 1910. Significantly, Njama's Mau Mau unit was initially stationed in the Aberdare forest reserve on the land formerly owned by his grandfather.[52] The landscape was invested with other forms of cultural memory. For instance, Mau Mau raiders killed Gray Arundel Leakey (Dr Louis Leakey's uncle) by burying him 'alive upside down, his feet left protruding from the earth'.[53] As appalling as this murder appeared, and as much as it seemed to confirm settler claims about Mau Mau's depravity, the method of execution had a straightforward rationale: the act was ordered by a Gikuyu seer who claimed that the colonizer would only be chased out of Kenya when a settler 'elder' had been killed in the same way as the British had killed Waiyaki (an early Gikuyu prophet) in one widely believed version of Gikuyu folk history.[54]

When Mau Mau groups moved, they were mindful of leaving the landscape and the forest foliage undisturbed,[55] of walking backwards to confuse trackers and of splitting up into groups and walking in different directions to throw the enemies' bloodhounds off the scent before meeting-up again at a rendezvous point.[56] Hence, Mau Mau's choreography of revolution became a highly reflexive act of writing on the landscape that largely flouted the colonizer's strategies of detection and containment in the early years of the insurgency. But beyond evading the colonizer's technologies of visibility, one of Mau Mau's most ingenious strategies was to stage its own absence in the landscape – for example, by setting up mock camps for the enemy to bomb or by sending a small detail to attack a Homeguard post in the Gikuyu reserve in order to prompt the immediate withdrawal from the forest of nearby government forces searching for Mau Mau.[57] Similar tactics of deflection were used to alleviate the sufferings of the civilian wing under security force control. In Nairobi, Mau Mau's urban wing was highly mobile, with its operatives executing informants in the back seats of moving taxis.

Separating the Women from the Boys

Women were Mau Mau's most transgressive principle. In the reserves and in the cities, they provided a largely invisible backbone to the movement and their

[51]   Throup, *Economic and Social Origins*, p. 240.
[52]   See Barnett and Njama, *Mau Mau from Within*, pp. 74, 85–6.
[53]   Edgerton, *Mau Mau*, p. 97.
[54]   Edgerton, *Mau Mau*, p. 97.
[55]   See Wamweya, *Freedom Fighter*, p. 143.
[56]   Itote, *'Mau Mau' General*, p. 73.
[57]   Itote, *'Mau Mau' General*, pp. 71–2.

contributions were made at the cost of enormous adversity and suffering. It was precisely the colonial assumption that Gikuyu women were backward[58] that contributed to the Kenyan government's underestimation of Mau Mau's passive or civilian wing. As a result, women were able to pass through the landscape largely undetected by colonial surveillance. Colonial discourses on women in Mau Mau built failure into the colonizer's look:

> When women's activism is described in pro-colonial historiography, two portrayals of women emerge. They project women as either victims of 'mau mau' or prostitutes who, through personal [read sexual] contact with male nationalists, were drawn to Mau Mau while resident in Nairobi. The view of women as victims of Mau Mau originates from the colonial record. Women are presented by colonial officials as physical and psychological victims of atavism . . . Women nationalists were relegated to the role of 'adoring female hangers-on'.[59]

These misguided notions of women as victims meant that they were able to conduct Mau Mau's business uninterrupted and unnoticed. Speaking of Mau Mau scouts, Itote says, 'Girls found it simpler to disguise themselves, or at least to be inconspicuous'[60] and that all a woman had to do to escape attention when cornered was to pretend to garden.

Mau Mau constructions of women were uneven. Karari Njama's memoir is perhaps the most revealing example of the ways in which 'femininity' was instrumentalized in Mau Mau narratives of the insurgency. He describes the administration of the Batuni oath (a corruption of the English military usage 'platoon'), during which the Mau Mau initiate's penis was inserted into a hole in a goat's throat. The fighters in the Aberdare Mountains referred to their lovers/sexual consorts as *kabatuni*, or 'small platoons',[61] establishing an obvious link between male virility, resistance and the diminution of women. The sexual imagery in the more advanced oathing procedures, such as the Batuni oath, was pervasive.[62] In addition, the leadership of Mau Mau referred to its enemies (loyalists, traitors and Homeguards) as *thata cia bururi*, 'the barren ones of the country',[63] thus constructing Mau Mau according to a narrative of male potency. Some (contested) accounts of oathing ceremonies point towards the use of women's private parts in the initiation of new

---

[58] See Wilson, *Kenya's Warning*, pp. 78–9. Wilson seems to suggest that one result of the women's backwardness is their unsophisticated agricultural methods. His implicit argument is that the settler is a better custodian of the land.

[59] Cora Ann Presley, *Kikuyu Women, the Mau Mau Rebellion, and Social Change in Kenya* (Boulder, Col.: Westview, 1992) p. 158.

[60] Itote, *'Mau Mau' General*, p. 78.

[61] Barnett and Njama, *Mau Mau from Within*, p. 242.

[62] See Maloba, *Mau Mau and Kenya*, p. 104–6.

[63] Barnett and Njama, *Mau Mau from Within*, p. 349.

fighters.[64] Njama's memoir marks a sexually ambivalent relation to women within the movement:

> To feed and defend women [I thought] is an unnecessary burden to our warriors. Sleeping with them would bring calamity to our camps, weaken our *itungati* [warriors] and, probably, they would become pregnant and would be unable to run away from the enemies, and they would be killed . . . For generations, women had been a source of conflicts between men.[65]

In other Mau Mau narratives – most notably in Kariuki's[66] – the struggles of female insurgents are either strategically omitted or received as textual asides.

Despite the lack of archival material dealing with the struggles and aims of women within Mau Mau, their role within the movement was crucial to its successes, and possibly to its survival. Women's roles

> included 'organization and maintenance of the supply lines which directed food, supplies, medicine, guns and information to the forest forces.' Those women who went to the forest were 'responsible for cooking, water-hauling, knitting sweaters etc.'
>
> Women formed the valuable link between the forest fighters and the passive wing in the reserves. Those women who went to the forests tended on the whole to be engaged in noncombatant roles, acting as 'transport, signals, medical corps and ordnance to their male counterparts.'[67]

Further, Mau Mau women in the reserves and in the city procured ammunition for the forest fighters by submitting to intercourse with Government forces. Karari Njama tells us that 'Bullets had become token payment [from security force personnel] to prostitutes who later sent them to our warriors',[68] and Edgerton confirms that some 'Mau Mau' women did seduce British soldiers in the hope of receiving a bullet or two in return'.[69] The Mau Mau prostitute and courier is an important figure. The male fighters forbade women to sleep with the enemy and yet it was precisely the prostitute who sustained the supply of guns and ammunition to the forests. Waruhiu Itote, who provides two anecdotes of women using their sexuality to obtain arms and ammunition, omits any mention of intercourse.[70] The prostitute subverts Mau Mau narratives of phallic heroism and Mau Mau's policing of female sexuality. She provides us with a model of sexwork-in-insurgency, a specifically female form

---

64 See Maloba, *Mau Mau and Kenya*, pp. 106, 195, n. 57.
65 Barnett and Njama, *Mau Mau from Within*, p. 242.
66 J. M. Kariuki, *Mau Mau Detainee* (Nairobi: Oxford University Press, 1963).
67 Maloba, *Mau Mau and Kenya*, p. 177, quoting Presley and Gachihi.
68 Barnett and Njama, *Mau Mau from Within*, p. 208.
69 Edgerton, *Mau Mau*, p. 168.
70 Itote, *'Mau Mau' General*, pp. 100–101.

of militancy in which sex is not capitulation but revolution. Her perilous journeys between the security forces and the rebels, from settlement to countryside and back again, meant that she shuttled between the extremities of the Emergency landscape in full view of the colonial surveillance apparatus and made an invaluable contribution to Mau Mau's military survival.

Inhabiting the Ground

Representations of the landscape are crucial to the political project of Ngugi wa Thiong'o's fiction. In many of the novels, landscape is intimately bound up with ideology. The landscape is a medium in which the conflicting ideologies that have contributed to Ngugi's subject-formation can be held in an ossified relation to one another. Ideological contradiction can thereby be held in abeyance. For example, consider the tree imagery in *Weep Not, Child*. Mwihaki, Njoroge's love interest, is described as 'a lone tree defying the darkness'[71] of the Mau Mau period. However, this description also implicates her in the Gikuyu traditionalist myth of origin that Ngotho recounts to Njoroge: 'But in this darkness, at the foot of Kerinyaga, a tree rose. At first it was a small tree and grew up, finding a way even through the darkness. It wanted to reach the light, and the sun. This tree had *Life*.'[72] In Christian discourse, the tree evokes the crucifix, which is sometimes depicted as the 'Tree of Life'. Furthermore, the tree imagery is implicitly linked to anti-colonial struggle, since Mau Mau insurgents hid in forests during the Emergency. Therefore, the tree is a figure that freezes the potentially disseminating force of competing ideologies (traditionalism, militant nationalism, Christianity, Gikuyu patriarchy). Since Njoroge never settles upon a progressive politics, nor takes up arms, nor acts upon his obvious attraction to Mwihaki, the fact that he chooses '*the* tree'[73] upon which to hang himself suggests that he is a failure in cultural-traditionalist terms (the tree as myth of origin), political/military terms (the forest as home of insurgency) and sexual terms (Mwihaki as lone tree defying the darkness of the Emergency); although the reader might object that these disparate modes of human experience are too seamlessly unified in Ngugi's landscape imagery. Moreover, just as Njoroge's education is an individual interest that runs contrary to the interests of the collective, his attempted suicide is an abandonment of social responsibilities that is only redeemed by the Messianic self-sacrifice it evokes. In Ngugi's next novel, *The River Between*, the conflicts between Christian ideology and Gikuyu traditionalist discourse are explicitly mapped out in the perennial geological antagonism of the

---

[71] Ngugi wa Thiong'o, *Weep Not, Child* (London: Heinemann, 1964; reprinted 1987), pp. 23–4.

[72] Ngugi, *Weep Not*, pp. 23–4.

[73] Ngugi, *Weep Not*, p. 135, my emphasis.

Makuyu and Kameno ridges, whose communities are divided over the issue of clitoridectomy.[74]

The gendering of the landscape is another crucial mechanism that allows Ngugi's narratives to stave off ideological ambivalence. In addition, this mechanism represses the gender-political agency of Gikuyu women. The feminized landscape effectively submerges Gikuyu women's contributions to the anti-colonial struggle, but at the price of sexual ambivalence elsewhere in the narratives. Since it is a defence against ideological contradiction, and a way of consolidating masculine prerogatives in culture, the landscape is a politically enabling signifier in Ngugi's fiction. In Ngugi's early novels, *Weep Not, Child* and *The River Between*, the gendering of the landscape is overt. For the settler, Howlands, possession of the land parallels sexual conquest, the 'farm was a woman whom he had wooed and conquered. He had to keep an eye on her lest she should be possessed by someone else.'[75] Whatever else divides him from Howlands politically and economically, the Mau Mau fighter, Boro, makes a strikingly similar analogy when he confronts Howlands, 'Together, you killed many *sons of the land*. You raped our women.'[76] Indeed, the motif of the 'raped' land is developed early in the novel, where the narrator locates the landscape within a discourse that links history with pathology: 'You could tell the land of Black People because it was red, rough and sickly, while the land of the white settlers was green and was not lacerated into small strips.'[77] Despite their different ideological positions, Howlands, Boro and the narrator all reciprocate a patriarchal discourse, for which 'woman' and the land are enabling signifiers. In effect, 'woman' becomes the contested terrain across which ideological struggles are waged. This representation is politically suspect, since the Gikuyu woman is allied with nature while her male counterparts dominate culture.

In Ngugi's middle fiction, the gendering of the landscape is linked to the changing political circumstances of the postcolony. For example, the Mau Mau detainee in 'The Return', Kamau, returns to find the landscape 'haggard', 'weary' and 'dull', and this change – along with the villagized settlements – reflects his irredeemably altered relationships with his community, family and wife.[78] Believing a love rival's lie that Kamau is dead, they have lost hope of his return and have allowed his wife, Muthoni, to abscond with the rival. In effect, the landscape equates the drained resources of a brutalized Kenyan population with the changes in Kamau's socio-sexual status. In 'Goodbye Africa' a former District Officer prepares to leave Kenya, but is haunted both by notions of the sorcery at work in the African landscape and by his former servant's political insubordination and the servant's sexual exploits with

---

[74] Ngugi wa Thiong'o, *The River Between* (London: Heinemann, 1965), p. 1.

[75] Ngugi, *Weep Not*, p. 127.

[76] Ngugi, *Weep Not*, p. 128, my emphasis.

[77] Ngugi, *Weep Not*, p. 7.

[78] Ngugi wa Thiong'o, *Secret Lives and Other Stories* (London: Heinemann, 1975; reprinted 1992), p. 49.

the officer's wife.[79] The former District Officer's crisis in political authority is thus filtered through a sexual crisis that permanently alters his sense of place.

A Grain of Wheat details the violence of the Emergency landscape in its acts of naming. Gikonyo's and Mumbi's names invoke the male and female archetypes ('Gikuyu' and 'Mumbi') in the Gikuyu myth of origin, but 'Gikonyo' also translates as 'navel' – and his name therefore evokes Mau Mau slang for the bombers that flew over the forests opening their underbellies to dispatch their cargoes.[80] The name of the village, 'Thabai', means 'stinging nettle' and this evokes both the starved home population's scavenging for food and the nettles inserted into women's vaginas as a means of torture in detention.[81] 'Thabai' therefore condenses the primarily female suffering that occurred on two sites in the Emergency landscape (the villagized settlements and the torture chamber). The title of the novel and the motif of sowing associated with it implicitly associates Mau Mau's bullets (which are dubbed 'maize grains') with cultural and spiritual rebirth through repossession of the land.[82] Since the novel genders Kenya female[83] and constructs resistance according to metaphors of insemination, women become vehicles for this rebirth.

The most covert patriarchal strategy of *A Grain of Wheat* is that it equates a complex national confrontation with an estrangement between spouses. Of course, the Emergency did fragment the lives of families and communities, and it would seem obvious to use a love-relationship as a model for social discord or social cohesion at the most nucleated level. However, even the Gikuyu homestead is a site of gender-codification in which male and female subjects are socially constructed and hierarchically organized. Before Mumbi is relocated to New Thabai by the colonial authorities, her hut is set on fire. This event is charged with Gikuyu cultural significances. First, the Gikuyu woman's hut (*Nyumba ya Mumbi* – 'House of Mumbi')[84] is the equivalent of a gynaeceum – all sexual relations between spouses take place in it (rather than in the husband's dwelling, the *thingira*) and children inhabit this hut prior to their initiation into adulthood via circumcision.[85] Second, *Nyumba* denotes the 'elementary [or nuclear-polygamous] family' in the Gikuyu community.[86] Third, *Nyumba ya Mumbi* is a traditionalist/nationalist construction of Kenya as the 'House of Mumbi'.[87] At the end of the novel, when Gikonyo's

---

[79] Ngugi, *Secret Lives*, pp. 71–9.

[80] Sicherman, *Ngugi wa Thiong'o*, p. 201.

[81] Barnett and Njama, *Mau Mau from Within*, p. 209.

[82] Ngugi wa Thiong'o, *A Grain of Wheat* (London: Heinemann, 1967; reprinted 1985), pp. 132, 175. General R.'s real name, 'Muhoya', means 'a tenant farmer', pointing towards his motivations for joining 'Mau Mau'.

[83] 'With us, Kenya is our mother,' says Kihika. Ngugi, *Grain*, p. 78.

[84] Sicherman, *Ngugi wa Thiong'o*, p. 228.

[85] Jomo Kenyatta, *Facing Mount Kenya* (London: Secker and Warburg, 1968), pp. 83–4.

[86] Sicherman, *Ngugi wa Thiong'o*, p. 228.

[87] Barnett and Njama, *Mau Mau from Within*, p. 182.

'reunion with Mumbi would see the birth of a new Kenya', the pregnant Mumbi that Gikonyo envisages in his carving has already had her reproductive and child-rearing functions yoked to the narrative of independent nationhood.[88] By framing Gikonyo and Mumbi's relationship in orature, Ngugi's conclusion evokes the myth of origin in which Gikuyu men overthrew an unjust matriarchy by impregnating the women simultaneously.[89] In the novel's own terms, resistance is aligned with male potency and Mumbi as character or as archetype of all Gikuyu women is situated conveniently on either side of the narrative present (in Gikuyu myths of historical origin and as a figure of deferred utopian nationhood). Gikonyo, whose mythical name (Gikuyu) bears the mark of modernity and is therefore part of the historical process, holds sway over the post-independence present.

Mumbi's infidelity marks a turning point in Ngugi's representation of the nation. The subsequent novels all construct Kenya as a prostituted economy and the gendering of the nation necessitates female characters who are 'fallen women'. In *Petals of Blood* the landscape becomes a medium for Marxist instruction[90] as, for example, when the schoolteacher Munira takes his pupils into the field and discovers an outlandish phallus (a worm) in a flower with 'petals of blood'.[91] The children ask Munira whether the eaten can eat back. When she recalls a comprador capitalist's act of sexually blackmailing her, Wanja's story of her decision to become a prostitute answers the children's question, 'If you have a cunt . . . if you are born with this hole, instead of it being a source of pride, you are doomed to either marrying someone or else being a whore. You eat or you are eaten.'[92] The representatives of the comprador class are all constructed in avaricious, bestial terms: Kimeria Hawkins ('hawk that swallows'), Raymond Chui/Chui Rimui ('chui' denotes 'leopard') and Nderi wa Riera ('vulture of the air').[93]

Wanja, whose 'deflowered' womanhood resonates quite powerfully with the Theng'eta flower's petals of blood, 'becomes a ready symbol for the ravaged state of Kenya'.[94] Constructed in terms of harvest imagery and allied with the landscape throughout the novel, Wanja's debasement is finally redeemed when she becomes pregnant. However, *Petals of Blood* reflects an anxiety about the sexually licentious

---

[88] Ngugi, *Grain*, p. 92.

[89] The myth – which contributes to the novel's equation of female sexuality with political misrule – is recounted in Ngugi, *Grain*, p. 11.

[90] This motif endures to the most recent novel. See the tilling imagery in relation to the 'one who reaps-where-he-never sowed', in Ngugi wa Thiong'o, *Matigari*, trans. Wangui wa Goro (Nairobi: Heinemann, 1987; reprinted 1990), p. 113.

[91] Ngugi wa Thiong'o, *Petals of Blood* (London: Heinemann, 1977; reprinted 1986), pp. 21–2.

[92] Ngugi, *Petals*, p. 293.

[93] Sicherman, *Ngugi wa Thiong'o*, pp. 209, 198, 224.

[94] Elleke Boehmer. 'The Master's Dance to the Master's Voice: Revolutionary Nationalism and the Representation of Women in the Writing of Ngugi wa Thiong'o', *The Journal of Commonwealth Literature*, 26:1 (1991), p. 193.

woman – namely, that she reverses or destabilizes gender roles. There is a curious moment in the novel in which Wanja and Karega leave the rest of the encamped Ilmorog villagers and encounter a hill. Wanja speaks:

'That! It is called the hill of uncircumcised boys. It is said that if a boy runs right round it, he will turn into a girl and a girl will turn into a boy. Do you believe that too?' 'No, I don't. We should have heard of cases of some who had tried and were changed into their opposites.' 'I wish it were true!' she said rather fiercely, almost bitterly.[95]

In a certain sense, Wanja's wish, or Ngugi's wish for her, has already been accomplished. Wanja's name, given to her by her playmates at school and by the Ilmorog townsfolk,[96] is Wanja Kahii ('kahii' denotes an uncircumcised boy),[97] because she was considered a tomboy in her youth. Karega might easily be read as 'Karego' ('small girl')[98] through a strategic orthographical slippage. The anxiety in the naming here, like Wanja's wish to change her gender in front of a feature in the landscape whose name she shares, forms part of a broader anxiety in Ngugi's later fiction. As Florence Stratton puts it, from Ngugi's perspective, '"a strong determined woman" is to all intents and purposes a man. The identification of his heroine with masculine values is Ngugi's response to the question of how to create a female national subject . . . [Rather] than rewriting nationalism, he rewrites woman.'[99] Like Wanja, Jacinta Wariinga (whose name means 'the flower . . . decorated with wire ornaments')[100] is rendered in terms of pastoral imagery in *Devil on the Cross* so that the narration constructs womanhood in precisely the same terms as the neocolonial acolytes debase it.[101] On the one hand, Wariinga refuses to be 'a mere flower . . . to decorate the doors and windows and tables of other people's lives'.[102] On the other hand, her breasts sway 'jauntily like two ripe fruits in a breeze'[103] and her 'clothes fit her so perfectly, it's as if she was created in them'.[104] This inconsistency in the

---

[95] Ngugi, *Petals*, p. 122.

[96] Ngugi, *Petals*, pp. 25, 264.

[97] Sicherman, *Ngugi wa Thiong'o*, p. 206.

[98] Presley, *Kikuyu Women*, p. 185.

[99] Florence Stratton, *Contemporary African Literature and the Politics of Gender* (London: Routledge, 1994), p. 163.

[100] Herta Meyer, *Justice for the Oppressed: The Political Dimension in the Language-Use of Ngugi wa Thiong'o* (Essen: Die Blaue Eule, African Literatures in English 4, 1991), p. 104.

[101] The Rich Old Man who has seduced Wariinga as a girl calls her 'My little fruit, my little orange, my flower to brighten my old age!' Ngugi wa Thiong'o, *Devil on the Cross* (London: Heinemann, 1980; reprinted 1987), p. 253.

[102] Ngugi, *Devil*, p. 216.

[103] Ngugi, *Devil*, p. 11.

[104] Ngugi, *Devil*, p. 217.

representation of Wariinga is implicit in Ngugi's attempt to confront Gikuyu women's oppression without confronting the Gikuyu traditional and neocolonial patriarchies. Furthermore, with Muturi's pistol on her person, Wariinga – biologically coded as female – is narratively and historiographically coded male.[105] Wariinga's political agency ultimately represses her femininity.

It seems to me that Ngugi's oeuvre attempts, and largely fails, to open up positive spaces of political agency for women.[106] Leaving aside the symbolic and institutional importance of clitoridectomy, which props up Ngugi's ideological positions from his first novel to his most recent,[107] the gendering of the landscape and the nation in Ngugi's fiction works to domesticate female sexuality and to privilege male political prerogatives. From the pristine, agrarian landscapes equated with motherhood in the early novels, to the polluted, grotesque landscapes equated with prostitution or sexual debasement in the later novels, Ngugi's heroines cannot take up an active role in culture unless they forfeit both their femininity and their sexuality. Where Ngugi does represent Mau Mau women, he never allows the characters to use their sexuality as a weapon in the struggle. Where he represents prostitutes or sexually uninhibited women, he denies them a meaningful contribution to the struggle in an ideological manoeuvre that the history of the Mau Mau prostitute contradicts.

In short, Ngugi's fiction largely repeats the colonizer's construction of Gikuyu women as static figures in the Emergency landscape. There is one exception to this rule. In *Matigari* Guthera will not prostitute herself with a policeman to rescue her father from execution during the Emergency years – he has acted as a Mau Mau courier, carrying bullets in his Bible. This representation initially represses the historical contribution of prostitutes to Mau Mau. However, Guthera does eventually sleep with a policeman (whom she considers an untouchable) in order to free Matigari from imprisonment and from his fate at the hands of the neocolonial government. By trading sex for Matigari wa Njiruungi's ('the patriots who survived the bullets' or the 'Kenyan Land and Freedom Army's') freedom, Guthera symbolically prostitutes herself for bullets/seeds ('Njiruungi')[108] and belatedly restores female sexwork-in-insurgency to Ngugi's narrative of the nation.

---

[105] For a similar argument, see Elleke Boehmer, 'The Master's Dance', p. 195.

[106] The two notable exceptions are Njeri (the Mau Mau fighter) and Wambui (the Mau Mau courier) in *A Grain of Wheat*.

[107] See the song (*maranjara*) performed during circumcision/clitoridectomy and in preparation for armed struggle. Ngugi, *Matigari*, pp. 4, 126. For an extended discussion of clitoridectomy and its importance to Gikuyu nationalism, see Brendon Nicholls, 'Clitoridectomy and Gikuyu nationalism in Ngugi wa Thiong'o's *The River Between*', *Kunapipi*, 25:2 (2003), pp. 40–55.

[108] For a fascinating explanation of Gikuyu polysemy in *Matigari*, see Ann Biersteker, '*Matigari ma Njiruungi*: What Grows from the Leftover Seeds of "Chat" Trees?', in Charles Cantalupo, ed., *The World of Ngugi wa Thiong'o* (Trenton, NJ: Africa World Press, 1995), pp. 141–58.

Chapter Eleven

The Garden and Resistance in Diasporic Literature: An Ecocritical Approach

Cynthia Davis

Luxuriant tropical landscapes belonging to other people have always engaged the European imagination. In early western art and literature, Edenic fantasies of fruitful abundance were enhanced by the apparently minimal effort required to sustain them. During the age of exploration, plants brought back from the so-called Second Eden inspired illustrations of exotic palms, ferns and fruit trees. Not surprisingly, the new plants were contextualized in a western setting. The banana, for example, 'often turned up as the tree of the knowledge of good and evil – though the jungle in which it allegedly grew bore a remarkable resemblance to neat, orderly European gardens'.[1] Some illustrators, such as the Flemish engraver De Bry, erred not only botanically but also morally, in distancing indigenous peoples from European viewers by portraying the former as barbaric and primitive. In the anonymous print 'The Unheard of Cruelties of the Iroquois' (1698), the so-called cruelties are not only quite recognizable 'to anyone familiar with Baroque paintings of Catholic saints being martyred, [but] the engraving was created by someone who believed that palm trees grew everywhere in the New World, including, apparently, Canada'.[2]

Literature also contributed to the 'othering' of tropical landscapes and inhabitants. In *The Tempest*, for example, Shakespeare links the trope of the New Eden with a clever European who dominates the 'brave new world' (V. i). Although Schneider argues that it is reductive to blame Shakespeare 'for the way in which British imperialists have justified colonial oppression on the model of Caliban's ineducability',[3] Tiffin maintains that the playwright did participate, albeit unconsciously, in 'a process of "fixing" relations between Europe and its

---

[1] William Warren, *The Tropical Garden* (London: Thames and Hudson, 1997), p. 7.

[2] Ellwood Parry, *The Image of the Indian and the Black Man in American Art* (New York: George Braziller, 1974), p. 12.

[3] Ben Ross Schneider, Jr., 'Are We Being Historical Yet?: Colonialist Interpretations of Shakespeare's *Tempest*', in Leeds Barroll, ed., *Shakespeare Studies*, vol. 23 (London: Associated University Press, 1996), p. 2.

"others"... [and] establish[ed] patterns of reading alterity'.[4] In other words, when Prospero distances Caliban with verbal abuse ('monster', 'thing of darkness', 'tortoise', 'poisonous slave') and denigrates his race and ancestry ('got by the Devil himself upon thy wicked dam'),[5] he seems to justify the fact that he has stolen his land and enslaved him. Nevertheless, Caliban comes out of his cave in resistance mode and continually tries to escape and to reclaim his tropical land of 'fresh springs ... brine pits ... berries ... fish ... wood'.[6]

This essay explores the garden landscape as a mode of resistance to the alienation of diasporic peoples implicit in Eurocentric texts as expressed in the work of seven African-American and Caribbean writers. The research is grounded in a 'Green Wave', or ecocritical approach, to diasporic literature. Influenced by Crosby's *The Columbian Exchange* (1972) and *Ecological Imperialism* (1986), ecocriticsm is 'concerned with environmental degradation and neocolonialist depredation of bioregions' and deconstructs writing about landscape as a political act.[7] The essay also responds to Slaymaker's call for more ecocritical analysis of Black Atlantic writing. While the term 'landscape' refers to indigenous plants in the Americas, it is used primarily to describe cultivated gardens. A distinction is made between botanic gardens that function as emblems of imperialist power and Eurocentric culture, and the personal, Afrocentric gardens of diasporic peoples.

The Caribbean and African-American writers discussed all work within a postcolonial framework, address the politics of landscape and a history of oppression, and protest the alterity of marginalized peoples. In addition, all explore the garden as a trope of resistance in ecological discourse. Zora Neale Hurston, Alice Walker, Gloria Naylor and Tina McElroy Ansa, as African-American women artists, respond to critic Barbara Christian's call for a Black, feminist presence; in their literary gardens they embrace Christian's exhortation to 'look low' and to celebrate the personal, vernacular voice of women who have hitherto been silenced. These four writers combine memory and gardening to re-establish communication with ancestral voices, and to correct the racist perspective of America's official history.

While overlap and commonalities certainly exist between African-American and Caribbean writers, the latter group, including Jamaica Kincaid, Jean Rhys and Ismith Khan, use the garden landscape, primarily the botanic garden, to explore structural relationships of power and institutionalized racism, and to interrogate the dangers of assimilationism in which the middle class privileges metropolitan culture to the exclusion of its own identity and spiritual strength.

---

[4] Helen Tiffin, 'Post-Colonial Literatures and Counter Discourse', in Bill Ashcroft, Gareth Griffiiths and Helen Tiffen, eds, *The Post-Colonial Studies Reader* (London: Routledge, 1995), p. 98.

[5] William Shakespeare, *The Tempest*, in *Major Plays and the Sonnets*, ed. G. B. Harrison (New York: Harcourt Brace, 1948), I. ii.

[6] Shakespeare, *The Tempest*, I. ii; II. ii.

[7] William Slaymaker, 'Letter', *PMLA*, 114:5 (1999), p. 1100.

As the conquest of landscape expanded, Europe's fascination with exotic flora and fauna included the thrill of possession. In the nineteenth century few major European capitals, 'however frigid, lacked some sort of facility for displaying the latest botanic wonders to the public'.[8] These gardens functioned, along with education, religion and language, 'to affirm the hegemony of universalist or Eurocentric concepts, codes and images'.[9] Jamaica Kincaid remembers that on Sundays in Antigua families dressed in their best clothes and strolled under the trees, reading the Latin labels identifying plants from other subject territories throughout the Empire. At the same time, their metropolitan counterparts in London's Kew marvelled at specimens brought from every corner of the Empire that they owned.[10]

In the colonial territories botanic gardens, originally established as collection stations for tropical plants, eventually became important research centres.[11] The first colonial garden, Pamplemousses, on the island of Mauritius, was planted by the French in 1735 in order to study sugarcane which 'turned out to be, next to disease, perhaps the most detrimental contribution of the Old World to the New'.[12] In 1764 the British established gardens on St Vincent and St Thomas; the former, the oldest botanic garden in the western hemisphere, still boasts a breadfruit tree from the original seedling brought by the infamous Captain Bligh on *The Bounty*. The garden in Port of Spain, Trinidad, has been in continuous operation since 1822, and Jamaica's four gardens, Bath, Cinchona, Hope and Castleton, were laid out between 1869 and 1881 by horticulturalists Nathaniel Wilson and Robert Thompson, who were trained by Joseph D. Hooker, the second director of Kew Gardens. As Brockway points out, 'this was the era of economic botany ... when every new plant was being scrutinized for its use as food, fiber, timber, dye, or medicine'.[13] In many ways, the botanic gardens 'resembled today's multinational corporations with their links to the military ... and their control of patents and franchises'.[14]

Even aesthetically botanic gardens contributed to the commodification of the tropical landscape and reinforced the power of the Empire. In the private sector, wealthy collectors like the Sixth Duke of Devonshire sent scouts all over the world in search of rare Brazilian lillies, Malaysian orchids and Madagascan palms for his greenhouse, which was, according to Warren, so tall that Queen Victoria was able to ride through it in the royal carriage. If the Duke's greenhouse looked anything like the Palm House at Kew, its height and long, curving iron ribs would have suggested

---

8　Warren, *Tropical Garden*, p. 7.

9　Simon During, 'Postmodernism or Post-Colonialism Today', in Ashcroft, Griffiths and Tiffin, *Post-Colonial Studies Reader*, p. 125.

10　Jamaica Kincaid, *A Small Place* (New York: Farrar, 1988).

11　Lucile H. Brockway, *Science and Colonial Expansion: The Role of the British Royal Botanic Gardens* (New York: Academic Press, 1979).

12　Herman J. Viola and Carolyn Margolis, *Seeds of Change* (Washington, DC: Smithsonian Institution, 1991), p. 12.

13　Brockway, *Science and Colonial Expansion*, p. 74.

14　Viola and Margolis, *Seeds of Change*, p. 8.

the ribbing of iron steamships, and by implication 'the extent of British maritime and colonial penetration of the entire world'.[15]

Not surprisingly, then, the tropical landscape has always been fraught with meaning in the literature of the Black Atlantic. V. S. Naipaul, visiting an estate in England, finds that an interrogation of the word 'gardener' leads him 'to Trinidad, to Port of Spain, to Indian indenture, to the canefields, slavery and the plantation and back to England and the landlord whose family wealth was based on imperial expansion'.[16] For writers like Naipaul, the very existence of plants in the New World – their selection, arrangement, traditions, properties and uses – has political, cultural and ecological implications in the postcolonial context. Jamaica Kincaid asks: 'What did the botanical life of Antigua consist of at the time Christopher Columbus saw it? To see a garden in Antigua now will not supply a clue.'[17] Montserrat, for example, when 'named' by Columbus in 1493, 'was a lush, tropical rain forest providing shelter and sustenance to Arawak Indians. Today, Montserrat's indigenous population and original landscape have vanished. The Arawaks were replaced first by the Irish … and then by African slaves. The rainforests were replaced by sugarcane.'[18] The imagery in Lorna Goodison's poem – 'the green cane growing/Tall flagging lances of veridian green' – suggests both the Empire and the military might behind it.[19]

Tall lances of imperial wrought-iron surround the formal garden in Port of Spain in Ismith Khan's *The Jumbie Bird* (1961); the garden is 'laid out like the lines of the Union Jack, in the centre of which stood the statue of Sir Ralph Woodford; it was he who had suggested bringing Indians to Trinidad after slavery was abolished'.[20] Now, to the chagrin of municipal authorities, the park is frequented by 'old and decrepit Indians like Mongroo and Kareem … many of them had left the sugar plantations long ago and come to the city … they had lost their trade, their ways of ploughing and sowing … and had come to spend rainy nights … only to be awakened by the steel-heeled policemen clacking at their ears'.[21] Despite Woodford Square's iron gates, formal paths and vigilant policemen, however, the landscape resists control. 'As the first rays of warm sunlight touch the grass there emerges a powerful pungence of the earth … the rich, moist air escapes, carrying with it the heady odours of purple poui … a million buds have burst open … and everything stands erect, seething with a kind of defiance … a violent urge to possess the earth.'[22] Defiant as the plants, the

[15] Viola and Margolis, *Seeds of Change*, p. 3.

[16] Helen Tiffin, 'Rites of Resistance: Counter-discourse and West Indian Biography', *Journal of West Indian Literature*, 3:1 (1989), p. 41.

[17] Jamaica Kincaid, *My Garden: Book* (New York: Farrar, 1999), p. 135.

[18] Viola and Margolis, *Seeds of Change*, p. 13.

[19] Lorna Goodison, *To Us, All Flowers are Roses* (Urbana: University of Illinois Press, 1995), p. 61.

[20] Ismith Khan, *The Jumbie Bird* (Harlow: Longman, 1961), p. 13.

[21] Khan, *The Jumbie Bird*, p. 19.

[22] Khan, *The Jumbie Bird*, p. 19.

old men ignore the Tourist Board, which periodically tries to dislodge them because they are 'an eyesore to the tourists from England and America who came to visit this beautiful tropical paradise'.[23]

Khan's young protagonist, Jamini, passes the old men in Woodford Square every day on his way to school. The men remind Jamini of his grandfather, with whose militant, anti-British values the boy must reconcile his opportunity to attend prestigious Queen's Royal College. Although the institution is only a mile away from Jamini's poor neighbourhood, the landscape of colonialism is such that he must traverse two cultures and hundreds of years of history to reach it. At school, the English boys ignore him because he does not play cricket and 'the few Indian boys talk and act just like the English'.[24] Jamini's loneliness is voiced by the Jumbie, an indigenous bird nesting in Woodford Square, whose cry, associated with death, links Jamini both with the old Indians, and with the demise of the old colonial order in Trinidad.

Khan thus uses the tropical landscape to interrogate colonial sites of marginalization and loneliness. The visitors to the public garden contrast the moral integrity of the disenfranchised poor with the spiritual emptiness of the Eurocentric middle class. The garden:

> was a place where tired shoppers came to rest their feet ... they were dwellers from the hidden hills and hamlets ... who knew no one in the great city ... they had their shoes strung about their necks as they squatted in the shade of a great sweeping Saman tree, unfolding their lunches from large-size handkerchiefs ... unconcerned with the city dwellers' laughter and humouring.[25]

Unlike the poor, the middle class visit the garden only in evening; their children are accompanied by nannies who warn them not to look at the country people, and 'particularly not to eat anything they might offer'.[26] In revealing that the affluent citizens of Port of Spain delegate the feeding of their children to servants and deprive them of cultural nourishment as well, Khan suggests that the legacy of the West Indian bourgeoisie is hypocrisy and spiritual sterility, the result of their self-created distancing from their heritage.

The hypocrisy of colonial society and the corruption of power, played out against a lush tropical backdrop, is foregrounded by Jean Rhys in her novel *Wide Sargasso Sea* and in her short stories. 'Goodbye Marcus, Goodbye Rose' (1976) is set in Jamaica's Hope Garden, but is clearly inspired by the Roseau Botanic Garden of Rhys's childhood on Dominica. In the story of a child's loss of innocence, Rhys reveals how the abuse of power is grounded in gender, race and class. Captain

---

[23]   Khan, *The Jumbie Bird*, p. 19.
[24]   Khan, *The Jumbie Bird*, p. 188.
[25]   Khan, *The Jumbie Bird*, p. 15.
[26]   Khan *The Jumbie Bird*, p. 15.

Cardew, a veteran of the nineteenth-century Indian campaigns, is not only a very handsome old man, but also a 'war hero'. For the second time he has appeared at Phoebe's house with a box of chocolates and an offer to take the 12-year-old girl for a walk. Her mother has impressed on her how kind it is of him to bother with a little girl like herself, and Phoebe is duly flattered. She takes him to 'the secluded part of the Garden that she'd spoken of'[27] and 'began to talk in what she hoped was a grown-up way about the curator, Mr. Harcourt-Smith, who'd really made the gardens as beautiful as they were. He'd come from a place in England called Kew.'[28] Suddenly, 'his hand, which had been lying quietly at his side, dived inside her blouse and clamped itself around one very small breast. "Quite old enough", he remarked.'[29]

In this predatory scene, the Caribbean garden becomes a site of corruption as two pillars of empire, the botanist and the soldier, alter landscape and despoil innocence with an impunity grounded in being white, male and upper class. The Captain's sin in the secluded garden is doubly hidden because Phoebe's mother, 'silent and reserved', has given her no words to express or to protest her violation. Although Phoebe is 'in a ferment ... she made up her mind that she would tell nobody ... it was a thing you could not possibly talk about ... also, no one would believe her ... and she would be blamed'.[30] As Kincaid suggests, speaking of the ecological exploitation of Antigua by European business interests, 'the only language ... [one] has in which to speak of the crime is the language of the criminal who committed the crime'.[31] However, the violation which makes it impossible for Phoebe to return to her place in Victorian society also opens her eyes to its hypocrisy and frees her from its restrictive codes. O'Callaghan points out that Rhys's Caribbean characters, typically white West Indian women, emotionally fragile and economically insecure, represent the 'ultimate outsider (whose) sensibility contributes to West Indian literature a concern for complexities ... an eye/ear for dissonances and false appearances in the social superstructure and a quest for realness'.[32]

Like 'Goodbye Marcus, Goodbye Rose', *Wide Sargasso Sea* (1966) depicts a tropical landscape indelibly tainted with the violence and cruelty of colonialism. Rhys sets a number of important scenes among West Indian flora. Antoinette, the narrator, is the same age as Phoebe: she recalls that 'our garden was large and beautiful as that garden in the Bible – the tree of life grew there. But it had gone wild. The paths were overgrown and a smell of dead flowers mixed with the fresh living

---

27 Jean Rhys, 'Goodbye Marcus, Goodbye Rose', in Jean Rhys, *Sleep it off, Lady* (New York: Harper & Row, 1976), 9. 26.

28 Rhys, 'Goodbye Marcus, Goodbye Rose', p. 26.

29 Rhys, 'Goodbye Marcus, Goodbye Rose', p. 26.

30 Rhys, 'Goodbye Marcus, Goodbye Rose', p, 27.

31 Kincaid, *Small Place*, p. 31.

32 Evelyn O'Callaghan, 'The Outsider's Voice: White Creole Women Novelists in the Caribbean Literary Tradition', *Journal of West Indian Literature*, 1:1 (1986), p. 86.

smell ... Orchids flourished out of reach or for some reason not to be touched.'[33] The lyricism of this passage suggests the original, pre-Columbian landscape of the Caribbean, now irretrievably altered. The Jamaican poet Mary Wolcott expresses a similar thought when she recalls 'the cruel deeds beneath the flowering limes'.[34] A second landscape scene involves the ruins of an old house, behind which is 'a wild orange tree covered with fruit, the leaves dark green. A beautiful place ... under the orange tree [were] little bunches of flowers tied with grass.'[35] This place of peace is an obeah shrine: indigenous vegetation has obliterated the old estate house and all that remains are offerings to the African gods. Rhys suggests that one possibility for spiritual regeneration in the Caribbean is through association with the Afrocentric past and the natural environment. Antoinette's fragmented self could become whole were she able to embrace her indigenous roots and establish an independent domicile in Jamaica, as her nurse advises her to do. Her dilemma is that she is 'a European receptacle housing a West Indian consciousness',[36] and thus unsure of her identity. 'What am I doing in this place and who am I ?' she asks poignantly.[37]

Unfortunately, Antoinette is not destined to achieve this integration of self with the Caribbean landscape. Although she, like Phoebe, is innocent, Rhys implies that she must suffer in order to expiate the guilt of her slave-owning ancestors. Antoinette's fate is foreshadowed in her recurring nightmare of a faceless man leading her to a terrible end: 'We are in an enclosed garden surrounded by a stone wall and the trees are different trees ... I stumble over my dress and cannot get up.'[38] The journey to this nightmare garden suggests that Antoinette, forced from her home and taken to an alien land, must imaginatively experience the Middle Passage endured by the family's slaves.

For Rhys, the landscape is a site to be interrogated in her continual search for truth and honesty. 'Even amid her happy moments as a child in Dominica ... [Rhys] saw beneath the lazy, surface calm the continued domination of blacks and the subordinate, reductive role of women.'[39] The tropics thus prove to be a complex image that suggests the search for ethnic and gender identity, the loss of innocence, the corruption of power and the despoilment of nature within the colonial context.

Like Rhys, Jamaica Kincaid maintains that violence, cruelty, and the perversion of nature stem from colonialism. Just as the Captain exploited Phoebe, Kincaid

---

[33] Jean Rhys, *Wide Sargasso Sea* (New York: Norton, 1999), p. 11.

[34] Mary Adela Wolcott (Tropica), 'The Undertone', in Alison Donnell and Sarah Lawson Welch, eds, *The Routledge Reader in Caribbean Literature* (London: Routledge, 1996), p. 42.

[35] Rhys, *Sargasso*, p. 62.

[36] Patricia Barber-Williams, 'Images of the Self: Jean Rhys and her French West Indian Counterpart', *Journal of West Indian Literature*, 3:3 (1989), p. 12.

[37] Rhys, *Sargasso*, p. 107.

[38] Rhys, *Sargasso*, p. 36.

[39] Thomas F. Staley, *Jean Rhys, A Critical Study* (Austin: University of Texas Press, 1979), p. 4 .

associates the plants in the Antigua Botanic Garden with 'our dominators ... their need to isolate, name, objectify, possess various parts, people, and things in the world'.[40] Revisiting the Garden as an adult, Kincaid remarks that 'accounts of botanic gardens begin with men who have sworn to forsake the company of women and have attached themselves to other things ... [such as] the capture, isolation and imprisoning of plants'.[41] For Kincaid, the whole concept of the botanic garden is fraught with implications of exile, displacement, objectification and 'the shameful qualities of imperialism and unjustified aggression'.[42]

In contrast to these ecologically incorrect sites, Kincaid offers her mother's Afrocentric yard where 'the leaves never stay on the trees, they are always yellowing and eventually falling down ... nothing behaves, nothing can be counted on to do so'.[43] The neighbours, on the other hand, strive for a British garden: they plant English roses and even decorate a tropical fern tree with Christmas lights. Kincaid thus opposes the aesthetic of the indigenous Caribbean garden with the European preference for artifice, Cartesian symmetry, right angles and the control of nature.

Unlike its European counterpart, function determines form in Afrocentric garden design since, according to Kincaid, medicinal folklore and botany are closely intertwined with aesthetics. Both healing plants, such as senna (*Cassia italica*), and okra (*Abelmoschus esculentus*) and deadly poisons (*Tephrosia sinapou*), made the journey with the bondsmen and women to the New World. Others were discovered upon their arrival: 'Since the Negro slave had brought with him an intimate knowledge of nature, he began to find substitutes for the plants he had used in his homeland.'[44] Like her African ancestors, Kincaid's mother grows the herb 'six sixty-six' not only because of its healing properties but because its deep green, oval leaves are intrinsically beautiful.

The aesthetic of the Afrocentric garden, as in other diasporic art forms, is grounded in harmony with nature and rejects the linear, preferring circular forms. For example, in the Caribbean 'gardeners do not make garden beds with straight lines and angles; paths meander; the corpus of dancers move in a circle, and the gyrating hips of individual dancers (rub-a-dub style) carve a circular pattern'.[45] Similarly, 'the Jamaican small farmer's repudiation of chemical fertilizers, export-oriented monocropping, and land reclamation schemes, promoted by development banks, is in keeping with an Afrocentric respect for nature, and represents a uniquely spiritual world view'.[46]

---

[40] Kincaid, *My Garden*, p. 143.

[41] Kincaid, *My Garden*, p. 151.

[42] Kincaid, *My Garden*, p. 148.

[43] Kincaid, *My Garden*, p. 45.

[44] William Ed Grime, *Ethno-Botany of the Black Americans* (Algonac, Mich.: Reference Publications, 1979), p. 63.

[45] Mervyn Alleyne, *Roots of Jamaican Culture* (London: Pluto Press, 1989), p. 161.

[46] Alleyne, *Roots*, p. 161.

Kincaid's Afrocentric garden aesthetic links her with African-American sisters Alice Walker, Zora Neale Hurston, Gloria Naylor and Tina McElroy Ansa. Like Kincaid, Walker makes a symbolic journey home and finds that after 22 years her mother's daffodils 'have multiplied and are now blooming from one side of the yard to the other' around 'the remains of a typical abandoned sharefarmer shack'.[47] Walker recalls that her mother 'adorned with flowers whatever shabby house we were forced to live in. And not just straggly zinnias ... she planted over fifty different varieties ... sunflowers, petunias, roses, dahlias, delphinium, verbena ... because of her creativity, even my memories of poverty are seen through a screen of blooms.'[48] In this transformative act, she resists the constraints of a racist and patriarchal system. Walker, in fact, refutes a narrowly hegemonic definition of creativity that excludes the artistry of her mother; rather, she defends gardening, sewing, letter-writing, journal-writing and story telling as redemptive and resistant acts.

Where Kincaid and Walker begin with personal memories and expand outward, Zora Neale Hurston, in her travels to Jamaica and Haiti, connects with broader racial memories as she investigates gardens associated with medicine, witchcraft and passion. From her opening description of Jamaica, whose 'land thrusts out its sensuous bosom to the sea',[49] Hurston links the garden with an Afrocentric, anthromorphic, feminine spirit. Country women run 'balm yards' where, in cleansing rituals, they bathe patients in nutmeg, rum, jasmine and lime juice. A bride is massaged on her wedding night by a herbalist with coconut oil and khus khus grass in order to make her more responsive to her husband, but unfaithful husbands are punished with deadly nightshade and dieffenbachia, which makes the tongue swell in the mouth. Hurston points out that food, aphrodisiac, medicine and poison exist on a continuum in the very same plant. The woman who knows the difference enjoys incalculable power and respect; but Hurston's characters, like Kincaid's and Walker's mothers, garden also for aesthetic reasons: 'the will to make life beautiful is quite strong', she tells us, and they go to great lengths to create 'an atmosphere of romance and mystery'.[50]

Unfortunately, according to both Christian and Alleyne, the aesthetic sensibility of such women has never been valued in a culture that privileges the logical and analytical over the spiritual. These 'artist-mothers', denied education and sometimes literacy, 'transformed the material to which they'd had access into their conception of Beauty: cooking, gardening, quilting, storytelling'.[51] To counteract this exclusion,

---

[47] Alice Walker, *In Search of Our Mothers' Gardens* (New York: Harcourt Brace, 1983), p. 244.

[48] Walker, *In Search*, p. 241.

[49] Zora Neale Hurston, *Tell My Horse: Voodoo and Life in Haiti and Jamaica* (New York: Harper & Row, 1990), p. 3.

[50] Hurston, *Tell My Horse*, p. 14.

[51] Barbara Christian, 'The Highs and Lows of Black Feminist Criticism', in Henry Louis Gates, Jr., ed., *Reading Black, Reading Feminist* (New York: Meridian, 1990), p. 44. See also Alleyne, *Roots of Jamaican Culture*.

Christian advises us to attend 'to body language, story telling and kitchen gossip, double-entendre, loud supper talk ... sashaying bodies, calypso, bantering and bambooshaying'.[52] Attending to the vernacular will enable 'the development of theories that will help us to properly see and understand the themes, motifs, and idioms, imagery and characters used by black women writers'.[53] Such literary strategies both signify resistance to the status quo and affirm the artistic abilities of many hitherto 'voiceless' women.

Hurston's and Walker's validation of black vernacular women's art is echoed by contemporary African-American writers who utilize the trope of the garden as a manifestation of authenticity and resistance. Tina McElroy Ansa and Gloria Naylor combine gardening and memory to correct the distorted, racist history of the American South. In *Mama Day* (1988) and *Ugly Ways* (1993), the protagonists have worked alone in their secret gardens for years and must now pass on to the next generation their knowledge, history and art. Their stories evolve slowly, for the narratives, which are organic and circular, privilege the oral tradition and are filtered through a number of sometimes conflicting voices. Mama Day's garden, for example, links a proud but tragic family history of slavery, madness and abandonment with the search for identity by her contemporary grandniece, Cocoa. Naylor suggests that the truth of the African-American experience in America, unavailable in official histories, can still be discovered in the gardens created and remembered by generations of women unable to leave a written record.

A garden, in fact, directly links Cocoa and Mama Day to the latter's great-grandmother, the slave Sapphira Wade. Except for a bill of sale dated 1819, there is no written record of Sapphira's existence, but despite a system that strove to deny individuality and personality, this official document inadvertently communicated several uniquely personal facts: Sapphira was of pure African descent and was a midwife and nurse. She was also suspected of practising witchcraft. These details, of course, connect Mama Day with her African culture. In the absence of records of birth, baptism, marriage and death, the legend of Sapphira Wade's potions, spells and magic is passed along generations of Sea Islanders, told by people sitting on porches shelling June peas. Unable to write her story, Sapphira's memories of African plant lore nevertheless enable her to frame a history of resistance and testify to a unique aesthetic which she passes on to her descendents.

Mama Day, 150 years later, still tends the garden Sapphira created: 'It was an old garden: a garden designed by a woman. A subtle arrangement of human hands had peach trees and pecan trees flowing into flowering bushes flowing into low patches of herbs ... those dried bundles of herbs over the mantel may have been ... [Mama Day's] but they hung on hooks that were rusted and ancient ... [Mama Day] was

---

[52] Christian, 'Highs and Lows', p. 45.
[53] Sherley Anne Williams, 'Some Implications of Womanist Theory', in Gates, *Reading Black, Reading Feminist*, p. 70.

not the first to use them.'[54] Like Sapphira, she is a healer and the isolated island community depends on her to know the exact dosage of chokecherry bark that could kill as easy as cure. Mama Day creates magic in her garden; she waves her cane over a patch of zinnias and 'the scarlet petals take flight ... and winged marigolds follow them into the air ... a thump of the stick: morning glories start to sing'.[55] Thus, Mama Day's legacy from Sapphira is not only the ability to cure but also the ability to transform reality in an only slightly more magical way than Alice Walker's mother did around her sharecropper cabin.

In Ansa's *Ugly Ways*, Mudear Lovejoy also 'magically transforms her life through her garden'. For 20 years, refusing to leave her home or to do any kind of housework, she stays in bed all day and gardens all night. She is famous in her small Georgia town for 'the whiteblooming garden ... [she] had grown especially to stand out at night ... the moonflowers, the stalks of ginger lily, the caladiums and hostas with their pale green and white stripes, the climbing peace roses and the iceberg roses ... [all] looked like spirits dancing in the autumn wind'.[56] Mudear has raised three daughters in this unconventional fashion. To them she is 'like some strange exotic mixed-up plant herself', which seems to give off noxious fumes as she makes the family miserable; at night, however, she exudes oxygen 'like a strange jungle plant that had reversed the natural order of the plant world'.[57]

The story, told in flashback by five family members, all of whom are baffled by her bizarre behaviour, gradually reveals that Mudear's pride will not allow her to tolerate the institutionalized racism of rural Georgia. Mudear's logic is, in fact, far less surreal than that of a society that predicates humanity on colour. Although Mudear would like to physically leave Georgia, she realizes that without a job or education she has nowhere to go. Instead, like the Sea Island slaves of legend who flew back to Africa, Mudear travels in spirit to her garden, an Edenic refuge of peace and beauty where she can assert her identity and express her thwarted creativity. Eventually, the daughters, all of whom had sworn not to have children, realize that Mudear's legacy is one of fertility and regeneration and they embrace a new pregnancy in the family.

It is just this *joie de vivre* in the face of adversity, passed on from generation to generation in the memories and gardens of women who have survived against all odds, that Walker affirms when she tells the story of the little lavender petunia bush her mother discovered in an abandoned sharecropper's garden: 'She said Stop! Let me go and get that petunia bush ... and they went home and she set it out in a big stump in the yard. And it never wilted, just bloomed and bloomed. Every time the family moved she took her petunia and thirty-seven years later when my daughter

---

54 Gloria Naylor, *Mama Day* (New York: Vintage, 1993), p. 225.

55 Naylor, *Mama Day*, p. 152.

56 Tina McElroy Ansa, *Ugly Ways* (New York: Vintage, 1993), p. 55.

57 Ansa, *Ugly Ways*, p. 55.

was born she brought me a piece of that same petunia bush.'[58]

It is through the garden that Walker, Ansa, Naylor, Hurston, Kincaid, Rhys and Khan ground themselves, literally and figuratively, in the New World. Establishing their connection with the African past in the hybridized present, they resist alienation and othering – whether based on race, gender or class – and affirm their claim on the landscape of the New World. Through garden and memory, the peoples of the Atlantic diaspora oppose the 'centralized, logocentric master narrative of European culture'.[59] Kincaid, now living in Vermont, emphasizes the primacy of memory and landscape when she realizes that her garden is 'an exercise in … remembering my own immediate past … the garden I was making (and am still making and will always be making) resembles a map of the Caribbean and the islands'.[60]

Today, as Slaymaker points out, the widespread interest in environmental literature and 'ecocrit' offers scholars the opportunity to deconstruct the Black Atlantic diasporic traditions through landscape and ecology. That a start has been made can be seen in current books, journal articles, university courses, reference works and sessions at academic conferences, but much research remains to be done in the field.

---

[58] Walker, *In Search*, p. 268.
[59] Ashcroft, Griffiths and Tiffin, *Post-Colonial Studies Reader*, p. 117.
[60] Jamaica Kincaid, *My Garden*, p. 8.

Chapter Twelve

Geographies of Liberalism: The Politics of Space in Colm Toibin's *Bad Blood: A Walk along the Irish Border* and *The Heather Blazing*

Conor McCarthy

I

Since perhaps the mid-1990s, Colm Toibin has come to assume the mantle of being Ireland's leading younger novelist. The only figure to rival him would be Roddy Doyle. They are of roughly the same generation, Toibin born in Wexford in 1955, Doyle in Dublin in 1958. They arrived on the scene of Irish fiction at roughly the same time: Toibin's *The South* was published in 1990, Doyle's *The Commitments* in 1988. They have also both achieved Booker Prize nominations: Toibin for his most recent novel, *The Blackwater Lightship*, in 1999, and Doyle with *The Van* and *Paddy Clarke Ha Ha Ha* in 1991 and 1993 respectively, with the latter winning the prize.

However, the differences between these authors are also significant. Doyle's books have been immensely commercially successful; his first three novels, the so-called *Barrytown Trilogy* (composed of *The Commitments*, *The Snapper* and *The Van*) have all been made into popular films. He has written successfully for television (*Family*) and the stage (*Brownbread*, *War*). But Toibin, ever since *The South* (which won the *Irish Times*/Aer Lingus Literature Prize in 1991), has been endowed with a 'literary' seriousness and hauteur that arguably still eludes Doyle. Moreover, Toibin has come to figure as a kind of intellectual in a way that, one suspects, Doyle has no wish to do. This may stem from their pre-literary backgrounds. Toibin had a successful career as a journalist before he turned to fiction. He published a collection of his journalistic pieces in 1990, *The Trial of the Generals* (a book that has oddly vanished from the list of his publications printed in his books by his metropolitan publishers, Picador and Vintage). In addition, Toibin has also been an editor of *Magill* magazine, an Irish current affairs publication, as well as appearing as a frequent reviewer and essayist. Doyle has not such a writerly history. He emerged out of the activities of the Passion Machine, the Dublin Northside popular theatre company founded by Paul Mercier in 1984. His plays were staged by the Machine in the St Francis Xavier (SFX) Centre before his fiction was published. The Passion Machine has been identified by the journalist and novelist Ferdia MacAnna with a principally working-class 'Dublin Renaissance', an allegedly 'non-literary' enterprise, at least at its founding moment.[1] So Doyle has not gone on to become the figure that Toibin's literary success has allowed him to be, as a commentator for such prestigious literary newspapers as the *London Review of Books* and the *New York Review of Books*, an editor[2] and essayist-intellectual, all activities and positions in which Doyle has shown little interest.

This status as a public intellectual offers us a starting point for a critique of Toibin's work, one that encompasses his 'factual' work alongside his fiction; that is, the critic is permitted to apply proximate frames of analysis to both genres of writing. Starting at least with his book on 'moving statues' (1985), Toibin has long had ambitions beyond quotidian journalism. The shuttling between these two kinds of writing – novels and a kind of anthropological or travel writing – suggests that Toibin is intent on intervening in the public sphere directly in both, and permits the critic's analysis to move from the travel genre to the novel, for it is Toibin's apparently successful self-construction as an intellectual that allows it to be said that his interventions take on a different valency from those of many of his contemporaries. It is precisely this background in the 'hard' world of journalism that might be argued to animate his elaborately minimalist prose. One could say that Toibin's spare style is an attempt to produce a kind of bleached naturalism that seeks to adhere in as empirically truthful a manner as possible to the 'facts'. But I would suggest that the fact that this style is employed as clearly in Toibin's travel writing as in his fiction undermines it and reveals it to be the rhetorical mode it pretends not to be. So, one could suggest that the repetition of the style in the two genres gives it a kind of deconstructive instability, quite to the contrary of its intentions. Its use in the fiction demonstrates its poetic basis when one turns to the 'factual' work, while its use in the travel writing reveals the realist ambitions of the fiction.

The two main texts I wish to examine here – the 'travelogue' *Bad Blood: A Walk along the Irish Border* and the novel *The Heather Blazing* – might be said to be Toibin's most explicitly 'Irish' work (though the more recent novel *The Blackwater Lightship* might modify that claim somewhat). Both may reasonably be said to deal with questions of geography and empire, or the geographical legacies of empire. *The Heather Blazing* is Toibin's second novel and juxtaposes the childhood and youth, and the mid-life crisis, of an Irish High Court judge who has grown up in the immediate post-Independence period. The travel account, *Bad Blood: A Walk*

---

[1] See Ferdia MacAnna, 'The Dublin Renaissance: An Essay on Modern Dublin and Dublin Writers', *Irish Review*, 10 (Spring 1991), p. 29.
[2] Toibin edited *Soho Square 6* (London: Bloomsbury, 1993).

Along the Irish Border, is a version of an earlier book, *Walking Along the Border*, published, with photographs by Tony O'Shea, by Toibin in 1987. The new edition was published in 1994.

The premise of *Bad Blood* is simple enough: in the summer of 1986, Toibin undertook to traverse the length of the border between Northern Ireland and the Republic of Ireland, from Lough Foyle between Co. Donegal and Co. Londonderry, to Carlingford Lough between Co. Down and Co. Louth. This was accomplished at a time of powerful strife even by the standards of the 'Troubles': the Hillsborough, or Anglo-Irish, Agreement, negotiated between the Thatcher and FitzGerald governments in 1985, had been revealed by the time of Toibin's journey to have had a deeply divisive effect on the communities of the North. Unionists were outraged that a treaty had been drawn up over their heads that accorded to the Republic a consultative role in the affairs of Northern Ireland, while northern Republicans were furious that the Agreement 'copperfastened' partition, by recognizing that the constitutional status of Northern Ireland would only ever change in accordance with the democratic will of the majority of the population. The Irish government saw the Agreement as a mechanism to restore some credibility to its main political partner in Northern Ireland, the Social, Democratic and Labour Party (SDLP), in the wake of the political successes of Provisional Sinn Fein since the Maze hunger strike crisis of 1981 and Mrs Thatcher's brusque dismissal of the conclusions of the New Ireland Forum of 1984. The British government saw the Agreement principally as a mechanism to improve security co-operation along the border. Such was the turbulence of the Unionist reaction, however, that the Agreement can now be said to have achieved neither of these aims.

But some remarks need to be made about Toibin's premise itself, before we look in some detail at the resultant text. Toibin's book is a travelogue, a narrative of a particular journey through a highly politicized space and time. It makes reference to events in the past, but it cannot be described as a work of history. Toibin's own status as journalist, writer and novelist gives the book the force of the literary, the honorific of 'culture', a dynamic evident in the shift from *Walking Along the Border*, with its large-scale, even 'coffee-table' format, to the A5 scale of the more serious 'text-only' 'book', *Bad Blood*. The text is about a particular experience, but Toibin's status and the manner of its writing elevate it into something more general, or 'universal'. The pared-down style suggests, among other things, the 'ordinariness' of the narrative voice. Anyone walking along the border would experience it in this way, it claims. The blank style suggests a narratorial Everyman.

But Toibin is not an Everyman. For a book by a journalist, the text displays a surprising lack of investigative zeal or historical research. It does not open with any kind of statement of purpose or self-description. Rather it throws the reader immediately into the flow of Toibin's experience:

> I walked out of Derry towards the border on a beautiful cloudless afternoon, past the broken-down public houses, past the abandoned shirt factory and the new housing estates

and the sailing boats on the Foyle. It was Saturday. I was wearing a rucksack. When I crossed the border I would turn right and take the road to Lifford.[3]

Here we have a casual tone of studied banality. The beauty of the afternoon is as significant as the 'broken-down public houses', 'the new housing estates', 'the sailing boats on the Foyle'. The date is no more specific than 'Saturday'. No further indication of the narrator's purpose is given than that he 'was wearing a rucksack'. This could be any walk, by anyone, almost anywhere. For the book to have begun with a self-description or a historical account of partition would have removed the possibility of the normal, but also normalizing, nature of this description. The reader is not invited to consider *why* the narrator is walking *where* he is or *what* the nature of the route is. The reader is given information on a pragmatic or empiricist 'need to know' basis. The reading-subject is interpellated, one might say, as being as incurious as Toibin's narrator seems to be.[4] So, we find here a mode of writing, a narrative style and authorial persona that aspires to neutrality or innocence, even. This is a highly debatable approach, since neither the context nor the narrative mode, nor space itself, are innocent or neutral.

II

There has been for some time a burgeoning field of study concerning cultural inscriptions of geopolitical space, as well as space more generally. French writers and theorists, such as Gaston Bachelard, Henri Lefebvre, Michel Foucault and Michel de Certeau, and the *Annalistes* school of French historiography, have revitalized historical and human geography, and have powerfully diverted these disciplines away from mere empiricism and positivism. More recently, Marxist geography, much of it influenced by Lefebvre, and led by writers such as David Harvey, Neil Smith and Edward Soja, has reasserted the crucial relationship between capitalist modes of production and social and political space. The point must be, fundamentally, that space and place are not simply inert facts of nature, waiting 'out there', somehow to be filled by human ideas, activities and history. Rather space is constructed, in an interaction between the natural world and human actions. This applies to private as well as public spaces: as Bachelard demonstrates in *The Poetics of Space*, even the most domestic and private spaces of the home are invested and

---

[3]   Colm Toibin, *Bad Blood: A Walk Along the Irish Border* (London: Vintage, 1994), p. 1. All further references will be to this edition, and will be marked in the text as *BB*.

[4]   I take my vocabulary here, of course, from Louis Althusser, most especially his essay 'Ideology and Ideological State Apparatuses (Notes towards an Investigation)', in his *Lenin and Philosophy and Other Essays*, trans. Ben Brewster (London: New Left Books, 1971), pp. 125–86.

given meaning by the human imagination.[5] In other words, space is not simply to be apprehended in positivist terms of depth, distance, area, length, volume. Rather, space is made by an endlessly proliferating and intermeshing network of human biographies that can be re-characterized as 'life paths in time-space'.

But it is more besides: such life paths both create and are created, humanly. Michel de Certeau writes of the way that we 'create' cities by walking through and around them. Walking, for de Certeau, is a willed act that can be both creative and resistant. It can create social spaces, and also offer a narrative of resistance to regulated or repressive spaces. Cities are bound together by the massing and flow of human paths. Social practices offer resistance to regulatory authority, since they spatialize rather than become localized under such authority.[6] We do not merely create spaces by traversing them. Space is created by the entire panoply of ways that human beings alter, design and mould their environment. Crucially, we can say that there are kinds of space produced in the modern post-Enlightenment world, the kinds of space produced under historical capitalism and under the aegis of the modern state. Frequently, these are represented, legitimized and also contested in discourse, including cultural discourse.

Famously, Raymond Williams wrote of the shifting representations of the land in English literature. He demonstrated brilliantly the relationship of the 'country house' poems of Andrew Marvell and Ben Jonson to the history of violent appropriation or extraction of labour surplus that was the condition of possibility of these new estates. Behind a poem like 'To Penshurst' lies an entire economy and social order which the poem obscures and justifies.[7] So the representation of space can be intimately bound up with the forms of power that have created and now regulate that space. Depending on the literary mode of production at the time, or the modality of production and dissemination and consumption of literature, that literature participates in, and may be influenced by, a variety of other discourses pertaining to the space in question.

If capitalism, represented in Williams by the early stages of English agrarian capitalism, is one major shaper of space in modernity, the state must be another, and here we move back towards territory more immediately relevant to the discussion of Toibin. One way to define the modern state, after all, is as a territory over which a single legitimate jurisdiction is exercised or which constitutes a form of spatialized sovereignty. The most obvious limit on this jurisdiction or sovereignty is the border that separates one state from another, thus linking the regulation of space with the state. But Toibin's narrative is an account of a summer spent walking along, around and near the border between two states. These states were created as a result of a

---

[5] Gaston Bachelard, *The Poetics of Space*, trans. Maria Jolas (Boston: Beacon Press, 1994).

[6] Michel de Certeau, *The Practice of Everyday Life*, trans. Steven Rendall (Berkeley: University of California Press, 1984).

[7] Raymond Williams, *The Country and the City* (London: The Hogarth Press, 1993), chs 3–6.

movement of secession from the British Empire.[8] The point that must immediately be made is that Toibin's text offers no historical understanding of this frontier. I shall argue that this would, in fact, be impossible given his chosen style, but it is first necessary to give an account, however brief and schematic, of that history.

As Ian Lustick has suggested, 'In the world as we know it in the 1990s, no fact is more obvious about states than the impermanence of their boundaries.'[9] Borders may change due to war or due to peaceful change, such as the reunification of Germany. Liam O'Dowd points out that the Irish border was created at roughly the same time as 'some of the least successful and most conflictual borders established this century'.[10] Locally, the point is that, as Michael Laffan has shown, there was nothing natural or inevitable about the creation of the Irish border.[11] Neither was the Irish border created in the institutional context of international negotiation. Unlike the post-1918 division of Silesia, for example, which was effected by means of democratic plebiscite and the mediation of four neutral countries, the partition of Ireland was seen as an affair internal to the United Kingdom. O'Dowd reminds us that it was, in fact, the product of a balance of force between Ulster Unionism and the British state, on the one hand, and the Free State and Ulster Nationalism, on the other. That balance, in the crucial phase of 1912–5, was tilted in Unionism's favour:

> Ulster Unionists ... won the right of self-determination in an historical conjuncture which maximised their power and influence. The outcome registered the concentration of Unionist-controlled industrial production and reflected the deep links between Unionist elites and the conservative and military establishments in Britain ... these groups ... had been able to shape the coalition government's policy in Britain and above all they had been able to mobilise concentrated armed force on the ground in what was to become Northern Ireland.[12]

The nineteenth-century Home Rule movement was superseded by the Government of Ireland Act of 1920, which legislated in effect for two 'Home Rule' parliaments, one in Belfast and one in Dublin. The resistance of Unionism to Home Rule had nevertheless issued in a form of Home Rule. In seeking to thwart nationalist, or as Ulster Unionists saw it, Catholic majoritarianism, they won their own majoritarian

---

[8]   I am indebted to the work of Joe Cleary in the discussion of the border that follows. For one of the very few sustained discussions of partition and Irish culture, see his *Literature, Partition and the Nation-state: Culture and Conflict in Ireland, Israel and Palestine* (Cambridge: Cambridge University Press, 2002).

[9]   Ian Lustick, *Unsettled States, Disputed Lands: Britain and Ireland, France and Algeria, Israel and the West Bank-Gaza* (Ithaca: Cornell University Press, 1993), p. 3.

[10]   Liam O'Dowd, *Whither the Irish Border? Sovereignty, Democracy and Economic Integration in Ireland* (Belfast: Centre for Research and Documentation, 1994), p. 11.

[11]   Michael Laffan, *The Partition of Ireland* (Dundalk: Dundalgan Press, 1983).

[12]   O'Dowd, *Whither the Irish Border?*, p. 11.

dispensation in the new Northern statelet. The Treaty of 1922, building on the Government of Ireland Act, had given more autonomy to the Oireachtas in Dublin, legislated for the formality of a Northern opt-out from an all-Ireland parliament and provided for a Boundary Commission to settle the border.

In practice, the working of the Commission was weakened and diluted. The Northern Ireland government, while accepting the Treaty's opt-out for Northern Ireland, refused to be bound by the Commission on the grounds that Northern Ireland had not been party to the Treaty. The British were wary of the Commission, lest it re-open the question of partition. If the prospect of major border alterations had originally been held out to Sinn Fein negotiators in 1921, the British government now argued for only minor rectifications. Crucially, it rejected the principle of plebiscites as the means to determine the wishes of the local inhabitants. Irish nationalist pressure for a plebiscite was countered with the suggestion that it would run foul of Ulster Unionist resistance. So, the status quo was confirmed by, if not force, then the threat of force, and not by democratic means.

As O'Dowd and Laffan suggest, few of those who actually helped to create the Irish border saw it originally as a frontier between nation-states. Yet, once in place, events, policies and the simple existence of two states as 'facts on the ground' combined to consolidate it. Most interestingly, it also served to effect various kinds of division or separation. It allowed British governments of all hues to separate Westminster politics from Irish 'domestic concerns'. To that extent, it even separated Unionists from British perceptions of overall national interest. Partition deeply divided Irish nationalists, breaking them into a range of bodies of opinion spanning straightforward rejection to short-term acceptance of what was felt to be a temporary settlement. Northern nationalism was divided between abstentionists and constitutionalists, and also between border inhabitants and those east of the Bann, and politicians and gunmen. Northern nationalists were sundered from their Southern brethren. And of course, nationalists were also separated from Unionists, who saw the Southern state as an external threat and Northern nationalists as a 'fifth column' intent on subverting the Northern state. Even in the South, nationalists divided over the Treaty (hence the Civil War and the emergence of Fianna Fail and Fine Gael as the dominant political parties), but further they faced the choice of either increasing and stressing their state's separateness from Britain or trying to develop links with the North. In the end, the logic of the existing Free State won out, and it prioritized its own economic, constitutional and socio-cultural agendas and interests. The ideological rupture thus effected in nationalism was compensated for in the 1937 Constitution's claim to the whole island as the 'national territory'.

Thus, there is a massive sedimented history lying behind the border as we come to it today. It is not merely a line on a map, but has itself acquired historical – institutional, economic, juridical and cultural – force. None of this is alluded to by Toibin. He merely notes that the Anglo-Irish Agreement 'signed the previous November by the British and Irish governments … had increased tension in the North, and sparked off a campaign by Protestants with the slogan "Ulster says No"

(*BB* 8). But this apparently not being a political book, he nowhere explains the real nature of the Agreement, which did not compromise British sovereignty in Northern Ireland to any significant degree. But what we must now consider, in returning to Toibin's text, is the way that what are aesthetic or literary choices, techniques, tropes and motifs may presuppose or imply a politics. The question, that is, is what is the link between Toibin's representation of the border (or his failure to do so) and his aesthetic strategies. After all, the border is, according to the book's blurb, 'the most dangerous strip of land in Western Europe'. But Toibin is not really interested in danger. He is ill-equipped for it. Much of his navigation is confused and haphazard. He carries only a Michelin road map, which does not mark a great many of the small roads that honeycomb the border region of Ireland. He finds that the best maps are those possessed by the British Army: 'He showed me his map ... The map was incredibly detailed, every house, every field, every road, carefully denoted and described. It would be impossible to go wrong with such a map' (BB 163). But he does not register the knowledge that maps are also a source, and sign, of power. He is himself offering a kind of map in his text, a map of the border itself, but it is one whose power lies in its cognitive/epistemological limitations. These are imposed by Toibin's use of language.

I would suggest that Toibin's style, and his mode of operation, constitute what might be called an impressionistic empiricism. This is conducive to a narrative mode of irony, as described by Hayden White.[13] Experience is seen to countermand the projections of theory or ideology or abstraction. Seamus Deane has caustically suggested, of Irish historical revisionist empiricism, that 'all good liberals are empiricists, but not all empiricists are good liberals'.[14] The point that follows is that Toibin's narrative voice is putatively liberal, but that this may be revealed to be severely circumscribed. When this empiricism is deployed by a mobile consciousness such as Toibin's narrator, we receive a view of the border that is characterized by a series of separated tableaux. Empiricism is constitutively sceptical about totality or abstraction. So, to historicize the border is beyond the reach of Toibin's narrative, as is the effort to see the border as the intersection of two states. The premise of Toibin's story is that the way to describe the border is to experience it physically. In a certain sense, the border is the 'plot'. But *Bad Blood* breaks into a series of somewhat discrete episodes, with no particular linking element other than Toibin's own consciousness: the hiring fair, the Lough Derg pilgrimage, the cruise on Lough Erne (*BB* 9–33, 33–49, 49–57). What is remarkable and damaging is the degree to which the border is allowed to dominate the narrative, while also, for the most part, going unanalysed. The point also is that Toibin's narrative voice is underwritten by a kind of meta-subject, that of the state conceived as the repository of modernity.

---

[13] Hayden White, *Metahistory: The Historical Imagination in Nineteenth-century Europe* (Baltimore: Johns Hopkins University Press, 1973), pp. 36–8.
[14] Seamus Deane, 'Wherever Green is Read', in Theo Dorgan and Mairin Ni Donnchadha, eds, *Revising the Rising* (Derry: Field Day, 1991), p. 97.

The frontier region and its people are clear to him, in that he can pass through them and render them narratively intelligible to the metropolis. But his clarity will never be that of the locals, in terms of their own knowledge of their own place, and Toibin is simply incurious as to what the locals think or know of him. Toibin's narrative remains resolutely outside the lives of the people he surveys. He produces a kind of knowledge that is predicated on an ironic distance from the people and experiences he chronicles. The Archimedean point from which such irony is possible is the state: the transparency of the people and the region to Toibin's surveillance mirrors their availability to the gaze of the state. Zygmunt Bauman neatly sums up the process of modernization when he suggests that before modernity the local tended to be unintelligible to the metropolis, but with the advent of modernity the reverse became the case – the metropolis attained to a transparent knowledge of the local, but the local lost any cognitive grip it ever had over the metropolis.[15] So, the very model of narrative voice offered by Toibin, that of a kind of naturalist objectivity, is the inscription of modernity, and in Ireland, that means the State.[16]

Of course, Toibin encounters local people along the way, and it is these encounters that are the stuff of his book. But it is worth noting that his project assumes the exotic or alien nature of these people to his readers. That Toibin's audience may be as much middle-class Dubliners as a wider readership in the United States and the United Kingdom does not reduce the effect of defamiliarization achieved here: none of Toibin's interlocutors would ever think of the border as he does. For them, it is a matter of smuggling, the security forces, sundered farms and families, price differences North and South, blocked roads and inconvenience, political rupture. To them, the idea of walking along the frontier would probably seem quixotic and self-indulgent. But Toibin seems oddly insouciant or careless in his attitude: he recounts his own fears at some of his encounters on the road, but he never reflects on the possible fears regarding *him* of the people whose localities he is passing through, a lone man on foot. He actually tells a young boy that he is an army foot patrol, and allows him to tell his friends the same story (*BB* 164). This episode, mentioned in passing, can be compared with a detailed description of a *faux pas* while staying at a guest house run by middle-class Protestants, where Toibin, identifying the soup he is served as borscht, mentions that the Pope is fond of it (*BB* 90–94). This incident is dwelt on with some self-deprecation and mortification on Toibin's part: 'I gave myself a good kick for mentioning the Pope. And for being surprised that the couple from Omagh signed themselves as British.' But for the most part, Toibin's narrative is unreflective and detached.

---

[15] Zygmunt Bauman, *Globalization: The Human Consequences* (London: Polity Press, 1998), p. 33.

[16] For further discussion of modernization as a governing concept in recent Irish cultural history, see Luke Gibbons, *Transformations in Irish Culture* (Cork: Cork University Press, 1996) and my *Modernisation, Crisis and Culture in Ireland, 1969–1992* (Dublin: Four Courts Press, 2000).

This extends to the border itself, which is refused a historical context, but is also allowed, as I suggested earlier, to dictate the narrative itself. For example, Toibin describes sectarian violence, such as the massacre of Protestants at Darkley, but his narrative never gives itself the space to consider the possibility of a relationship between this sentiment and the border. Toibin, the peripatetic narrator, permits himself only to see the facts on the ground before him. His narrative, especially when dealing with violence, does not explicitly try to comment or register any emotion. His description of the killing of James Graham illustrates this well:

> I met Michael Harding, the curate in Derrylin ... I asked him about the shouts for joy that Father Gaffney had heard, the whoops which he had told me that the IRA had given as they escaped after killing James Graham. Had he heard them too? ... What did they sound like? I wanted to know. It was a wild howl, he said. Yes, but what exactly did it sound like? He did it for me in a high-pitched voice.
> 'Ya-hoo, ya-hoo, ya-hoo,' they screamed when they killed the third Graham brother (*BB* 102).

This is the last paragraph of a chapter, and is placed in this way to allow the horror of the attitude of the murderers to work its own power, without embellishment or superfluous comment. This suggests a number of things. First, that the incident has been rendered factually. Second, that further comment is unnecessary and, third, that further comment is in fact *impossible*. This, in turn, suggests an ambivalent attitude to language, at once of exorbitance and of modesty. Exorbitance, because it implies that events *can* be rendered accurately if one employs the correct rhetorical register and, modesty, because it suggests that extreme events or experiences cannot be rendered at all. This ambivalence works also on the level of the narrative as a whole. On the one hand, Toibin suggests that the Border can only be described in terms of empirical experience, as a series of discontinuities. On the other, he nevertheless covers its entire length. His local hesitancies and uncertainties do not deter the forward progress of his narrative, whose geographical logic cannot be gainsaid. He seems to be telling us that his project is an impossible one, yet he goes ahead and carries it through.

Toibin deviates from the border to describe certain events or experiences such as the Lough Derg pilgrimage or the service at Darkley. The assumption here must be that these institutions, powerful symbols of conservative Roman Catholicism and of the 1859 Protestant Revival in Ulster, are symptomatic of the border. Yet, as Toibin himself writes, Lough Derg has been a place of pilgrimage since the twelfth century. To include it in a narrative on the border is therefore, arguably, unhistorical. The implication is also of an equivalence in religious fervour, and that the normality of religious practice is of a conservative kind. The Lough Derg scene is one where Toibin's status as mere observer becomes more than usually clear, as it is shot through with an ironic detachment that he does not bring to Darkley. Darkley is more morally difficult to be openly irreverent about because of the terrible attack perpetrated on its worshippers by the Irish National Liberation Army, an offshoot of the Official IRA, in 1983. But Lough Derg is described at length. The problem is that, viewed simply through the eyes of a sceptical empiricist observer, we receive no impression as to what the rituals might mean to a believer:

> Having followed the instructions of the leaflet once, I discovered that the entire process had to be repeated three more times on the way around three identical beds: St Brendan's Bed, St Catherine's Bed, St Columba's Bed. People moved with a slow, quiet zeal as though they were working in a field, kneeling down and standing up again, moving around a small piece of ground before kneeling once more. All this ritual just added up to one Station. It was going to have to be repeated nine times before I got off the island, and the first one hadn't even finished yet (*BB* 40).

Inevitably, Toibin perceives Lough Derg mediated by the work of earlier writers: Sean O'Faolain, Patrick Kavanagh, Seamus Heaney. But such literary precedents do not help him to understand, in anything other than the most superficial manner, the motivations of his fellow pilgrims:

> The car park beside the pier where the boats were moored was full of big, shiny cars. I had imagined that the sort of people who came here were poor, from the small farms, from the edges of the towns and cities. One look at the car park put me right on that (*BB* 36).

The point here is doubled: Toibin has nursed a class prejudice that can only envisage fervent old-fashioned ritual as part of the faith of poor, ill-educated people. But he can now cast aspersions on the sincerity of the pilgrims as he finds them, by noting their relative material wealth. Darkley, however, is rendered in a more sober manner. At Lough Derg, Toibin's sceptical and ironic relation to Catholicism is given free play, but at Darkley he has no purchase at all on the ritual he witnesses, and he can only offer humanist generalization:

> The long room began to fill up now, this Sunday afternoon. Most of the congregation looked like ordinary members of a farming community. All the women wore hats. There was a lanky young man across from me who was standing up, with his arms spread out. Except for this, and the accordion and drums at the top of the room, it could have been a small congregation at prayer on a Sunday anywhere in Ireland (*BB* 179).

In Toibin's description, the service he attends is intercut with an account of the fatal INLA assault of 1983. While the service continues, 'the British Army appeared outside'. A little later, 'the British Army moved around the building'. Finally, 'I stood outside as the army drove away down the hill' (*BB* 180–82). A contrast is therefore set up between the offensive and dreadful penetration of the hall by the terrorists and the circumspection and non-intrusiveness of the Army. It is difficult not to reach the conclusion that the Army is seen as the condition of possibility of the service. So, Toibin, in spite of himself, shows us how this is clearly not a 'small congregation at prayer on a Sunday anywhere in Ireland'.

III

Francis Spufford notes that travellers are 'notoriously bad at saying why'.[17] Travellers tend not to clarify their motives, so we cannot expect to understand them in the way that we understand a realist fictional character, who is established for us by an omniscient narrator. Accordingly, Toibin never offers a justification for his journey. He neither evinces a particular original curiosity or quest for novelty, nor a personal emotional reason for his movement. His narrative offers itself, tautologically, as its own rationale. Furthermore, we have no access to his interior world, as we would with a realist fictional character. Toibin's narrative constructs him as a blank cipher, amenable to endless redefinition by each encounter, a space to be filled by the empirical realities of which he is the neutral observer. His isolation from social ties, as with other travel writers, produces a narrative voice that is apparently representative and universal, yet his leisure and mobility separate him from both the people and the places he travels among, and serve to render them exotic. They are also rendered exotic to his reader, and this sense is accentuated by the moments when he decides that he needs a break from the rigours of his journey and retires to the Tyrone Guthrie Centre, at Annaghmakerrig, Co. Monaghan. This only adds to the sense that the journey is one mediated through a literary sensibility. Hence also the encounters with Eugene McCabe, John McGahern and Seamus Heaney. Annaghmakerrig, the former home of the great Irish-American theatre director, was left to the Republic when he died and now functions as a state-sponsored artists' refuge. Conveniently, it also conforms to the liberal-humanist and pluralist ethic that Toibin stands for, even down to its demographic balance:

> The result of the divorce referendum was made known the following Friday morning … the country had voted no. I was in Monaghan, at Annaghmakerrig, the house which Sir Tyrone Guthrie had left to the Irish nation as a retreat for artists … Guthrie's presence was everywhere in the house: the books in each room were his books, with inscriptions from colleagues and friends … He specified in his will … that the artists should eat together in the evening. The house was supported by the Arts Councils, North and South; people came from both sides of the border. The area around the house was still a mixed society, with thriving Church of Ireland, Presbyterian and Catholic congregations (*BB* 49).

Here we find, neatly juxtaposed, a powerful sign of Irish conservatism, and the harmony of a pluralist oasis in the desert of border sectarianism. The harmony of the confessional communities mirrors that of the artistic community. In the absence of any historical explanation as to why this tolerant balance of religion might obtain, we are left with an idealized and moralized demography. A few pages later,

---

[17] Francis Spufford, *I May Be Some Time: Ice and the English Imagination* (London: Faber and Faber, 1996), p. 2.

figures, including a sile-na-gig, carved in the stonework of a Hiberno-Romanesque church, are invested in even more crudely explicit terms. The clerical figures

> seemed to be joining the rest of the population, North and South, in saying 'No'. Their mouths were on the word for eternity. 'No. No. No'. 'Ulster says No.' 'The Republic says No'. The first figure [the sile-na-gig] ... looked as though she could survive in any environment. Her hands ... were ... displaying her pudenda. She had a fixed grin on her face, which seemed to express the joys of lust. 'Yes', she was saying, 'yes, yes, yes' (*BB* 51).

This passage reads and reduces the divorce referendum result, and the entire Northern question, into early Christian statuary. The result becomes, in this formulation, merely clerically derived. Further, it becomes a hypostatized negation, infinite, transhistorical. Into it is collapsed the history of colonization, partition, the Troubles. Into it is collapsed the Loyalist slogan, 'Ulster says no', and its difference from the specific referendum result in the Republic. Real fears of voters are traduced. Under this all-consuming rubric, the two states, North and South, are rendered alike and equal in their essentialized sectarianism. Over against this image Toibin places the sile-na-gig, putting the words of Molly Bloom in her mouth. As a symbol of liberated and liberal desire, this image is almost unanswerable. The trope of reading the environment deployed here is all the more striking when compared to the unwillingness to read the *border* for what it is, especially when it is remembered that the border is itself the condition of possibility of Toibin's liberalism.

The contrast of female sexuality and patriarchal authority is also present in *The Heather Blazing*, along with a spatial economy that separates the domestic and the public/political. This novel, published in 1992, tells the story of Eamon Redmond, a High Court judge in the contemporary Republic. Its form is cyclical, with chapters dealing with Redmond's mature years juxtaposed with an account of his childhood in Wexford. As a middle-aged man, he retains a holiday home in Wexford, which he frequently retreats to with his wife, Carmel. The location of the Redmond cottage atop a cliff overlooking a beach is a matter of some significance. As Neil Corcoran has astutely pointed out, with the passing of the years the cliff is gradually eroded by the constantly encroaching sea, and neighbouring houses are claimed again by nature in the process. Parallel to this geophysical erosion occurs an erosion of Redmond's ethical and political background and inheritance.[18] The problem of this figure, of course, is that it naturalizes and, to that extent, makes inevitable the change it signifies. In a novel that is interested to offer a history of the modern Republic in capsule form, this is an oddly unhistorical formulation.

We first meet Redmond when he is about to deliver a judgement relating to the responsibilities of the State with regard to the hospital care of a handicapped child. His decision is that the State has no duty of care to the handicapped child, and if the

---

[18] Neil Corcoran, *After Yeats and Joyce: Reading Modern Irish Literature* (Oxford: Oxford University Press, 1997), p. 98.

hospital wishes to discharge the child, it is entitled to do so and place the burden of responsibility back on the parents. The difficulty, of course, is that the family is not necessarily equipped to provide this care. But Redmond is clear and unswerving. A little later, in a pattern that repeats throughout the book, Redmond prepares to travel to his cottage in Wexford. His wife informs him that their unmarried daughter, Niamh, is pregnant. For Carmel and Eamon Redmond, this comes as a shock:

> 'She went to England to have an abortion, and she couldn't face it. She was in the hospital and everything; she had paid her money. I told her that we'd do what we could for her, I told her that I was pro-life all the way. I felt so sorry for her. Imagine Niamh having an abortion. So she's going to have the baby and she's going to keep it. Eamon, I wrote her a cheque. But it's a terrible thing to happen, isn't it?'[19]

This is the crucial juxtaposition in the novel: the public judgement, the private crisis. Later, Redmond is faced with a case that explicitly mirrors his daughter's situation. He judges that a school is entitled to expel a pupil who has become pregnant. But the process of erosion has become apparent:

> that was all he knew: the law, its letter, its traditions, its ambiguities, its codes. Here … he was being asked to decide on something more fundamental and now he realized that he had failed and he felt afraid.
>
> He took a biro from a drawer and began to make squiggles on a pad of paper. What was there beyond the law? 'Law'; he wrote the word. There was natural justice. He wrote the two words down and put a question mark after them. And beyond that again there was the notion of right and wrong, the two principles which governed everything and came from God. 'Right' and 'wrong'; he wrote the two words down and then put brackets around them and the word 'God' in capitals beside them.
>
> … the idea of God seemed more clearly absurd to him than ever before … yet the courts and the law ultimately depended for their power on such an idea. He crossed out the word 'God' (*HB* 85–6).

Redmond realizes that he has 'no strong moral views' and has 'ceased to believe in anything' (*HB* 90). Just before he goes out to deliver his judgement, it occurs to him that the clause of *Bunreacht na hEireann* (the Constitution of the Republic) that describes the family as the fundamental social unit never specifies what exactly makes up a family. Thus, it might be open to him to view the pregnant girl and her child as a family, which would then guarantee her rights under the Constitution. But he retreats from the ramifications of this possibility (*HB* 91–2). His own daughter, Niamh, is bitterly critical of his decision when he meets her later at the cottage in Cush. 'Do you think I should be expelled as well?', she asks him (*HB* 99). So, the consequences of Redmond's public position are immediately flung back at him.

---

[19] Colm Toibin, *The Heather Blazing* (London: Picador, 1993), p. 11. All further references will be to this edition and will be marked in the text as *HB*.

The movement from present to past, from Redmond's adulthood to his childhood and youth, offers Toibin's readers a deliberately privileged and ironic vision of the man. The very title of the novel, *The Heather Blazing*, is a line from a famous Republican ballad, 'Boolavogue', about the Rising of 1798. In Toibin's hands, of course, this takes on a distinctly ironic meaning. We, as readers, know much more of Redmond than his wife or children. We are given, in stark detail, Redmond's grim and disease-haunted childhood, invested as it was with a powerful sense of history. His father was a teacher, and amateur historian, who contributed a column, 'Scenes from Enniscorthy's Past', to the local newspaper, the *Enniscorthy Echo*, and organized a museum in the town dedicated to the United Irishmen's Rising of 1798. Redmond's childhood is rendered as desolate and ascetic, lived in the shadow of history, and of the Catholic Church. It is scored with the pain of death and suffering: his grandfather dies, his uncle Stephen dies, his father dies, his mother is already dead. History is a living tradition that can be experienced personally, as when father and son, in the company of the priest, collect rebel pikes from an elderly couple who can claim a connection with the Rising itself:

'Our grandmother now on our mother's side', the woman spoke, 'she was brought up here. It was the time of the evictions. Sure, they used to own from here out to the road … She knew about the men of "Ninety Eight"', the woman looked into the fire and then back at the two visitors. 'She would have been too young to remember it, but they told her about it, and it was she who always said that they came down this way and that was the end of them then. That's all I remember now' (*HB* 23).

This history is impressed on the very person of Eamon Redmond, who is named for Eamon De Valera (*HB* 25). Redmond, one could say, is a direct inheritor of the 'whig-nationalist' narrative of Irish history.[20] He is inserted into and interpellated by a nationalist-republican metanarrative of Irish history, made up of rebellion and resistance. In his late teens, Redmond makes a political speech, introducing De Valera to a crowd in Enniscorthy (*HB* 167–9). He is greeted and praised by Sean Lemass, and much later in his career he meets Charles Haughey (*HB* 220–22). He is thus affiliated with crucial personalities in the development of Fianna Fail and, indeed, of the country. De Valera figures as the father of the nation-state. Lemass represents the turn to exogenous economic development and pragmatism of the early 1960s. Haughey represents both the hope engendered by that modernization and the shadow cast over that hope by dubious politics, an intimate relationship with powerful business interests and the Northern crisis, mediated by the Arms Trials. The scene with Haughey is notable:

'Will we hold the two seats in Wexford?' he asked Uncle Tom.
'It'll be hard without Dr Ryan, but we'll do it'.

---

[20] Brendan Bradshaw, 'Nationalism and Historical Scholarship in Modern Ireland', *Irish Historical Studies*, xxvi (1988–89), p. 329.

[…]

'Otherwise we could run this man here,' Haughey said, putting his hand on Eamon's shoulder. 'But we've other things in mind for him'. He smiled and then became serious again (*HB* 221).

A little later, Haughey tells Redmond, 'You're for the bench' (*HB* 222). So, Haughey is revealed to be a provocateur, but one for whom Redmond is content to work. Even at the time of Toibin's writing, Haughey's was a controversial and divisive name. Redmond's association with Haughey links him with Southern nationalist irredentism, exemplified by Haughey's role in the 1970 Arms Crisis, where he, Neil Blaney and Kevin Boland, all Fianna Fail ministers, were charged with smuggling weapons to the IRA. The link with Haughey also associates Redmond with a new aggressive bourgeoisie that emerged in the 1960s, the first political leaders in the history of the State not to have a personal history of involvement in the revolutionary period.

The effect of parallel narratives in this novel, one recounting Redmond's rise to the position in which we first meet him, and the other describing the death of his wife and his reconciliation with his lone-parent daughter in middle age, is of ironic counterpoint. Bereavement produces a lonely, self-contained, emotionally invertebrate young man during Redmond's initial rise, but it functions as a kind of punishment and produces the social space for reconciliation during his middle age. The ascent to the pinnacle of the legal profession is set off against a mounting confusion in middle age, as Redmond is forced to reassess long-held assumptions. But there is also a geographical element to this contrast. The narrative of Redmond's childhood is one, as in any *Bildungsroman*, of gradually widening circles of geosocial mobility and experience: exile from the family home, school, the Law Library in Dublin, mixing with senior politicians. The narrative of Redmond's maturity is, in contrast, one of the effort to escape from the Four Courts in Dublin and retire to the seaside cottage at Cush, in Wexford. In effect, it is one of return, to the space of childhood, the primary site of affect and emotion. This seems a classically humanistic trope, where the public or political world is conquered by the private or personal one. Against the warm potential of familial reconciliation and redemption, the hypocrisy and impersonality of the political world stand no chance. Redmond's childhood geography is represented as one of seamlessly joined political and familial activity in Wexford, but his geography of middle age is one of a split between Wexford and Dublin, the private and the public, with the former winning out over the latter. It is entirely appropriate, then, that the novel should be entitled with a phrase from one of the most famous ballads about 1798, 'Boolavogue' – a phrase that writes revolutionary politics into the very landscape while resolutely inscribing the depoliticization of that space in the forward progress of the narrative. Indeed, one could go so far as to say that the novel narrates, and spatializes, the 'end of history' in the Irish context: the crisis of Redmond's nationalism is the crisis of

Irish nationalism, its hollowing out from within by the corrosive power of personal hypocrisy and the subversive power of sexuality and the personal sphere.

Toibin's writing, then, in both *Bad Blood* and *The Heather Blazing*, embodies 'incredulity towards metanarratives',[21] one might say, in its Irish manifestation, a kind of hybrid between liberalism and postmodernism.[22] Liberalism in Ireland has meant in the last 30 years a stress on individual freedoms, mostly in the private sphere. It has moved forward, hand-in-hand, with a powerful repressive state apparatus[23] and with the move to economic neoliberalism that has produced the so-called 'Celtic Tiger'. But, as suggested earlier, it is also matched by a literary mode that refuses totality of representation, either historically or spatially, as a coercive abstraction. This mode insists instead on local detail and personal interaction, and it displays a fundamental unwillingness to confront concepts or structures as influences on human behaviour. It is to this extent that Toibin's writing can be argued to manifest the geographical imagination of Irish liberalism.

---

[21] Jean-Francois Lyotard, *The Postmodern Condition: A Report on Knowledge*, trans. Geoff Benington and Brian Massumi (Manchester: Manchester University Press, 1984), p. xxiv.

[22] See Terry Eagleton, 'Revisionism Revisited', in his *Crazy John and the Bishop, and Other Essays on Irish Culture* (Cork: Cork University Press, in association with Field Day, 1998), p. 325.

[23] See Michael Farrell, *The Apparatus of Repression* (Derry: Field Day, 1986).

Select Bibliography

Alaimo, Stacy, *Undomesticated Ground: Recasting Nature as Feminist Space* (Ithaca: Cornell University Press, 2000)

Alexander, Mrs, *A Missing Hero* (London: Chatto & Windus, 1901)

Alleyne, Mervyn, *Roots of Jamaican Culture* (London: Pluto Press, 1989)

Andrews, J. H., 'The French School of Dublin Land Surveyors', *Irish Geography*, 5 (1967)

——, 'The Irish Surveys of Robert Lythe', *Imago Mundi*, 19 (1965)

——, *Shapes of Ireland: Maps and their Makers, 1564–1839* (Dublin: Geography Publications, 1997)

Andrews, M., *Landscape and Western Art* (Oxford: Oxford University Press, 1999)

Angier, Carole, *Jean Rhys: Life and Work* (London: Andre Deutsch, 1990)

Arnold, David, *Colonizing the Body: State Medicine and Epidemic Disease in Nineteenth-century India* (Berkeley: University of California Press, 1993)

Ashcroft, Bill, Gareth Griffiths and Helen Tiffin, eds, *The Post-Colonial Studies Reader* (London: Routledge, 1995)

Bachelard, Gaston, *The Poetics of Space*, trans. Maria Jolas (Boston: Beacon Press, 1994)

Ballantyne, Andrew, *Architecture, Landscape and Liberty: Richard Payne Knight and the Picturesque* (Cambridge: Cambridge University Press, 1997)

Barber-Williams, Patricia, 'Images of the Self: Jean Rhys and her French West Indian Counterpart', *Journal of West Indian Literature*, 3:3 (September 1989)

Barrell, J., 'The Public Prospect and the Private View: The Politics of Taste in Eighteenth-century Britain', in S. Pugh, ed., *Reading Landscape: Country – City – Capital* (Manchester: Manchester University Press, 1990)

Barrington, G. W., *Remarkable Voyages and Shipwrecks. Being a popular collection of extraordinary and authentic sea narratives relating to all parts of the Globe* (London: Simpkin, 1880)

Bauman, Zygmunt, *Globalization: The Human Consequences* (London: Polity, 1998)

Beckett, Urusula à, *In Extenuation of Sybella*, (London: Stanley Paul, 1910)

Bell, H. Hesketh, *Glimpses of a Governor's Life: From Diaries, Letters, and Memoranda* (London: Sampson, 1946)

Berger, John, *Ways of Seeing* (London: Pelican, 1984)

Berman, Bruce and Lonsdale, John, *Unhappy Valley: Conflict in Kenya and Africa – Violence and Ethnicity* (London: James Currey, 1992)

Blake, Susan L., 'A Woman's Trek: What Difference Does Gender Make?', in Chaudhuri, Nupur and Margaret Strobel, eds, *Western Women and Imperialism: Complicity and Resistance* (Bloomington: Indiana University Press, 1992)

Boehmer, Elleke, 'The Master's Dance to the Master's Voice: Revolutionary Nationalism and the Representation of Women in the Writing of Ngugi wa Thiong'o', *The Journal of Commonwealth Literature*, 26:1 (1991)

Bohls, Elizabeth, *Women Travel Writers and the Language of Aesthetics, 1716–1818* (Cambridge: Cambridge University Press, 1995)

Booth, A. R., *The United States Experience in South Africa, 1784–1870* (Cape Town: A. A. Balkema, 1976)

Bourchier, Helen *The Ranee's Rubies* (London: Anthony Treherne, 1902)

Bourdieu, Pierre *The Logic of Practice* (Cambridge: Polity Press, 1990)

Bowden, Mrs. G., *Nella of Pretoria* (London: Digby, Long, 1907)

Bradshaw, Brendan, 'Nationalism and Historical Scholarship in Modern Ireland', *Irish Historical Studies*, xxvi (1988–89)

Bridges, Yseult, *Child of the Tropics: Victorian Memoirs*, ed. Nicholas Guppy (Port-of Spain: Aquarela Galleries, 1988)

Bristow, Joseph, *Empire Boys: Adventures in a Man's World* (London: HarperCollins, 1991)

Brockway, Lucille, H., *Science and Colonial Expansion: The Role of the British Royal Botanic Gardens* (New York: Academic Press, 1979)

Bruce, Catherine, 'Finding England Everywhere: Regional Identity and the Construction of National Identity, 1890–1940', *Ecumene*, 6:1 (1999)

Burns, Patricia, *Fatal Success: A History of the New Zealand Company* (Auckland: Heinemann Reed, 1989)

Cadell, H. M., *Ida Craven*, 2 vols (London: King, 1876)

Cameron, Charlotte, *A Durbar Bride* (London: Stanley Paul, 1912)

Canny, Nicholas *The Origins of Empire*, vol. 1 (Oxford: Oxford University Press, 1998)

Cantalupo, Charles, ed., *The World of Ngugi wa Thiong'o* (Trenton, NJ: Africa World Press, 1995)

Carr, Emily, *The Complete Writings of Emily Carr* (Vancouver: Douglas and MacIntyre, 1997)

Cassin, Freida, *With Silent Tread; A West Indian Novel* (St John's, Antigua: G. A. Uphill, 1890)

Chaudhuri, Nupur and Margaret Strobel, eds, *Western Women and Imperialism: Complicity and Resistance* (Bloomington: Indiana University Press, 1992)

Christian, Barbara, 'The Highs and Lows of Black Feminist Criticism', in Henry Louis Gates, Jr., ed., *Reading Black, Reading Feminist* (New York: Meridian, 1990)

Clark, H. F., *The English Landscape Garden* (Gloucester: Sutton, 1980)

Clarke, G. N., 'Taking Possession: The Cartouche as Cultural Text in Eighteenth-century American Maps', *Word & Image*, 4:2 (April–June 1988)

Clery, Joe, *Literature, Partition and the Nation-state: Culture and Conflict in Ireland, Israel and Palestine* (Cambridge: Cambridge University Press, 2002)

Clough, Marshall, *Mau Mau Memoirs: History, Memory, Politics* (Boulder, Col.: Lynne Rienner, 1998)

Cohen, Phil, 'From the Other Side of the Tracks: Dual Cities, Third Spaces, and the Urban Uncanny in Contemporary Discourses of "Race" and "Class"', in Gary Bridge and Sophie Watson, eds, *A Companion to the City* (London: Blackwell, 2000)

Colquhoun, Combe, Mrs Kenneth, *Cecilia Kirkham's Son* (Edinburgh: Blackwood, 1909)

Colquhoun, M. J., *Every Inch a Soldier*, 3 vols (London: Chatto & Windus, 1888)

——, *Primus in Indis: A Romance*, 2 vols (London: Chapman and Hall, 1885)

Comer, Krista, *Landscapes of the New West: Gender and Geography in Contemporary Women's Writing* (Chapel Hill: University of North Carolina Press, 1999)

Corcoran, Neil, *After Yeats and Joyce: Reading Modern Irish Literature* (Oxford: Oxford University Press, 1997)

Cosgrove, Denis and Daniels, Stephen, eds, *The Iconography of Landscape: Essays on the Symbolic Representation, Design and Use of Past Environments* (Cambridge: Cambridge University Press, 1988)

Cosgrove, Denis E., ed., *Mappings* (London: Reaktion Press, 1999)

——, *Social Formation and the Symbolic Landscape* (London: Croom Helm, 1984)

Crais, C., 'The Vacant Land: The Mythology of British Expansion in the Eastern Cape, South Africa', *Journal of Historical Sociology*, 25:2 (1991)

Croker, Bithia Mary, *A Bird of Passage*, 3 vols (London: Sampson Low, 1886)

——, *Her Own People* (London: Hurst and Blackett, 1903)

Crommelin, May, *The Mountain-Heart of Jamaica*, *Jamaica Pamphlets*, 22, item 31 (Kingston: National Library of Jamaica, 1898)

——, *Pink Lotus: A Comedy in Kashmir* (London: Hurst and Blackett, 1914)

Crook, D. P., *Benjamin Kidd: Portrait of a Social Darwinist* (Cambridge: Cambridge University Press, 1984)

Crosby, Alfred, *Ecological Imperialism* (Cambridge: Cambridge University Press, 1993)

Curtis, Anthony, *The Pattern of Maugham* (London: Hamish Hamilton, 1974)

Cuthbell, Edith E. (writing as 'An Idle Exile'), *Indian Idylls* (Calcutta: Thacker, Spink, 1890)

De Certeau, Michel, *The Practice of Everyday Life*, trans. Steven Rendall (Berkeley: University of California Press, 1984)

De Vere, Aubrey, *The Poetical Works of Aubrey De Vere* (London: Kegan Paul, 1884)

Dehan, Richard, *The Dop Doctor* (London: William Heinemann, 1910)

Dell, Ethel M., *The Top of the World* (London: Cassell, 1920)

——, *The Way of an Eagle* (London: Ernest Benn, 1912)

Denoon, Donald, *Settler Capitalism: The Dynamics of Independent Development in the Southern Hemisphere* (Oxford: Oxford University Press, 1983)

Derrida, Jacques, *The Truth in Painting*, trans. Geoff Bennington and Ian McLeod (Chicago: University of Chicago Press, 1987)

Despard, Charlotte (writing anonymously), *The Rajah's Heir*, 3 vols (London: Smith, Elder, 1890)

Diver, Maud, *Captain Desmond, V.C.* (London: George Newnes, 1931)

Dixon Hunt, John, *The Figure in the Landscape: Poetry, Painting, and Gardening during the Eighteenth Century* (Baltimore: Johns Hopkins University Press, 1976)

——, *Gardens and the Picturesque: Studies in the History of Landscape Architecture* (Cambridge, Mass.: MIT Press, 1992)

Douglas, A. Elizabeth, *The End of the Trek: A Story of South Africa* (London and New York: Andrew Melrose, 1923)

——, *Shadowed Blood* (London and New York: Andrew Melrose, 1925)

Douglas, Mary, *Purity and Danger: An Analysis of Concepts of Pollution and Taboo* (London: Routledge, 1966)

Douglas, Olivia, *Olivia in India: The Adventures of a Chota Miss Sahib.* (London: Hodder and Stoughton, 1913)

Drennan, William, *Fugitive Pieces, in Verse and Prose* (Belfast: Finlay, 1815)

Duff-Fyfe, Ethel, *The Nine Points* (London: John Long, 1908)

Dunlap, Thomas, *Nature and the English Diaspora: Environment and History in the United States, Canada, Australia and New Zealand* (Cambridge: Cambridge University Press, 1999)

During, Simon, 'Postmodernism or Post-colonialism Today', in Bill Ashcroft, Gareth Griffiths and Helen Tiffin, eds, *The Post-Colonial Studies Reader* (London: Routledge, 1995)

Duval Smith, A., 'Markets shape Clinton's Itinerary', *Mail and Guardian*, 20 March 1998

Dyer, Richard, *White* (London: Routledge, 1997)

Eagleton, Terry, *Crazy John and the Bishop, and Other Essays on Irish Culture* (Cork: Cork University/Field Day Press, 1998)

Edge, K. M., *The Shuttles of the Loom* (London: John Murray, 1909)

Edgerton, Robert, *Mau Mau: An African Crucible* (New York: Ballantine, 1989)

Edwood, May, *The Autobiography of a Spin. A Story of Anglo-Indian Life* (Calcutta, Bombay and London: Thacker and Spink, 1893)

Eldred-Grigg, Stevan, *A Southern Gentry: New Zealanders who inherited the Earth* (Christchurch: Reed, 1980)

Ellis, J. J., *Passionate Sage: The Character and Legacy of John Adams* (New York: Norton, 1993)

Eustace, Alice, *Flame of the Forest* (London: Mills & Boon, 1927)

Everett-Green, E., *The Double House* (London: Stanley Paul, 1914)

Fairburn, Miles, *The Ideal Society and its Enemies: The Foundations of Modern New Zealand Society, 1850–1900* (Auckland: Auckland University Press, 1989)

Fairweather, John R., 'White-Settler Colonial Development: Early New Zealand Pastoralism and the Formation of Estates', *ANZJS*, 21:2 (1985)

Farrell, Michael, *The Apparatus of Repression* (Derry: Field Day, 1986)

Ferguson, Niall, *Empire: How Britain made the Modern World* (London: Allen Lane, 2003)

Ferguson, Samuel, *Lays of the Western Gael, and Other Poems* (Dublin: Sealy, 1888)

Fieldhouse, D. K., *The Colonial Empires: A Comparative Survey from the Eighteenth-century* (London: Macmillan, 1982)

Foley T. and Ryder, S., eds, *Ideology and Ireland in the Nineteeth Century* (Dublin: Four Courts, 1998)

Froude, James A., *The English in the West Indies: or The Bow of Ulysses* (London: Longmans, 1909)

Fussell, Paul, *Abroad: British Literary Traveling between the Wars* (Oxford: Oxford University Press, 1980)

Gaunt, Mary, *Reflection - in Jamaica* (London: Ernest Benn, 1932)

Gibbons, Luke, 'Race against Time: Racial Discourse and Irish History', *Transformations in Irish Culture* (Cork: Cork University Press, 1996)

Gilpin, W., *Observations on the River Wye, and Several Parts of South Wales, etc. relative Chiefly to Picturesque Beauty* (London: Blamire, 1782)

Gilroy, Amanda, *Romantic Geographies: Discourses of Travel, 1775–1844* (Manchester: Manchester University Press, 2000)

Gilroy, Paul, *The Black Atlantic* (London: Verso, 1993)

Glass, Ruth, *London's Newcomers: The West Indian Migrants* (Cambridge, Mass.: Harvard University Press, 1961)

Goodison, Lorna, *To Us, All Flowers are Roses* (Urbana: University of Illinois Press, 1995)

Graham, J. M., *The Land of the Lotus* (Bristol: Arrowsmith, 1914)

Gray, Maxwell, *In the Heart of the Storm: A Tale of Modern Chivalry* (London: Newnes, 1903)

Green, Martin, *Dreams of Adventure, Deeds of Empire* (London: Routledge, 1980)

Grewal, Inderpal, *Home and Harem: Nation, Gender, Empire, and the Cultures of Travel* (London: Leicester University Press, 1996)

Grier, Sydney C., *England Hath Need of Thee* (Edinburgh: Blackwood, 1916)

Grime, William, ed., *Ethno-Botany of the Black Americans* (Algonac, Mich.: Reference Publications, 1979)

Hadfield, Andrew and Maley, Willy, eds, *Representing Ireland: Literature and the Origins of Conflict, 1534–1660* (Cambridge: Cambridge University Press, 1993)

Hall, Stuart, 'Cultural Identity and Diaspora', in Laura Chrisman and Patrick Williams, eds, *Colonial Discourse and Post-Colonial Theory: A Reader* (Hemel Hempstead: Harvester, 1993)

Hamer, Mary, 'Putting Ireland on the Map', *Textual Practice*, 3:2 (Summer 1989)

Harasym, Sarah, *The Post-Colonial Critic: Interviews, Strategies, Dialogues* (New York: Routledge, 1990)

Hardiman, James, *Irish Minstrelsy, or Bardic Remains of Ireland*, 2 vols (London: Joseph Robbins, 1831)

Harker, Richard, Mahar, Cheleen and Wilkes, Chris, eds, *An Introduction to the Work of Pierre Bourdieu: The Practice of Theory* (New York: St. Martin's Press, 1990)

Harley, J. B., 'Maps, Knowledge and Power', in Denis Cosgrove and Stephen Daniels, eds, *The Iconography of Landscape* (Cambridge: Cambridge University Press, 1988)

——, 'Meaning and Ambiguity in Tudor Cartography', in Sarah Tyacke, ed., *English Map-Making, 1500–1650* (London: The British Library, 1983)

——, 'Silences and Secrecy: The Hidden Agenda of Cartography in Early Modern Europe', *Imago Mundi*, 40 (1988)

Hatch, Elvin, *Respectable Lives: Social Standing in Rural New Zealand* (Berkeley: University of California Press, 1992)

Hayes-McCoy, G. A., 'Contemporary Maps as an Aid to Irish History, 1593–1603', *Imago Mundi*, 19 (1965)

Helgerson, Richard, 'The Land Speaks: Cartography, Chorography, and Subversion in Renaissance England', *Representations*, 16 (Fall, 1986)

Horner, Arnold, 'Cartouches and Vignettes on the Kildare Estate Maps of John Rocque', *Quarterly Bulletin of the Irish Georgian Society*, XIV: 4 (Oct.–Dec. 1971)

Howarth, Anna, *Katrina: A Tale of the Karoo* (London: Smith, Elder, 1898)

——, *Nora Lester* (London: Smith, Elder, 1902)

——, *Sword and Assegai* (London: Smith, Elder, 1899)

Howell, N., 'South Africa might have been an American Colony', *Cape Times*, 3 September 1938

Hulme, Peter, *Colonial Encounters: Europe and the Native Caribbean, 1492–1797* (London: Methuen, 1986)

——, 'Islands and Roads: Hesketh Bell, Jean Rhys and Dominica's Imperial Road', *The Jean Rhys Review*, 11:2 (2000)

——, *Remnants of Conquest: The Island Caribs and Their Visitors, 1877–1998* (Oxford: Oxford University Press, 2000)

Hurston, Zora Neale, *Tell My Horse: Voodoo and Life in Haiti and Jamaica* (New York: Harper & Row, 1990)

Hussey, Christopher, *The Picturesque: Studies in a Point of View* (Hamden: Archon, [1927] 1967)

Huxley, Elspeth, *Back Streets, New Worlds* (London: Chatto & Windus, 1964)

Jacobs, Jane, *Edge of Empire: Postcolonialism and the City* (London: Routledge, 1996)

Janowitz, Anne, *England's Ruins: Poetic Purpose and the National Landscape* (Oxford: Blackwell, 1990)

Kariuki, J. M., *Mau Mau Detainee* (Nairobi: Oxford University Press, 1963)

Kenyatta, Jomo, *Facing Mount Kenya* (London: Secker and Warburg, 1968)

Khan, Ismith, *The Jumbie Bird* (Harlow: Longman, 1961)

Kincaid, Jamaica, *My Garden: Book* (New York: Farrar, 1999)

——, *A Small Place* (London: Virago, 1988)

Kipling, Alice M. (writing as Beatrice Grange), *The Heart of a Maid* (Allahabad: A. H. Wheeler, 1890)

——, (writing as Mrs J. M. Fleming) *A Pinchbeck Goddess* (London: William Heinemann, 1897)

Kolodny, Annette, *The Land before Her: Fantasy and Experience of the American Frontiers, 1630–1860* (Chapel Hill: University of North Carolina Press, 1984)

Korte, Barbara, *English Travel Writing: From Pilgrimages to Postcolonial Explorations* (London: Macmillan, 2000)

Kristeva, Julia, *Strangers to Ourselves*, trans. Leon S. Roudiez (London: Harvester, 1991)

Kröller, Eva-Marie, 'First Impressions: Rhetorical Strategies in Travel Writing by Victorian Women,' *Ariel*, 21:4 (October, 1990)

Laffin, Michael, *The Partition of Ireland* (Dundalk: Dundalgan Press, 1983)

Lamming, George, 'The Coldest Spring in Fifty Years: Thoughts on Sam Selvon and London', *Kunapipi*, 20:1 (1998)

——, *The Emigrants* (Ann Arbor, Mich.: University of Michigan Press, 1994)

——, *The Pleasures of Exile* (London: Michael Joseph, 1960)

Lassner, Phyllis, 'The Game is Up: British Women's Comic Novels of the End of Empire', in Graeme Harper, ed., *Comedy, Fantasy and Colonialism* (London: Continuum, 2002)

Lee, R., *The African Wanderers: or, The Adventures of Carlos and Antonio. Embracing Interesting Descriptions of the Manners and Customs of the Western Tribes, and the Natural Productions of the Country* (London: Grant, 1850)

Livingstone, David N., 'The Moral Discourse of Climate: Historical Considerations on Race, Place and Virtue', *Journal of Historical Geography*, 17:4 (1991)

Lockhart, L. C. M., *Fire of Life: A Domestic Chronicle* (Edinburgh: Blackwood, 1924)

Lonsdale, Thorunn, 'Reconstructing Dominica: Jean Rhys's "Pioneers, Oh, Pioneers"', *Journal of the Short Story in English*, 26 (1996)

Lustick, Ian, *Unsettled States, Disputed Lands: Britain and Ireland, France and Algeria, Israel and the West Bank–Gaza* (Ithaca: Cornell University Press, 1993)

Lynch, Mrs. Henry, *The Mountain Pastor* (London: Darton, 1852)

——, *The Wonders of the West Indies* (London: Seeley, 1861)

McAleer, Joseph, *Passion's Fortune: The Story of Mills & Boon* (Oxford: Oxford University Press, 1999)

MacAnna, Ferdia, 'The Dublin Renaissance: An Essay on Modern Dublin and Dublin Writers', *Irish Review*, 10 (Spring, 1991)

McCarthy, Conor, *Modernisation, Crisis and Culture in Ireland, 1969–1992* (Dublin: Four Courts, 2000)

McElroy Ansa Tina, *Ugly Ways* (New York: Harcourt Brace, 1993)

MacInnes, Colin, *Absolute Beginners* (London: Allison, 1980)

——, *City of Spades* (London: Allison, 1980)

McIntyre, David, *British Decolonization, 1946–1997: When, Why and How did the British Empire Fall?* (Basingstoke: Macmillan, 1998)

MacKenzie, John M,. ed., *Imperialism and the Natural World* (Manchester: Manchester University Press, 1990)

Mahar, Cheleen, 'On the Moral Economy of Country Life', *Journal of Rural Studies*, 7:4 (1991)

Maloba, Wunyabari, O., *Mau Mau and Kenya: An Analysis of a Peasant Revolt* (Bloomington: Indiana University Press, 1993)

Mansfield, Charlotte, *"For Satan Finds ..."* (London: Holden, 1917)

——, *Gloria: A Girl of the South African Veld* (London: Holden & Hardingham, 1916)

——, *Red Pearls* (London: Holden & Hardingham, 1914)

Mansfield, Katherine, *The Collected Letters of Katherine Mansfield*, ed. Vincent O'Sullivan and Margaret Scott (Oxford: Oxford University Press, 1984–96)

——, *The Katherine Mansfield Notebooks*, ed., Margaret Scott (Canterbury: Lincoln University Press, 1997)

——, *Katherine Mansfield: Selected Stories*, ed., Angela Smith (Oxford: Oxford University Press, 2002)

——, *Poems of Katherine Mansfield*, ed., Vincent O'Sullivan (Oxford: Oxford Unversity Press, 1988)

Marais, J. S., *The Colonisation of New Zealand* (London: Oxford University Press, 1927)

Marchand, Annabella Bruce, *Dirk: A South African* (London and Calcutta: Longmans, Green, 1913)

Maughan-Brown, David, *Land, Freedom and Fiction: History and Ideology in Kenya* (London: Zed, 1985)

Merton, Ray, *My Cousin's Wife* (London; Digby, Long, 1892)

Miles, Robert, *Gothic Writing, 1750–1820: A Genealogy* (London: Routledge, 1993)

Mills, Sara, *Discourses of Difference: An Analysis of Women's Travel Writing and Colonialism* (London: Routledge, 1991)

Milne Rae, Mrs., *A Bottle in the Smoke: A Tale of Anglo-Indian Life* (London: Hodder & Stoughton, 1912)

Mitchell, W. J. T., ed., *Landscape and Power* (Chicago: University of Chicago Press, 1994)

Monkland, Mrs. (writing anonymously), *The Nabob at Home; or, The Return to England*, 3 vols (London: Henry Colburn, 1842)

Moore, Thomas, *Poetical Works* (London: Longman, 1841)

Moray, Gerta, 'Emily Carr and the Traffic in Native Images', in Lynda Jessop, ed., *Antimodernism and Artistic Experience: Policing the Boundaries of Modernity* (Toronto: University of Toronto Press, 2001)

Morgan, Marjorie, *National Identities and Travel in Victorian Britain* (London: Palgrave, 2001)

Muddock, J. E., *The Great White Hand or The Tiger of Cawnpore: A Story of the Indian Mutiny* (London: Hutchinson, 1896)

Muir, Richard, *Approaches to Landscape* (Basingstoke: Macmillan, 1999)

Mutwa, Credo, *My People: The Writings of a Zulu Witchdoctor* (London: Penguin, 1977)

Nash, Thirza, *The Ex-Gentleman* (London: Jarrolds, 1925)

Nasta, Susheila, 'Setting up Home in a City of Words: Sam Selvon's London Novels', *Kunapipi*, 18:1 (1991)

Naylor, Gloria, *Mama Day* (New York: Vintage, 1993)

Newton, Margaret, *Glimpses of Life in Bermuda and the Tropics* (London: Digby, Long, 1897)

Ngugi Wa Thiong'o, *A Grain of Wheat* (London: Heinemann, 1985)

——, *Petals of Blood* (London: Heinemann, 1986)

——, *The River Between* (London: Heinemann, 1965)

——, *Secret Lives and Other Stories* (London: Heinemann, 1992)

——, *Weep Not, Child* (London: Heinemann, 1987)

Norwood, Vera, *Made from this Earth: American Women and Nature* (Chapel Hill: University of North Carolina Press, 1993)

O'Callaghan, Evelyn, 'The Outsider's Voice: White Creole Women Novelists in the Caribbean Literary Tradition', *Journal of West Indian Literature*, 1:1 (October 1986)

O'Dowd, Liam, *Whither the Irish Border? Sovereignty, Democracy and Economic Integration in Ireland* (Belfast: Centre for Research and Documentation, 1994)

O'Farrell, Mary Ann, *Telling Complexions: The Nineteenth-century English Novel and the Blush* (Durham, NC: Duke University Press, 1997)

Page, Gertrude, *The Rhodesian* (London: Hurst and Blackett, 1912)

Palgrave, Mary E., *A Promise Kept* (London: National Society's Depository, 1887)

Parry, Ellwood, *The Image of the Indian and the Black Man in American Art* (New York: George Braziller, 1974)

Patterson, Sheila, *Dark Strangers: A Study of West Indians in London* (London: Penguin, 1965)

Peard, Frances M., *The Ring from Jaipur* (London: Smith, Elder, 1904)

Penny, F. E., *Dark Corners* (London: Chatto & Windus, 1908)

——, *Love in the Hills* (London: Chatto & Windus, 1913)

——, *A Mixed Marriage* (London: Methuen, 1903)

——, *The Rajah* (London: Chatto & Windus, 1911)

——, *The Sanyasi* (London: Chatto & Windus, 1904)

Percival, R., *An Account of the Cape of Good Hope* (London: Baldwin, 1804)

Perrin, Alice, *The Anglo-Indians* (London: Methuen, 1912)

——, *East of Suez* (London: Anthony Treherne, 1901)

Peterson, Margaret, *Dust of Desire* (London: Andrew Melrose, 1922)

Petrie, P., ed., *Morrell's narrative of a voyage to the south and west coast of Africa* (London: Whittaker, 1844)

Phillips, Jock, *A Man's Country? The Image of the Pakeha Male: A History* (Auckland: Penguin, 1987)

Phipps, C. M. K., *Douglas Archdale. A Tale of Lucknow* (London: London Literary Society, 1885)

Pinter, Harold, *The Caretaker* (London: Methuen, 1978)

——, *The Room and the Dumb Waiter* (London: Methuen, 1979)

Pollard, Eliza F., *The White Dove of Amritzir. A Romance of Anglo-Indian Life* (London: Partridge, 1897)

Porter, A., ed., *The Loss of the Ship 'Hercules', 16 June 1796* (Port Elizabeth: Historical Society of Port Elizabeth, 1975)

Pound, Francis, *Frames on the Land: Early Landscape Painting in New Zealand* (Auckland: Collins, 1983)

Pratt, M. L., *Imperial Writing: Travel Writing and Transculturation* (London: Routledge, 1992)

Pratt, Stephanie, 'From the Margins: The Native American Personage in the Cartouche and Decorative Borders of Maps', *Word & Image*, 12:4 (Oct.–Dec. 1996)

Presley, Carol Ann, *Kikuyu Women, the Mau Mau Rebellion, and Social Change in Kenya* (Boulder, Col.: Westview, 1992)

Preston, Rebecca, 'The Scenery of the Torrid Zone: Imagined Travels and the Culture of Exotics in Nineteenth-century British Gardens', in Felix Driver and David Gilbert, eds, *Imperial Cities: Landscape, Display and Identity* (Manchester: Manchester University Press, 1999)

Proctor, James, 'Descending the Stairwell: Dwelling Places and Doorways in early Post-war Black British Writing', *Kunapipi*, 20:1 (1998)

Ramchand, Ken, '*The Lonely Londoners* as a Literary Work', *World Literature in English* (Autumn, 1982)

Raphael, Frederic, *Somerset Maugham and his World* (London: Thames and Hudson, 1976)

Rhys, Jean, *The Collected Short Stories* (New York: Norton, 1987)

——, 'Goodbye Marcus, Goodbye Rose', in Jean Rhys, *Sleep It Off, Lady* (New York: Harper & Row, 1976)

——, *Smile Please: An Unfinished Autobiography* (London: Penguin, 1981)

——, *Wide Sargasso Sea* (London: Penguin, 1968)

Rosenthal, E., *Stars and Stripes in Africa,* 2nd edn (Cape Town: National Books, 1968)

Salmond, Anne, *Two Worlds: First Meetings between Maori and Europeans, 1642–1772* (Honolulu: University of Hawaii Press, 1991)

Savi, E. W., *Baba and the Black Sheep* (London: Hurst and Blackett, 1914)

——, *A Blind Alley* (London: Digby, Long, 1911)

Schneider, Ben Ross, Jr., '"Are We Being Historical Yet?": Colonialist Interpretations of Shakespeare's Tempest', in Leeds Barroll, ed., *Shakespeare Studies*, vol. 23 (London: Associated University Press, 1996)

Selvon, Sam, *The Lonely Londoners* (London: Longman, 1994)

Seymour, Susanne, 'Historical Geographies of Landscape', in Brian Graham and Catherine Nash, eds, *Modern Historical Geographies* (Harlow: Pearson, 2000)

Shakespeare, William, *Major Plays and the Sonnets*, ed., G. B. Harrison (New York: Harcourt Brace, 1948)

Sicherman, Carol, *Ngugi wa Thiong'o: The Making of a Rebel* (London: Hans Zell, 1990)

Sinfield, Alan, *Literature, Politics and Culture in Postwar Britain* (London: Athlone, 1997)

Slaymaker, William, 'Letter', *PMLA*, 114:5 (October 1999)

Spufford, Francis, *I May Be Some Time: Ice and the English Imagination* (London: Faber and Faber, 1996)

Staley, Thomas F., *Jean Rhys: A Critical Study* (Austin: University of Texas Press, 1979)

Steel, Flora Annie, *The Builder* (London: John Lane, 1928)

——, *King-Errant* (London: John Lane, 1912)

——, *Mistress of Men* (London: William Heinemann, 1917)

——, *On the Face of the Waters* (London: William Heinemann, 1897)

——, *A Prince of Dreamers* (London: William Heinemann, 1908)

Stepan, Nancy Leys, *Picturing Tropical Nature* (London: Reaktion, 2001)

Stevenson, Nora, *African Harvest* (London: Thornton Butterworth, 1928)

Stewart, Jay and Macnair, Peter, *To the Totem Forests: Emily Carr and Contemporaries interpret Coastal Villages* (Victoria: Art Gallery of Greater Victoria, 1999)

Stockley, Cynthia, *The Claw* (London: Hurst and Blackett, 1911)

——, *Dalla the Lion-Cub* (London: Hutchinson, 1924)

——, *Kraal Baby* (London: Cassell, 1933)

——, *The Leopard in the Bush: A Sequel to Dalla the Lion-Cub* (New York: G. P. Putnam, 1928)

——, *Pink Gods and Blue Demons* (London: Cassell, 1920)

——, *Ponjola* (London: Constable, 1923)

——, *Poppy: The Story of a South African Girl*, (5th edn., London: Hurst and Blackett,1910)

——, *Tagati (Magic)* (London: Constable, 1930)

——, *Virginia of the Rhodesians*, (4th edn., London: Hutchinson, 1903)

Stoneham, C. T., *Mau Mau* (London: Museum Press, 1953)

Stout, B., *Narrative of the loss of the ship 'Hercules', commanded by Captain Benjamin Stout, on the coast of Caffraria, the 16th of June, 1796; also a circumstantial detail of his travels through the southern deserts of Africa, and the colonies, to the Cape of Good Hope. With an introductory address to the Rt. Honourable John Adams, President of the Continental Congress of America* (London: J. Johnson, 1798)

Strathern, Marilyn, *After Nature: English Kinship in the late Twentieth Century* (Cambridge: Cambridge University Press, 1992)

Stratton, Florence, *Contemporary African Literature and the Politics of Gender* (London: Routledge, 1994)

Supriya, Nair, *Caliban's Curse* (Ann Arbor, Mich.: University of Michigan Press, 1996)

Swan, Annie S., *Love Grown Cold* (London: Methuen, 1902)

Symmonett, Ethel Maud, *Jamaica: Queen of the Carib Sea* (Jamaica: Mortimer C. De Souza, 1895)

Tabler, E. C., 'Notes and Queries', *Africana Notes and News*, 17:2 (June 1966)

Teltscher, Kate, *India Inscribed: European and British Writing on India 1600–1800* (New Delhi: Oxford University Press, 1995)

Thom, Ian M., *Emily Carr: Art and Process* (Vancouver: Vancouver Art Gallery, 1998)

Thomas, Nicholas, *Colonialism's Culture: Anthropology, Travel and Government* (Princeton: Princeton University Press, 1994)

Thomas, Sue, 'The Tropical Extravagance of Bertha Mason', *Victorian Literature and Culture*, 27:1 (1999)

Throup, David W., *Economic and Social Origins of Mau Mau* (London: James Currey, 1987)

Tiffin, Helen, 'Post-Colonial Literatures and Counter-discourse', in Bill Ashcroft, Gareth Griffiths and Helen Tiffin, eds, *The Post-Colonial Studies Reader* (London: Routledge, 1995)

——, 'Rites of Resistance: Counter-discourse and West Indian Biography', *Journal of West Indian Literature*, 3:1 (1989)

Todorov, Tzvetan, *The Conquest of America: The Question of the Other* (New York: Harper & Row, 1984)

Toibin, Colm, *Bad Blood: A Walk Along the Irish Border* (London: Vintage, 1994)

——, *The Heather Blazing* (London: Picador, 1993)

Toler, D. A., 'Clinton goes Big-game Hunting in Africa', *Mail and Guardian*, 20 March, 1998

Travers, John, *Sahib-Log* (London: Duckworth, 1910)

Varley, John, 'John Rocque: Engraver, Surveyor, Cartographer and Map-Seller', *Imago Mundi*, 5 (1965)

Vidler, Anthony, *The Architectural Uncanny: Essays in the Modern Unhomely* (Cambridge, Mass.: MIT Press, 1992)

Viola, Herman J. and Margolis, Carolyn, *Seeds of Change* (Washington, DC: Smithsonian Institution, 1991)

Walker, Alice, *In Search of Our Mothers' Gardens* (New York: Harcourt Brace, 1983)

Wamweya, Joram, *Freedom Fighter* (Nairobi: East African Publishing House, 1967)

Warren, William, *The Tropical Garden* (London: Thames and Hudson, 1997)

Waswo, R., 'The Formation of Natural Law to justify Colonialism, 1539–1689', *New Literary History*, 27:4 (1996)

Webster, Elizabeth Charlotte, *Bullion: A Tale of Buried Treasure and the Bush* (London: Eldon Press, 1933)

——, *Pot Holes: An Adventure of the Diamond Fields* (London: Chapman and Hall, 1928)

Webster, Wendy, 'Elspeth Huxley: Gender, Empire and Narratives of the Nation, 1935–64', *Women's History Review*, 8:3 (1999)

——, *Imagining Home: Gender, 'Race' and National Identity, 1945–64* (London: UCL Press, 1998)

Welu, James A., 'The Sources and Development of Cartographic Ornamentation in the Netherlands', in David Woodward, ed., *Art and Cartography: Six Historical Essays* (Chicago: University of Chicago Press, 1987)

Werner, A., 'Her Ride', *The Captain of the Locusts* (London: T. Fisher Unwin, 1899)

White, Hayden, *Metahistory: The Historical Imagination in Nineteenth-century Europe* (Baltimore: Johns Hopkins Press, 1973)

Whitlock, Gillian, '"A Most Improper Desire": Mary Gaunt's Journey to Jamaica', paper presented to the Ninth International ACLALS Conference, University of the West Indies, Mona, Jamaica (13–20 August, 1992)

Wilkes, Christopher, *Re-inventing Capitalism: History, Structure and Practice in the Formation of Social Classes in New Zealand* (Palmerston North: Massey University, 1993)

Williams, Raymond, *The Country and the City* (London: Hogarth, 1985)

Williams, Sherley Anne, 'Some Implications of Womanist Theory', in Henry Louis Gates Jr., ed., *Reading Black, Reading Feminist* (New York: Meridian, 1990)

Williamson, Tom, *Polite Landscapes: Gardens and Society in Eighteenth-Century England* (Baltimore: Johns Hopkins University Press, 1995)

Wilson, Christopher, *Kenya's Warning: The Challenge to White Supremacy in our British Colony* (Nairobi: The English Press, 1954)

Wilson, Rob, *The American Sublime: The Genealogy of a Poetic Genre* (Madison: University of Wisconsin Press, 1991)

Wilson, Thomas M. and Donnan, Hastings, eds, *Border Identities: Nation and State at International Frontiers* (Cambridge: Cambridge University Press, 1998)

Wolcott, Mary Adela, 'The Undertone', in Alison Donnell and Sarah Lawson Welsh, eds, *The Routledge Reader in Caribbean Literature* (London: Routledge, 1996)

Woodell, S. R. J., *The English Landscape: Past, Present, and Future* (Oxford: Oxford University Press, 1985)

Woodward, David, ed., *Art and Cartography: Six Historical Essays* (Chicago: University of Chicago Press, 1987)

Wylie, I. A. R., *The Daughter of Brahma* (London: Mills & Boon, 1912)

——, *The Rajah's People* (London: Mills & Boon, 1910)

Zinn, H., *A People's History of the United States, 1492 – the Present* (New York: HarperCollins, 1995)

Index

abbey(s)
  Gaelic 30
  of Timoleague 89
  ruined 79, 80, 85
Aberdare forest 181, 186
  mountains 14, 187
absences 24
abstraction 214, 223
abundance, natural 50
Achebe, Chinua: *Things Fall Apart* 9
Act of Union with Ireland 31, 80, 82
  with Scotland 80
Adams, John 7, 45, 47, 53, 54, 57, 58–9
adventure(s) 6, 8, 10, 108, 171
aesthete, Europeanized 153
aesthetic
  appreciation 80
  cogency 148
  criteria 119
  Fauvist 147, 155
  field 65, 66, 67–70
  preferences, western 48
  productions 104
  sensibility 203
  theories 161
aesthetics 3, 7, 8, 103, 202
aestheticization 80
Africa 1, 4, 127, 129, 134, 135, 137, 165
  American investment in 58
African(s) 46
  alleged 'savagery' 54
  American experience in America 204
  as workers and consumers 63
  good 181–2
  stereotypical assumptions 179
Africana Notes and News 61
agriculture 66, 70, 77
  British 73
  commercial 55, 58
  Maori 77
  methods, modern 115

Alexander, Mrs: *A Missing Hero* 129, 134
Algeria 13, 14
alienation 161, 162, 170, 171, 172, 173,
  175, 196, 206
aliens, bodily and metaphoric 162
allegory, political 170
Alleyne, Mervyn 203
alterity 29, 196
Althusser, Louis 210 n.4
America 7, 24, 45, 104, 204
  Central 104
  North 6, 12, 52 n.22
  'postcolonial' 16
  South 104
American Embargo Act of 1807 62
Americans 47, 57
Amsterdam 22
ancestry, European 105
Andrews, John 20, 29, 40
Andrews, Malcolm 5
Anglo-Irish
  Agreement 209, 213, 214
  relations 27, 30, 42, 43
animals 76
  as a tactical resource 185
  importation 67, 74, 77
  wild 48
Annaghmakerrig 218
Annalistes school 210
Ansa *see* McElroy Ansa
Antigua 115, 197, 198, 200
  Botanic Garden 201, 202
antiquarianism, Irish 38
antiquities, Irish 81
Antrim Valley, Dominica 116
Antwerp 22
anxiety/anxieties
  modernist 10
  of black/white encounters 176
  postcolonial 10
Aotearoa 65, 67, 78

Arawak Indians 198
Arcadia 7, 65, 66, 67, 69, 70, 74, 75, 77, 99
architecture 3, 161
Ards peninsula 2
Arnold, Matthew 100
art 3, 69
    black vernacular women's 204
    diasporic 202
    experimental 12
    First Nation 148, 149
    historians 3
    history 5
    indigenous 149
    modernist 12
artifice 202
artist-mothers 203
artists
    African-American women 196
    as recorders of the environment 69
    British picturesque 67
    Irish 80, 81
assimilationism 196
atlases 42–3
Auckland 69
Austen, Jane 120
Australia 69, 75, 76, 114
authenticity 132, 204
authority 2, 5, 30, 38, 54, 96, 178
    British 14
    colonial 9
    imperial 8
    metropolitan 16
    patriarchal 219
    political 88, 191
authors *see* writers

Bachelard, Gaston: *The Poetics of Space*
    210
Baker, David 20
ballad, nationalist 81
    'Boolavogue' 221, 222
'balm yards' 203
banana 195
banks 71, 73
Barbados 100
    Tourist Association 108
barbarians, true 9

barbarism, domestic 160
Baring, Governor Evelyn 183
Barlow, Joel 45 n.1
Barrell, John 52
Barrington, George Winslow
    Remarkable Voyages 61
Barrow, John 61, 62
Bartlett, Richard 21, 40
Bartram, William 52 n.22
basement rooms 171, 176
Bath, Alexander: 'Map of Cork' 36–8, 39
Bauman, Zygmunt 215
Beaufort, Daniel Augustus 30
    'A New Map of Ireland' 29, 31, 32, 38
Beckett, Ursula à 136
behaviour
    European codes of 68
    native 98
Belfast 34, 212
Bell, Henry Hesketh 9, 10, 111, 115–6,
        118, 119, 120, 121, 122, 123, 124,
        125, 126
    'A Scheme for Expenditure' 115, 117
    publicity leaflet 120
Berger, John 26
Berlin 12
Bermuda 96
Bhaba, Homi 148
Bildungsroman 222
Black British history 12
Blake, Susan 94, 97
Blakemore, M. J. 17
Blaney, Neil 222
Bligh, Captain 197
bloodstock 76
Bloom, Molly 219
Blundell, Michael 183 n.29
boarding-house culture 13
Boer War 130, 135
Boers 130
Bohls, Elizabeth 7
Boland, Kevin 222
botany 197, 202
boundaries 142, 143, 154, 155, 163, 170,
        173, 178
Bounty, The 197
bourgeoisie, West Indian 199

Bowden, Mrs G.
  Nella of Pretoria 133
Bradbury, Malcolm 12
Brenan, Gerald 12
Bridges, Yseult 103
  Child of the Tropics 102
  'Victorian Memoirs' 102–3
Britain 3, 4, 5, 10, 13, 20, 40, 52, 53, 57,
    66, 70, 71, 72, 83, 115, 124, 164, 165,
    167, 170, 173
'Britannia' 26, 27, 42
British, the 1, 78
British airforce 14
British Army 214, 217
British Columbia 141
British East India Company 45
British government(s) 209, 213
British Isles 120
British Parliament 180
British Somaliland 13
Brixton 164
Brockway, Lucile H. 197
Brontë, Charlotte 119, 120
  Jane Eyre 111, 119–20
Brown, Capability 4
Brownrigg, John
  'Survey of the Grand Canal' 26 n.33
brutality 179, 180, 181
Bunn, David 52 n.25
Bunreacht na hEireann 220
Burke, Edmund 8, 51, 114
  The Sublime and the Beautiful 7
Burma 13
bush, the 11, 76, 152
Bushman/Bushmen 50, 54–5
business 65, 67, 70, 78, 200, 221

California 12
Camden, William 25
Cameron, Charlotte: *A Durbar Bride* 132
Canada 11, 16, 114, 141, 148
Canary Wharf 162
Canterbury 75, 76
'Canterbury Pilgrims' 75
Cape, the 7, 57, 62
  eastern 6, 45, 47, 51, 52, 59, 61, 63
  western 7, 47, 51, 52

Cape Town 45, 47
capital 70, 71, 72, 73, 74, 75, 76
  types of 66–7
capitalism 53 n.28, 71, 211
Caribbean, the 4, 8, 15, 18, 93, 159, 173
Caribs 125
Carlingford Lough 15, 209
Carolina 6
Carpenter, Benjamin 62 n.68
Carr, Emily 11, 12, 141, 142–51, 152, 156
  field studies 147
  paintings 143
    Big Raven 149, 150
    Guyasdom's Zonoqua 146
    Indian Church 145
    Tanoo, Queen Charlotte Islands 143,
      144
    Totem Mother, Kitwancool 156–7
    Zunoqua of the Cat Village 149, 151,
      157
  writing
    Klee Wyck 143, 149
    The Book of Small 142, 156
cartography 19, 20, 40
  promotional 31 n.42
Cary, Joyce
  Mister Johnson 9
Cassin, Frieda
  With Silent Tread; A West Indian Novel
    105–6
castle(s), ruined 79, 80, 82
Catholic Emancipation 42
Catholicism 88, 89, 216, 217
Cawnpore 139
Celtic Tiger 223
Ceylon 13, 115
Chairman Mao 178
Chamberlain, Joseph 9, 10, 111, 114, 115,
    116, 118, 120, 123
charts 22, 42, 68
children 120, 145
Christian, Barbara 196, 203, 204
Christianity 1, 189
church
  Anglican 76
  building a 136
  Hiberno-Romanesque 218

Monotheism 145
  of Ireland 21
  Presbyterian 76, 218
Churchill, Captain 112, 122
cities 12, 71, 211
city, the 160, 161, 171, 172
citizen, political status of 53
Civil War 80
civilization 54, 70, 84, 87, 137, 142
Clarke, G. N. 25
class(es) 71, 75, 76, 161, 167, 199, 206
  comprador 192
  middle 167, 196, 199
  transformation 66
  working 164, 165
Claudian Ideal 69
climate 54, 111, 119, 120, 125
  English 107
  ideal 119
  temperate 125
  tropical 116, 121, 125
climatic zones 118
Clinton, Bill 62–4
clitoridectomy 190, 194
club, the 124
Co. Donegal 86, 209
Co. Down 31, 209
Co. Londonderry 209
Co. Louth 209
Co. Meath 86
Co. Monaghan 218
Co. Wicklow 82
Coetzee, J. M.
  Waiting for the Barbarians 9
Cohen, Phil161, 162
Colonial Institute 114
colonial officials, black 183
colonialism 15, 94, 171, 176, 177, 201
colonist(s) 2, 5
  British 78
  European 15, 65
  white 114
colonization 152, 153, 219
  in reverse 161
colonized 91, 142, 148
colonizer 142, 148, 179
colony/colonies, the 9, 114

ex-slave 108
  self-governing 114
  tropical 114
colour 124, 125, 205
  issues of 111
  problem 162
  shock 164, 165, 168
colourist motif 156
Colquhoun, M. J.
  Every Inch a Soldier 136
Columbus, Christopher 102, 198
commerce 38
Committee on Colonial Lands 70
Commonwealth 72, 159
Commonwealth Immigrants Acts 159
communal punishments 181
community/communities
  artistic 218
  Asian 162
  black 160
  Caribbean, in Britain 12, 13
  colonial 65
  confessional 218
  development of 175
  ethnic minority 164
  homosocial 126
  inclusive cultural 172
  Irish 162
  Italian 162
  Jewish 162
  Polish 162
  private 165
  rural 65, 66
  'virtual' 85
  West Indian 162, 165, 174
  white 124, 160
concentration camps 180, 181
Condé, Mary 10–11
conflict 80, 82, 83, 189
conflicted parentage 135
Conrad, Joseph
  Heart of Darkness 142
consciousness, historical 81, 87
consciousness-raising, cultural 81
conservatism, Irish 218
constructs, cultural 155
consumerism, new 167

continuity 15
control 1, 5, 8, 9, 14, 36, 38, 71, 114, 135,
  172, 198
  ideological 83
  of nature 202
  of resources 70, 73
  of the landscape 179
  white, of Kenya 177
'Conway Castle' 82–3, 87
Cook's second voyage to the Pacific 69
Corcoran, Neil 219
Corfu 12
Cork 21 n.18
Cosgrove, Denis 2–3, 5, 34, 38, 53 n.28
country house, English 4
countryside 70, 74
crafts, First Nation 148
creativity 203, 205
credit 72, 77
creole(s) 94, 99
  stereotypical 106
  West Indian 111
  white 104
  white West Indian 106, 108
creolization 171
Croker, B. M.
  Her Own People 133
Crommelin, May 103, 108
  Pink Lotus 132
  'The Mountain-Heart of Jamaica' 96, 100
Crosby, Alfred
  Ecological Imperialism 196
  The Columbian Exchange 196
Cuba, US invasion 118
cultivation 48, 50
culture 70, 88, 163, 173, 194, 209
  African 204
  difference 160
  distinctiveness 87
  European 104
  expectations of the 'feminine' 97
  First Nation 149
  imperial 126
  male 7
  metropolitan 196
  nineteenth-century bourgeois British 65, 67
  occupied 176

  of consumption 162
  relativism 54
  shock 170
curfews 181, 182
Cyprus 13

D'Sonoqua 149
Daily Mail 132 n.33
Daniels, Stephen 34
Darkley 216, 217
Davis, Cynthia 14
Davis, Thomas 81
  'Irish Antiquities' 86
De Bry 195
de Certeau, Michel 210, 211
De Valera, Eamon 221
de Vere, Aubrey:
  'Ode: The Curse of Cromwell' 88–9
Deane, Seamus 214
decay 38, 79, 83, 87, 90
decline, imperial 165
decolonization 121
deep structures 147
defamiliarization 215
deferred disclosure 175
degeneration
  colonial 126
  physical and moral 111
Dehan, Richard: *The Dop Doctor* 128
de-historicization 87
Delamore, Lord 14 n.26
Dell, Ethel M. 132
  The Way of an Eagle 127
democracy 58
Denoon, Donald 72
dependencies 114
depoliticization 222
Derrida, Jacques 42
  The Truth in Painting 40
destinations 93
destiny 78
  the African's 182
destruction 79
  civilizing 69
  signs of 83
detention camps 180
determinism, geographic 68

Devonshire, Sixth Duke 197
diaries 98
diaspora 173
    Atlantic 206
    theory 160
diasporic peoples 196
Diego Martin 103
discourse(s) 6, 211
    American imperial 45
    British political 6
    Christian 189
    class 161
    colonial 8, 18, 25, 97, 142, 177, 187
    colonialist 93, 94
    cultural 4, 211
    ecological 196
    emigrant 7
    feminine 8, 104
    Gikuyu 189
    Irish aesthetic 8
    masculinist high seas adventure 6
    multiple 103, 104
    nineteenth-century nationalist 86
    of Englishness 160
    of femininity 94, 97, 99
    of feminism 94
    of historical adventure 102
    of imperialism 99, 104
    of the nation 169
    on women 187
    patriarchal 190
    picturesque 8
    race 161
    racist 162
    romantic 8
    self-referentially split 104
    shipwreck fable 6
    sublime 7, 8
    travel narrative 6
discovery 97, 99, 108
disease(s) 117, 130
disjunction 80
displacement 202
divorce referendum 218, 219
domestic customs 163
domination of blacks 201
Dominica 5, 9, 16, 111–26, 199

Dominicans 116
domino theorists 13
Donnan, Hastings 15
doubles 154
doubling 142, 145, 153, 154, 155
Douglas, A. Elizabeth
    Shadowed Blood 135
    The End of the Trek 130
Douglas, Mary 146–7
Downpatrick 31, 34
Doyle, Roddy
    Barrytown Trilogy 207
    Brownbread 207
    Paddy Clarke Ha Ha Ha 207
    Family 207
    The Commitments 207
    The Snapper 207
    The Van 207
    War 207
dread 161, 162, 166, 167
Drennan, William 87, 89, 91
    'Glendalloch' 82, 83
Driver, Maud
    Captain Desmond, V.C. 138
Dublin 21, 207, 208, 212, 213, 222
Dubliners 215
Duff-Fyfe, Ethel
    The Nine Points 136
Duncan, Archibald
    The Mariner's Chronicle 60
Duncan, William: 'County of Dublin' 34
    n.45
Dunedin 75
Durrell, Lawrence 12
Dutch 1, 7, 58, 63
    East India Company 56
    Empire 56

ecocriticism 196, 206
economic and political structures 65, 66,
    70–73
Eden 102, 103, 195
Edge, K. M.
    The Shuttles of the Loom 127
Edgerton, Robert B. 14, 188
Edwood, May
    The Autobiography of a Spin 136

El Dorado 103
Eliot, George
  The Mill on the Floss 129
Eliot, T. S.
  The Waste Land 172
Elizabeth 86
emigration 160
empire/Empire 10, 11, 15, 16, 17, 83, 114,
    142, 155, 157, 197, 198, 208
  British 11, 89, 212
  building 131
  end of 170
  Roman 11
Empire Windrush 12, 160
empiricism 214
  impressionistic 214
  Irish historical revisionist 214
enabling signifiers 190
Enclosure Movement 73
enclosures 51
England 20, 26, 45, 76, 79, 80, 87, 90, 103,
    120, 168, 169
English 63
English Anglicans 75
English System 73
Englishness 118, 123, 124, 170
enterprise 111
entrapment 171
environment
  domesticated 34
  European 70
  New Zealand 69
  primeval 182
envy 162
erosion 185, 219, 220
estate houses 76
estate owners 116
estrangement 161, 171, 191
ethnicity/ ethnicities 156, 160, 162
ethnographical 'facts' 98
Europe 3, 12, 67, 76, 104, 119
Eustace, Alice
  Flame of the Forest 132
Everyman 209
evolution 70
exclusion 161, 203
exile 160, 202, 222

exotic 93, 103, 106, 108, 175, 215,
    218
  flora and fauna 197
  tales of the 47
  vegetation 129
exotica 69
exoticism 100
experience 214, 216, 222
  British colonial 16
  tourist 133 n.38
exploitation
  ecological 200
  economic 47
  of poor 88
exploration 68
export(s) 38, 42, 71
  American, to the Cape 62 n. 69
  for American markets 64

face as landscape 127
Fairbairn, Miles 65 n.1, 70
famine 181
Fanon, Frantz
  Black Skin, White Masks 13
fantasy/fantasies
  Edenic 195
  female 131
  settler 177
  stereotypical pakeha 155
farm 73, 76, 77
farmers 65, 67, 72, 76, 78
  British 73 n.25
  yeoman 74, 76
farming
  dairy 77
  ladder 75
  potential 48
Fauves 147
Fauvist style 147, 148
fear(s) 2, 9, 155, 161, 166, 171, 215
female empowerment 146
female travel writer(s) *see* women travel
    writers
femininity 157, 146, 187, 194
Ferguson, Samuel 89
Fergusson, J. D. 147, 148, 155
fertility 205

Fianna Fail 213, 221, 222
Fine Gael 213
fiction 100, 127, 134, 141, 208
  experimental forms 152
  imperialist 133 n.41
  romantic 127–39
finance, international 73
First Nation Haida people 143, 145, 148
Fitzgerald government 209
'flats' 116, 120
flora, West Indian 200
follies, architectural 80
Forbes, Vernon S. 61
foreigner(s) 141, 157, 162
  within the self 142, 143, 145, 149,
     153, 157
foreignness 141, 143
forest(s) 184, 189
  clearing 74
  destruction 77
  disappearance of 69
  gendered 149
  physical 149
  primeval 114
Foucault, Michel 17, 18, 210
Fowler, Gordon 115, 116, 120, 121
France 13, 31, 56, 58, 148
Frazer, John de Jean
  'The Holy Wells' 88
Free Church of Scotland 75
free trade 55, 56, 57, 58, 63
freedom 173
  'British' 83
  Irish 84
  of the Welsh 83
  spirit of 84, 88, 90
French revolution 30
freshness 129
Freud 161, 164, 165
frontier 213, 215
Froude, James Anthony 114, 116, 122,
  23, 126
  The English in the West Indies 112
Furlong, Thomas 89
Fussell, Paul 12
future, the Irish 85

Gainsborough 67
Ganges 138
garden(s) 3, 66, 137, 195–206
  Afrocentric 196, 202
  attitude to 15
  botanic 15, 152, 196, 197, 202
  British/ English 11, 137, 202
  Caribbean 200, 202
  cultivated 196
  European model 15
  first colonial 197
  Indian 138
  landscape 76
  literary 196
  management 137
  nightmare 201
  of the Moghul Emperors 137
  secret 204
gardener 198
gardening 196, 203, 204
  botanical 5
  landscape 80
Gaunt, Mary 97, 98, 102, 103, 108
  *Harmony, a Tale of the Old Slave Days in
    Jamaica* 102
  Reflection – in Jamaica 96, 100
gaze
  aesthetic 65
  colonial 67
  idealized and symbolic 66
  of the state 215
gender 94, 96, 149, 191, 193, 199, 206
gendering 157, 192
genocide 152
genre(s) 6, 162, 208
  continental exploration 47
  literary 68
  male 8
  maritime survival 47
gentrification 34
gentry 74, 76
geography
  historical 3, 5
  Marxist 210
geomorphology 2
George II 22
Georgia 205

georgic mode 111, 119
Germany, reunification of 212
ghosts 81, 85
Gibb, Harry Phelan 148
Gibbons, Luke 79, 80
Gikuyu
  civilians 180
  elders 185
  folk history 186
  linguistic code 176, 177
  myths of origin 189, 191, 192
  patriarchy 189, 194
  population 182
  prophet 186
  reserve 182
  subjects 179
  woman's hut 191
  women 180, 187, 190, 192, 194
Gilpin, William 4, 8, 51
Gilroy, Amanda 6
Gilroy, Paul 170, 173
globe(s) 22, 24
God 68, 100, 103, 185, 220
  the Great Artist 68
gods, African 201
Gold Coast 13
Goodison, Lorna 198
goodwill 43
gothic 162
  effects 88
  fiction, Anglo-Irish 85
  tradition 85
Government of Ireland Act 212, 213
Graham, James 216
Graves, Robert 12
Gray, Maxwell
  In the Heart of the Storm 139
Great Famine 88, 89
Greek myth 100
Green, Martin 10
Green Wave 196
Greenwood, Mrs Sarah 73
grief, national 82
Group of Seven 148
guardianship 43
guidebook 133 n.38
gypsies 155

Haiti 203
Hall, Stuart 172 n.52
Hamer, Mary 36
Hardiman, James
  Irish Minstrelsy 89
Hargreaves, John 29
Harley, J. B. 6, 17–19, 25, 31, 40, 42
  Concepts in the History of Cartography
    17
  'Deconstructing the Map' 18
  'Historical Geography and the
    Cartographic Illusion' 18
  'Maps, Knowledge and Power' 17
  'Silences and Secrecy' 18, 30
Harmony district 102
harp, Irish 26, 42
Harvey, David 210
Haughey, Charles 221–2
haunted places 83
haven, safe and sexless 12
Hayes-McCoy, G. A. 20
health 111, 119, 120
Heaney, Seamus 217, 218
Helgerson, Richard 25
Henry VIII 89
Hercules 45, 48, 52, 60, 61
heritage
  distancing from 199
  mixed 131
hero, face of 127
heroes, conquering 10
heroine(s) 10, 127, 194
  identification with masculine values
    193
  identity 131
  importance 131
  romantic 134
  South African 131
high farming 73
high theory 18
Hillsborough Agreement 209
historical records 81
historiography 81
  African 14
  French 210
history/histories 152, 221
  America's official 196

Caribbean 100
cultural 168
distorted, of American South 204
end of 222
family 204
imperialist versions of native 81
Irish 80, 82, 221
national 79
of cartography 6, 17, 25
official 204
shared 173
Hodges, William 7, 69
   Waterfall in Dusky Bay 69
holy wells 88
home 12, 107, 131, 159, 160, 163, 168, 169,
   171, 172, 176, 210
   'unhomely' 162, 168
homeland 170
homelessness 161
homosexuality 166
Hooker, Joseph D. 197
Hooper, Glenn 6
Horner, Arnold 24
horticulture 15
House of Commons 114
houses 174, 176
   multiple occupancy 163, 165, 171
   West Indian-tenanted 165
housing 170, 171
Howarth, Anna
   Katrina: A Tale of the Karoo 130
   Nora Lester 133
Hulme, Peter 9, 18
   Colonial Encounters 18
humanism, heroic 70
humanity 205
Humphreys, David 45 n.1
hunting 76
Hurston, Zora Neale 15, 196, 203, 204, 206
husbandry 31
Huxley, Aldous 12
Huxley, Elspeth 163, 164, 165, 171
   Back Streets, New Worlds 162
hypocrisy 199, 200

iconography 17
   Celtic 38

Irish nationalist 80
   racist 177
ideal, notion of 119
idealism 173
identification(s) 172, 173, 175
identity 160, 172 n.52, 196, 201, 205
   Canadian 149
   Caribbean 170, 172 n.52
   construction of 171
   creation of British national 80
   cultural 81, 160
   diasporic 15
   ethnic 201
   gender 201
   Irish national 82
   masculine British 94
   national 122, 152
   pan-Caribbean West Indian 170
   politics of 159
   search for 204
   Welsh 83
ideological history 62
ideology/ideologies 14, 68, 69, 103,
   157, 214
   Christian 189
   competing 189
   imperial 123
   of British nationhood 80
   of Unionism 31
   political 104
image/ images
   iconic 93
   mirror 153
   of cemetery 145
   of English gentry 74
   of exportable worth 30
imagery
   Arcadian 65, 73
   landscape 189
   map 25
   pastoral 193
   sexual 187
   tree 189
immigrant(s)
   Caribbean to Britain 160
   presence of 163
   to New Zealand 65, 66, 74, 78

immigrant–host relations 164
immigration 160, 164
   context and language 170
   European 77
   West Indian 162
immorality 119
Imperial Road 115, 121, 122
imperialism 111, 159, 160
Imperialism, New 114
import-export businessmen 70
imported flora and fauna 77, 78
imports, British 73
income, average 75
independence
   Caribbean political 173
   Indian 13
   Irish 82
   Kenyan 180
India 4, 16, 127, 132, 134, 136, 137
   hill stations 118 n.23
Indian indenture 198
Indian Mutiny 139
Indians 138
indigenous people(s) 145, 153, 195
inhabitants, native 45
innocence 99, 129, 171, 199, 200, 201, 210
insecurity 169, 173
insurgents
   female 188
   Kenyan 176
   Rockite 85
   Mau Mau 183, 186, 189
insurrection 31
International Geographical Congress 121
internment camps 14
interpretation of scenery 139
IRA 216, 217, 222
Ireland 2, 6, 16, 20, 24, 26, 29, 30, 31, 40,
     42, 43, 76, 79–91, 215
   Arms Crisis 222
   Boundary Commission 213
   Constitution of the Republic 213, 220
   difference to other cultures 87
   Home Rule movement 212
   rebellion 82, 221
   Rebellion of 1798 221
   Republic of 209, 218, 219

   separateness from Britain 213
   Treaty of 1922 213
Irish, the 81, 198
Irish border 15, 211, 212, 213, 214, 215,
   216, 219
Irish Free State 213
Irish government 209
Irish National Liberation Army (INLA)
   216, 217
Irish Times/Aer Lingus Literature Prize 207
Irishness 8, 38, 87
irony 214, 215, 221, 222
Itote, Waruhiu 188

Jacobs, Jane 160
Jamaica 16, 96, 102, 105, 107, 197, 201,
   203
   Bishop of 106
   Hope Garden 197, 199
James, Winifred 93
Janowitz, Anne 79, 80
Johannesburg 130
Johnson, David 6
Jonson, Ben 211
Jordan, Vernon 63
journals 98
Joyce, James 11

kabatuni 187
Kaffraria 55
Kariuki, J. M.
   Mau Mau Detainee 188
Karoo, the 130
Kavanagh, Patrick 217
Kennedy, Dane 121
Kenya 13, 14, 16, 191
   Africa Union 180
   agricultural campaign 185
   as a prostituted economy 192
   Central and Rift Valley Provinces 182
   Emergency 177, 182, 189
   Hola detention camp 180
   Homeguard 183, 187
   Kameno ridge 190
   Land and Freedom Army 178 n.5,
     185, 194
   Land Consolidation programme 181

Makuyu ridge 190
Manyani concentration camp 184
Operation Anvil 180
Operation Bullrush 181
Operation Dante 181
Operation First Flute 181
Operation Hammer 181
Operation Hannibal 181
Operation Jock Scott 180
Operation Schlemozzle 181
'Prohibited Areas' 182
Rehabilitation programme 180, 181
'Special Areas' 182
treatment of prisoners 180
Villagization programme 180, 181
Kenyatta, Jomo 186
Kew Gardens 152, 197
Palm House 197
Khan, Ismith 196, 206
The Jumbie Bird 198–9
Kidd, Benjamin
The Control of the Tropics 118
Kimberley 129
Kincaid, Jamaica 15, 196, 197, 198, 200,
201, 202, 203, 206
mother's Afrocentric yard 202
A Small Place 108
King's African Rifles 183
kinship 114
Kipling, Alice M.
A Pinchbeck Goddess 133
The Heart of a Maid 135
Kipling, Rudyard 132 n.33, 133
Klee Wyck 143, 1345
Knight, Richard Payne 4
knowledge
building, European 93
form(s) of 5, 3
historical 81
lack of 21
spatial 178
koumaras 155
Kristeva, Julia 141, 142, 152
Kröller, Eva-Marie 98, 104

La Malinche 1
labour 35

disparity 38
forced 181, 182
surplus 72, 211
labourers 72, 76
Lady's Pictorial 132
Laffan, Michael 212, 213
Lake District 119
Lambeth 165
lament 84
Lamming, George 13, 160, 161, 170, 173,
174, 175, 176
The Emigrants 170, 171, 172–6
land 40, 45, 58, 66, 70, 76, 122
African 47, 63
alien 201
as a type of capital 66
class view 67
coded as female 126
colonial acquisition 47
control of 66, 71, 73, 88
Crown 72, 73
cultivation 45
cultural role 65
dealers 71
emptiness 50
foreign 160
freehold 71, 72
grazing 71
imperial 53
Irish 6, 27
law 46
male attachment to 11
management 77; Maori 65, 72
monopoly 72
ownership 14, 46, 70, 71, 76, 185
primary responses to 2, 5
privately owned 72
'raped' 190
redistribution 72, 73
repossession 191
Southern African 64
speculation 68, 72
speculators 7, 65, 71
use of 69
Land Settlement Finance Act 72
landlord–tenant relationship 73
landowners 70, 74, 76, 114

landscape(s) 4, 5, 8, 11, 34, 45, 50, 67 n.5, 111, 119, 127, 128, 143, 153, 156, 192, 196, 222
  aesthetic approaches 2
  African 53
  alien 131
  American 11, 30
  animist 145
  appreciation 3, 8, 24, 45, 52
  as a cultural concept 5
  as a historical narrative 15
  as a politically enabling signifier 190
  as a site of contestation 15
  as accomplice 130
  as adversary 130
  as 'already known' 103
  as female 126
  as repository of significance 184
  as spectacle 107
  attitudes to 137
  British 163
  British Columbian 147
  Brontëan 120
  Caribbean 201
  colonial 2, 4, 10, 111, 183;
  commodification 197
  concept of 2, 53 n.28
  creation of 67
  desecration, British 14
  deserted 88
  domestic 160
  English 80
  exotic 63, 93, 98
  female 143
  feminized 190
  fusion with culture 146
  garden 196
  gardening 3
  gendered responses 14
  gendering 190, 194
  historical context 3
  hostile 170
  ideal 8, 111
  ideology of representation 2
  imperial 111, 112
  in art 52
  Indian 5, 138, 139
  integrity 133
  internalizing 142
  interpretation 5
  Irish 2, 6, 24, 40
  Jamaican 100
  Kenyan 14, 178
  Kenyan Emergency 182, 189, 191, 194
  literal and metaphoric 141
  literary 171
  male attachment to 11
  mixed 121
  moral connotations 118
  naming 40
  natural 78
  New Zealand 67
  non-European 11
  notion of 67
  of colonialism 199
  of London 13
  of moderation 120
  of the eastern Cape
  of the mind 171
  owning 40
  physical 90
  politics of 19
  pre-colonial 55
  primal 104
  psychological 129
  reading 135, 136, 154
  real 129
  reconfiguration 40
  relationship of Mau Mau with 184
  representations 14, 189
  respect for 134
  response to 136
  Romantic psychological 91
  scale of 134–5
  second-order 66
  sexualized 116
  social 171
  South African 128
  spiritual significance 18
  sympathetic sensory 185
  threat 139
  traumatized 91
  tropical 97, 195, 197, 198, 199
  urban 167

West Indian 98, 106, 108
language
   attitude to 216
   feminized 114
   of space 171
   of the sublime 112, 114
Law of the Father 142
Le Vaillant, Francois 47, 48
Leakey, Dr Louis 186
Leakey, Gray Arundel 186
lease-in-perpetuity 72
leasehold system 72
leaseholders 71, 72
leases, long-term 73
Lee, Mrs R.
   The African Wanderers 127
Lefebvre, Henri 210
legitimacy 38
Leinster 20
Lemass, Sean 221
Lessing, Doris
   The Grass is Singing 11
letters 68, 78, 98
Lewis, Samuel
   Atlas of Ireland 41, 42–3
liberalism 219, 223
Libya 13
life paths 211
'Lines, Written at Kenilworth Castle,
   Warwickshire' 85–6
literary strategies 204
literary studies 18
literature 65, 195, 211
   environmental 206
   of the Black Atlantic 198
   sociological 160
Liverpool School of Tropical Medicine
   117–8
local, the 215
Lockean imperative 116
Lockhart, Acton Don 122
London 12, 13, 22, 155, 159, 164, 166, 167,
   170, 171, 172, 173, 197
   Dockland 162
   School of Tropical Medicine 117–8
London Review of Books 208
loss 8, 90

Lough Derg pilgrimage 214, 216, 217
Lough Erne 214
Lough Foyle 15, 209
Low, Gail 12–13
loyalty 107
Lucknow 139
Lustick, Ian 212
Lynch, Mrs Henry 95, 100, 102, 103, 104,
   106–7, 108
   The Mountain Pastor 94
   The Wonders of the West Indies 95
Lythe, Robert 20

Maasai 178, 184
MacAnna, Ferdia 208
Macaule/ay, Rose 80
MacInnes, Colin 13, 161, 165, 166
   Absolute Beginners 166–8
   City of Spades 166
Maclise. Daniel 81
   Installation of Captain Rock 81
   Marriage of Strongbow and Aoife 81
MacManus, Henry
   Reading the Nation 81
Macmillan, Harold 13
madness 119, 124, 204
magazine(s) 155
   ladies' 132
   Magill 207
   Melbourne 152
Mahar, Cheleen Ann-Catherine 7
Mahehu, Paul 183
Mahupuku, Maata 154
Majorca 12
Mandeville 106
Mangan, James Clarence 89–91
   'Lament over the Ruins of the Abbey of
   Teach Mologa' 89
   'Siberia' 90
   'To the Ruins of Donegal Castle' 86
Mansfield, Charlotte 136
   "For Satan Finds..." 135
   Gloria: A Girl of the South African Veld
   129
   Red Pearls 134
Mansfield, Katherine 11, 12, 141, 142, 143,
   152–7

drafts for stories 154
'How Pearl Button was Kidnapped'
    155–7
notebooks and journals 152, 154
short stories 141
stories about children 142
'Summer Idylle' 154
'To Stanislaw Wyspiansky' 152
Manson, Patrick
    Tropical Diseases 117
Maori(s) 7, 65, 67, 68, 72, 77, 153, 154, 155
Maoritanga 77, 78
map(s) 2, 6, 16, 20, 40, 43, 99, 213, 214
    allegorical content 26
    apolitical nature 26
    Armagh county 22
    as agents of change 36
    as instruments of control 19
    as political documents 19
    as source and sign of power 214
    British 29
    captions 19
    cartouche(s) 6, 19, 22, 24, 25, 26, 27,
        29, 30, 31, 32, 33, 34, 37, 38, 39, 40,
        42, 43
    Cork 22
    cultural meaning 17
    deconstructionist reading 1
    decorative detail 6, 19, 25, 42
    Dublin 22
    emblem 25
    fictional status 36
    frontispiece 25
    global, of Empire 160
    historical context 17, 19
    humanist reading 18
    Irish 20, 21
    Kilkenny 22
    lettering 6, 19
    meaning 40
    message of 25, 30, 34, 36, 38, 42, 43
    of Ireland 6, 22, 40, 43
    of North America, late eighteenth-
        century 25
    ornamentation 22, 24
    political context 19, 24, 38
    purpose(s) 25, 38, 40

scales 24
symbol 25
symbolism 6, 19, 25, 38
Thurles 22
totality 19
mapmakers in Low Countries 22
map-making 68
mapping 24, 40, 99, 146
    conventions 36
    moral 120
    of Ireland 21
Marchand, Annabella Bruce
    Dirk: A South African 129
margin, the 146
marginalization 161, 198
marginalized people 196
markets
    British 72
    overseas 67
Marvell, Andrew 211
Marxist instruction 192
'Mary of the *Nation*' 88
    'The Old Castle' 84–5, 87
Maryland 25
masculinity, white 111
matriarchy 192
Mau Forest 178
Mau Mau 13–14, 177–89
    bullets 191
    civilian wing 186, 187
    insurgency 14
    memoirs 183
    psychological warfare 183
    scouts 187
    spiritual dimensions 185
    supplies of arms and ammunition 188
    urban wing 186
    women 186–9, 194
Maugham, Somerset 10, 12
Mauritius 197
Maze hunger strike 209
McCabe, Eugene 218
McCarthy, Conor 15
McCarthy, Denis Florence:
    'The Pillar Towers of Ireland' 87
McElroy Ansa, Tina 196, 203, 204, 206
    Ugly Ways 204, 205

McGahern, John 218
meaning 4, 67, 84, 198, 211
measuring concepts of 146
  equipment 24
méconnaissance 75
media 160
memorialization 15
memory/memories 186, 196, 204, 205, 206
merchants 71, 73
Mercier, Paul 208
Merton, Ray
  My Cousin's Wife 136
metanarrative(s) 221, 223
metaphor(s)
  for heroine 127
  for personal fate 90
  for 'virtual' community 85
  gardens 137
  jewels 102
  mausoleum 82, 91
  of rooms 176
  of the cage 173
  spatial 163
  spatialized 162
  tomb 89
metropolis 215
Middle Passage 201
Middleham 115, 116, 118, 120, 125
migrants
  West Indian 163
  white 9
migration 5, 171
  British 71
  Caribbean post-war 12, 16, 159
  West Indian 168
  Windrush 171
Miles, Robert 162
militancy, female form 188–9
military
  British 14, 178
  coercion 83
  fortifications 2
  might 198
Mills & Boon 132
Mills, Sarah 93, 94, 98, 99
  Discourses of Difference 97
Milton 106

mirror, the 26, 29, 155
miscegenation 125, 164
misrule, British 88
mission civilisatrice 13
Missouri Compromise 58 n.52
mixed race 137
mobility, upward 75
modernism 11, 12
modernity 192, 214, 215
modernization 215, 221
  economic 114
  of Dominica 115
monasteries 89
monastery, ruined 82
Montserrat 198
Moore, Thomas 8, 84, 85, 87, 88, 89
  Captain Rock 85
  Irish Melodies 83
  'The Harp That Once through Tara's
    Halls' 83–4
moral
  inferiority 137
  purpose and virtue 66
morality 70
Morrell, Captain Benjamin 59 n.54
Mother England 43, 107
Mountjoy, Lord 21
moving statues 208
Muddock, J. E.
  The Great White Hand 139
Muir, Richard 2, 36
mythology, colonial 182

Naipaul, V. S. 176, 198
Nairobi 180
name(s) 145, 154, 155 , 156, 191, 193
  suburban English 137
naming 120, 191, 193
Napoleon III, Emperor 76
narrative(s) 216
  figure 99
  forms, feminine 97, 98–99, 104
  literary 98
  of the past 173
  parallel 222
  social exploration 162
  style 210

telling 108
tension 167
Nash, Thirza
  The Ex-Gentleman 128
Nasta, Susheila 171
Nation newspaper 81, 84
nation 160
nation building 17, 79
nation-state(s) 213, 221
national belonging 160
nationalism 21, 82, 193, 222
  African 14
  cultural 81
  Irish 26, 87, 223
  militant 189
nationalist impulse, West Indian 94
nationalists, Irish 213
nationhood 192
Native Americans 29, 58
Native Companion, The 152
native/s 1, 168
  assent 47
  European 159
  Irish 6
  of the Pacific 70
  real 125
  society 93
  to go 125
  white 163
'natural'
  definitions 155;
  essentialist notions of 154
natural history, records of 69
naturalization 87
nature 67, 70, 80, 88
  as pictorial representation 68
  development and domination 66
  European attitude towards 15
  harmony with 202
  perversion of 201
  sublime force of 3
Naylor, Gloria 196, 203, 204, 206
  Mama Day 204–5
Nduru, Brigadier Nyama 183
neighbourhood 160
Nelson 70, 74, 76
neutrality 210

'New Britain' 7
new Britain 67
New England 25
New Ireland Forum 209
New World 1, 104, 202, 206
New York 12
New York Review of Books 208
New Zealand 7, 11, 16, 65–78, 152
  as an ideal landscape 66
  borrowings 71
  class structure 66
  colonization 73, 76, 152
  Company 70
  economy 71, 72, 73
  exports 71, 72
  imports 71–2
  lack of history 152
  Land Wars 77
  Liberal government 72, 73
  Liberal Party 72
  male culture 74
  North Island 76, 77, 141, 153
  per capita income 76
  population 71, 74
  Provincial Councils 71
  social patterns 75
  South Island 71, 74, 75, 76, 77, 78
  working conditions 76
New Zealander 153
Newgrange 86
Newton, Margaret 96, 98, 99, 100, 102,
    103, 108
  *Glimpses of Life in Bermuda and the
    Tropics* 95–6
Ngai 185
Ngugi wa Thiong'o 14, 189–194
  A Grain of Wheat 191
  Devil on the Cross 193
  'Goodbye Africa' 190–91
  Matigari 194
  Petals of Blood 192
  political project 189
  subject-formation 189
  'The Return' 190
  The River Between 189, 190
  Weep Not, Child 189, 190
Nicholls, Brendon 14

nicknames 172
Nigeria 13
Nilgiri Hills 138
Njama, Karari 186, 187, 188
Norman-Gaelic conflict 81
norms, English 125
North American Free Trade Agreement for
    Africa 63
North American viewer 48
North Carolina 52 n.22
Northern Ireland 209
    government 213
    nationalism 213
    Republicans 209
    Unionists 209, 213
Notting Hill riots 167
novel(s) 16, 105, 127, 132, 133, 136
    'End of Empire' 166
    of migration 171
    of the Indian Mutiny 139
    romantic 139
novelist(s), female 10, 11, 133

O'Callaghan, Evelyn 8, 9, 200
Ó Coileáin, Seághan 89
O'Donnell, Red Hugh 86
O'Dowd, Liam 212, 213
O'Faolain, Sean 217
O'Neill, Hugh 40
O'Shea, Tony 209
oak tree(s) 5, 34, 77, 106
oath(s) 178, 183, 187
oathing ceremonies 187
obeah shrine 201
objectification 202
obligation 114
observer-position 53
officer class 14
Oireachtas 213
oppression 88
    colonial 195
    history of 196
    of Gikuyu women 194
oral tradition 204
Orange Free State 135
Ordnance Survey of Ireland 36, 40
Orinoco river 103

Osborne, John
    Look Back in Anger 166
Otago 75
Other(s) 108, 141, 142, 149, 155, 178
    as a savage 142
    attraction of 156
    culturally displaced 30
    the colonized 11, 142
othering 154, 195, 206
'our ways' 165
outsider, ultimate 200
ownership 2, 13, 29, 40, 185

Page, Gertrude
    The Rhodesian 135
painters
    British 8
    modernist 11
painting(s) 3, 65, 67–70, 77
    ideal genre 68–9
    codes of the genres 69
    landscape 68, 78
    narrative Irish 81
    topographical 7, 68, 69, 81
    watercolour landscape 69
pakeha 141, 154, 155
Palgrave, Mary E.
    A Promise Kept 136
Pamplemousses 197
Panofsky, Irwin 17
Paris 147
partition of Ireland 212, 213, 219
Passion Machine 208
pastoral tone 35
pastoralism 77
paternalism 43, 63, 71, 76
patriarchy 142, 143, 145, 154, 157, 189
patriotism 152
Patterson, Sheila 164, 165, 168, 171
    *Dark Strangers A Study of West Indians
        in London* 164
peace 80
Peacock, Joseph
    Glendalough 81
Peard, Frances M 136
Penny, F. E.
    A Mixed Marriage 138

Love in the Hills 138
The Sanyasi 137
Percival, Captain Robert 56 n.43
Perrin, Alice 136
The Anglo-Indians 134
Petty, Sir William: 'The Down Survey' 40
Philips, Jock 74
Phipps, C. M. K.
Douglas Archdale 139
picturesque 5, 45, 51, 52, 67, 79, 86, 103,
    112, 119
Pinter, Harold 13, 160, 165, 166, 168, 170
A Slight Ache 168
The Caretaker 168
The Dwarfs 168
The Room 168, 169–70
pioneer
    cultivators 122
    inexperienced 123
    taint of 152
place 210
    based struggles 159, 160
    belonging to Britain 4, 93, 108
    of refuge 174
    sense of 191
plantation(s)
    coffee 115
    colonial 10
    house 103
    sugar 112
planter(s)
    class, new white 115, 121
    homosocial 121
    ideal 121
    new 122
    pioneer 126
    sexual company across the racial divide
        121
    society 10
    young 121
plantocracy, white 114
plants
    healing 202
    indigenous in the Americas 196
    Latin labels 197
    new 195
    New World 198

tropical 197
    wealthy collectors 197
pleasure, aesthetic 4
plebiscite(s) 212, 213
poem(s) 16, 198
    British 89
    chronicle history 80
    country house 211
    English ruin 79, 81, 82, 85, 87
    Irish 89
    Irish ruin 79, 85–91
    pioneer 125
    political meaning 79
    ruin 80, 84
poet(s)
    English 106
    Irish 80
    Jamaican 201
    Romantic 99
poetic licence 99
poetics
    of Caribbean identity 170, 173
    urban 172
poetry
    Irish 79, 86, 91
    topographical 79
poison(s) 202, 203
politics 52, 70, 88, 221
    internal British 25
    revolutionary 222
Pollard, Eliza F.
    The White Dove of Amritzir 139
pollutant, imagined 162
Polynesia 69
Pope, Alexander 125
Pope, the 215
population
    civilian 181, 184
    European racist 77
    indigenous 78
    Kenya 179
    mixed 121
Port of Spain 197, 198, 199
Porter, A. 62
Portuguese 1
possession 34, 35, 36, 97, 100, 114, 169,
    190, 197

Post-Impressionist concern 147
post-independence 171, 192
postmodernism 223
post-structuralism 18
potency, male 187, 192
poverty, rural 51
power 20, 66, 67, 70, 131, 157, 159, 211,
    214, 223
  abuse of 199
  colonial 2
  corruption of 199, 201
  emblems of 19
  erotic 138
  of romantic love 139
  of the Empire 197
  of the landscape 147
  structural relationships of 196
  Welsh 83
Pound, Francis 67, 69
  Frames on the Land 68
Prague 12
Pratt, Mary Louise 93, 94, 98, 99, 104, 107
Pratt, Stephanie 29
prejudice
  against female authors 132 n.3
  class 217
  colonial 104
prestige 66
Price, Uvedale 4
primitivism 70
Pringle, Thomas 52 n.25
print: 'The Unheard of Cruelties of the
    Iriquois' 195
prison 174
privacy of British national character 160
private/public divide 165
privilege, European 94
Procter, James 171, 173
production 65, 66, 67, 70, 178
  capitalist modes 210
  commercial 72
  cultural 78
  dairy 72
  estate 71
  European 72
  farm 65
  indigenous 72

literary mode 211
  Maori kin-based 77
  primary 72, 73
  rise in 73
  rural 70
  social relations 78
productivity 14, 15, 30, 31, 111, 114,
    116
profits 66
promoters, colonial 119
promotion, colonial 31
promotions, modern day tourist 108
proprietorship 43
prosperity 114
prostitute(s) 188, 192, 193
prostitution 193
protectionism 58
protectionist policies 55–6
Protestant Revival 1859 216
Protestants 213, 215, 216
proto-nationalism, West Indian 105, 107
publishers 132
Puerto Rico, US invasion 118
putti/putto 22, 24

Queen Victoria 197

race 111, 136, 161, 163, 169, 199, 206
  affiliations 167
  difference 111
  distinction, openly 114
  exclusivity 121
  memories 203
  relations 164, 167
racialization 160
racially coded distinction 116
racism 160, 196, 205
  animosity 174
  perspective 196
Rae, Milne
  A Bottle of Smoke 137
Ramble district 100
Ramchand, Ken 171
reading public 47
reading-subject 210
rebirth, cultural and spiritual 191
Reformation 80

regeneration 201, 205
religion 88, 89, 99, 216, 218
renaming 120, 143
representation(s) 25, 36, 223
    allegorical 42
    colonial 97
    feminized 26
    military 27 n.35
    of black cultures 162
    of Mau Mau 182–3
    of the city 161
    of the countryside 67
    of the land 211
    of space 211
    picturesque 80
    racist 167
requerimiento 1
resident(s) 164, 171, 174
    white 165
resistance 13, 21, 57, 88, 89, 182, 187, 191,
        192, 196, 204, 211, 221
revival 85, 89, 90
rhetoric
    of 'anti-conquest' 99
    of contamination 181, 183
    of discovery 93, 108
Rhodes, Cecil 130, 136
    monument at Groote Schuur 135
Rhodesia 137
Rhys, Jean 10, 15, 111, 121, 122, 196,
        201, 206
    After Leaving Mr McKenzie 10
    'Goodbye Marcus, Goodbye Rose'
        199–200
    'Pioneers, Oh Pioneers' 9, 111, 121, 122–6
    Smile Please 115
    Wide Sargasso Sea 102, 199, 200
Rhythm 155
Rice, Anne Estelle 155
Rice, Susan 63
Rich, George 76
rights, black British 176
rituals 170, 217
Riviera, the 12
road-building
    in Dominica 5, 9, 115
    in New Zealand 7

Rocque, John 21–2
    'A Plan of the City and Suburbs of
        Dublin' 22–4
    Kildare estate maps 24
romance 8, 102, 108, 172
    failure of 131
    fiction 11, 127
    narratives 10
    of empire 10
romantic 45, 48, 50, 52, 86, 99
    sentimentalism 167
Romanticism 6, 112
    European 104
    mainstream 79
rooms 171, 172, 173, 174, 175, 176
Rooseveldt, Theodore 63 n.73
Rosa, Salvator 69
rose(s) 118, 202
Roseau 112, 121
    Botanic Garden 199
rosiness 118
Royal Irish Academy 20, 30
ruin(s) 3, 7–8, 79–91
    aestheticization 80
    ancient 81
    as object-in-itself 81
    English 81, 87
    haunted 84
    Irish 5, 79–91
    manufactured 80
    'naturalized' 79
    relationship with natural landscape 79
    restoration 86
    the soul in 84
rule
    British/English 88, 139
    European 93
    imperial 137
    Kenyan colonial 177
runholders 75
runholding 71
rusticity 31
Ryder, Sean 8

satire 123
savage 142
savagery 153

Savi, E. W.
  Baba and the Black Sheep 138
Saxton's book of county maps 25
Schneider, Ben Ross 195
science, empirical 118
scientific 'facts' 93
Sea Islanders 204
sealers 66
Second World War 12
sectarianism 218
security 169, 174, 176
seeing 68, 108
  conventions of 67
  Ideal 67
  Picturesque 67
  Sublime 67
  Topographic 67
self, the 11, 108, 141, 142, 154, 157
  civilized 142
  duality in 152
  fragmented 162
  integration with Caribbean landscape 201
  sense of 155,159
  separation from 142
  war within 152
self-confidence 31
self-determination, national 26
self-image 114
  national 26
self-government 13
self-legitimation 179
Selvon, Sam 13, 161, 170, 171, 172, 173,
    174, 176
  The Lonely Londoners 170, 171, 175
settlement(s) 116, 164, 171, 172, 173, 174
  alien 165
  villagized 190, 192
  West Indian 171
settler(s)
  American 51
  British 61
  Caribbean 170
  Dutch 45, 51, 55–8
  English 56, 59
  farms 50
  honorary 72
  ideal 120

in New Zealand 73, 74, 75
invasion 145
Kenyan 178
political imagination of 182
potential 25
relations with Bushmen 55
social lives 120–1
white 111
Seymour, Susanne 2
sex 137, 154, 189, 190, 191, 194
sexuality 111, 124, 223
  female 188, 194, 219
  heroine's 138
sexwork-in-insurgency 188, 194
Shakespeare 154, 195
  The Tempest 195–6
Sharpe, Alfred 7, 69
  A View of Wenderholm 69
sheep 71, 72, 77, 78
ship 173, 175
shipwreck(s) 60, 61
sile-na-gig 219
Silesia 212
Sinfield, Alan
  *Literature, Politics and Culture in
    Postwar Britain* 168
Sinn Fein, Provisional 209, 213
Sistheutl 149
slave-owning ancestors, guilt of 201
slavery 58, 172, 204
slaves 201
  African 198
  Sea Island 205
Slaymaker, William 196, 206
slippage
  linguistic 178
  orthographical 193
smallpox 130
Smith, Angela 11
Smith, Bernard 65 n.1, 70
Smith, Neil 210
Smith, Sir Thomas 1–2
snake 29
social Darwinism 153
Social, Democratic and Labour Party
    (SDLP) 209
social forces/social fields 70

social markers of class distinction 66
social relations 65, 66, 73–5, 78
social unit, fundamental 220
society 173
  colonial 199
soil erosion 185
Soja, Edward 210
solidity 34, 176
Somali ethnicity 184
sorcery 190
South Pacific 1
South Africa 16, 129, 130, 133
South Carolina 25
Southern Africa 6, 45, 58
  economic attractions 47
  native inhabitants 53–8, 60, 61
space 6, 12, 159, 160, 170, 171, 210,
    211
  African 178
  colonial 178, 182, 184
  communal 174
  control and manipulation of 36
  geopolitical 210
  metropolitan 170
  narratorial and writerly 172
  of childhood 222
  political 210
  social 67, 210, 211, 222
spaces
  actualized 172
  of political agency for women 194
  of the West Indian community 174
  prohibited 183
  racialized 169
  regulated or repressive 211
  sacrosanct 183
  unsullied white 162
'spades' 166, 168
Spain 12
Spanish conquistadors 1
Speed, John 25
Speke, Captain 96
spirituality native Irish 88
Spivak, Gayatri 178 n.5
sports 76
Spufford, Francis 218
squatters 71

St Francies Xavier Centre 208
St Thomas 197
St Vincent 197
stability 30
starvation 76
state 214, 215
  independent political Irish 81
  modern 211
  unified British 83
Steedman, Andrew 61
Steel, Flora Annie
  A Mistress of Men 137
  A Prince of Dreamers 137
  King-Errant 137
  On the Face of the Waters 132 n.33
  The Builder 137
stereotypes 98, 108
Stevenson, Nora
  African Harvest 128
Stockley, Cynthia
  Kraal Baby 129
  Poppy: The Story of a South African Girl
    132 n.33, 134
  Tagati (Magic) 137
  The Claw 128
Stout, Benjamin 7, 45–64
  Dedication to John Adams 46, 47, 60
  *Narrative of the loss of the ship
    'Hercules'* 6, 47, 48, 58–61, 62, 63
stranger(s) 165
  being a 162
  influx of 163
  proximity of 170
  recognition of the 141
strategy, colonial military 179, 180, 181
Stratton, Florence 193
street(s) 12
strike of workingmen 70
struggle, anti-colonial 189, 190
subculture(s)
  British 13
  minority and youth 167
subjugation of Welsh 83
sublime, the 3, 45, 51, 52, 67, 69, 99, 100,
    102, 103, 108, 111, 112, 116, 120
  imperial 114
  Wordsworthian 90

subtitles 131
success, commercial 36, 38
Sudan 13
sugarcane 197, 198
suicide 119
superiority
  moral 119
  threat to 131
suppression
  of Catholicism 88
  of culture(s) 82
  of Welsh freedom 83
supremacy, white 104
surveying equipment 22, 24
surveyors 40
suspicion 155
Swahili 178
Swan, Annie S.
  Love Grown Cold 130
symbolism 143, 160
  cartographic 40
  Christian 155
  Irish 38
Symmonett, Ethel Maud 98, 99–100, 104–5,
  106, 107, 108
  Jamaica: Queen of the Carib Sea 95, 103

Table Bay 47
Tabler, E. C. 61
Tambouchis 53
taste 3, 4
Taylor, Alexander: 'A New Map of Ireland'
  25–9, 30
Teach Molaga 89, 90
technologies of the visible 178, 186
Tegg, Thomas 60
temperance 124, 125
temperature 118, 119
temperate 118–9
tenure 46
territoriality 13, 34, 42
territorization 160
territory/territories 5, 11, 168, 211
  colonial 2, 197
  defence of 168
  fictional 139
  ritualized marking 170

textuality 171
Thatcher government 209
Thatcher, Mrs 209
Thom, Ian 147
Thompson, Robert 197
threat
  139, 177
  from American traders 56
Tiffin, Helen 195–6
tiki, Maori 156
time-space 211
Tintern Abbey 91
Toibin, Colm 15–16, 207–23
  aesthetic strategies 214
  as intellectual 207, 208
  as observer 216, 217, 218
  Bad Blood: A Walk along the Irish Border
    208, 209, 214–19, 223
  journalism 207, 208
  narrative voice 214
  readership 215
  style 208, 209, 214
  The Blackwater Lightship 207, 208
  The Heather Blazing 208, 219–23
  The South 207
  The Trial of the Generals 207
  Walking Along the Border 209
Toler, Deborah 64
tomb 89, 145
topography
  ideological 115
  synchronic spatial 171
torture 9, 181, 191
totalizing 79
totem pole 148;
  female 147
tourism 8, 25, 63, 69
tourist(s) 25, 166
tower, round 30, 82
trade 26, 27, 30, 36, 38, 42, 62
traders 66
  American 56
transculturation 104
transformation 7
  of the land 34, 65
trauma 81, 82
travel 6, 12

books 68
diarist, first-person 104
  writer(s) 93, 96, 97, 218
travel writing(s) 6, 12, 45, 47, 61, 93, 208
  confessional form 97, 98, 99, 104
  generic conventions 97
  relationship to fiction 98
  women's 93–109
travel narrative(s)
  British 8
  female-authored 98
  forms 47
  nineteenth-century 97
travellers 25, 218
  American 59
  British lady 8, 93
  female 97
  motives 218
travelogue(s) 9, 15, 16, 209
  West Indian 97
treasure 114
trigonometrical survey, first 40
Trinidad 102, 103, 197, 198, 199
'Troubles', the 209, 219
truth, objective 104
Tyacke, Sarah
  English Map-Making 1500–1650 17
Tyrone Guthrie Centre 218

Ulster 20–21, 40, 219
  Nationalism 212
  Unionism 212
  Unionists 213
unbelonging 160
uncanny 161, 165, 172
unconscious 161
underworld 166
unheimlich 161
unhomely 161, 176, 182
unhousing 162, 163
unity, national 80
United Kingdom 212, 215
United States 73 n.25, 76, 215
unsuitability of white people to life in the
    tropics 118
urban frontline 162
urban rioting 168

urban sociology 164
urban uncanny 161, 162, 165, 171, 174,
    176

value(s) 67
  eurocentric 15;
  European 104
  feminocentric 94
  for home culture 102
  masculine 193
  militant, anti-British 199
  national 4
  of the past 85
  social 66
  truth 97, 98, 99
  use- 68
Vancouver 147
  Fine Arts Society 148
  Ladies' Art Club 148
vanity, female 132
veldt 11, 128 (veld)
Venezuela 103
Vermont 206
viewpoint, elevated 50, 52, 116
vice 119
Vidler, Alec
  The Architectural Uncanny 161
violence 182, 201, 216
  imperial 83
  of colonialism 51, 200
  of history 82
  political 82
  racial 168
  recreational 9
  sectarian 216
  successful 46, 47
Virginia 6
virility 187
visitors, foreign 107
VOC (Dutch East India Company) 56
voice(s)
  ancestral 196
  narrative 124, 125, 214, 215, 218
  personal, vernacular, of women 196
  of adventurous male hero 97
vulnerability 51
Waiyaki 186

Walckenaer, C. A. E.
    Collection de voyages en Afrique 60
Walker, Alice 15, 196, 203, 204, 205, 206
walking 211, 215
Wakefield, Edward Gibbon 70, 73, 75
Wakefield settlements 66
Wallas, Chief J. J. 149
war 130, 212
Ward, H. G. 70
Warren, William 197
way of life, British 4
wealth 66, 102, 114
    aesthetic/material 102
    agricultural 66, 68
Webster, Elizabeth Charlotte
    *Pot Holes: An Adventure in the Diamond
        Fields* 130
Webster, Wendy 164, 165, 170
    *Imagining Home: Gender, 'Race' and
        National Identity* 160
Wellington 141, 152
Welsh 82
Welu, James 22
Werner, A. 131
West Indies 8, 93, 94, 102, 103, 107, 114,
    165
Wexford 207, 222
whalers 66
White, Hayden 214
whiteness 119 n.28, 121
    ideological 118
    true 118
whites-only club 124
Whitlock, Gillian 96, 102
Whitman, Walt 125–6
Wilkes, Christopher 71
Williams, Raymond 211
Williamson, James 42
    'A Map of the County of Down' 31, 33,
        34, 35
Wilson, Nathaniel 197
Wilson, Richard 69
Wilson, Thomas M. 15
'wind of change' 13
Windley, Mr Edward 183
Wolcott, Mary 201
woman/women 193

and colonialism 94
as gardeners 137 n.69
as victims 187
colonial 131
construction of 157
creole 94, 104
diminution of 187
European 99
'fallen' 192
in New Zealand 70, 74
of the woods, wild 146, 149
painter 141
role of 201
sexually licentious 192–3
suffering of 191
travel writers 7, 8, 93, 94, 97, 98,
    108
travellers 8
voiceless 204
white Antiguan 105
white West Indian 200
writer(s) 98, 134, 141
writers of romance 127–39
womanhood 193
Woodford, Sir Ralph 198
Woodford Square 198, 199
'woodkerne' 6
wool 71, 72
Wordsworth 99, 119
work 36, 38, 70, 111, 119
workplace 160
world view, colonial 96
worth 30
writer(s) 12, 135
    African-American 196, 204
    black women 204
    British 8
    Caribbean 12, 159, 196
    creole 107
    creole women 104, 106, 108
    colonialist 102
    female 132 n.33
    'male' female 132
    modernist 11
    relationship with the landscape 102
    white creole 108
writing 77, 78, 112

anthropological 208
about landscape as a political act 196
about trivial things 96, 97
Black Atlantic 196
current Caribbean women's 108
imaginative 132
nationalist 85, 87
promotional 6, 7, 106
Romantic 119

settler 53
  women's 134
Wylie, I. A. R. 132

Xhosa 53, 54

Yssassi, Cristoval 102

Zimbabwe ruins 135